In the Shadow of War and Empire

Studies in Global Social History

VOLUME 52

Studies in the Social History of the Global South

Series Editors

VOLUME 4

The titles published in this series are listed at *brill.com/shgs*

In the Shadow of War and Empire

Industrialisation, Nation-Building, and Working-Class Politics in Turkey

By

Görkem Akgöz

BRILL

LEIDEN | BOSTON

The publication of this work was supported by the Open Access Publication Fund of Humboldt-Universität zu Berlin.

Published with the support of the Gerda Henkel Foundation, Duesseldorf.

Cover illustration: Workers at the Bakırköy spinnery, 10 April 1950. Courtesy of Ergin Aygöl

The Library of Congress Cataloging-in-Publication Data is available online at https://catalog.loc.gov

Typeface for the Latin, Greek, and Cyrillic scripts: "Brill". See and download: brill.com/brill-typeface.

ISSN 2590-3144
ISBN 978-90-04-41674-1 (hardback)
ISBN 978-90-04-68714-1 (e-book)
DOI 10.1163/9789004687141

This book is printed on acid-free paper and produced in a sustainable manner.

To Neriman, the tobacco worker
Sabiha, the neighbourhood tailor
and Behçet, the soul mechanic
for the light they shed on the child inside me

Contents

Foreword

Görkem Akgöz has written an important and original book. Not only is the subject new, so is the methodology used. She explores new paths and she does so convincingly.

Her greatest merit is probably that she connects two spheres that usually remain separate: on the one hand, the "public" sphere of economic development, industrial politics, and business management—what Marx called the "noisy sphere, where everything takes place on the surface and in full view of everyone"—and on the other hand, "the hidden abode of production, on whose threshold there hangs the notice 'No admittance except on business'." Akgöz places the developments in one textile company in Istanbul, the Bakırköy Cloth Factory, in a broad economic and political context from the 1840s onward. She situates the fortunes of the enterprise and its workforce during the downturn and collapse of the Ottoman Empire and in the subsequent state-led industrialization in Republican Turkey until the 1950s. Creatively exploiting hitherto unused sources, she then leads the reader in the second part into the everyday world of the women, men and children within the company walls, their lives, problems, ambitions and actions. She has an eye for contradictions and differences. The workers about whom she has been able to find biographical data—often only after persistent sleuthing—are described as individuals with their individual idiosyncrasies, some very courageous, others less so. Always Akgöz guards against stereotypes and simplifications.

By tracing the lines of development from the mid-nineteenth to the mid-twentieth century, Akgöz mines new ground, for as she herself rightly writes, the story of Turkish industrial relations in the 1930s and '40s is "a largely neglected history." In recent decades, Turkish labour history has undergone tremendous development. After earlier historians had already explored institutional aspects, others have expanded the field to broader questions, concerning labour relations and workers' struggles. But this initially focused on the Ottoman period and the first years of the Republic. Akgöz follows subsequent developments, during the world economic crisis and etatist attempts at import substitution. In doing so, she simultaneously lays the groundwork for a more in-depth analysis of Turkish society after World War II.

By paying attention both to wider social relations and to the feelings and actions of concrete workers, Akgöz makes the age-old opposition between structure and agency manageable. Historians are constantly faced with a dilemma: the more they focus on real individuals the more social processes and structures on a larger scale move to the background. And the more intensely they focus on structures and large-scale processes the more individual actors with their personal histories are erased. Each approach has its price. Akgöz does not choose either approach, but combines them fruitfully.

In doing so, she adopts a feminist perspective. She recognizes that the working class is extremely heterogeneous and complex at all levels. She leaves the "single-axis framework" of the "white, male industrial worker" behind and sketches a multi-dimensional picture of interacting factors that, in combination, keep people in subordinate social positions in different ways. Akgöz exposes intersections between class, gender, religion, ethnicity, and age, among others. The analysis of such intersections is difficult. It has even been argued, that it is almost impossible to simultaneously keep more than two concepts such as gender and class in play. Akgöz's study nevertheless succeeds in unifying the importance of aspects heuristically.

With her creative and complex approach, Akgöz demonstrates that while a single narrative can never tell the whole story, a so-called Grand Narrative remains possible. Like spotlights, each separate perspective generates a great deal of light, but also leave something in the shade and may even blind the observer. In combination however they can create an unprecedentedly rich picture.

In the Shadow of War and Empire is undoubtedly a landmark in the social historiography of the Global South.

Marcel van der Linden
International Institute of Social History, Amsterdam

Acknowledgements

This book has been a long time in the making. From the beginning, it emanated from concerns that were at once political and personal. These concerns only grew over time, and the writing was shaped and buffeted by a huge amount of contemporary change. I began contemplating this book more than ten years ago in Amsterdam. Back then, I had a job waiting for me in Turkey, my home country, and I naively thought that I would spend the early years of my academic career learning to teach and writing my book. Little did I know that these years would be spent mostly on political activism. In the end, I could only begin writing after I had to flee my home country in 2017, and found myself settled in Berlin. Since then, its progress has fluctuated with the ups and downs in the political situation in Turkey, and it was finally finished under circumstances dramatically different to those in which I began writing it.

Many people and institutions have contributed to the completion of this study, and it is a pleasure to be able to acknowledge this. The dissertation that lies behind this book was supervised by Marcel van der Linden, who, among other things, taught this converted social scientist to think like a historian. His support continues to this day. The International Institute of Social History in Amsterdam provided me with office space, library facilities, and, most important of all, supportive and intellectually stimulating colleagues. Among those, *sevgili hocam* Touraj Atabaki has a special place in my heart.

This book has been substantially improved by the intellectual engagement provided by colleagues at re:work, where I have found a home away from home in the last five years. The pleasure of exchanging ideas and information with other scholars of labour, and the joy of watching their projects come to fruition, has greatly enriched my writing. I am especially thankful to Felicitas Hentschke for her continuous support over the years.

Without the generosity of two funding agencies, this project would have been impossible. A three-year Gerda Henkel Fellowship allowed me to begin writing; additional support came from an Einstein Stiftung Grant. I cannot thank enough the numerous librarians and archivists who provided guidance and access to the sources that form the empirical foundation of this book. I am especially indebted to Geran Özdeş Çelik, Elifcan Çoruk, Bülent Erdem, Daniella Greca, and Zeynep Ecem Pulaş. My special thanks go to Ergin and Nebahat Aygöl, Sibel Bozdoğan, İlhan Öden, Emre Öncü, Ediz and Esin Tenşi, and Turgay Tuna for the photographs they shared with me.

The book also bears the stamp of many people who contributed in diverse ways to its completion. Numerous scholars and colleagues have read and commented on various parts of the book. Hasan Ashraf, Pınar Dönmez, Şirin Fulya Erensoy, Eda Güçlü, Rick Halpern, Nurçin İleri, Ezgi Pehlivanlı, Christian Strümpell, Gürsan Şenalp, Onurcan Taştan, Alp Eren Topal, and Nitin Varma commented on particular chapters. A number of other colleagues have offered helpful criticism and/or have engaged me in enormously useful discussions about the ideas in this book. Aslı Odman has been an unwavering intellectual support and a true friend, generously sharing her ideas and insights. At Brill, Alessandra Giliberto has been a model editor; she remained warmly encouraging without ever rushing the final product, even as deadline followed deadline. Special thanks go to Helen Veitch, who meticulously copy edited the manuscript. I also gratefully acknowledge the stimulating and invaluable comments of the two anonymous readers of the manuscript.

In the wider world, the range of my gratitude is equally great. No amount of academic support, intellectual stimulation, or financial aid would have enabled me to finish this project without the nurturing I received from family and loving friends. I am grateful to my parents, Meliha and Haluk, my brother Gürcan, and my entire extended family for the unconditional love and support they showered me with. Fiti and Piti have been my rocks as always; Supurna Banerjee, Seda Cantekin, Cem Dinler, Anıl Duman, Yasemin Erensoy, Sebastian Großmann, Sevda Hamzaçelebi, Dimitra Kofti, Georg Mayer, Hakan Mıhçı, Sevinç Topuzoğlu Mıhçı, Duygu Nesli, Nico Pizzolato, Özlem Sarıyıldız, Açalya Temel, and Regina Tunke have accompanied me through the long and strange trip this book has taken me on. But there is no one to whom I am more indebted than Pieter Verstraete, who has been an unflinching supporter of my writing projects over the past few years. He not only read the several drafts, he also listened to practically every little detail that made or did not make to the final manuscript. He has also provided an enormous amount of care and love labour during the time of the writing.

I dedicate this book to my beloved grandmothers, Neriman and Sabiha, who, like most women, carried the double burden of paid work with unpaid care work, while at the same showering me and my cousins with the gift of unconditional love; and to my soulmate, Behçet, for healing the child in me during the twelve years we spent cheek to cheek, *anne seni çok seviyor ömrümün baharı.*

Maps, Figures and Table

Maps

Figures

Table

Abbreviations

AKP	Justice and Development Party (*Adalet ve Kalkınma Partisi*)
CHP	Republican People's Party (*Cumhuriyet Halk Partisi*)
DIP	Democrat Labour Party (*Demokrat İşçi Partisi*)
DISK	Confederation of Progressive Trade Unions of Turkey (*Türkiye Devrimci İşçi Sendikaları Konfederasyonu*)
DP	Democrat Party (*Demokrat Parti*)
ICFTU	International Confederation of Free Trade Unions
ILO	International Labour Organization
MKP	National Development Party (*Milli Kalkınma Partisi*)
TKP	Communist Party of Turkey (*Türkiye Komünist Partisi*)
TSEKP	Socialist Party of the Workers and Peasants of Turkey (*Türkiye Sosyalist Emekçi ve Köylü Partisi*)
TSP	Socialist Party of Turkey (*Türkiye Sosyalist Partisi*)
Türk-İş	Confederation of Turkish Trade Unions (*Türkiye İşçi Sendikaları Konfederasyonu*)
WFTU	World Federation of Trade Unions

Introduction

Postimperial Synchrony: Industrialisation and Nation-Building as Entwined Processes

Shortly before the First World War would cast a further shadow over the "sick man of Europe," Rosa Luxemburg was working on the publication of a series of lectures she had delivered at the central school of the German Social Democratic Party. The then crumbling Ottoman Empire was one of the examples Luxemburg cited in what would become a popular work of economic history and theory on the complexity and unevenness of capitalist development:

> A country like Turkey [has] a large surplus of imports, amounting in many years to almost double the quantity of exports. How can Turkey … afford the luxury of such a copious filling of the "gaps" in [her] "national economy"? … Do the Western powers offer the crescent … each year a present of several hundred million marks, in the form of all kinds of useful goods, out of Christian charity? Every child [knows] that … Turkey [is] actually up to [her neck] in the jaws of European usurers, and [has] to pay the British, German and French banks an enormous tribute in interest. … Turkey has virtually no industry of its own, and cannot conjure this out of the ground of its medieval peasant subsistence agriculture with its primitive cultivation and tithes. … And so not only the whole of the population's needs for industrial goods, but also everything necessary for transport construction and the equipment of army and navy, has to be imported ready-made from Western Europe and constructed on site by European entrepreneurs, technicians and engineers.[1]

Two decades later, the leadership of the Republic of Turkey, the last nation-state to emerge from the ashes of the Ottoman Empire, decided it was time to break free from the shackles of underdevelopment so masterfully described here by Luxemburg. This gave rise to the first attempt outside the Soviet Union to set out an industrial plan. The preface to the first five-year plan of 1934 echoed Luxemburg's analysis in an equally powerful tone, suggesting that the German-speaking Turkish bureaucrats may even have read her work, which had been published posthumously in 1925. The text referred to Western Europe

1 Peter Hudis, ed., *The Complete Works of Rosa Luxemburg*, vol. 1 (London: Verso, 2013), 113–114.

 | DOI:10.1163/9789004687141_002

and the eastern shore of North America as "the workbench of the world" that had destroyed the productive means of non-industrialised societies by selling them their manufactured products. The rationale for the plan, again similar to Luxemburg's analysis, foreshadowed the basic premises of the Latin American *dependencia* school by more than three decades.[2] For countries such as Turkey, this unequal exchange between industrial and agricultural nations, the authors of the plan argued, resulted in *de jure* independence but *de facto* dependence.

The industrialised powers, for their part, were able to set aside their existing conflicts to join forces in an effort to retain the agricultural countries as raw material producers, which they saw as a way of controlling their national markets. The onset of the Great Depression affected the latter more adversely than the former, but the crisis of the entire liberal world of the nineteenth century, as Eric Hobsbawm put it, also had a silver lining: the core countries temporarily lost their grip on the periphery, presenting a small window of opportunity for the underdeveloped nations to turn the tide.[3] The crisis of world capitalism, the planners asserted, was a chance for the Turkish state to reverse the peripheralisation of the country by quickly building national industry.[4]

And so, postimperial Turkey emerged from long years of war and economic destruction with a new developmentalist plan to embark on an ambitious import substitution model of national industry-building. This was before state-led import substitution industrialisation would spread throughout the developing world in the years after 1945.[5] The new economic policy was baptised

---

2 Andre Gunder Frank, "The Development of Underdevelopment," in *Latin America: Underdevelopment or Revolution*, ed. Andre Gunder Frank (New York: Monthly Review Press, 1969); Colin Leys, "Underdevelopment and Dependency: Critical Notes," *Journal of Contemporary Asia* 7, no. 1 (1977), 92–107.

3 Eric Hobsbawm, *Industry and Empire* (Suffolk: Penguin, 1969), 210; Andre Gunder Frank, *Capitalism and Underdevelopment in Latin America: Historical Studies of Chile and Brazil* (New York: Monthly Review Press, 1967), 149.

4 Korkut Boratav, "Büyük Dünya Bunalımı İçinde Türkiye'nin Sanayileşme ve Gelişme Sorunları: 1929–1939" in *Tarihsel Gelişimi İçinde Türkiye*, ed. Orhan Kurmuş et al. (Ankara: Makina Mühendisleri Odası, 1977), 3–4.

5 Clark Kerr, John T. Dunlop, Frederick H. Harbison, and Charles A. Myers, *Industrialism and Industrial Man: The Problem of Labour and Management in Economic Growth* (Cambridge: Harvard University Press, 1960), 271; Zivi Yehuda Hershlag, *Turkey: The Challenge of Growth* (Leiden: E.J. Brill, 1968), 74; Gunnar Myrdal, *Asian Drama: An Inquiry into the Poverty of Nations* (New York: Pantheon Books, 1972), 248–249; Charles Issawi, "De-industrialization and Re-industrialization in the Middle East Since 1800," *International Journal of Middle Eastern Studies* 12, no. 4 (1980), 474; Korkut Boratav, "Kemalist Economic Policies and Étatism," in *Atatürk: Founder of a Modern State*, eds. Ali Kazancıgil and Ergun Özbudun (London: C. Hurst & Company, 1981), 175; Zivi Yehuda Hershlag, *The Contemporary Turkish Economy* (London: Routledge, 1988), ix; Haldun Gülalp, "Capitalism and the Modern

"etatism," a term used by French protectionists and socialists in the 1890s, which, in the economic life of the 1920s, came to mean direct state intervention. In 1935, the Republican People's Party (*Cumhuriyet Halk Partisi*, hereafter the CHP) adopted etatism as a party principle. Two years later, etatism made it into the constitution as one of the six principles of the republic, together with republicanism, populism, secularism, reformism, and nationalism. By the mid-1930s, Kemalism, the official ideology of the republic named after its founding leader, Mustafa Kemal, had a strong industrial component. As industry and technology were celebrated as the centrepieces of state-building, a factory system took shape in the 1930s consisting of old Ottoman factories and newly built ones. State factories emerged as key sites of entanglement, where questions of nation-building, class formation, and modernisation were intimately tied together. They were expected not only to buttress Turkey's hard-won political independence with economic independence from the advanced industrialised countries, but also to set the standard for relations between capital and labour throughout the country.

The republic was barely ten years old when it embarked on state-led industrialisation. The first decade was characterised by turmoil, politically as well as economically. The Kemalist leadership engaged in a radical and wide-ranging programme of superstructural reforms to address the institutional and legal framework and cultural issues of the 1920s. After violently suppressing the first armed Kurdish rebellion under the republican regime in 1925, the government enacted the Law for the Maintenance of Order (*Takrir-i Sükûn Kanunu*), endowing itself with virtually absolute powers. It was at this point that authoritarian state-building began to gather momentum. By the time state-led industrialisation had begun, that momentum was in full swing.

The simultaneity of the two processes of postimperial nation-building and state-led industrialisation lies at the heart of this book. *In the Shadow of War and Empire* is a tale of these two distinct yet connected histories and the ways in which the interactions between them shaped and were shaped by working-class politics. The industrialisation efforts of the 1930s and 1940s

Nation-State: Rethinking the Creation of the Turkish Republic," *Journal of Historical Sociology* 7, no. 2 (1994), 155; Alfred Bonne, *Studies in Economic Development* (London: Routledge, 1998), 107–108; Haldun Gülalp, "The Eurocentrism of Dependency Theory and the Question of 'Authenticity': A View from Turkey," *Third World Quarterly* 19, no. 5(1998), 954; Alan Richards, John Waterbury, Melani Cammett, and Ishac Diwan, *A Political Economy of the Middle East* (Boulder: Westview Press, 2013), 239; M. Erdem Özgür and Eyüp Özveren, "Turkey's Attempt to Break the Fetters Before the Ladder was Kicked Away, 1929–1947," in *Political Economy of Development in Turkey 1838-Present*, eds. Emre Özçelik and Yonca Özdemir (London: Palgrave Macmillan, 2022), 113.

and their consequences have their origins in the underdevelopment of the Ottoman Empire, an examination of which is essential for understanding the key characteristics and global connections of Turkey's interwar economic policy. I therefore swerve the chronological marker that severed Turkey's national present from her imperial past and reject the received wisdom that compares the Turkish republic to an "immaculate conception."[6] My first contention is that Turkey's interwar state-led industrialisation can only be properly understood through a broader analysis of postimperial nation-building, one which neither reduces it to state actions nor ignores the relative autonomy of industrial relations.

If the aim is to trace the historical continuities in peripheral industrial development, there could hardly be a better starting point than a factory that was central to the two rounds of state-led industrialisation, separated by almost a century. And it is here that the story begins, at one of the old imperial factories that was taken over by the republican regime. *In the Shadow of War and Empire* explores the close relationship between nation-building and workplace relations under state-led industrialisation. The book offers a site-specific history of Ottoman and Turkish industrialisation through the lens of a mid-century cotton factory in the "Turkish Manchester," the name chosen by the Ottomans for the industrial complex they had built on the northern shore of the Marmara Sea in the 1840s, which was taken over by the republican state in 1923. The building of this industrial complex marked a turning point in the prolonged process of the Ottoman state's resistance and accommodation to capitalism in the mid-nineteenth century. During the interwar period, the factory was at the centre of another attempt by a new political regime to resist foreign control. In the contemporary words of one of the country's most prominent Marxist theorists, the factory was "the secret to and the basis of Turkish state capitalism."[7] Both the imperial and the republican regimes had vested their hopes in this factory on their path to catching up with European industrialisation. The Ottomans, for their part, failed. This failure served as political capital for the republican Turks, who staked their ambitious industrialisation policy on the promise of transforming the semi-colonial Ottoman socioeconomic and geographic structure into a sovereign and autarkic nation-state. The Bakırköy Cloth Factory, together with three other old Ottoman and newly built state factories, would come to symbolise that transformation.

---

6 Selim Deringil, "The Ottoman Origins of Kemalist Nationalism: Namık Kemal to Mustafa Kemal," *European History Quarterly* 23 (1993), 165.

7 Hikmet Kıvılcımlı, *Türkiye İşçi Sınıfının Sosyal Varlığı* (Istanbul: Bozkurt Matbaası, 1935), 51.

The empirical core of this book consists of an analysis of labour relations at a single state factory. Yet it has much more to say, by implication, not only about early republican Turkey, but also about nation-building and industrialisation in late-latecomer economies. Late Ottoman and early republican Turkey offers a unique opportunity to unpack the peripheral industrialisation and political economy of development because it serves as a critical juncture where political regime change and industrial development ideals intertwine. By placing these two processes within and against their wider historico-geographical field, this book elucidates the diverse array of international and domestic forces that shaped the political economy of underdevelopment, nation-building, and working-class politics in republican Turkey.

In writing this book, my aim is to strip etatism of its celebratory excess and highlight the critical role of nation-building in the construction of a new labour regime. *In the Shadow of War and Empire* is concerned with how workers, who were recategorised from imperial subjects to citizens, lived and worked through this transformation, struggling to be heard amid the thunder of nationalist developmentalism. The story of Turkish industrial relations in the 1930s and 1940s is reflective of many broader economic, political, and social trends in republican Turkey. Yet this is a largely neglected history, and one which has considerable wider significance for our understanding of the many meanings of work and working-class politics in the development of modern Turkey.

1 The Story: From Economic Colonialism to Economic Nationalism

It would not be inaccurate to describe the atmosphere of policymaking in the first years of the republic as "the urge to have done with empire." The speed of the republican state's superstructural and legislative reforms in the 1920s struck the international community as remarkable. Things were much slower in the economic realm though, because of the imperial commitments inherited from the latter part of the nineteenth century. The temporary economic provisions of the Treaty of Lausanne (1923), with regard to the Ottoman debt and customs tariffs in particular, hampered state capacity to assume the role of an autonomous policymaker. To begin with, this entailed Turkey relinquishing her right over the regulation of its trade regime and monetary policy. In addition to its massive international debt, the country was suffering in the face of the physical destruction of warfare and the financial and human cost of the population exchange with Greece, which meant, among other things, the loss of a significant portion of its skilled urban labour force. Despite its efforts, the republican regime was unable to reduce its dependency on the early industrialised economies during the first years of its existence.[8]

Then came the shock of the Great Depression. Turkey was one of the primary-goods producing countries hit hardest by the deflation that followed the 1929 crash. The vulnerability of the Turkish economy revealed that legal and cultural reforms were not enough to banish the Ottoman past to oblivion. The regime had already set up a temporal dichotomy between the Ottoman past and the republican present thanks to the superstructural changes. Following the global capitalist crisis, this dichotomy now shifted to the realm of economic policy, positioning factory-based industrialisation as the key symbolic site for revolutionary vigour and radical change. By the early 1930s, the state elite and middle-class intellectuals were becoming increasingly attuned to the depiction of the Ottoman economy as a colonial dependency controlled by European foreign interests. They argued that sustained industrialisation was the only way to transform the economic geography of a semi-colonised empire into a robust national economic entity.[9]

Perhaps the clearest expression of this came from a pro-government journalist, who resorted to racialised images of slave labour and Asian colonialism to describe the condition of the young republic. Prior to etatism, he lamented, Turkish cotton was "only as worthy as a Negro's sweat." But hope reigned by the end of the 1930s, he argued, as each rotation of the spindles erodes "part of our Asianness."[10] By the middle of the decade, industrialisation and economic nationalism would become key issues in Kemalist modernisation. The image of the belching industrial smokestacks, referred to "Atatürk's minarets" by a group of foreign experts, dominated the political and intellectual landscape to an extent that is difficult to imagine in the present-day era of deindustrialisation.[11] The project of modernisation was now synonymous with

8 Çağlar Keyder, *The Definition of a Peripheral Economy: Turkey 1923–1929* (Cambridge: Cambridge University Press, 1981), vii; Haldun Gülalp, "Patterns of Capital Accumulation and State-Society Relations in Turkey," *Journal of Contemporary Asia* 15, no. 3 (1985), 334; Zvi Yehuda Hershlag, *The Contemporary Turkish Economy* (London; New York: Routledge, 1988), 1–3; Feroz Ahmad, *The Making of Modern Turkey* (London: Routledge, 1993), 94; Korkut Boratav, *Türkiye İktisat Tarihi* (Istanbul: Gerçek Yayınevi, 1993), 37; Korkut Boratav, "İktisat Tarihi (1908–1980)" in *Türkiye Tarihi 4: Çağdaş Türkiye 1908–1980*, ed. Sina Akşin (Istanbul: Cem Yayınevi, 2008), 311.

9 Vedat Nedim Tör, "Müstemleke İktisadiyatından Millet İktisadiyatına," *Kadro* 1, no. 1 (1932), 8–11; Bilsay Kuruç, *Belgelerle Türkiye İktisat Politikası, 1933–1935*, vol. 2 (Ankara: Ankara Üniversitesi Yayınları, 1993), 175, 269.

10 Cemal Kutay, "Değişme," *Ulus*, 18 May 1939.

11 Max Weston Thornburg, Graham Spry, and George Soule, *Turkey: An Economic Appraisal* (New York: The Twentieth Century Fund, 1949), 105–106.

industrialisation, and the image of the factory embodied the republic's eagerly anticipated future.

The distasteful memory of the Ottoman external debt, financial deficit, and dependence on European industrial technology and skills intensified the rush to construct a manufacturing industry that would both lighten the import burden and develop the essential basic elements of industrial management: adequate capital resources, competent management, skilled labour, and a responsive internal market for the later stages of industrialisation. The Kemalist leadership claimed that Turkey had no more time to lose; she needed to move fast to overcome the centuries-long inertia and catch up with Western industrial modernity. A desire to accelerate history and sweat out the lingering poison of the Ottoman influence underscored policymaking. The first five-year industrial plan reflected that sense of urgency, and, similarly to the import substitution industrialisation attempts that would be planned in later decades, focused on the manufacture of previously imported simple consumer goods for which internal markets and local raw materials existed and labour-intensive production methods could be employed.

The result was successful. The implementation of the industrial plan began in 1934 and, by the end of the decade, Turkey was already producing basic consumption goods that had previously been imported. Industry's contribution to gross national product increased from 11.4 per cent between 1923 and 1929 to 16.9 per cent between 1933 and 1939.[12] Large-scale government investment together with infusions of private capital resulted in a great expansion of the textile, cement, and sugar industries, as well as the creation of certain new ones such as paper, glass, rayon, iron, and steel. The index of physical output of medium-scale and large-scale industry increased from thirty-five in 1930 to one hundred in 1939, and the overall index of industrial output increased from sixty-four in 1938 to 115 in 1950. By the end of the 1930s, dependence on textile and foodstuff imports had fallen, while the share of capital goods had increased from 14.5 per cent to 37.2 per cent of total imports.[13] The government

12 Boratav, "İktisat Tarihi (1908–1980)," 328; Korkut Boratav, "Kemalist Economic Policies and Étatism," in *Atatürk: Founder of a Modern State*, eds. Ali Kazancıgil and Ergun Özbudun (London: C. Hurst & Company, 1981), 179.

13 United Nations, Department of Economic and Social Affairs, *The Development of Manufacturing Industry in Egypt, Israel and Turkey* (New York: United Nations, 1958), 17; Bonne, *Studies in Economic Development*, 108; Zivi Yehuda Hershlag, *Introduction to the Modern Economy of the Middle East* (Leiden: Brill, 1964), 198; Şevket Pamuk, *Uneven Centuries: Economic Development of Turkey Since 1820* (Princeton: Princeton University Press 2018), 278; William Hale, "Ideology and Economic Development in Turkey 1930–1945," *Bulletin British Society for Middle Eastern Studies* 7, no. 2 (1980), 108.

also managed to repay a good proportion of its external debt, and attain a balanced budget.[14] In 1945, the state was employing more than 100,000 workers in its factories. Five years later, this figure had reached 150,000, that is, fifteen per cent of the almost one million workers in manufacturing out of a total population of 12.6 million.[15]

Shortly before the government's second industrial plan, which aimed to expand and roll out state industries, the shadow of another war would extend across the world.[16] Turkey did not participate in the war, but the country nevertheless suffered severely amid the pressures on the global war economy. Industrial output decreased during the early years of the war as a result of intense shortages of imported machinery and spare parts as well as the toll that military conscription took on the already instable labour supply. In face of the fifty per cent fall in wheat production, the government initially tried to intervene through price controls, but abandoned this path in 1942. A hike in prices followed, resulting in a thirty per cent decrease in real wages.[17] In the pages to follow, the reader will encounter state workers describing their impoverishment during the war years. Meanwhile, the formation of the wartime black market economy and widespread smuggling gave rise to the social category of war profiteers.

Private industrialists, who had accumulated a sizeable amount of capital thanks to wartime inflation, threw their weight behind a rival, more pro-business political party formed by a RRP splinter group. It was baptised the Democrat Party (*Demokrat Parti*, hereafter the DP), as a direct criticism of RRP rule.[18] Etatism, which by 1945 had enveloped all major fields of the economy, represented one of the major lines of division between the Democrat Party and the CHP, and, as such, came under increasing scrutiny. At the same time, the emergent and profoundly different postwar politico-economic order forced the CHP to drop its long-standing policy of protectionism. The tensions of the Cold War developed quickly and intensely in Turkey, the furthest

14 Yakup Kepenek and Nurhan Yentürk, *Türkiye Ekonomisi* (Istanbul: Remzi Kitabevi, 1994), 59, 61; Pamuk, *Uneven Centuries*, 189–190; Boratav, "Kemalist Economic Policies," 179.

15 Ahmet Özeken, "Türkiye Sanayiinde İşçiyi Barındırma Problemi," *Sosyal Siyaset Konferansları Dergisi* 3 (1950), 104; United States Bureau of Labour Statistics, *Summary of the Labour Situation in Turkey* (Washington: International Cooperation Administration Office of Labour Affairs, 1956),15; Ahmet Makal, "Türkiye'nin Sanayileşme Sürecinde İşgücü Sorunu, Sosyal Politika ve İktisadi Devlet Teşekkülleri: 1930'lu ve 1940'lı Yıllar," *Toplum ve Bilim* 92 (2002), 38.

16 Şevket Pamuk, "Political Economy of Industrialization in Turkey," *MERIP Reports* 93 (1981).

17 Boratav, "İktisat Tarihi (1908–1980)," 335; Pamuk, "Industrialization in Turkey," 26.

18 Osman Okyar, "The Concept of Etatism," *Economic Journal* 75, no. 297 (1965), 106.

geographical outpost of the non-communist world. With an eye to admission to the new international organisations, and under pressure from Soviet territorial demands, the country came under the increasing influence of the North Atlantic coalition-in-the-making. To qualify for International Monetary Fund membership and to benefit from the Marshall Plan, the government initiated a major shift in economic policy involving devaluation and a set of foreign trade liberalisation measures. Etatist priorities gave way to agricultural development and export promotion; state resources were diverted to infrastructural investments to expand markets, and foreign credit became an important financial resource.[19] The tide had turned by the end of the 1940s, opening up a whole new chapter in republican Turkish history. In 1950, the CHP lost power after twenty-seven years of uninterrupted rule. *In the Shadow of War and Empire* narrates this series of events, and analyses the historical outcomes as well as their impact on industrialisation in modern Turkey.

2 The Argument: Controlling Labour on and beyond the Shop Floor

If one side of the Janus face of state-led industrialisation as it developed in 1930s Turkey entailed a sense of anxious but hopeful urgency, the other side displayed pure fear. Rapid industrialisation meant the rapid growth of an industrial working class. This is where the Turkish ruling elite's complicated relationship with Western modernity enters the equation, signifying both an ideal to catch up with and a dark example to avoid repeating at all costs. The rulers desired all that industrial modernity represented, except for the violent history of class strife and class struggle. In 1935, the economic affairs minister assured the nation that Turkey's shortcut to industrial modernity was safe because the policymakers knew the bumpy roads that the industrialised countries had taken all too well.[20] He held up the 1936 Labour Code, which was modelled on Italian fascist legislation of 1935, as the strongest evidence of that "wisdom" and assured the public that it would "clear away the clouds of class consciousness once and for all."[21]

---

19 Kepenek and Yentürk, *Türkiye Ekonomisi,* 84, 122; Pamuk, *Uneven Centuries*, 206; Gülalp, "Patterns of Capital Accumulation," 336; İlhan Tekeli and Selim İlkin, *Savaş Sonrası Ortamında 1947 Türkiye İktisadi Kalkınma Planı* (Ankara: ODTÜ Yayınları, 1974), 15–24.

20 Kuruç, *Belgelerle* 2, 269.

21 Recep Peker, the General Secretary of the Republican People's Party, speaking during parliamentary discussions on the labour code. TBMM Tutanak Dergisi (Records of the Grand National Assembly), 8 June 1936, Session 5, vol. 12, Meeting no. 75, 83–84.

From the very beginning, and although industrial employment remained modest up until the 1950s, Turkish industrialists acted out of fear of "the dark side" of industrialisation, that is, its potential to spread subversive ideologies. It was this fear that propelled the ruling elite to act as if it faced a large, militant, and organised industrial labour force, and to subdue the language and politics of class under the language and politics of the nation. Two interrelated factors came to their rescue here: the timing of industrialisation and etatism as a republican constitutional principle. Together, they fuelled a nationalist narrative of industrial work, mobilising a work ethic that concealed the unequal and coercive relations of production and, thus, subordinating class divisions in service to the nation.

Throughout the early republican period, the ruling elite would refer to the legacy of the Independence War with searing intensity. If the Ottoman Porte, a synecdoche for the central government of the Ottoman Empire and named after the gate leading to the principal state departments in Istanbul, embodied a purely self-interested and disloyal ruler, the republican parliament embodied a selfless and patriotic leader who had proven his loyalty in the liberation struggle. As the temporal marker of that break, the memory of the Independence War was central to the nationalist ethics of sacrifice for the rapid reconstruction of the country. Industrialisation, according to this official historiography, meant a revered effort to reconstruct a country that no longer belonged to a privileged few but to the entire Turkish nation. The time was ripe to demand a patriotic effort in the form of work. An International Labour Office report from 1949 described two prevailing aspects of public opinion with respect to the labour question in Turkey: the sense of national unity generated by the independence movement and the distrust of labour based on often inaccurate knowledge of developments in other countries.[22]

By placing the state at the heart of the industrialisation drive, etatism built on the ideal of industrial labour as patriotic service. Combined with populism, etatism as a constitutional principle safeguarded the Turkish state against the infiltration of class interests, promising developmental benefits to the nation as a whole. This set the Turkish case apart from the well-known Latin American populism of the same period. While the latter rested on a cross-class coalition of workers and industrialists, the former either rejected the existence of class altogether or subsumed it under a supra-class state. It followed logically that etatism was a class-neutral and nationalistic development plan; it

22 International Labour Office, *"Labour Problems in Turkey," Report of a Mission of the International Labour Office* (Geneva: ILO, 1950), 17.

was a powerful political and ideological concept as much as a pragmatic economic policy. The government succeeded in institutionalising the concept of a neutral state above class that would intervene directly in the socioeconomic order to minimise foreign economic dependence, eliminate class inequality, and prevent the emergence of class-based politics. Under etatism, workers would come up against this ideal whenever they attempted to challenge both the external and internal regulation of labour. This effectively dismissed the exploited status of labour in public discussion.

But where did industrial workers belong in this official narrative? To borrow from Satish Deshpande's work on Nehru's socialism, Kemalist industrialisation imagined the "patriotic producer" at the heart of the nation, surrounded by the apparatus of state-led planning; Turkish state factories anteceded "the temples of modern India" by two decades.[23] The myth and the reality of the Turkish revolution gave etatism the ideological legitimisation it needed to call upon workers without giving them a voice in the national polity. State factories became the centrepieces of postimperial nation-making, and state workers epitomised the ideal of the patriotic producer. In contrast to a private factory, where a profit-making ethos would dominate, a state factory was a thoroughly and openly politicised space where workers were expected to toil for the benefit of a developmentalist regime.

In the field of industrial relations, etatism, again in the official discourse, meant the replacement of colonial and exploitative industrial relations with modern and egalitarian ones. From the beginning of state-led industrialisation, labour protectionism was one of the most important elements of the narrative drawing a contrast between the empire and the republic. In the words of the first labour minister, the fundamental difference between the republican regime and "the previous periods of backwardness" was the recognition of the value of work and workers:

> The mentality that looked down on workers shook our country to its core and has left it on verge of ruin. Representing an attempt at a new life, our republican regime considers it one of its main duties to provide the

23 Charles A. Myers, *Labour Problems in the Industrialization of India* (Cambridge, MA: Harvard University Press, 1958), 7; Satish Deshpande, "Imagined Economies: Styles of Nation-Building in Twentieth Century India," *Journal of Arts and Ideas* 25, no. 26 (1993), 25; Srirupa Roy, *Beyond Belief: India and the Politics of Postcolonial Nationalism* (Durham: Duke University Press, 2007), 134; Jonathan Parry and Christian Strümpell, "On the Desecration of Nehru's 'Temples': Bhilai and Rourkela Compared," *Economic and Political Weekly* 43, no. 19 (2008), 47–57.

> rights and dignity of workers … The Turkish worker is not a mere productive machine for us, but a citizen on whose health, safety, and dignity we place a great deal of care.[24]

His pride in Turkish labour policy was widely shared. The first director of the Bakırköy Factory under etatism confidently explained his managerial vision to a European visitor: "If we take care from the outset not to create an exploited proletariat, if we make our workers feel that this factory belongs to the state and, therefore, to them, and if we really keep all the doors open to them to advance—why shouldn't we succeed?"[25] After a visit to the Bakırköy Factory in 1945, a journalist claimed: "the worker finds a heaven at [state] factories."[26] Another journalist described workers at Bakırköy as "shining, happy, and proud people."[27] Throughout the period, and especially until the emergence of a labour press after 1946, such celebratory reporting abounded, setting out state factories as exemplary national workplaces that provide their workforce with superior social and economic citizenship rights and serve as a model for ideal industrial relations for the whole nation.

The state ideology of class harmony found its strongest expression in the institutionalisation of compulsory arbitration that, once again, combined the claim to the supra-class character of the Turkish state with the fear of class conflict. Compulsory arbitration made perfect sense to a prominent contemporary social policy expert, who argued that because the state, as the largest industrial employer, by definition protected the public interest, it would also protect the interests of workers.[28] Turkey thus diverged from other contexts of state-led industrialisation, where the state intervened actively in the labour-management relationship, first to protect labour, and then, when labour grew too strong, to control it through compulsory arbitration and other methods of repression. The Turkish state had already "clipped the wings" of the labour movement quite effectively in the 1920s, that is, before the state-led industrialisation arrived in full force.[29] In the absence of the right to strike and collective agreements, the state served as the dominant and decisive voice in industrial

24 Sadi Irmak, "Yurdun En Büyük İşçi Sendikası Kömür Havzasında Kuruldu," *Türk İşçisi*, 12 April 1947.

25 Lilo Linke, *Allah Dethroned: A Journey Through Modern Turkey* (London: Constable and Co., 1937), 308.

26 Abidin Daver, "Bakırköy Fabrikasında," *Cumhuriyet*, 19 November 1945.

27 Sedat Saip Altuğ, "Sümerbank Bakırköy Pamuklu Sanayii Müessesesi Yüz Yaşında," *Mensucat Meslek Dergisi* 4, no. 1 (1951), 28–32.

28 Cahit Talas, *İçtimai İktisat* (Ankara: S.B.F. Yayınları, 1961), 298–299.

29 Kerr et al., *Industrialism and Industrial Man*, 92–93.

disputes. At the same time, it largely abstained from intervening in wage determination processes, where, despite the appearance of bureaucratic rules and regulations for state industries at least, individual contracts remained the exclusive instrument regulating employment relationships. In the 1930s, foreign experts criticised the lack of any consistent wage policy at state factories; by the mid-1950s, a prominent contemporary sociologist observed that wages at state factories were determined on the basis of "social justice and moral deliberation."[30] Although the 1936 Labour Code empowered the government to issue minimum wage rates, only a few of these were actually issued. The situation remained unchanged even after the emergence of a trade union movement because unions were not able to play an effective role in arbitration. Wages remained low, and productivity problems persisted.[31] The employers' solution to this, including the managers of state factories, was further work intensification.

The reality of shop-floor relations simply did not square with the contemporary representations of state factories and their workers. Neither does it tally with the descriptions of worker passivity found in various scholarly pieces on the period, writing that positions state action central to an analysis based mainly on state-produced archival material. Re-embedding agency at the workplace level is important for two reasons. First, under conditions of repressive industrialisation, where class-based organisations are banned, workplace resistance requires particular attention. Second, in workplaces where the state plays the role of both employer and regulator, connecting worker agency to state formation and nation-building is key to understanding the making of working-class citizenship.

The ideology of patriotic labour failed to a large extent on the shop floor for a number of reasons. In spite of nationalist propaganda, serious and chronic problems of poor efficiency and low productivity characterised the operations of state factories from the very beginning. As early as 1934, industrial policymakers, who were closely following developments in both Europe (especially Germany) and the Soviet Union, underlined the need to rationalise industrial

30 Ziyaeddin Fahri Fındıkoğlu, "Türkiye'de Sınai Sosyoloji Araştırmaları 1-Defterdar Fabrikası," *Feshane Mensucat Meslek Dergisi* 2, no. 12 (1954), 393; Görkem Akgöz, "Experts, Exiles, and Textiles: German 'Rationalisierung' on 1930s Turkish Shop Floor," *International Review of Social History* 66, no. 2 (2021).

31 ILO, "Labour Problems in Turkey," 188; United States Bureau of Labour Statistics, Summary, 23; Kurthan Fişek, *Devlete Karşı Grevlerin Kritik Tahlili* (Ankara: Ankara Üniversitesi Siyasal Bilgiler Fakültesi Yayınları, 1969), 47; Toker Dereli, *Aydınlar, Sendika Hareketi ve Endüstriyel İlişkiler Sistemi* (Istanbul: Istanbul Üniversitesi İktisat Fakültesi Yayını, 1974), 88; Talas, *İçtimai İktisat*, 299.

production and sought the help of foreign experts to reorganise production and implement scientific methods of labour control. The renovation of the Bakırköy Factory in 1934 was therefore meant to signify a mentality change, from the simple financial control of industrial enterprises to the combination of rational work and patriotic labour.[32] But the operation of the Bakırköy Factory, and other state factories for that matter, remained trapped between the bottlenecks of centralised planning and the reality on the shop floor. There was a considerable gap between formal planning and practical execution, pointing to the fact that Turkish planning and centralisation were open-ended processes rather than a top-down implementation as in other contexts of planned industrialisation.[33]

Foreign and local experts alike agreed that the problems facing Turkish industry went beyond technical issues of productivity. The two main problems for state factories were "the deep sickness" of skills shortages combined with the inefficiency of worker control. The micro-level study of industrial relations offered in this book reveals that a strictly authoritarian world of labour lay hidden behind the ceremonial façade of a scientifically managed, worker-friendly industrial landscape. Industrial managers resorted mainly to work intensification to increase productivity, relying heavily on the iron rule of the foreman on the shop floor. The foremen fell back on tight supervision, abuse, profanity, and threats in order to maintain or increase work effort. In 1943, a foreign expert referred to the operational basis of state textile factories as "the anxiety to increase production," comprised of a lack of scientific labour control and a managerial mentality of getting the most out of the workers and the machines.[34] Supporting evidence came in the 1950s from a local expert, who wrote that industrial policymakers had omitted to consider giving labour its fair share in the benefits of rationalisation in order to secure its cooperation.[35] In the cacophony produced by nationalist pride and the anxiety of underdevelopment, redistribution remained a distant idea, and state workers toiled for low wages and for long hours under a regime of repressive industrial relations.

---

32 Kuruç, *Belgelerle* 2, 269; "Başvekil Hz. Sümer Bank Fabrikalarını Tetkik Ettiler," *Cumhuriyet*, 22 November 1933; "Yeni Daireleri Dün Açıldı," *Haber-Akşam Postası*, 14 August 1934.

33 Stephen Kotkin, *Magnetic Mountain: Stalinism as a Civilization* (Oakland: University of California Press, 1997); Alina-Sandra Cucu, *Planning Labour: Time and the Foundations of Industrial Socialism in Romania* (New York: Berghahn, 2019).

34 Hösli, *Bakırköy Bez Fabrikası Hakkında Rapor*, 1943. Archival Collection of the Republic of Turkey Prime Ministry Supreme Audit Board.Amb. /Db.No: K.A./255.07.02.01.06.1241, 19.

35 Cahit Talas, "Verimliliğin Arttırılmasında Psikolojik ve Manevi Amiller," *Çalışma Vekâleti* 1, no. 1 (1953), 98.

Various scholars have shown that state-led industrialisation was directed by the general logic of capital accumulation. Except for a brief period in the early 1930s, when the scope of active state involvement provoked intense conflict within the ruling bloc, industrial policymakers were largely in agreement that etatism meant a mixed economy in which state and private investment were complementary. By 1935, private enterprise was defined as the "basic idea" in the party programme. The state used the relative autonomy it enjoyed under etatism to develop the socioeconomic and institutional infrastructure required to expand the sources of capital accumulation and mechanisms of surplus extraction.[36] Between 1932 and 1939, the total amount of private capital invested in industry increased by more than eighty-six per cent.[37] By the beginning of the war, a prominent economic historian wrote, the country had already passed the critical first threshold on the difficult road to industrialisation, thanks to the increase in the rate of accumulation.[38] In 1939, thirty-four per cent of all factories were in the hands of private industrialists. The process accelerated during the war years, taking the figure to forty-five per cent by 1945.[39] Industrial workers came out of the war overworked, exhausted, and impoverished. Having seized the exceptional opportunity for profiteering, private capital emerged from the war years with unprecedented rates of accumulation

---

36 Fişek, *Grevlerin Kritik Tahlili*, 5; Yahya Sezai Tezel, "Turkish Economic Development 1923–1950: Policy and Achievements" (PhD diss., University of Cambridge, 1975), 171; İlhan Tekeli and Selim İlkin, *Uygulamaya Geçerken Türkiye'de Devletçiliğin Oluşumu* (Ankara: ODTÜ İdari İlimler Fakültesi, 1982), 336; Berch Berberoğlu, *Turkey in Crisis: From State Capitalism to Neo-colonialism* (London: Zed Books, 1982), 58; Bilsay Kuruç, *Mustafa Kemal Döneminde Ekonomi* (Istanbul: Bilgi Yayınevi, 1987), 53; Kuruç, *Belgelerle 2*, 225; Boratav, *Türkiye İktisat Tarihi*, 57; Boratav, "İktisat Tarihi (1908–1980)," 325; Kepenek and Yentürk, *Türkiye Ekonomisi*, 70, 83–84; Pamuk, "Industrialization in Turkey," 26; Galip Yalman, "The Turkish State and Bourgeoisie in Historical Perspective: A Relativist Paradigm or a Panapoly of Hegemonic Strategies?" in *The Politics of Permanent Crisis; Class, Ideology and State in Turkey*, eds. Neşecan Balkan and Sungur Savran (New York: Nova Science Publishers Inc., 2002), 29–30; Taha Parla and Andrew Davison, *Corporatist Ideology in Kemalist Turkey: Progress or Order?* (Syracuse: Syracuse University Press, 2004), 128; Gülten Kazgan, *Türkiye Ekonomisinde Krizler (1929–2001), "Ekonomi Politik" Açısından bir İrdeleme* (Istanbul: Bilgi Üniversitesi Yayınları, 2005), 78–81; Gülten Kazgan, *Türkiye Ekonomisinde Krizler, 1929–2001*, 81; Korkut Boratav, *Türkiye'de Devletçilik*, 2nd ed. (Ankara: İmge Kitabevi, 2017), 356–357; Richards et al., *A Political Economy of the Middle East*, 43, 178.

37 Fişek, *Grevlerin Kritik Tahlili*, 41.

38 Boratav, "Kemalist Economic Policies," 186.

39 Mehmet Şehmus Güzel, "İkinci Dünya Savaşı Boyunca Sermaye ve Emek," in *Osmanlı'dan Cumhuriyet Türkiye'sine İşçiler*, eds. Donald Quataert and Erik Jan Zürcher, trans. Cahide Ekiz (Istanbul: İletişim Yayınları, 1998), 221.

achieved mainly through speculation and black-marketing.[40] The burden of industrialisation fell on the peasants and the industrial workers.[41]

In the Shadow of War and Empire joins this critical chorus to expand on the point further. Etatism served as the "nursemaid" of Turkish capitalism by providing it with lucrative credit options, expanding the national market, increasing the available technology and know-how, and developing industrial labour and management skills; it also created a labour regime that accelerated, aided, and nurtured private capital accumulation.[42] Based on a new state-sponsored ideology of industrial work that combined nationalism and the ideal of harmonious industrial relations, both at the workplace and the national levels, the 1935 party programme institutionalised the nascent nationalistic labour regime. The 1936 Labour Code, the 1938 Associations Act (*Cemiyetler Kanunu*), and the 1940 National Defence Act (*Milli Korunma Kanunu*) added to these restrictions. The emergent labour regime had long-term consequences for the structure of industrial relations in Turkey in the way that it would shape state, employer, and trade union policies in subsequent decades.

My argument is premised on there being more to labour control than the sphere of production. The labour market is a mental and cultural—as well as an economic— structure, where historical actors negotiate a socially and culturally desirable order. The articulation of state and cultural discourse plays a central part in the constitution of labour control regimes. Building on the discursive representations of a class-neutral state on the one hand, and of "the national economy" and the worker-citizen's place in it on the other, etatism

40 Gülalp, "Patterns of Capital Accumulation," 335–336; Ali Yaşar Sarıbay, "The Democratic Party, 1946–1960," in *Political Parties and Democracy in Turkey*, eds. Martin Heper and Jacob M. Landau (New York: I.B. Tauris, 1990), 120.

41 S.C. Wyatt, "Turkey: The Economic Situation and the Five-Years Plan," *International Affairs* 13, no. 6 (1934), 833–834; Robert V. Kerwin, "Private Enterprise in Turkish Industrial Development," *Middle East Journal* 5, no. 1 (1951), 27; Alec Alexander, "Turkey," in *Economic Development: Analysis and Case Studies,* eds. Adamantios Pepelasis, Leon Mears, and Irma Adelman (New York: Harper & Brothers Publishers, 1961), 475; David Waldner, *State Building and Late Development* (Ithaca: Cornell University Pres, 1999), 204–205; Pamuk, "Industrialization in Turkey," 26; Barkey, *The State and The Industrialisation,* 5; Boratav, *Türkiye İktisat Tarihi,* 53–54; Boratav, "Kemalist Economic Policies," 178; Korkut Boratav, *Türkiye İktisat Tarihi 1908–2009* (Istanbul: Imge, 2003), 53–54, 79; Pamuk, *Uneven Centuries*, 189.

42 James M. Barker, *The Economy of Turkey: An Analysis and Recommendations for A Development Program* (Baltimore: The Johns Hopkins Press, 1951), 161–162; Necdet Serin, "Industrialization Policy of Turkey Since 1923," *Ankara Üniversitesi SBF Dergisi* 20, no. 2 (1965), 199; William Hale attributes the phrase "nursemaid of capitalism" to the economic affairs minister, Celal Bayar. See: William Hale, *The Political and Economic Development of Modern Turkey* (London: Croom Helm, 1981), 56.

played a central role in shaping both the real and discursive contours of the labour regime. Industrial policymakers resorted to etatism to ideologically mobilise and motivate workers to commit their labour power to the process of industrialisation. Such discourses were not only at work in legislation pertaining to industrial relations; they were also embedded and integrated into the regimes of labour control at the workplace level. The regime's perception of its industrial workforce affected the management of industrialisation both on the shop floor and at the commanding heights of the economy.

As the state tried to mould industrial class politics into nation-building, the rhetorical devices of history and public memory became a contested terrain where employers' demands for a labour imbued with patriotic motives clashed with workers' demands for their share in the fruits of national development. The workplace emerged in this process as a crucial site of struggle, where workers, managers, and industrial policymakers would act on particular hegemonic representations of class and national identities. Besides working time and wage payments—the two main sources of major struggle within capitalist production relations—workplace politics manifested themselves as a negotiation of power over the boundaries between the identities of class and nation. In the 1930s and 1940s, workers contested the national narrative of industrial work and its accompanying labour control regime. The subtle, yet pervasive, worker agency expressed, first, at the micro-scale of the workplace and, then, in the trade union movement culminated in the rising tide of worker militancy in the 1960s and 1970s.

3 The Historiography: Industrial Workplace in Global Labour History[43]

A narrative of crisis had pervaded the discipline of labour history for more than two decades by the time I joined the field in the mid-2000s.[44] This sense

43 I have formulated most of the ideas in this section in dialogue with the members of the working group Workplaces: Pasts and Presents (formerly known as Factory History) of the European Labour History Network (https://socialhistoryportal.org/elhn/wg-workplaces). See also Görkem Akgöz, Richard Croucher and Nicola Pizzolato, "Back to the Factory: The Continuing Salience of Industrial Workplace History," Labor History 61, no. 1 (2020), 1–11.

44 Jeffrey Cox, "Labour History and the Labour Movement," *Journal of British Studies* 25 (1986), 233–241; James Epstein, "Rethinking the Categories of Working-Class History," *Labour/Le Travail* 18 (1986), 195–208; Charles Bergquist, "Labour History and Its Challenges: Confessions of a Latin Americanist," *The American Historical Review* 98, no. 3 (1993), 757–764; Marcel van der Linden, ed., *The End of Labour History?* (Cambridge: Cambridge University Press, 1994); Laura L. Frader, "Dissent over Discourse: Labour History, Gender and the Linguistic Turn," *History and Theory* 34, no. 3

of a crisis was a response first and foremost to the socio-political problems of the 1980s. Two of these problems directly concerned the field of labour history. First, the argument that the "forward march of labour" had been halted cast doubt on the political primacy of working-class movements.[45] Second, the very idea of work as the cornerstone of modern society was coming under intense critical scrutiny.[46] Although unspecified, the category of work at stake here was industrial work, as evident in the term coined by social scientists to describe the new social order: post-industrial. Manufacturing had little contemporary resonance, they contended, and the once-emphasised industrial working class was now a marginal phenomenon.

One prominent approach that developed as a response to the perceived crisis of labour history was that of global labour history. By questioning an agenda that was seen as focusing on male workers in industry and other large-scale operations, global labour history broadened the geographical and thematic foci of traditional labour history. As research on non-industrial societies outside Western Europe and North America proliferated, labour historians began to transcend the traditional dichotomies between free and unfree labour, paid and unpaid work, and formally and informally organised workers.[47]

But what happened to the study of the industrial workplace when labour history found a new home? As the steady fragmentation of work and workplaces induced historians to explore previously neglected categories of workers, the potential of the industrial workplace for understanding the workings and logic of capitalism ceased to impress. In their efforts to counterbalance the disproportionate focus on industrial workers and the industrial workplace, labour historians this time relegated industrial work to the margins of the discipline and de-centred the workplace as a site of value production, exploitation, and class. Leon Fink observed that the new insights of labour history were coming

---

(1995), 213–30; Geoff Eley and Keith Nield, "Farewell to the Working Class?" *International Labour and Working-Class History* 57, no. 1 (2000), 30.

45 Eric Hobsbawm, "The Forward March of Labour Halted?" *Marxism Today* 22, no. 9 (1978), 279–286; Gareth Stedman-Jones, *Languages of Class: Studies in English Working Class History, 1832–1982*, (Cambridge: Cambridge University Press, 1983).

46 André *Gorz, Farewell to the Working Class: An Essay on Post-Industrial Socialism* (London: Pluto Press, 1982); Jeremy Rifkin*, The End of Work: The Decline of the Global Labour Force and the Dawn of the Post-Market Era* (New York: Tarcher, 1995).

47 Marcel van der Linden, *Workers of the World: Essays toward a Global Labour History* (Leiden: Brill, 2008); Marcel van der Linden, "Labour History Beyond Borders," in *Histories of Labour: National and International Perspectives*, eds. Joan Allen, Alan Campbell, and John Mcllroy (Decatur: Merlin Press, 2010), 359–360; Lex Heerma Van Voss, "Whither Labour History? Histories of Labour: National and International Perspectives," *International Review of Social History* 58, no. 1 (2013), 97–106.

at a cost of certain blinders, with the marginalisation of industrial labour in the global labour history framework being one of them.[48]

The move away from the historical study of industrial work and the industrial workplace is problematic in two ways. First, in the last two decades or so, factories have received attention almost exclusively at times of crises, such as the Rana Plaza collapse, the Foxconn suicides, and the liquidation of large public-sector companies in developing countries. But, in a world awash with manufactured goods, factories have not disappeared. Nor have they lost their relevance to capitalism. On the contrary, they remain significant sites of employment that are crucial to capitalism. The relocation of industrial production has created more factory jobs in developing economies without entirely destroying them in the developed world. Moreover, the tide seems to have turned at the level of economic policy, as evident from Donald Trump's promise to revive American industry, former British chancellor George Osborne's aspiration for "a Britain carried aloft by the march of the makers," and India's Narendra Modi's "Make in India" slogan for his development agenda. More recently, the technological "reshoring" of manufacturing jobs has been on the agenda for industrial capitalists. And then there is the capital flight taking unexpected directions. For example, the Taiwanese multinational company Foxconn established workshops in Central and Eastern Europe, a region which has become the electronics industry's second-tier global location, just behind East Asia.[49] The 2019 Netflix hit documentary *American Factory*—and the first film produced by Barack and Michelle Obama's production company—tells the story of a Chinese auto-glass manufacturing company opening a division in a shuttered General Motors factory near Dayton, Ohio, in 2016. Last but not least, companies within the service sector (call centres) and logistics and distribution (warehouses) have adopted the factory as a model of production, where workers are highly regimented and their activities constantly measured against metric performance standards, provoking arguments that they constitute present-day "Satanic mills."[50] Overall, these developments suggest that the

48 Leon Fink, "The Great Escape: How a Field Survived Hard Times," *Labour: Studies in Working-Class History of the Americas* 8, no. 1 (2011), 115.

49 Rutvica Andrijasevic and Devi Sacchetto, "China May be Far Away but Foxconn is On Our Doorstep," accessed 5 June 2013, https://www.opendemocracy.net/en/china-may-be-far-away-but-foxconn-is-on-our-doorstep/; Rutvica Andrijasevic and Devi Sacchetto, "Made in the EU: Foxconn in the Czech Republic," *WorkingUSA: The Journal of Labour and Society* 17 (2014).

50 Peter Bain and Phil Taylor, "Entrapped by the 'Electronic Panopticon'? Worker Resistance in the Call Centre," *New Technology, Work and Employment* 15, no. 1 (2000); Moritz

factory's "invisibility" in both current and historical agendas is less an outright disappearance and more a matter of marginalisation and disqualification.[51]

Second, the body of scholarship on the industrial workplace is highly unevenly distributed between the global north and the global south because of inequality in the means of research production, including but not limited to the complex politics of archival work. Within global relations of unequal academic exchange, local processes of state and class formation have shaped national historiographies.[52] By the time the factory and industrial work ceased to impress historians with its potential for understanding capitalism, industrial workplaces in much of the global south had been explored in only the most peripheral way.[53] Though it is true that the extent of scholarship on industrial labour is significantly smaller in contexts outside Western Europe and North America (the socialist scholarship on the industrial workplace, especially after 1945, should of course be included here), the difference is not only a matter of quantity. The subject has taken different paths in "the north" and "the south." Even if the historical shift to the industrial workplace was systemic and global in character, it was definitely not uniform or linear. Historically, capitalism created a variety of labour relations both within and between industrial workplaces.

To begin with, and mostly based on a series of global antinomies on working-class formation such as traditional versus modern, co-optation versus autonomy, and resistance versus integration, history written outside Europe has mostly been "the historiography of '(not) yet,' of absences."[54] Similarly to the problematisation of the absent bourgeoisie as "the collective hero of western civilisation" in Soviet historiography, or the "dominance-without-hegemony"

Altenried, *The Digital Factory: The Human Labor of Automation* (Chicago: Chicago University Press, 2022).

51 Jackie Clarke, "Closing Moulinex: Thoughts on the Visibility and Invisibility of Industrial Labour in Contemporary France," *Modern & Contemporary France* 19, no. 4 (2011).

52 Marcel van der Linden, "Labour History: The Old and the New and the Global," *African Studies* 66, no. 2–3 (2007), 174; Gabriel Winant, Andrew Gordon, Sven Beckert, and Rudi Batzell, "Introduction: The Global E.P. Thompson," *International Review of Social History* 61 (2016), 1.

53 It should be noted that significant differences in labour historiography exist in the global south. Latin America and South Africa, for example, saw a wave of historical studies on industrial labour in the 1970s. Interest in labour history preceded this wave by a decade due to the strong influence of the British university tradition. See: Marcel van der Linden, "The 'Globalisation' of Labour and Working-Class History and Its Consequences," in *The Global History of Work: Critical Readings: Vol. 1: Work and Workers in Context*, ed. Marcel van der Linden (*London:* Bloomsbury Publishing, 2019), 138–139.

54 van der Linden, "The 'Globalization' of Labour and Working-Class," 142.

thesis in Indian historiography, the dominance of state over society and the implications of a missing native bourgeoisie have been most prevailing paradigms in Ottoman and Turkish historiography.[55] In India, for example, historians cited the weakness of capitalist development and the persistence of "premodern" non-class loyalties as evidence for the unthinkability of a working class, let alone a class-conscious working class.[56] In the same vein, when I first expressed my interest in the labour history of the early republican period, a prominent Turkish historical sociologist asked me whether there even existed a working class worthy of study at all.

The enduring resilience of the law and the state in studies on Turkey's working-class history misses the complexity of labour-state relations. As a latecomer to issues being raised by social and transnational history, scholarship in Turkey has remained largely state-centred, policy-oriented, and insular. Reduced to the prey of state ideology and manipulation, the working class is usually presented as an ideal construct at the service of state ideology, whereas the state is conceptualised as a more or less autonomous bureaucratic apparatus.[57] Because labour historians have tended to reduce class formation to

55 Şerif Mardin, "Center–Periphery Relations: A Key to Turkish Politics?" *Daedalus* 102 (1972), 169–191; A. J. Toynbee, "The Ottoman Empire's Place in World History," in *The Ottoman State and Its Place in World History,* ed. Kemal Karpat (Leiden: Brill, 1974), 15–34; Halil İnalcık, "Turkey Between Europe and the Middle East," *Foreign Policy* 7 (1980), 12–21; Lewis H. Siegelbaum and Michael Morgan, "'State' versus 'Society' in Tsarist and Soviet History," *Radical History Review* 28, no. 30 (1984), 96; Metin Heper, *The State Tradition in Turkey* (Walkington: Eothen Press, 1985); Binnaz Toprak, "The State, Politics, and Religion in Turkey," in *State, Democracy and the Military: Turkey in the 1980's*, eds. Metin Heper and Ahmet Evin (Berlin: Walter de Gruyter, 1988), 119–137; Ranajit Guha, *Dominance Without Hegemony: History and Power in Colonial India* (Cambridge: Harvard University Press, 1997); Susie Tharu, "Citizenship and Its Discontents," in *A Question of Silence? The Sexual Economics of Modern India,* eds. Mary E. John and Janaki Nair (New Delhi: Zed Books, 1998), 224; Chitra Joshi, "Histories of Indian Labour: Predicaments and Possibilities," *History Compass* 6, no. 2 (2008), 439–454.

56 Rajnarayan *Chandavarkar,* "'*The Making* of the Working Class': E. P. Thompson and Indian History," *History Workshop Journal* 43, no. 1 (1997), 179.

57 Dereli, *Sendika Hareketi*, 283–284; Ahmet İnsel, "Devletçiliğin Anatomisi," in *Cumhuriyet Dönemi Türkiye Ansiklopedisi* 2 (Istanbul: İletişim Yayınları, 1984), 419–442; Ahmet İnsel and Cengiz Aktar, "'*Devletin Bekası*' İçin Yürütülen Çağdaşlaşma Sürecinin Toplumsal Sorunları," *Toplum ve Bilim* 31, no. 39 (1987), 39; Yıldırım Koç, "1923–1950 Döneminde CHP'nin İşçi Sınıfı Korkusu," *Mülkiyeliler Birliği Dergisi* 170 (1994), 43–44; Yıldırım Koç, "Türkiye'de 1923–1946 Döneminde Mülksüzleşme ve İşçi Sınıfının Oluşumu," *Mülkiyeliler Birliği Dergisi* 174 (1994), 14–28; M. Bülent Varlık, "Izmir Sanayi İşçileri Birliği-1932," *Mülkiyeliler Birliği Dergisi* 155 (1995), 35–40; M. Bülent Varlık, "Izmir İşçi-Esnaf Kurumlar Birliği Yardım Talimatnameleri (1935–1936)," *Kebikeç-İnsan Bilimleri İçin Kaynak Dergisi* 4 (1996), 195–201; M. Bülent Varlık, "Izmir İşçi ve Esnaf Birlikleri Genel Bürosu Nizamnamesi

stages of economic development, they have rarely passed through the gate of the industrial workplace to analyse the social relations *in* production, including regimes of labour control, changes in the labour process and technology, shop-floor cultures, and the production of gender, ethnic, and racial difference on the shop floor.[58] Historians have mistaken state and management discourse and objectives for what actually happened inside the workplace because they viewed the industrial workplace as the derivative of external orientations to work rather than as a source of conflict and identity. Because working-class formation and political development seem to have occurred in a sphere external to the workplace, the rank-and-file politics of workers and their mentalities, identities, and everyday experiences have virtually escaped scholarly attention.[59]

The challenge facing historians of industrial labour, especially in the global south, is to take the recent historiographical and theoretical insights and bring them to bear on the industrial workplace. By interweaving the history of the industrial workplace with questions of national and transnational movements of labour and capital, memory, state policy, and national ideology, we can view

(1935)," *Kebikeç-İnsan Bilimleri İçin Kaynak Dergisi* 5 (1997), 201–205; M. Şehmuz Güzel, *Türkiye'de İşçi Hareketleri 1908–1984*, (Istanbul: Kaynak Yayınları, 1996), 136–137; Hakkı Uyar, "CHP Izmir İşçi ve Esnaf Cemiyetleri Birliği (1935)/Devletin İşçi Sınıfı ve Örgütlenme Girişimi," *Tarih ve Toplum* 160 (1997), 14–20; Makal, "Sanayileşme Sürecinde İşgücü Sorunu ve Sosyal Politika," 44.

58 A new wave of research decentres the state in labour history, but still, most of it refers mainly to the working-class experience outside the workplace: See, for example: Catherine Alexander, *Personal States: Making Connections between People and Bureaucracy in Turkey* (New York: Oxford University Press, 2002); Can Nacar, "'Our Lives Were Not as Valuable as an Animal': Workers in State-Run Industries in World-War-II Turkey," *International Review of Social History* 54 (2009), 143–166; Nurşen Gürboğa, "Compulsory Mine Work: The Single-Party Regime and the Zonguldak Coalfield as a Site of Contention, 1940–1947," *International Review of Social History* 54 (2009), 115–142; Yiğit Akın, "The Dynamics of Working-Class Politics in Early Republican Turkey: Language, Identity, and Experience," *International Review of Social History IRSH* 54 (2009), 167–188; Caroline E. Arnold, "In the Service of Industrialization: Etatism, Social Services and the Construction of Industrial Labour Forces in Turkey (1930–50)," *Middle Eastern Studies* 48, no. 3 (2012), 363–385; Barış Alp Özden, "Health, Morality and Housing: The Politics of Working Class Housing in Turkey, 1945–1960," *New Perspectives on Turkey* 49 (2013), 91–120; Ali Sipahi, "Convict Labour in Turkey, 1936–1953: A Capitalist Corporation in the State?," *International Labour and Working-Class History* 90 (2016), 244–265.

59 Anna Sailer, *Workplace Relations in Colonial Bengal: The Jute Industry and Indian Labour 1870s-1930s* (London: Bloomsbury, 2022), 9; Paul Thompson and Chris Smith, "Labour Power and Labour Process: Contesting the Marginality of the Sociology of Work," *Sociology* 43, no. 5 (2009), 916; Richard Coopey and Alan McKinlay, "Power Without Knowledge? Foucault and Fordism, c. 1900–50," *Labor History* 51 (2010), 114.

history in our own regions in a new light. The economic, social, and political transformations of the industrial workplace have not only mirrored but also shaped national and global shifts; a study of its history presents a way of approaching broader historical processes while engaging with specifically local questions.

We are lucky to have a base to build on for a more totalising and less particularistic history of the industrial workplace. Industrial workplace-based research in labour history and in fields adjacent to labour history have left behind a theoretically and empirically rich tradition. From the renowned American Hawthorne study within a social psychology framework in the 1920s and 1930s, to the anthropologically informed studies of factories in the 1940s, and the expansion of British industrial anthropology and sociology in the 1950s and 1960s, shop-floor studies have grown central to social theory.[60] In the 1960s, autonomous Marxists coined the term "social factory" to explain how the capital accumulation process escapes the confines of the factory and extends into society as a whole.[61] In the 1970s, labour process theory revitalised sociological studies of work by focusing on how the indeterminacy of labour power generated struggle and resistance on the shop floor.[62] It became commonplace for researchers of industrial workplaces to challenge abstract conceptions of workplace conflict and class struggle, and to conceptualise industrial conflict

60 Elton Mayo, *The Human Problems of an Industrial Civilization* (New York: MacMillan, 1933); Mass Observation, *War Factory* (MO: London, 1943); Elton Mayo, *The Social Problems of an Industrial Civilization* (London: Routledge & Kegan Paul, 1949); Eric Batstone, Ian Boraston, and Stephen Frenkel, *Shop Stewards in Action: The Organization of Workplace Conflict and Accommodation* (Oxford: Blackwell, 1979); Carol S. Holzberg and Maureen J. Giovannini, "Anthropology and Industry: Reappraisal and New Directions," *Annual Review of Anthropology* 10, no. 1 (1981), 317–360; Sheila Cunnison, "The Manchester Factory Studies, the Social Context, Bureaucratic Organisation, Sexual Divisions and Their Influence on Patterns of Accommodation between Workers and Management," in *Custom and Conflict in British Society*, ed. R. Frankenberg (Manchester: Manchester University Press, 1982), 94–139; Isabel Emmett and D.H.J. Morgan, "Max Gluckman and the Manchester Shop-floor Ethnographies," in *Custom and Conflict in British Society*, ed. R. Frankenberg (Manchester: Manchester University Press, 1982), 140–165.

61 Mario Tronti, "Factory and Society," trans. Guio Jacintoh, *Operaismo in English*, accessed 17 January 2022, https://operaismoinenglish.wordpress.com/2013/06/13/factory-and-society/.

62 Michael Burawoy, *Manufacturing Consent: Changes in the Labour Process Under Monopoly Capitalism* (Chicago: University of Chicago Press, 1979); *The Politics of Production: Factory Regimes Under Capitalism and Socialism* (London: Verso, 1985); P.K. Edwards,"Understanding Conflict in the Labour Process: The Logic and Autonomy of Struggle," in *Labour Process Theory*, eds. D. Knight & H. Willmott (London: Palgrave Macmillan, 1990), 125–152.

beyond its overt, organised expression and incorporate it into their analyses of the daily experiences of workers and their representatives, composing a far more complex picture of the past.

Scholars theorising the workplace in historical studies joined this concerted effort, drawing on labour process theory and social history. Arguing that the worker's worldview was formed above all at the point of production, they called for the study of workers within the workplace itself, the site where "working people and the capitalists confronted each other [and] the labour process is actualized" and where "the theory and practice of industrial relations strategies meet, founder, are successful or modified."[63] Analyses at this level offer a view into the nitty-gritty of formal and informal mechanisms of political mediation on the shop floor.

Recent studies have begun to recognise the centrality of the workplace and shop-floor organisation to an understanding not only of working-class experience and the process of intersectional identity formation, but also of wider social developments. They have conceptualised the industrial workplace beyond a local and inward-looking unit, to incorporate different angles beyond the exclusive focus on labour relations. Through new interpretative lenses, they have addressed a range of questions such as the construction and reconstruction of social identities in relation to the experience of work, the production of social difference both in relation to labour and social practices, and the discourses around it.[64] There has also been an upsurge in interest

---

63 David Montgomery, *The Fall of the House of Labor: The Workplace, the State, and American Labour Activism, 1865–1925* (New York: Cambridge University Press, 1987); David Brody, "Labor History in the 1970s," in *The Past Before Us: Contemporary Historical Writings in The United,* ed. Michael Kammen (Ithaca: Cornell University Press, 1980), 252–269; Jeremy Brecher, "Uncovering the Hidden History of the American Workplace," *Review of Radical Political Economics* 10, no. 4 (1978), 20; Richard Price, "'What's in a Name?' Workplace History and 'Rank and Filism'," *International Review of Social History* 34, no. 1 (1989), 64.

64 Peter Winn, *Weavers of the Revolution: The Yarur Workers and Chile's Road to Socialism* (Oxford: Oxford University Press, 1986); Diane Lauren Wolf, *Factory Daughters: Gender, Household Dynamics, and Rural Industrialization in Java* (Berkeley: University of California Press, 1992); Kevin Yelvington, *Producing Power: Ethnicity, Gender, and Class in a Caribbean Workplace* (Philadelphia: Temple University Press, 1996); Thomas Miller Klubock, *Contested Communities: Class, Gender, and Politics in Chile's El Teniente Copper Mine, 1904–1951* (Durham, NC: Duke University Press, 1998); Angela Vergara, *Copper Workers, International Business, and Domestic Politics in Cold War Chile* (University Park, PA: Pennsylvania State University Press, 2008); Samer S. Shehata, *Shop Floor Culture and Politics in Egypt* (Albany: SUNY Press, 2009); Victoria Basualdo, "Shop-Floor Labour Organization in Argentina From Early Peronism to the 'Proceso' Military Dictatorship," *Working USA: The Journal of Labour and Society* 14, no. 3 (2011), 305–332; Sailer, *Workplace Relations*; Hanan Hammad, *Industrial Sexuality: Gender, Urbanization, and Social*

in the anthropological study of the industrial workplace. Recent work on the anthropology of industrial labour has focused on the experience of flexible work on fragmented shop floors, that is, the unequal employment status between regular and casual, or between company and contract workers. Underlining how Taylorist and flexible forms of production are recombined and reconnected on the same shop floor, anthropologists have analysed labour relations among workers enjoying different work statuses and benefits while working in the same industrial workplace, sometimes doing the exact same job. Anthropologists have also underlined the intricate connections between the local workplace and global markets. By linking localised centres of production with wider global relationships and forces, they have shown how chains of production and consumption relate to industrial relations.[65] The time is ripe for a cross-fertilisation between history and other disciplines, from anthropology to critical organisational studies and geography, and to explore the industrial workplace as a key place to challenge the models of a linear and uniform progress of capitalism and to analyse its combined and uneven development across time and space.

This book joins the recent efforts to open up the national histories of labour based on modernisation theories by attending to the worker's concrete experience at the point of production. In exploring the complex dimensions of class as a lived experience and structured determination, it strives to overcome the

---

Transformation in Egypt (Austin: University of Texas Press, 2016); Prerna Agarwal, "The War at The Workplace: Calcutta's Dockworkers and Changing Labour Regime, 1939–1945," *International Review of Social History* 67, no. 3 (2022). A new generation of researchers revitalised the study of the socialist industrial workplace, which was previously limited to a predictably 'party' and teleological frame, by addressing a multitude of previously neglected questions. See: Renata Kirin and Marina Blagaić, "The Ambivalence of Socialist Working Women's Heritage: A Case Study of the Jugoplastika Factory," *Narodna Umjetnost* 1, no. 150 (2013), 40–73; Rory Archer and Goran Musić, "Approaching the Socialist Factory and Its Workforce: Considerations from Fieldwork in (Former) Yugoslavia," *Labor History* 58, no. 1 (2017), 44–66; Cucu, *Planning Labour*; Goran Musić, *Making and Breaking the Yugoslav Working Class: The Story of Two Self-Managed Factories* (Budapest: Central European University Press, 2021).

65 Geert De Neve, "Towards an Ethnography of the Workplace: Hierarchy, Authority and Sociability on the South Indian Textile Shop Floor," *South Asia Research* 21, no. 2 (2001), 133–160; Massimiliano Mollona, "Factory, Family and Neighbourhood: The Political Economy of Informal Labour in Sheffield," *The Journal of the Royal Anthropological Institute* 11, no. 3 (2005), 527–548; Jonathan Parry, "Sex, Bricks and Mortar: Constructing Class in a Central Indian Steel Town," *Modern Asian Studies* 48, no. 5 (2014), 1,242–1,275; Dimitra Kofti, "*Moral Economy of Flexible Production: Fabricating Precarity Between the Conveyor Belt and the Household*," *Anthropological Theory* 16, no. 4 (2016), 433–453; Christian *Strümpell*, "The Anthropology of *Work* and *Labour*," *Ethnoscripts* 19, no. 2 (2017), 5–14.

divide between the micro level of the production floor and the macro level of state policy, doing history "from the bottom up, all the way to the top."[66] It treats the Bakırköy Factory not as the background to the story, a closed and inward-looking unit behind-the-scenes, but as a "contact zone," that is, a seemingly static locality made up of circulations of capital, labour, and industrial expertise, as well as the politico-economic visions of different state regimes.[67] Both in history and in cinema, the global perspective in any close-up is implicit, argues Carlo Ginzburg.[68] The close-ups in this book focus on workers' everyday practices that are replete with agency, and I build on them to reconnect worker agency to the wider societal structures it is embedded in.

4 The Book: Sources, Themes, and Organisation

In the Shadow of War and Empire offers a broad variety of perspectives and voices through which to examine both the official and celebratory narratives as well as the critical counternarratives on etatism. Throughout the book, the reader will hear from bureaucrats, intellectuals, foreign and local industrial experts, employers, managers, and, last but not least, workers themselves. To present these diverse voices, I draw on a broad range of sources, including state documents, inspection reports, travel writing, memoirs, workers' files, oral interviews, and periodicals.

Turkey's relatively weak archival infrastructure and its historically modest levels of popular literacy have tempted scholars of labour to opt for textual analyses of the discourses generated by dominant groups. This has impeded the pressing task of undoing the elite-centred historiography. Materials that allow us to see and understand what workers were doing and thinking, or data of any kind on the actual work process, are hard to find in Turkey. As are worker voices on how they experienced work, how they made sense of their lives and the wider forces operating in society, and how they lived with the demands and constraints of industrial labour. For the brief period of trade unionism covered

66 Stephen Mihm, "Interchange: The History of Capitalism," *Journal of American History* 101 (2014), 504.

67 Christian G. De Vito and Anne Gerritsen, "Introduction," in *Micro-Spatial Histories of Global Labour*, eds. Christian G. De Vito and Anne Gerritsen (London: Palgrave Macmillan, 2018), 1–28, 7.

68 Interview with Carlo Ginzburg by Nicolas Weill, accessed 28 February 2023, https://www.versobooks.com/blogs/5536-carlo-ginzburg-in-history-as-in-cinema-every-close-up-implies-an-off-screen-scene.

here, there are virtually no documents actually produced by the unions. As a whole, the scant, scattered, and mostly normative nature of historical material has been a major constraint in writing this book. Partly to overcome this difficulty, I dynamically move between different scales of analysis. In order to demonstrate the complex and varied ways in which nation-building and industrialisation interacted on and off the factory floor, I have pieced together Bakırköy workers' life trajectories from slim and sketchy material, highlighting the embeddedness of their experiences and the choices available to them in the larger context of hierarchical relations of power and domination. Although I have not been afraid to indulge in reasoned and informed speculation or comment, I have tried not only to explicitly note such instances but also to keep them to a minimum.

Since they present workers' voices most clearly, a few words on the workers' files are warranted. In the mid-2000s, the workers' files were still at the factory site. In my first attempt to view them, I was told they had been lost. After spending more than a year going back and forth between government offices, I learnt that they had become dark archives, meaning that they lay uncatalogued and inaccessible to researchers in the basement of the Republican Archives. Six months of persistence later, I gained extremely limited access to specific records following a process of personal negotiation. During the two months of my permitted access, I was able to request files based on limited information (namely, name, staff number, birth place, and date) on Excel sheets covering all state workers. Under these circumstances, finding the file of a worker who worked in the Bakırköy Factory in the 1930s or 1940s felt like winning the lottery. Not being allowed to photograph or copy the documents, I took handwritten notes. I spent several years pestering the national archives for further access to these files, but to no avail.

This severely limited archival access served to silence the voices of child workers. They were certainly there, and they were many. But their voices could not be found in the archives. With female workers, I had slightly more success, but almost all of the very few files that belonged to women were empty, except for their initial employment forms. Despite my efforts to recruit alternative sources through which women could speak, I could not overcome the gendered silences of documentation and history. At this point, I can only hope for further studies that investigate in more detail how class and gender interacted on the shop floor.

The book comprises two parts. Part 1 covers the state strategies of industrialisation, first, in the mid-nineteenth-century Ottoman Empire and, then, in republican Turkey. From the construction of the Bakırköy Factory in the 1840s to the implementation of etatism in the 1930s, it focuses on the political economy and macro processes of peripheral industrialisation. The central themes here are postimperial state discourses, labour legislation, spatiality of development, and local labour markets. With Part 2, we enter the gates of the Bakırköy Factory, but without losing sight of the relations of production, the external regulation of labour, and the worker experience outside the workplace. The experience-near analysis of the lived reality of state-led industrialisation on the shop floor here builds on the macro processes described in Part 1. By reducing the scale of historical analysis, I redirect the reader's gaze toward the dense textures of workers' everyday lives, social relationships, and political agency. Relationships and bargaining at the point of employment, gender relations on the shop floor, and the development of the trade union movement are among the central themes I explore.

The general approach adopted in terms of organisation of this book has been that of narrative analysis. The chapters follow a chronological order. The first chapter locates the politico-economic underpinnings of 1930s Turkish state-led industrialisation within the nineteenth-century peripheralisation of the Ottoman economy. In order to ground the story in place and time, it starts with Ottoman efforts to catch up with European manufacturing by constructing an industrial complex they proudly crowned the "Turkish Manchester." The chapter presents a multi-level analysis of the political economy of Ottoman underdevelopment, the urban industrial geography of Istanbul, the financially and industrially prominent Armenian Dadian family, the technology and technical expertise transfer from Europe, and the multi-ethnic character of the Ottoman industrial workforce. An analysis of how this history was rewritten completely during the republican period sets the tone for the remainder of the book.

Chapter 2 finds Turkey in the midst of the Independence War, and follows her through the first decade of her struggles and ambitions. The central focus of this chapter is the diverse array of international and domestic forces that brought about the policy change from an open economy in the 1920s to a mixed economy of protectionism and etatism in the 1930s. Besides the politico-economic and policy determinants of state-led industrialisation, I also attend to the intra-elite conflicts, specifically the politics of foreign industrial expertise, the debate on the institutional framework of industrialisation, and the multiple failed attempts to enact a Turkish labour code. The winning party in these class conflicts within the state apparatus would go on to direct etatism as a capitalist project of industrialisation with a clear vision of class relations in the coming years.

But what was the territorial logic that lay behind state-led industrialisation? Chapter 3 starts with this question, and explains how the Turkish state elite desperately tried to undo the uneven geographical development that was left behind by the Ottoman economy under the domination of foreign capital. The spatial configuration of development thinking reflected the postimperial anxieties associated with transforming Turkey into an economically and culturally integrated nation-state. Together with a nationalised and expanded railway network, industrial site selection in interwar Turkey was part of a state strategy to achieve national consolidation and effective statehood. This chapter offers an important correction to the treatment of state industries as a unified entity by examining the differences between the old industrial centres and the new industrial sites in terms of local labour market dynamics. The historically uneven spatial development of capitalism produced considerably divergent outcomes in terms of labour recruitment and stability, as well as the conditions of labour reproduction. It was local rather than national forces that shaped labour market outcomes, especially with regards to its gender dynamics.

Shop-floor industrial relations sit at the centre of the analysis in Chapter 4. I take issue with the prevalent arguments on state workers' working and living conditions in the 1930s and 1940s, attending to the physical conditions of production, the factory administrative structure, employment and wage policy, labour control strategies, social provisions, and housing problems. This chapter brings the disjuncture between ideological prescription and everyday practice to the fore by examining the micro-physics of power. The failed attempt at rationalising production, repressive shop-floor management practices, and isolated and individualised worker resistance are the main themes.

Building on the extended histories of workers' shop floor experiences through their petitions, Chapter 5 depicts the factory as a space of everyday work charged with political meaning, and traces the day-to-day conflicts and compromises that took place on the shop floor in the 1940s. The Turkish state factory, like any other industrial workplace under capitalism, was a contested terrain where norms were negotiated and redefined. A two-way struggle between labour and management, however unequal the terms, over the drawing of lines of authority characterised daily interactions on the shop floor. Midway into the 1940s, a significant change occurred in the direct manifestation of class relationships over the control of the job and the line of authority. This chapter explains that change through a study of the links between the political system, industrial legislation, and the emergence of new patterns of industrial conflict.

With chapter 6, we enter the fast-changing world of workers in postwar Turkey to track down the rise of labour as a political category. Focusing on the early trade union movement, I build on the premise that workplace relations and working-class politics are not merely expressions of structural class positions, and argue that worker subjectivity contains shifting and contradictory positions that cannot be understood without paying due attention to labour relations on the shop floor. I specifically follow the life trajectories of two trade unionists during the 1950s who adopted two different insider's critiques of the mainstream political direction taken by the union movement, and paid for their political choices. Their life stories reveal the multiple working-class political positions that were extinguished or submerged.

I now invite the reader to a century-long industrial walk in Istanbul. We will set off with enthusiastic Ottoman industrialists and their curious but cautious European visitors, continue with ambitious republican policymakers and idealistic factory managers, and end with disillusioned but increasingly determined worker-citizens. An industrial workplace overlooking the Marmara Sea, which once lay outside the city walls but was later incorporated into the city, will be our vantage point to look upon this action-packed history.

PART 1

CHAPTER 1

The "Turkish Manchester"

Factories in Nineteenth-Century Istanbul

On one of the hottest days in the middle of August 1847, Charles MacFarlane, a Scottish writer known as much for his historical and travel works as for his novels, was walking up the hill to the village of Safraköy. Twenty years after his first visit to the imperial capital, he had returned to see whether the "revolting conditions of the Government and the people" had been as greatly improved as he had been told. What he and his company saw from their vantage point was in direct contrast to the conditions in the hill-top village. Seeing the latter was like a journey to a past frozen in time, for nothing had changed in the "barren" scenery of the backward empire. The sight at the bottom of the hill in the distance, however, was bustling with tall industrial chimneys and furnaces, the symbols of the empire's prospects:

> We ascended to the hill village of Saffra-keui ... The high road to Adrianople ... traversed the undulating plain beneath us ... from that height we saw the tall chimneys of the iron works, blast-furnace, and cotton mill near Macri-keui, and the immense enclosures and buildings, and engine-houses for all manner of manufactories that were to be at Zeitoun Bournu; the Armenians having, years ago, persuaded the Sultan that the proper way to improve the country was to begin by establishing in it all manner of manufactures, and so prevent the issue of money to England, France, and Germany; and that by importing a hundred or two of foreign workmen, and making them teach their arts to the people of the country, they could soon create a Turkish Manchester and Leeds, a Turkish Birmingham and Sheffield at Zeitoun Bournu, and produce (between that place and Macri-keui) every article that could be needed.[1]

The hill where MacFarlane stood was to the northeast of the western boundary of the industrial complex in Küçük Çekmece. Located on the European shore of the Marmara Sea, the complex stretched almost fifteen kilometres

1 Charles MacFarlane, *Turkey and Its Destiny: The Result of Journeys Made in 1847 and 1848 to Examine into the State of That Country,* vol. 1 (London: John Murray, 1850), iii, 57–8.

© GÖRKEM AKGÖZ, 2024 | DOI:10.1163/9789004687141_003

east-to-west on the coastline to the Yedikule corner of the Istanbul land walls. It was bounded by the road to Edirne (Adrianople) in the north, while the Marmara Sea constituted its natural southern border. It was divided into two parts. Closer to the city walls was the district of Zeytinburnu, where an iron foundry and machine works was located. It was called the Grande Fabrique because it was the largest industrial enterprise at the time. The second part was located a couple of kilometres west of the foundry toward Bakırköy (or, Macri-keui, as it was known to foreigners then). It housed a boatyard designed to build steamships, as well as other industrial plants and a model agricultural farm.[2]

MAP 1 Nineteenth-century Istanbul
INSTITUT FRANÇAIS D'ETUDES ANATOLIENNES—MAP ARCHIVES

Approximately five months later, MacFarlane and his company were in Bakırköy and walking in the direction of the iron works when they saw an iron steamboat construction site on the bank of a little creek. Some thirty metres away were the walls of the "*Barouth-Khaneh*," the Imperial Powder Works (*Baruthane-i Amire*). The two sites were in such close proximity that sparks from the steam engine's chimney would fly over the walls of the the boat construction site to land near the furnace and two forges of the gunpowder works. There had already been explosions at the gunpowder works even before the

2 Edward C. Clark, "The Ottoman Industrial Revolution," *International Journal of Middle East Studies* 5, no. 1 (1974), 67; Wolfgang Müller-Wiener, "15. –19. Yüzyıllar Arasında Istanbul'da İmalathane ve Fabrikalar" in *Osmanlılar ve Batı Teknolojisi: Yeni Araştırmalar, Yeni Görüşler*, ed. Ekmeleddin İhsanoğlu (Istanbul: Edebiyat Fakültesi Basımevi, 1992), 78; Tevfik Güran, "Tanzimat Döneminde Devlet Fabrikaları" in *150. Yılında Tanzimat*, ed. Hakkı Dursun Yıldız (Ankara: Türk Tarih Kurumu Yayınları, 1992), 250.

arrival of their inflammable neighbours; they now looked to be inevitable. But this was not the only planning quandary. The iron boat "looked like a reel in a bottle," for its building site "had no exit to the sea except by a narrow mouth chopped up by a sandbank." Once the steamboat was ready to get afloat, the English builder Mr Phillips explained, the Ottomans would have to spend a large sum of money to clear up the mouth of the water and they would lose more money on what was already a preposterously expensive project. The Englishman had previously told the Ottoman managers of the industrial complex that building the ship at the Imperial Arsenal at the Golden Horn would be much more rational. He was confused and frustrated because the Ottomans rebutted his suggestion and just carried on with their existing plan. MacFarlane, on the other hand, had a better insight into the reasons behind such irrational decision-making and bad management practices: "I, however, understood why they had selected this cul-de-sac, this unsightly and perilous hole. It stood within their regions—it was within the kingdom of the Dadians, which extended from the land-walls of Constantinople to their other powder-works at St. George, on the lake called Ponte Piccolo [Küçük Çekmece], five miles beyond San Stefano [Yeşilköy]. Overall, in this region the Dadians were lords paramount."[3]

In this "kingdom of the Dadians" (or, *Dadyans,* as it is written in Turkish), there stood also a textile mill. Having been established as a small calico plant by Ohannes Dadian in the 1840s, this factory had survived the Ottoman Empire to become one of Turkey's major state textile factories—Bakırköy Bez Fabrikası, or as it was popularly known, "*Basmahane*" (lit., calico house). The history of the Bakırköy Factory, much like other large factories of the period, constitutes a formative chapter in Ottoman modernisation efforts that had developed in the nineteenth century as a response to two political and economic developments. Politically, the central government needed to ward off the provincial forces, often through armed conflict, resulting in heavy military expenses. Economically, the penetration of world capitalism into the empire during the nineteenth century introduced trade competition, foreign lending, and exchange rate instability. The construction of the industrial complex was part of an Ottoman economic policy of crash industrialisation in the 1840s. But it was too little, too late to overcome the mounting pressure of European manufacturing, especially in the textile sector.

The emergence and failure of the Turkish Manchester project, besides being an important chapter in the complex history of the empire's capitalist

3 Charles MacFarlane, *Turkey and Its Destiny,* vol. 2, (London: John Murray, 1850), 220.

integration, has been a significant motif in the republican industrial discourse. However, before delving into the details of this attempt, as well as the associated hegemonic politics of memory, a historiographical note is due. In describing this attempt as a failure, I am fully aware of the pitfalls of the standard modernisation theory dichotomies of Ottoman tradition and Western modernity. Recently, Ottoman historians have challenged the conventional and deterministic historical discourses of imperial decline and break-down that failed to grasp the complexities of the empire's final century.[4] At a time when approaches to the eighteenth and nineteenth centuries as a period of multifaceted transformations are gaining ground, my use of the term "failure" requires specification. The story is more complicated and complex than an all-encompassing failure of the late Ottoman industry, or even more particularly of the textile industry. While some textile industries withered irreversibly in the nineteenth century, others recovered after the initial onslaught of European imports to the extent that there was a general revival of Ottoman manufacturing in the final quarter of the nineteenth century.[5] A linear account of Ottoman economic decline and de-industrialisation in the era of European industrial hegemony would therefore be nothing more than a flat story.

The main issue at stake here is the comparative lack of mechanised factories, or, following the language of MacFarlane's Ottoman guides, the lack of an Ottoman development of a Manchester-style industrial infrastructure. Their heightened hopes for the growth of modern industry soon gave way to disillusionment. In the second half of the nineteenth century, the Middle East and North Africa had far less industrialisation than Latin America or East Asia.[6] My focus in this book is on machine-based and factory-located manufacturing;

4 Frederick F. Anscombe, "Islam and the Age of Ottoman Reform," *Past and Present* 208, no. 1 (2010), 159–189; Olivier Bouquet, "Is it Time to Stop Speaking about Ottoman Modernisation?" in *Order and Compromise: Government Practices in Turkey from the Late Ottoman Empire to the Early 21st Century*, eds. M. Aymes, B. Gourisse and É. Massicard (Leiden: Brill, 2015), 45–48; Ali Yaycıoğlu, *Partners of the Empire: The Crisis of the Ottoman Order in the Age of Revolutions* (Stanford: Stanford University Press, 2016), 9–12; Murat R. Şiviloğlu, *The Emergence of Public Opinion: State and Society in the Late Ottoman Empire* (New York: Cambridge University Press, 2018), 1–22; Özgür Türesay, "The Political Language of *Takvīm-i vekayi*: The Discourse and Temporality of Ottoman 'Reform' (1831–1834)," *European Journal of Turkish Studies* 31 (2020); Alp Eren Topal, "Tanzimat Politics Revisited: New Sources and Novel Approaches," *Journal of the Ottoman and Turkish Studies Association* 8, no. 1 (2021), 463–464.

5 Donald Quataert, "Ottoman Manufacturing in the Nineteenth Century" in *Manufacturing in the Ottoman Empire and Turkey, 1500–1950*, ed. Donald Quataert (Albany: State University of New York Press, 1994), 87, 103.

6 Charles Issawi, *An Economic History of the Middle East and North Africa* (New York: Columbia University Press, 1982), 155.

I do not discuss rural industry, or urban homes and workshops, which were widespread and remained the locale of most Ottoman manufacturing in their own right.

For the early republican state elite and middle-class intellectuals, the Ottoman failure to establish a modern industry came to symbolise the backward and semi-colonial imperial economy, which they contrasted with the dynamism and autarky of the republic. With the beginning of state-led industrialisation in the 1930s, references to Ottoman industrialisation failure multiplied. At the same time as the Ottoman factories in Istanbul were fast becoming republican modal factories, the industrialisation efforts of the 1840s were either completely disregarded or ridiculed. But, despite its shortcomings, the nineteenth-century Ottoman industrialisation effort bequeathed a physical infrastructure as well as experience in industrial management and labour that would shape the industrial geography of Istanbul. And so, before we delve into industrialisation in post-1923 Turkey, we need to take an industrial walk through nineteenth-century Istanbul. In the following pages, I will take the reader on a guided tour of key issues and sites of Ottoman industrialisation and the political uses of its memory.

1 The Ottoman Military-Industrial Complex

In the second half of the eighteenth century, the Ottoman economy was under increasing pressure from head-to-head competition with European manufacturers, on the one hand, and military exigencies, on the other.[7] Following his accession to the throne in 1789, Sultan Selim III (r. 1789–1807) embarked on a series of reforms, at the centre of which was a programme of military reorganisation to create a professional army along European lines. Originally the name given to the new army, *Nizam-ı Cedid* (lit., New Order) eventually came to encompass the entire reform programme. Industrialisation policy aligned with the primacy of military reform, focusing mainly on military enterprises such as gunpowder mills, cannon factory, and small textile workshops.[8] Only a few

---

7 Donald Quataert, "Introduction," in *Manufacturing in the Ottoman Empire and Turkey, 1500–1950*, ed. Donald Quataert (Albany: State University of New York Press, 1994), 4; Mehmet Genç, "Ottoman Industry in the Eighteenth Century: General Framework, Characteristics, and Main Trends," in *Manufacturing in the Ottoman Empire and Turkey, 1500–1950*, ed. Donald Quataert (Albany: State University of New York Press, 1994), 66.

8 Abdülkadir Buluş, "Osmanlı Tekstil Sanayi Hereke Fabrikası," (PhD diss., Istanbul University, 2000), 11; Enver Ziya Karal, *Osmanlı Tarihi: Islahat Fermanı Devri, 1856–1861*, vol. 6 (Ankara: Türk Tarih Kurumu, 2007), 249; Stanford J. Shaw, *Between Old and New: The*

of these establishments approximated the scale and organisation of a modern industrial workplace. The majority remained barely larger than artisan shops, operating on low technology and employing eight to twenty workers.[9] The state production units primarily produced goods for a limited market; there was minimal interest in scaling up production through cheaper unit costs.

Among the few factories catering to the civilian market were a woollen mill and a paper factory constructed in 1805 in Beykoz, a picturesque village with a rich water source at the northern end of the Bosphorus on the Anatolian side.[10] In the textile sector, Selim III tried to protect local manufacturing against imports by banning the use of certain imported fabrics such as English broadcloth and encouraging the elite to use locally manufactured textiles. A contemporary visitor to a silk factory that had been built in Üsküdar, a district bordering on the north of Beykoz, reported fifteen hundred hands working at a thousand looms. Following the new dress reform under Mahmud II, under which rich figured clothing was replaced with plain dress, the numbers fell to 300 hands at 750 looms.[11]

In 1807, the Janissary corps, the elite infantry units that were central to the old military establishment, led a popular revolt. This culminated in the collapse of the New Order and ultimately resulted in dethroning the Sultan.[12] In the following two decades under Sultan Mahmud II's reign (r. 1808–1839), few, if any, industrial attempts were made.[13] The establishment of machine-operated factories worthy of the name would have to wait until the advent of the modern army.[14] In 1826, following the abrogation of the Janissaries, Mahmud II initiated a wide-ranging military, fiscal, and bureaucratic reform programme entailing the establishment of a new army through mass conscription.[15] As the

---

Ottoman Empire under Sultan Selim III, 1789–1807 (Cambridge: Harward University Press, 1971), 138–44.

9 Genç, "Manufacturing," 67.

10 Adnan Giz, "Istanbul'da İlk Sınai Tesislerin Kuruluş Yılı: 1805," *Istanbul Sanayi Odası Dergisi* 2, no. 23 (1968), 25–26; Kevork Pamukçiyan, "Dadian Ohannes Bey," *Istanbul Ansiklopedisi*, vol. 8 (Istanbul: Koçu Yayınları, 1966), 4,194; Önder Küçükerman, *Geleneksel Türk Dericilik Sanayi ve Beykoz Fabrikası: Boğaziçi'nde Başlatılan Sanayi* (Istanbul: Sümerbank, 1988), 14.

11 Charles White, *Three Years in Constantinople: Or, Domestic Manners of the Turks in 1844*, vol. II (London: Henry Colburx, 1845), 263.

12 Ali Yaycıoğlu, "Guarding Traditions and Laws-Disciplining Bodies and Souls: Tradition, Science, and Religion in the Age of Ottoman Reform," *Modern Asian Studies* 52, no. 5 (2018), 1,543.

13 Clark, "Ottoman," 66.

14 Ömer Celal Sarc, *Tanzimat ve Sanayimiz* (Istanbul: Maarif Matbaası, 1940), 12–3.

15 Gültekin Yıldız, *Neferin Adı Yok: Zorunlu Askerliğe Geçiş Sürecinde Osmanlı Devleti'nde Siyaset, Ordu ve Toplum (1826–1839)* (Istanbul: Kitapevi, 2009), 15–130.

new European-style professional army, *Asakir-i Mansure-i Muhammediye* (lit., the Victorious Muhammadan Troops) replaced the Janissaries; the old brightly coloured uniforms made of luxurious materials gave way to dull-coloured clothing made of coarse materials.[16] For the already struggling Ottoman clothmakers, this came as a further blow for it meant the end of a certain degree of protection from foreign competition.[17]

By the end of the eighteenth century, cotton and silk textiles, the two most emblematic textile products of the empire, were being locally produced and even exported, with cotton being the second most important sector of the Ottoman economy after grains. The empire's self-sufficiency in cotton textiles continued until the 1820s, mainly because the French Revolutionary and Napoleonic Wars provided some respite for the region. Thereafter, European competition went into full throttle.[18] Initially, it was mainly the small manufacturers in the urban centres of the empire who suffered, while home production continued, albeit with difficulty. The crisis gradually expanded geographically and spilled over into other sectors toward the mid-century. During the reigns of Mahmut II and Abdülmecid I (r. 1839–1861), the Ottoman textile market came increasingly under European dominance as the empire turned into a raw materials supplier for European manufacturing and a market for their products.[19] The international export market disappeared for wool, cotton, and linen

---

16 Darin Stephanov, "Sultan Mahmud II (1808–1839) and the First Shift in Modern Ruler Visibility in the Ottoman Empire," *Journal of the Ottoman and Turkish Studies Association* 1, no. 1–2 (2014), 135.

17 Donald Quataert, *Ottoman Manufacturing in the Age of the Industrial Revolution* (Cambridge: Cambridge University Press, 1993), 3–4.

18 Issawi, *Middle East and North Africa*, 151.

19 Sarc, *Sanayimiz*, 12–3; Halil İnalcık, "Osmanlı Pamuklu Pazarı, Hindistan ve İngiltere: Pazar Rekabetinde Emek Maliyetinin Rolü," *ODTÜ Gelişme Dergisi*, special issue (1979–80), 13; Charles Issawi, *The Economic History of Turkey, 1800–1914* (The University of Chicago Press: Chicago, 1980), 275; Murat Çizakça, "Incorporation of the Middle East into the European World-Economy," *Review (Fernand Braudel Center)* 8, no. 3 (1985), 373; Önder Küçükerman, *Hereke Fabrikası* (Istanbul: Sümerbank, 1987), 20; Şevket Pamuk, *The Ottoman Empire and European Capitalism, 1820–1913* (Cambridge: Cambridge University Press, 1987), 110–114; Rıfat Önsoy, *Tanzimat Dönemi Osmanlı Sanayii ve Sanayileşme Politikası* (Ankara: Türkiye İş Bankası Kültür Yayınları, 1988), 21; Nazif Öztürk, "XIX. Yüzyılda Osmanlı İmparatorluğu'nda Sanayileşme ve 1827'de Kurulan Vakıf İplik Fabrikası," *Vakıflar Dergisi* 21 (1990), 23; Emre Dölen, *Tekstil Tarihi* (Istanbul: Marmara Üniversitesi Teknik Eğitim Yayınları, 1992), 382; Donald Quataert, "The Age of Reforms: 1812–1914," in *An Economic and Social History of the Ottoman Empire, 1300–1914*, ed. Halil İnalcık and Donald Quataert (Cambridge: Cambridge University Press, 1994), 903–906; Halil İnalcık, *Osmanlı İmparatorluğu: Toplum ve Ekonomi* (Istanbul: Eren Yayıncılık, 1996), 311–3; Halil İnalcık, *Türkiye Tekstil Tarihi Üzerine Araştırmalar* (Istanbul: Iş Bankası Yayınları, 2008),

clothmakers, but expanded for the export of rugs, lace, embroideries, and raw silk. The overall effect was an expansion in the size of the market accompanied by a steady shrinkage in the already miniscule importance of the Ottoman industrial economy at the global level.[20]

With worsening terms of trade exacerbated by an expanding military budget, the Ottoman statesmen gradually recognised the unsustainability of their dependence on foreign manufacturing. Their vision of achieving military parity retained primacy, but there was also now a burgeoning recognition of the wider significance of industrialisation for economic development. Ottoman modernisers, arguing that traditional manufacturing methods could not compete with European factories, began to advocate for the establishment of large, modern factories.[21] There were two factories established in the 1820s and 1830s that symbolised the intricate relations between the Ottoman state's modernisation efforts and its industrial policy.

The first factory, which was established in 1826 after Mahmud II had abolished the Janissaries, was an imperial spinning mill, *İplikhane-i Amire* (Imperial Spinnery; also known as *Riştehane-i Amire*). It was located in Eyüp, a district at the confluence of the Kağıthane and Alibey streams at the head of the Golden Horn. Three palaces were demolished to make way for the building site for this factory. One foreman and 106 workers used animal power to operate fourteen spinning wheels with 120 spindles to produce cotton yarn and rope mainly for the navy and the new corps.[22] The factory was also known as the "rope barracks" (*İplik Kışlası*) because part of it accommodated soldiers.[23] Later on, the building was partially converted to a prison for petty criminals, with prison labour also utilised in the factory. The prison labourers' situation was described as "falling into disaster" by the head imam of the neighbourhood.[24]

"No traveller should leave Constantinople without paying a visit to the Fez Manufactory of Eyoub," insisted the British traveller Julia Pardoe after witnessing Feshane, the Imperial Fez Factory (*Feshane-i Amire*) in 1836: "The building,

---

79; Vedit İnal, "The Eighteenth and Nineteenth Century Ottoman Attempts to Catch Up with Europe," *Middle Eastern Studies* 47, no. 5 (2011), 737.

20 Quataert, *Ottoman Manufacturing*, 15–16.

21 Vedit İnal, "Ottoman Attempts," 737; Nazif Öztürk, "İplik Fabrikası," 27; Quataert, *Ottoman Manufacturing*, 10.

22 Öztürk, "İplik Fabrikası," 31–6.

23 Hakkı Göktürk, "Bahariye Adaları," *Istanbul Ansiklopedisi*, vol. 4 (Istanbul: Koçu Yayınları, 1960), 1,850.

24 *New Redhouse Turkish-English Dictionary, Eighth Edition* (Istanbul: Redhouse Press, 1968), 544; Reşad Ekrem Koçu, "Bahariye," *Istanbul Ansiklopedisi*, vol. 4 (Istanbul: Koçu Yayınları, 1960), 1,850; Öztürk, "İplik Fabrikası," 33.

which is entirely modern, and admirably adapted to its purpose, stands in the port, near the palace of Azme Sultane, on the site of an ancient Imperial residence."[25] Feshane was the last sizeable military factory founded before the Tanzimat reforms. The fez had been introduced to the army in 1826; three years later it was being worn by all civil servants. And it was because it removed the visible distinction between non-Muslims and Muslims that the headdress became a key marker of modernisation.[26] The Ottomans had initially imported their fezes from Austria, France, and Tunisia. In 1828, they brought twenty-three foremen from Tunisia to start local manufacturing. When the first production unit, Darüssinae, located in Kadırga, proved to be too small, production was moved to an imperial seaside residence in the Golden Horn in 1839. With the installation of mule-powered wool weaving looms in 1843, the factory expanded into carpet and gabardine production as well. Between 250 and 300 workers worked at Feshane during this period, manufacturing 300,000 fezes every year, the majority of which were for the troops, whilst the remainder were handed over to the bazaars. Yet, the volume of local production was not enough to curb the increase in European imports, making technological and organisational improvements inevitable. In 1844, the management of Feshane was handed over to Belgian experts, who succeeded in increasing production levels by importing machinery from their country.[27]

The industrial site selection for these two factories points to the mentality shift in Ottoman development thinking. Three imperial palaces were demolished for the construction of the imperial mill, another imperial residence was transformed into a fez workshop, and other factories were either built in the place of or located inside old imperial buildings.[28] The ornate imperial edifices were erased from the urban fabric to make space for the architectural symbol of European development, "with its prominent chimneys and clerestoried

25 Julia Pardoe, *The City of the Sultan: Domestic Manners of the Turks in 1836* (London: Henry Colburn, 1837), 117.

26 Donald Quataert, "Clothing Laws, State, and Society in the Ottoman Empire, 1720–1829," *International Journal of Middle East Studies* 29, no. 3 (1997), 412–3.

27 Ömer Alageyik, "Türkiye'de Mensucat Sanayiinin Tarihçesi," *Sümerbank* 16 (1967), 9; "Defterdar Fabrikası Tarihçe" *Sümerbank* 1, no. 1 (1961), 24; Müller-Wiener, "İmalathane ve Fabrikalar," 75–6; Edward C. Clark, "The Emergence of Textile Manufacturing Entrepreneurs in Turkey, 1804–1968" (PhD diss., Princeton University, 1969), 29; M. A. Ubicini, *Letters on Turkey: An Account of the Religious, Political, Social, and Commercial Condition of the Ottoman Empire*, vol. 1 (London: John Murray, 1856), 341–3; Güran, "Devlet Fabrikaları," 239–41; Clark, "Textile Manufacturing," 28; Karal, *Osmanlı Tarihi*, vol. 6, 242.

28 Müller-Wiener, "İmalathane ve Fabrikalar," 71; Doğan Kuban, *Istanbul, An Urban History: Byzantion, Constantinopolis, Istanbul* (Istanbul: The Economic and Social History Foundation, 2004), 349.

roofs over large sheds."[29] Architectural grandeur gave way to functional spaces to reverse the image of a stagnating, oriental empire. A century later, scholars would mourn the loss of the elegant wooden palaces by the Golden Horn to textile factories, calling it the sacrifice of modernity.[30] But to reform-minded Ottomans, factories pointed to a bright future. In the contemporary *Sefaretnames*, that is, documents recounting the journeys and experiences of Ottoman ambassadors in foreign lands to be presented to the Sultan, factories were recurrently cited as a source of wealth and power.[31] "Industry and science—factories and schools," wrote Bernard Lewis, "were the talismans by which both Mahmud II in Turkey and Muhammad Ali in Egypt tried to conjure up the wealth and power of Europe, and thus maintain the European-style armies which were their prime concern."[32]

Inspired by the success of Feshane, the Ottoman state established several new factories. A small water-powered spinning and weaving mill was built in Sliven (Bulgaria) in 1836 to produce woollen cloth for military uniforms. The factory director was Polish, the foremen were German, and the workers, Bulgarian. Initially a state-owned factory, it was later rented out to private capital.[33] A calico factory in Izmit, a broadcloth factory in Sliven, and a weaving factory in Zeytinburnu followed. The machinery of the calico factory in Izmit was renewed around the same time as Feshane.[34] In addition to these state investments, private industrial investment also took hold in the 1820s. Entrepreneurs, both local and foreign, built factories and imported technology. Steam-driven silk reeling got off the ground in Salonika and Bursa in the 1830s.[35] Between 1831 and 1840, military establishments such as the shipyard, cannon factory, and small arms factories started embracing steam power as well.[36]

---

29 Sibel Bozdoğan, *Modernism and Nation Building: Turkish Architectural Culture in the Early Republic* (Seattle: University of Washington Press, 2002), 19.

30 Vedat Eldem, *Osmanlı İmparatorluğu'nun İktisadi Şartları Hakkında Bir Tetkik* (Istanbul: Türkiye İş Bankası Kültür Yayınları, 1970), 216; Kuban, *Istanbul*, 349.

31 Bernard Lewis, *The Emergence of Modern Turkey* (London: Oxford University Press, 1968), 457.

32 Lewis, *Modern Turkey*, 131.

33 *Türkiye'de Pamuk İpliği ve Pamuklu Dokuma Mensucat Sanayii* (Ankara: Türkiye Ticaret Odaları, Sanayi Odaları ve Ticaret Borsaları Birliği, 1958), 4–9.

34 Karal, *Osmanlı Tarihi*, vol. 6, 241–2.

35 Clark, "Textile Manufacturing," 41–6.

36 İlhan Tekeli & Selim İlkin, "Osmanlı İmparatorluğu'nda 19. Yüzyıl'ın İkinci Yarısında Nafia Programları ve Teknoloji Gelişimi Üzerine," *Dünü ve Bugünüyle Toplum ve Ekonomi* 3 (1993), 136.

Despite the monopoly protection they received, the state factories could not reduce the empire's import dependency on textiles. Even those larger in size mainly adopted artisanal practices and concentrated on the final stages of manufacturing.[37] They suffered from fuel and raw material insufficiencies, dilapidated machinery, transportation, and other economic infrastructural problems.[38] They were also poorly managed, with the military elite serving as supervisors instead of technically trained personnel. When William Fairbairn, a prominent Scottish shipbuilder and inventor of the riveting machine, visited the public works in Istanbul on the Sultan's invitation in 1839, he found the imperial dockyards, small-arms manufactory, cannon foundries, powder mills, and rope factory in "a very primitive state."[39] Though new machinery had been introduced shortly before his arrival, it was far from perfect and "the native workman appeared to me to be at a loss how to work and manage machinery of such a complicated character."[40] Another foreign visitor to the Ottoman factories of the 1830s also noted the elaborate and expensive machinery falling rapidly to ruin at the cloth and paper factories in Beykoz.[41] The partial use of the imperial mill as a prison was also a result of poor management.[42] Still, some establishments were improved and continued operation.[43] A tannery, leather goods, and shoe factory established in 1810, as well as Feshane, for example, survived the Ottoman Empire to become two of the largest state-owned factories in republican Turkey.

By the end of the 1830s, another industrial centre of the empire was on the ascent, the fate of which would be inextricably bound up with the industrialisation of the imperial capital. Fascinated by the military reforms carried out by Sultan III, the governor of Egypt, Muhammad Ali Pasha, had decided to pursue an ambitious economic and military agenda to transform his province into a semi-independent union. His industrialisation plan, launched in the 1810s, encompassed military production, agricultural processing, and textiles. By the 1830s, a thirty-thousand-strong workforce was labouring across thirty cotton mills in Egypt.[44] The Porte was eyeing Muhammad Ali's industrial and military

37 Clark, "Ottoman," 67.

38 Issawi, *Middle East and North Africa,* 154; Clark, "Ottoman," 67.

39 William Fairbairn, *The Life of Sir William Fairbairn Bart,* ed. William Pole (London: Hansebooks, 2017), 168.

40 Ibid., 174.

41 Pardoe, *City of the Sultan,* 22.

42 Öztürk, "İplik Fabrikası," 27, 33.

43 Müller-Wiener, "İmalathane ve Fabrikalar," 73.

44 Joel Beinin, "Formation of the Egyptian Working Class," *Middle East Research and Information Project,* no. 94 (1981), 14.

success with fear and fascination.[45] Compared with Egypt, factory production in Turkey remained limited, with an industrial workforce of five thousand labouring mainly in Istanbul and its hinterland.[46]

But manufacturing suffered a fatal blow when the Ottomans were forced to sign the Anglo-Ottoman Commercial Treaty of Balta Liman in 1838 in return for European military support against Muhammad Ali's revolt. The agreement represented an utter surrender to the European laissez-faire system since the Ottomans had to abolish most state monopolies and other import-export controls.[47] The treaty also marked the beginning of a series of agreements with European powers through which the Ottoman internal market would be incorporated into the world economy. The tariff rate on imports was reduced to nominally low levels until World War I. At the same time, domestically produced commodities were subjected to a twelve per cent internal customs duty when transported within the empire.[48] The barriers standing in the way of European merchants were thus dismantled, causing imports, especially of textiles, to soar. As in other contexts of delayed industrialisation, the semi-colonial conditions of dependency made it difficult for Ottoman manufacturing to take off.

Despite the differences in their scope and success, the factories in the two industrial centres of the empire shared three characteristics. First, the industrial efforts were all largely geared toward military and palace use, rather than any large-scale production for a mass market. Second, labour, especially skilled labour, and industrial expertise were scarce. Forms of unfree labour and an extensive dependence on foreign engineers, supervisors, and workers were widespread. Third, by the 1840s, both industrial plans had failed. Muhammad Ali's factories survived until 1841 mainly thanks to the protection provided by the monopolies. But, after his defeat in 1841, he, too, was forced to implement the conditions of the 1838 Anglo-Ottoman treaty. Thereafter these industries underwent a rapid decline. In Turkey, most factories had been abandoned by 1849.[49] But, before this final blow, the 1840s would witness yet another ambitious industrial move.

45 Pamuk, *Ottoman Empire and European*, 127.

46 Issawi, *Middle East and North Africa*, 155.

47 Şevket Pamuk, *Osmanlı-Türkiye İktisadî Tarihi 1500–1914* (Istanbul: İletişim Yayınları, 2005), 164, 205–9.

48 Pamuk, *Ottoman Empire and European*, 113.

49 Beinin, "Egyptian Working Class," 14; Issawi, *Middle East and North Africa*, 154–155; Şevket Pamuk & Jeffrey G. Williamson, "Ottoman De-Industrialization, 1800–1913: Assessing the Magnitude, Impact, and Response," *The Economic History Review* 64, no. 1 (2011), 14.

2 Ottoman Industrialisation in the 1840s

It is perhaps ironic that the largest and broadest industrial effort by the Ottomans came in the 1840s, that is, shortly after the Anglo-Ottoman commercial treaty forced the Ottomans to surrender their monopolies and tariff authority to foreign powers. However, besides an almost complete surrender to European laissez-faire, the decade of the 1830s culminated in an Ottoman modernisation programme known as *Tanzimat* (lit., reorganisation), aimed at administrative, economic, and military centralisation and rationalisation. If the centralisation of bureaucracy is the practical ally of capitalism, we can argue that the Tanzimat was a political corollary to the trade agreement of 1838.[50] The Ottomans were now engaged in heated debates on the best strategy for economic development, focusing on the two familiar and interconnected axes that would come to dominate economic policy discussions well into the first decades of the republic, as we shall see in the next chapter: agricultural versus industrial development and liberalism versus protectionism."[51]

In the 1840s, the Ottoman state tried once more to bridge the growing technical and technological gap with Europe. State investment in industry peaked when the state allocated a large part of the Imperial Privy Purse (*Hazine-i Hassa*) budget to industrial development projects, and launched a great variety of industries under the name of *Fabrika-i Hümayun* (Imperial Factories). This new wave of industrialisation displayed five main differences from previous attempts. To begin with, the new establishments were partially mechanised and employed larger workforces. They were built in places such as Izmit, Hereke, Bursa, Kayseri, Konya, and also Balkan cities, expanding the industrial geography of the empire. State establishments constituted the largest part of industrial investment, but private industrial investment, partly local and partly foreign in origin, grew in this period as well. Industrial sectors also expanded and diversified. Last but not least, the perception of industrialisation as an economic policy changed. Instead of being merely a method for reducing import dependency for military requirements, local industrial production became a goal in itself.[52]

The Turkish Manchester project embodied this policy change. The construction of this agro-industrial complex began in 1843 under the full administrative and operational control of a prominent Armenian family, the Dadians.

---

50 Stefanos Yerasimos, *Az Gelişmişlik Sürecinde Türkiye* (Istanbul: Belge Yayınları, 1986), 14.

51 Deniz T. Kılınçoğlu, *Economics and Capitalism in the Ottoman Empire* (New York: Routledge, 2015), 24.

52 İnal, "Ottoman Attempts," 737–8.

From the late eighteenth to early twentieth centuries, six subsequent generations of Dadians held the office of *Barutçubaşı,* the directorship of the imperial Ottoman powderworks. Thanks to their practical and empirical industrial knowledge, they played a founding role in the industrialisation efforts of the Ottoman state by establishing imperial factories producing gunpowder, weaponry, paper, silk, cotton, and cast iron around the capital as well as Izmit, Bursa, and Izmir (Smyrna).[53] The family owed their rise to industrial leadership to a technical failure at the end of the eighteenth century.

3 The Dadian Family

In 1794, Selim III had commissioned a Frenchman of Spanish extraction to build a horse-driven mill for the Imperial Powder Works to produce European quality gunpowder. When the pulley of the mill broke, to the great annoyance of the Sultan, the foreign secretary sent word to his watchmaker, Arakel Dadian. A self-educated Armenian, Arakel was a jack of all trades; he worked as a goldsmith, a watchmaker, a miller, and a weaver. He repaired the pulley, and built a completely new one. The Sultan then asked Arakel to construct a water mill for the Azadlı Gunpowder Factory in Küçük Çekmece. Impressed by the success of this construction, he appointed Arakel to chief gunpowder maker in 1795. Arakel then managed to mechanise the entire gunpowder production process; he transformed parts of the plant into mechanical workshops and built different kinds of machinery including weaving looms.[54]

Ohannes Dadian, Arakel's third son, began working at the gunpowder factory in 1813 at the age of fifteen, a year after the death of his father, and his older brother Simon Amira Dadian became the chief gunpowder maker. Ohannes learnt machine building from Armenian foremen. He was the director of the paper factory in Beykoz between 1820 and 1822, and the weaving mill in Eyüp between 1826 and 1829.[55] Initially the two brothers, Ohannes and Simon, were entrusted with constructing the imperial spinning mill, but they failed and

53 Anahide Ter Minassian, *A Family of Armenian Amiras: The Dadians* (MA: Armanian Review, 1992), 1–4.

54 Müller-Wiener, "İmalathane ve Fabrikalar," 67–8; Muzaffer Erdoğan, "Arşiv Vesikalarına Göre Istanbul Baruthaneleri," *Istanbul Enstitüsü Dergisi* 2 (1956), 130; Kevork Pamukçiyan, "Dadian veya Dad (Arakel Amira)," *Istanbul Ansiklopedisi* 8 (Istanbul: Koçu Yayınları, 1966), 4,188; Pars Tuğlacı, *Dadian Ailesi'nin Osmanlı Toplum, Ekonomi ve Siyaset Hayatındaki Rolü* (Istanbul: Pars Yayın, 1993), 2.

55 Pamukçiyan, "Dadian veya Dad," 4,194; Küçükerman, *Dericilik Sanayi*, 14.

resigned. In 1827, Ohannes invented two machines, one for the small arms factory and the other for the rope factory. He presented both machines in the palace garden to Mahmud II, who rewarded the inventor with praise and a handsome payment.[56]

After his brother Simon's death, Ohannes acquired the title of *Barutçubaşı* in 1832. When he visited France and England to enhance his knowledge of chemistry in 1835, he was also ordered to examine the broadcloth manufacturing process. He came back with new machinery and a memorandum to be presented to the Porte:

> As broadcloth [needed by the military] cannot be woven in this country, it has to be imported from Austria and France … If it was locally produced, this would mean a great saving, and, at the same time, employment for several thousands of workers. With the use of steam engines in Europe, the work of a hundred [workers] can be accomplished by fifteen or twenty, and production costs are greatly reduced as a result. Such machines are absolutely essential here. Experts in this field should be brought from Europe, and it would then be possible in quite a short space of time to manufacture the broadcloth required locally.[57]

With these words, Ohannes summarised the expectations placed by the Ottomans on local manufacturing: to produce basic consumer goods, to reduce the foreign trade deficit, to follow and transfer the European technical and technological developments, and to create employment.

Ohannes's next task was a double order: starting broadcloth production at Feshane and finishing the construction of a broadcloth factory in Sliven without delay. In the meantime, he continued building and repairing machines, impressing Abdülmecid I, who, after a visit to the Imperial Powder Works, exempted the Dadian family from all forms of taxation.[58] This success was followed by the construction of a broadcloth factory in Izmit, a cotton mill (later silk factory) in Hereke, and an iron foundry in Zeytinburnu, the Grande Fabrique, under Ohannes's control. He made two more visits to Europe and returned with English machinery, engineers, and European workers.[59] Between 1842 and 1844, he was in Paris and London. *The Times* reported favourably on his activities in Great Britain, from where he sent back home "a complete

56 Tuğlacı, *Dadian Ailesi*, 196.
57 Ibid., 14.
58 Ibid., 23, 96.
59 Minassian, *Dadians*, 4.

woollen-mill, a silk-mill, a complete set of tools for works for the repair of steam-engines, and various mechanical instruments."[60] Besides his recognition as an inventor and industrial expert at the Ottoman palace, Ohannes also succeeded in becoming a member of industrial societies in France, England, and Scotland. During his 1847 mission to import new machinery from Europe, his two sons accompanied him. He returned with European mechanics, chiefly Germans. He went on to build the first iron boat of the empire at Zeytinburnu, the location where MacFarlane remarked on the flying sparks.[61]

By the time of the iron foundry's construction in 1843, Ohannes Dadian had established and was in control of a variety of state factories. These comprised a small arms factory in Dolmabahçe, a silk factory in Hereke, a nail factory in Yeşilköy, a leather factory in Beykoz, a broadcloth factory in Izmit, a carpet weaving and a yarn factory in Hereke, and a steam-powered mill in Istanbul.[62] The broadcloth factory in Izmit was the second largest state factory built during that time. It was built in 1843 using European construction techniques and equipped with the finest available machinery. This factory was initially run by a British manager, and it employed two hundred workers. In 1846, it was turned into a state factory to produce wool yarn and cloth for military use to a quality equal to European manufacturing.[63] With the money earned from the management of the Izmit Factory, the Dadian brothers established another factory some thirty kilometres away on the northern shore of the Marmara Sea in Hereke in 1843.[64] This factory started as a cotton mill using English and German machines and operated by Italian and French workers.[65] But before the end of the 1840s, with new machines brought over from Austria by Ohannes Dadian, production shifted to fancy silk products for the palace.[66] The cotton machinery was then transferred to Istanbul in 1850 and used at the Bakırköy Factory.[67]

---

60 "Manufactories in Turkey," *The Times*, 28 December 1843, 7.

61 Pamukçiyan, "Dadian veya Dad," 4,194–6; MacFarlane, *Turkey and Its Destiny*, vol. 2, 598; Tekeli & İlkin, "Nafia Programları," 138.

62 Tuğlacı, *Dadian Ailesi*, 25.

63 Güran, "Devlet Fabrikaları," 245; "Hereke Fabrikası," *Sümerbank Aylık Endüstri ve Kültür Dergisi* 1, no. 1 (1961), 30; MacFarlane, *Turkey and Its Destiny*, vol. 2, 435–6, 449–53; Clark, "Ottoman," 68.

64 Tuğlacı, *Dadian Ailesi*, 200.

65 Güran, "Devlet Fabrikaları," 248–9; Eldem, *Osmanlı İmparatorluğu'nun İktisadi Şartları*, 119.

66 Güran, "Devlet Fabrikaları," 248; Donald Quataert, *Manufacturing and Technology Transfer in the Ottoman Empire: 1800–1914* (Istanbul and Strasbourg: The Isis Press, 1992), 30.

67 Alageyik, "Mensucat Sanayi," 9; MacFarlane, *Turkey and Its Destiny*, vol. 2, 461–8.

In line with MacFarlane's description of "the Kingdom of Dadians," the family enjoyed extensive authority over industrial decisions ranging from site selection, machinery purchasing, hiring, to manufacturing, and were subject only to imperial control through fund allocation.[68] Ohannes Dadian used this authority to construct the new industrial complex away from the already existing industrial centres in Istanbul and its hinterland. The selection of Zeytinburnu as the site for the industrial complex signalled an important shift in the industrial geography of Istanbul. Until then, the state-funded imperial factories were concentrated in three major zones: Beykoz on the Asian side of the Bosporus, the entire Golden Horn area, and, beyond Istanbul to the east, in the textile town of Izmit and the adjacent village of Hereke, outside the city proper. With the construction of the Turkish Manchester on the Marmara coast, industrial activity moved further to the southwest of the city, a spatial move that would change the urban fabric in the following decades.

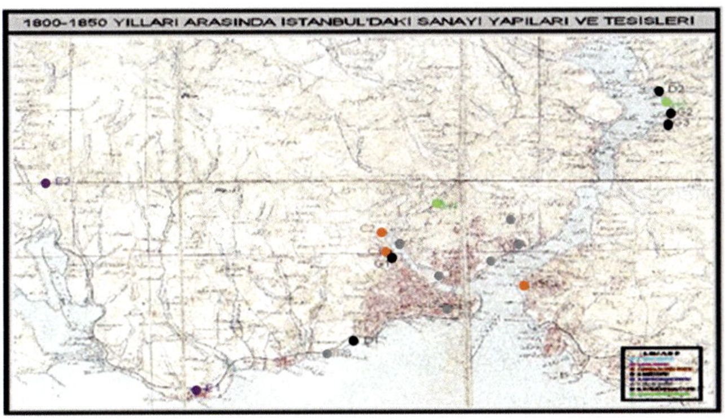

Legend
A. Energy
B. Foodstuff
C. Garment and Textile
D. Leather Production
E. Chemicals
F. Mining-based industries
G. Soil-based Industries
H. Forest-based Industries

MAP 2 Industrial buildings and enterprises in Istanbul, 1800–1850
GÜL KÖKSAL, "ISTANBUL'DAKİ ENDÜSTRİ MİRASI İÇİN KORUMA VE YENİDEN KULLANIM ÖNERİLERİ" (PHD DISS., ISTANBUL TEKNİK ÜNİVERSİTESİ, 2005), 236

68 Clark, "Textile Manufacturing," 34–6.

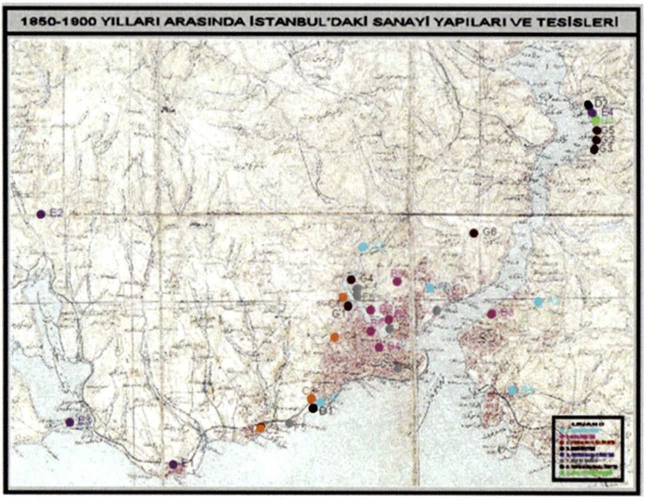

Legend

A. Energy
B. Foodstuff
C. Garment and Textile
D. Leather Production
E. Chemicals
F. Mining-based industries
G. Soil-based Industries
H. Forest-based Industries

MAP 3 Industrial buildings and enterprises in Istanbul, 1850–1900
IBID., 237

4 The Agro-Industrial Complex

As the Ottoman industry expanded and technologically improved, its need for technical maintenance increased. By the end of the 1830s, if a steam engine at the gunpowder plants, shipyards, or small arms factories broke down, it would either be replaced or sent to Europe for repair. The construction of an iron factory, the Grand Fabrique, lay at the heart of the plan for the industrial complex to end this dependency.[69] After an unsuccessful site search in Haliç, Ohannes Dadian, together with British engineers, visited several possible sites and estimated the construction cost.[70] They chose Çubuklu, a

69 Tuğlacı, *Dadian Ailesi*, 19.

70 Müller-Wiener, "İmalathane ve Fabrikalar," quoted in Didem Boyacıoğlu, "Osmanlı Fabrika Yapılarının Kentsel Mimari Analizi" (PhD diss., Istanbul Technical University, 2013), 27.

neighbourhood in the Beykoz district on the Anatolian side of the Bosphorus in Istanbul, and Zeytinburnu as the most appropriate sites. Because Çubuklu was far from residential areas, workers' accommodation would be a problem. In Zeytinburnu, there was a large inn to serve as worker accommodation, and the nearby Yedikule could potentially house workers; for engineers, Bakırköy had rental houses.[71] In the end, most workers lived in the barracks constructed on the site. The area only became a working-class neighbourhood with the construction of the railway that connected Küçükçekmece to Yedikule in the 1870s.[72]

The two Dadian brothers finished the construction of the iron foundry in 1844.[73] The foundry was set up in a square enclosure with some 210 to 240 metres on one side and an adjacent two-storey barracks with a central corridor of 200 metres in length. At first, it produced a wide variety of products including pumps, small machines, steam engines, swords, ploughs, locks, cannons, iron rails, pipes, pen knives, and razors mainly for the military and for small producers in the area.[74] After the 1850s, however, production began to focus on guns and ammunition, and eventually this was their exclusive output.[75] The industrial complex incorporated the establishments that were already in the area such as the Imperial Powder Works, a second gunpowder factory in Azadlı, Küçük Çekmece, a salt basin to the east of the complex, and old tanneries and candle workshops in Kazlıçesme.[76] As mentioned in the introduction of this chapter, a boatyard was constructed in Bakırköy, where the first steamship of the empire was assembled, albeit mostly with pre-fabricated material

71 Boyacıoğlu, "Osmanlı Fabrika Yapıları," 28.

72 Ayhan Han, "İstanbul'da Sanayi Bölgesi Planlamasının Bir Örneği Olarak Zeytinburnu Demir Fabrikası" (unpublished manuscript, 17 May 2021).

73 Tuğlacı, *Dadian Ailesi,* 183–4; Pamukçiyan, "Dadian Ohannes Bey," 4,195.

74 MacFarlane, *Turkey and Its Destiny,* vol. 2, 606; Clark, "Textile Manufacturing," 31.

75 Müller-Wiener, "İmalathane ve Fabrikalar," 67–8.

76 Clark, "Textile Manufacturing," 33; Erol Özvar, "Osmanlılar Zamanında Zeytinburnu," in *Surların Öte Yanı, Zeytinburnu,* ed. Burçak Evren and Alper Çeker (Istanbul: Zeytinburnu Belediye Başkanlığı, 2003), 54.

from England.[77] There was also a small and short-lived professional school in the complex to teach and train technical personnel.[78]

The site featured an ambitious model farm devised as the nucleus of agricultural development and improvement. The Ottomans tasked an American agricultural expert, Dr Davis, with producing cotton. Besides his expertise in agricultural science and cotton seeds, Dr Davis had brought his four emancipated slaves from South Carolina and he had plans to build South Carolina-style plantations throughout eastern Thrace. The emancipated slaves, whom MacFarlane described as "the best agricultural labourers we ever saw in Turkey," constructed a ginhouse with six cotton gins of English make, which ended up going to rust because there were no hands to attend to them.[79] The industrial farm was left to its fate eventually, and the frustrated Dr Davis quit in 1848.[80] The fate of the factory he produced the cotton for proved to be more complicated.

5 The Construction of the Basmahane

The native manufactory that was to be supplied by cotton produced on the model farm was a textile mill, Basmahane, near Bakırköy. Located between Yeşilköy and Zeytinburnu, several kilometres west of the iron foundry, the site was situated conventionally along a smooth coastline in the vicinity of abundant water sources such as the Çırpıcı stream. The suburban quarter of Constantinople known as Hebdomon (Lat. Ad Septimum) dates back to the late fourth century. Initially serving as a military district, it developed as an area of imperial resorts and retirement villages. After being looted and destroyed several times, the district lost this function and was eventually abandoned to its fate. In an archaeological excavation on the factory site in 2013, a variety of Byzantian architectural ruins were found dating back to between the sixth and thirteenth centuries. Some of these ruins were partially destroyed during the construction work at the factory site in 1933 and 1944.[81]

The district came to be known as Makro Hori (lit., long village, as it extended two kilometres along the coastline) in the late Byzantine period. The name

77 MacFarlane, *Turkey and Its Destiny,* vol. 2, 219–21, 615–6.

78 Adnan Giz, "Istanbul'da İlk Sanayi Mektebinin Kuruluşu," *Istanbul Sanayi Odası Dergisi* 3, no. 35 (1969).

79 Clark, "Ottoman," 68; MacFarlane, *Turkey and Its Destiny,* vol. 1, 59–70, 63; vol. 2, 629–34.

80 Clark, "Ottoman," 73–74.

81 Ö. Emre Öncü and Sırrı Çölmekçi, "Yeni Araştırmalar: Bakırköy Eski Sümerbank Arazisinde Yürütülen Arkeolojik Kazılar," *Mimar.ist* 18, no. 61 (2018), 30–7.

was adapted to Makrıköyü (with "köy" meaning village in Turkish) when it was captured by the Ottomans in the fourteenth century and turned into a district of gardens and orchards full of sacred springs under Ottoman rule. Until the seventeenth century, it remained a Greek village. By the mid-century, the village had a mosque. After Ohannes Dadian constructed the gunpowder works in the district, the number of Armenian residents increased. By the last quarter of the nineteenth century, the district was once again a summer resort with predominantly Turkish residents.[82] When the first railway connecting Istanbul to Sofia was constructed in 1874, Makriköy became one of the six stations connecting the suburbs to the city centre.[83] It was eventually renamed Bakırköy in 1925 when the republican state changed the place names of foreign origin. The district became a suburb of Istanbul on 30 May 1926; as of 1952, it was home to 48,000 Turks, 1,435 Jews, and 6,860 Armenians.[84]

The available information on the early years of the factory is scattered and contradictory. Many sources give the year of establishment as 1850.[85] This information, which is based on hearsay rather than archival research, has remained commonly accepted. In 1951, the factory celebrated its centenary, although in 1949, Fazlı Turga, a one-time director of the Bakırköy Factory had given 1840 as the year of the factory's establishment and even provided details about the operation of the factory in the early 1840s.[86] The factory was established as a weaving mill to produce calico, Turga wrote, and with the instalment of the famous Platt brothers spinning machinery in 1843, it became one of the most modern factories of the time.[87] Later publications uncritically reproduced the incorrect date of 1850, endowing it with the status of truth. Interestingly, some historians repeated the mistake even after citing MacFarlane's 1847–1848

82 Reşad Ekrem Koçu, *Istanbul Ansiklopedisi*, vol. 4 (Istanbul: Koçu Yayınları, 1960), 1,892–1,894.

83 Zeynep Çelik, *19. Yüzyılda Osmanlı Başkenti: Değişen İstanbul* (Istanbul: Tarih Vakfı Yurt Yayınları, 1998), 82–83.

84 Ziyaeddin Fahri Fındıkoğlu, "Türkiyede Sınai Sosyoloji Araştırmaları 1," *Mensucat Meslek Dergisi* 7, no. 6 (1954), 195–6.

85 Engin Kırlı, "Osmanlı Tekstil Sektöründe Meydana Gelen Gelişmeler Çerçevesinde Basma Fabrikası'nın Kuruluşu ve Faaliyetleri, 1846–1876" (PhD diss., Marmara University, 2015), 162; Hüsamettin Toros, *Türkiye Sanayii Devlet İşletmeleri* (Istanbul: Güven Basımevi, 1954), 109; Kemalettin Apak, Cevdet Aydınelli, and Mehmet Akın, *Türkiye'de Sanayi ve Maadin İşletmeleri* (Izmit: Selüloz Basımevi, 1952), 187; Zafer Toprak, "Tanzimat'ta Osmanlı Sanayii," *Tanzimat'tan Cumhuriyet'e Türkiye Ansiklopedisi*, vol. 5 (Istanbul: İletişim Yayınları, 1985), 1,345; Alageyik, "Mensucat Sanayi," 9.

86 Sedat Saip Altuğ, "Sümerbank Bakırköy Pamuklu Sanayii Müessesesi Yüz Yaşında," *Mensucat Meslek Dergisi* 4, no. 1 (1951), 31.

87 Fazlı Turga, "Pamuk Dikiş İplikleri ve Bunların Numaralanması," *Feshane Mensucat Meslek Dergisi* 2, no. 2 (1949), 28–29.

visit to the factory. And then there are other scholarly sources that cite 1840, or even 1839, as the year of establishment.[88] The most reliable source so far is a recent dissertation by Engin Kırlı. Based on a rich array of primary sources, Kırlı found that the decision to build the factory, which was cited either as *Veliefendi Basma Fabrikası* (Veliefendi Calico Factory because it was located next to the Veliefendi Stream) or *Basma Fabrika-i Hümayunu* in the archives, dates back to 1845. Construction started the following year, and production began on a limited scale in 1847. It took another nine months before the factory was working at full capacity.[89]

Confusion continues about the factory's ownership status and physical characteristics. Among the inaccurate claims made by historians are the following: Ohannes Dadian established the mill originally as a private enterprise; the famous Armenian architect Garabed Balian designed the factory building as a four-floor stone or brick building; the factory was transferred to the imperial treasury in 1850; production stopped in 1860; the factory management was transferred to the Quartermaster General's Department of the Ministry of War in 1867; and there was no renovation or renewal efforts in the second half of the nineteenth century.[90] Kırlı's archival findings contradict these claims. The Bakırköy Factory was a state factory from the very beginning; it was funded by the Imperial Privy Purse and controlled and managed by Ohannes Dadian.[91] The building had three storeys and was indeed designed by Garabed Balian.[92] In 1848, MacFarlane described the factory as "an extensive cotton-mill, calico manufactory, and print works" erected "in a swampy hollow near the sea, and the choked-up mouth of another creek."[93] The site was notoriously unhealthy, he claimed, remembering having been advised against passing through so as to avoid malaria fever.

In the initial years, the factory imitated English broadcloth designs using wooden printing blocks, which MacFarlane claimed that the Dadians seized from John Duckworth after firing him.[94] Later on, the factory gained fame by producing Turkish and Arabic designs and motifs.[95] The factory primarily manufactured calico, but silk and cotton cloth, a cotton or linen percaline

88 Karal, *Osmanlı Tarihi,* vol. 6, 257.

89 Kırlı, "Basma Fabrikası'nın Kuruluşu," vii, 37, 49.

90 Alageyik, "Mensucat Sanayi," 9; Müller-Wiener, "İmalathane ve Fabrikalar," 79; Eldem, *Osmanlı İmparatorluğu'nun İktisadi Şartları,* 119.

91 Kırlı, "Basma Fabrikası'nın Kuruluşu," 18, 37–8.

92 Ibid., 40.

93 MacFarlane, *Turkey and Its Destiny,* vol. 2, 616.

94 Ibid., 617.

95 Alageyik, "Mensucat Sanayi," 9.

known as "kirpas," shirts, handkerchiefs, and gloves were also produced in the early years. By 1852, kirpas production surpassed calico, and calico production stopped completely in 1861. Kirpas remained the primary product of the factory until the collapse of the Ottoman Empire.[96]

The factory was initially managed by the Ministry of Imperial Factories (*Fabrika-i Hümayun Nezareti*). In 1857 it came under the management of the Privy Purse. An extensive renovation followed this transfer: the factory site was extended, forested, and surrounded by walls; a water pool, a mosque, and workers' barracks for single workers were constructed.[97] Management was transferred again in 1876, to the Quartermaster General's Department of the Ministry of War (*Harbiye Nezareti Levazimati Askeriye Dairesi*). This saw production shift to nettle cloth, tent canvas, and dress fabric for the army. Contrary to the claims that the factory was never renovated, there were waves of construction and also new machinery installations. Production soared during the Crimean War, for example, and a workers' barracks was built to ease the discontent of the overworked labourers.

Until 1857, the factory operated at a loss. Between 1857 and 1864, profits were minimal. But after 1867, an increase in production brought with it a substantial increase in profits. Although it did not stop, production slowed down in the first half of the 1860s, possibly due to the increase in cotton yarn prices caused by the American Civil War. Difficulties in yarn provision continued until the end of the century, forcing the factory to buy yarn from the Yedikule Spinnery.[98] After 1865, production increased substantially making the factory a profitable enterprise. Renovations intensified between 1864 and 1869, and by the 1870s, in addition to the production units, the factory had a garden, workers' housing, a coffee house, a general store, and a public bath.[99] But production interruptions remained commonplace. For example, in 1890 a worker demanded a transfer to the Feshane Factory, complaining of loss of wages due to production outages at the Bakırköy Factory. But the factory began producing new types of products in the 1890s. In addition to tent canvas, it now also produced home textiles.[100]

Ohannes Dadian had complete control over the planning and construction of the factory from the very beginning. According to Kırlı, he was the first

96 Kırlı, "Basma Fabrikası'nın Kuruluşu," 164–6, 181–2.

97 Altuğ, "Sümerbank," 30.

98 Eldem, *Osmanlı İmparatorluğu'nun İktisadi Şartları*, 119.

99 Kırlı, "Basma Fabrikası'nın Kuruluşu," 73–86, 94, 98, 112, 232, 511, 512.

100 Ibid., 539–40.

manager as well. However, MacFarlane tells a detailed story of two Duckworth brothers that Ohannes Dadian had brought from Lancashire to manage the factory. He placed the brothers in a farmhouse, situated on an area of land where the native workers refused to live because of the bad conditions. It was not long before they both died of malarial fever. John Duckworth, the son of one of the brothers, then became the director, but shortly afterward, he found himself in a conflict with the Dadian brothers and got fired.[101] Ohannes himself was fired in 1850, probably following an investigation into the Dadians concerning allegations of corruption.[102] A Muslim Ottoman, Hurşit Efendi, replaced Ohannes. Kırlı cites his negative report on the factory spinners as evidence of Ohannes Dadian's faulty planning back in 1846, as well as of his inefficient and corrupt management until 1850. There were other accusations of corruption directed at Ohannes regarding his management of other state factories in the same period. He lost the management of Hereke and Izmit Factories in 1850 as well.[103] It is said that the family managed to regain their personal property and continued to hold the title of *Barutçubaşı* until later in the century.[104] Some hundred years later, however, the republican industrialists would erase this Armenian Ottoman industrialist's name from the history of the Bakırköy Factory.

6 Labour in State Factories

In the 1850s, there were around five thousand women and men working in Ottoman state factories. Despite the small size of the factory workforce, state factories suffered from the Ottoman economy's chronic problem of labour scarcity, and thus resorted to a variety of mechanisms. Initially, the locally recruited unskilled workers for state factories were found among convicts of misdemeanour offenses, who would work off their sentences, and army conscripts.[105] The state also tried to recruit civilian workers through incentives

101 MacFarlane, *Turkey and Its Destiny*, vol. 2, 616–7.

102 *The Times*, 23 January 1850.

103 Kırlı, "Basma Fabrikası'nın Kuruluşu," 58, 476–7.

104 Clark, "Ottoman," 73.

105 Zafer Toprak, "Tanzimat'ta Osmanlı Sanayii," *Tanzimat'tan Cumhuriyet'e Türkiye Ansiklopedisi* v (Istanbul: İletişim, 1986); Zafer Toprak, "Tanzimattan Cumhuriyet'e Osmanlı Ekonomisinde Gelişmeler: Tarım, Ticaret, Sanayi," *1885–1985 Türkiye Ekonomisinin 100 Yılı ve Izmir ve Izmir Ticaret Odası Sempozyumu* (Izmir: Izmir Ticaret ve Sanayi Odası,

such as military duty exemption.[106] Last but not least, orphaned children toiled in the Ottoman state factories.[107]

Due to the shortage of skilled labour and lack of industrial expertise, state factories of the 1840s were heavily dependent on foreign workers, foremen, and managers.[108] Basmahane also employed European men from the beginning of its operation.[109] Already in 1844, Ohannes Dadian was blaming the foreigners for the losses made by the factory. They slacked off, he claimed, despite their high paycheques. In fact, their wages made up only a part of the yearly losses, still Ohannes sent some of them back to their home countries. He complained about their unwillingness to train the native workers, arguing for the need to open technical schools. The dependency on foreign foremen can be assumed to have reduced over time, as we as can see from the decrease in their number. In 1857, seven European foremen worked at the factory; by 1864, there was only one.[110]

The lack of discipline among the local workers was also cited in archival documents. A 1846 document, for example, described textile workers as "obstinate" and "unable to tell good from bad." They left the factory after a few months of work, and thus perpetuated the dependency on foreign workers.[111] Already in 1848, MacFarlane was critical that hardly any work was done at the good English machinery. Most workers lounged about with their hands in their pockets: "Some had gone home, and others, vexed by arrears of pay, were wishing that they had never come." Foreign workers also received their share of his disdain. The foreign stocking weavers had made a few dozen stockings, he wrote, but their chief pocketed the money he made by selling the Dadians some worthless machinery and had gone back to Nottingham. Because the model farm proved to be a failure, the factory used English cotton yarn to weave calico. The manager presented the final product to Sultan Abulmecid as "triumphant evidence of the progress his subjects were making in manufacturing."

1986), 24; Quataert, *Ottoman Manufacturing*, 34; Donald Quataert, "19. Yüzyıla Genel Bakış: Islahatlar Devri, 1812–1914," in *Osmanlı İmparatorluğu'nun Ekonomik ve Sosyal Tarihi, 1600–1914*, eds. Halil İnalcık and Donald Quataert, trans. Ayşe Berktay, Süphan Andıç and Serdar Alper (Istanbul: Eren Yayıncılık, 2004), 1,012.

106 Güran, "Devlet Fabrikaları," 238.

107 Quataert, "Ottoman Manufacturing," 94.

108 Ayhan Aktar, *Kapitalizm, Az Gelişmişlik ve Türkiye'de Küçük Sanayi* (Istanbul: Afa Yayınları, 1990), 161–16; Akın Sefer, "British Workers and Ottoman Modernity in Nineteenth-Century Istanbul," *International Labor and Working-Class History* 99 (2021), 147–66.

109 MacFarlane, *Turkey and Its Destiny*, vol. 2, 616; Karal, *Osmanlı Tarihi*, vol. 6, 257–8.

110 Kırlı, "Basma Fabrikası'nın Kuruluşu," 136, 400, 431.

111 Ibid., 432.

The production costs must have been very high, he concluded, for not only the spinners and weavers but also because the bleachers and dyers, pattern-designers, and block-cutters were Englishmen waiting most of the time idle for cotton supplies.[112]

The factory used an ethnically and religiously mixed workforce. Of a total of 120 employees in the factory in 1849, nineteen were African slaves. Kırlı cites an archival document mentioning that "the ruler of Africa, Bernuh," sent these Muslim-named slaves to the Ottoman Empire in 1844, but he does not pursue this lead.[113] Most probably, these slaves were sent from the African state of Niger known as the Bornu (or Borno) Empire (1396–1893), a caliphate and an ally to the Ottoman Empire.[114] These slaves worked at Bakırköy and Hereke Factories, and in accordance with the common practice of freeing slaves after seven to nine years of service in the Ottoman Empire, they were freed by 1859. Those who wanted to stay were treated as free factory hands afterward. In 1864, there were eight freed slaves working at the Bakırköy Factory.[115]

Of the 310 workers in 1852, 155 were Muslim, including the African slaves. In 1864, there were 190 Muslim and 106 non-Muslim workers at the factory. In 1876, these numbers were 279 and 77, respectively.[116] Clearly, the workforce composition was changing to the advantage of the Muslim population, but the reasons behind this change are unbeknown to us. Also unknown is the composition of the non-Muslim workforce at the factory. According to MacFarlane, the Dadians "barred out the Greeks from all their establishments" and preferred to employ "their people."[117] Indeed, with the construction of the Imperial Powder Works in Bakırköy in the eighteenth century, the number of Armenians in the district increased to the effect of doubling the population.[118] In the 1830s and 1840s, the Dadians built an Armenian church and a school in the vicinity at the request of the Armenian workers.[119] Arguably, the

112 MacFarlane, *Turkey and Its Destiny,* vol. 2, 619–21.

113 Kırlı, "Basma Fabrikası'nın Kuruluşu," 461–3.

114 Paul E. Lovejoy, *Transformations in Slavery: A History of Slavery in Africa* (New York: Cambridge University Press, 2012), 72.

115 Kırlı, "Basma Fabrikası'nın Kuruluşu," 463–4.

116 Ibid., 452, 401, 456.

117 MacFarlane, *Turkey and Its Destiny,* vol. 2, 622, 465.

118 *Istanbul Ansiklopedisi,* vol. 4 (Istanbul: Koçu Yayınları, 1960), 1894.

119 Tuğlacı, *Dadian Ailesi,* 74. In 2005, the name of this street was changed from "Mabet" to "Dadian" by the Republican People's Party-controlled Bakırköy Municipality (https://hyetert.org/2005/01/31/ermeni-ismi-neden-sokak-ismi-olmasin/, accessed 23 September 2020). But the ruling party-controlled Istanbul Metropolitan Municipality did not approve the name change. Until 2018, the two municipalities confronted each other six times over this name change (https://www.cumhuriyet.com.tr/yazarlar/ali-sirmen/Dadian-soka

availability of labour, especially Armenian labour, played a role in the selection of the Zeytinburnu district for the industrial complex. In accordance with the common practice of employing orphans from *ıslahhanes* (lit., reform houses), that is, vocational state orphanages, at Ottoman state factories, students from an orphanage managed by Yedikule Surp Pırgiç Ermeni Hospital worked at the iron foundry.[120] Already in 1836, an imperial decree had ordered the collection of thousands of Armenian youngsters "from eight to fifteen years of age" from Anatolia to work at factories in Istanbul, including the iron foundry, under extremely harsh conditions.[121]

As is the case historically, female labour was widespread in Ottoman textile factories. Pardoe wrote about the five hundred women—Greeks, Armenians, Jews, and Turks—at Feshane in 1836.[122] Factory production co-existed with other forms of production such as the putting-out system.[123] In 1848, MacFarlane was struck to see Armenian and Greek women from the "poverty reigned ... dreadful" factory district anxiously waiting for a distribution of work at Feshane.[124] In 1951, the then director of the Bakırköy Factory claimed that women were first employed at the factory during World War I.[125] This was certainly not the case, but it shows us how the republican industrialists sought to represent the Ottoman industrial experience. I will address the politics of these representations in the coming chapters.

7 The Demise and Memory of Tanzimat Industrialisation

The Ottoman industrialisation effort lost its momentum rather quickly. Already in the mid-1850s, an empty central treasury was making it increasingly difficult to meet the costs of industrial investment.[126] The majority of the

kin-garip-oykusu-1266175, accessed 23 September 2020). Finally, in February 2019, the street name was changed to Dadian once again and after the ruling party lost the control of the Metropolitan Municipality in March 2019, the name stayed Dadian.

120 Mustafa Kurt, Kemalettin Kuzucu, Baki Çakır, and Kemal Demir, "19. Yüzyılda Osmanlı Sanayi Sürecinde Kurulan Devlet Fabrikaları: Bir Envanter Çalışması," *OTAM* 40 (2016), 260; Tuğlacı, *Dadian Ailesi*, 25.

121 Hagop Levon Barsoumian, "Armenian Amira Class of Istanbul" (PhD diss., Colombia University, 1980), 204.

122 Julia Pardoe, *City of the Sultan*, 178.

123 Clark, "Textile Manufacturing," 28.

124 MacFarlane, *Turkey and Its Destiny*, vol. 2, 623.

125 Altuğ, "Sümerbank Bakırköy," 31.

126 Clark, "Textile Manufacturing," 30; Müller-Wiener, "İmalathane ve Fabrikalar," 79.

160 industrial enterprises either disappeared or were out of operation by the end of the 1850s.[127] There were three sets of reasons behind the failure of this attempt at industrialisation.

To begin with, the Ottoman industrial enterprises had started off as expensive investments because they were equipped with foreign machines, employed foreign technicians, used foreign raw materials, and were often managed by foreigners.[128] A Belgian worker aptly summarised the paradoxical character of the "native" industries in 1848:

> It would be very odd if we could not turn out a piece of the finest cloth occasionally, seeing that we have the best machinery of England and France, that the finest wools for the purpose are imported via Trieste from Saxony and the best wool countries, and that we Belgians and Frenchmen work it. You could not call it Turkish cloth—it is only cloth made in Turkey by European machinery, out of European material and by good European hands.[129]

Corruption reigned supreme in the management of the factories. For example, there was a French director of a state textile factory who presented imported cloth as local goods to the Sultan for years and escaped when caught. Lack of coordination and disregard for expert advice were widespread. During the construction of the iron foundry, for example, an Armenian foreman disregarded the calculations of European experts regarding the construction of a chimney. The chimney subsequently collapsed, causing the death of thirty workers.[130]

The second set of reasons concerns the cut-throat competition between Ottoman and European wares, especially in the textile industries. The consecutive trade agreements with European powers banned the Ottoman state from protecting local industries. A government-commissioned report from 1868 stated that in the last three to four decades, the number of cloth-making looms in Istanbul had fallen from 2,750 to twenty-five. Between 1827 and 1850, English imports increased by 842 per cent and cotton textiles made up 85 per cent of total imports. The decline continued into the next century, with the import of cotton textiles increasing some hundredfold between 1820 and 1914. International competition thus struck many fatal blows to the empire's industrialisation efforts.[131]

---

127 Önsoy, 55; Clark, "Ottoman," 73; Dölen, *Tekstil Tarihi*, 402.

128 Clark, "Textile Manufacturing," 29.

129 MacFarlane, *Turkey and Its Destiny*, vol. 2, 453.

130 Ibid., 620; Sarc, *Sanayimiz*, 14.

131 Ibid., 14; Karal, *Osmanlı Tarihi*, vol. 7, 255; Charles Issawi, "De-industrialization and Re-industrialization in the Middle East Since 1800," *International Journal of Middle Eastern*

Last but not least were the problems related to domestic infrastructure and policy. Due to the inefficiency of transport infrastructure, for example, as well as inapt environmental conditions such as malarial swamps, factory operations became even more expensive. And the lack of a rational and consistent economic policy only aggravated these problems. It is true that at least some of the Ottoman statesmen recognised the interconnectedness of industry with other economic activities such as agriculture, financial administration, commerce, and public works. But any efforts to come up with a solid economic policy remained isolated and superficial as the cumbersome Ottoman bureaucracy kept busy with fiscal considerations at the expense of developmental policies.[132]

By the mid-1860s, the Ottoman state had made another attempt at industrialisation. An industrial improvement commission (*Islah-ı Sanayi Komisyonu*) was established in 1864, organising industrial exhibitions and opening industrial schools. Under Abdülaziz's rule (r. 1861–1876), the Bakırköy Factory was renovated, resulting in an increase in production. In the 1870s, private factories expanded rapidly in number, and after the 1880s the state established additional industrial entities as well. But this second wave remained modest in its effect; the Ottomans failed in redefining their terms of participation in the international economy. Industrial production proved limited compared with the handicraft sector, and the import burden continued to grow. In the textile sector, cotton gradually took over as the fibre of choice. Per capita cotton textile consumption was almost three times as high as that of woollen and other cloth put together by the 1910s. Between 1820 and World War I, the volume of cotton imports increased over a hundredfold and their share in domestic consumption increased from less than five per cent to more than eighty per cent.[133]

By the end of the Tanzimat period in 1876, the Grand Vizier Sadrazam Hayrettin Paşa succinctly described the industrial situation in the empire:

Studies 12, no. 4 (1980), 470; Önsoy, *Sanayileşme Politikası*, 18; Vedat Eldem, *Osmanlı İmparatorluğu'nun İktisadi Şartları Hakkında Bir Tetkik* (Ankara: Türk Tarih Kurumu, 1994), 65–6.

132 MacFarlane, *Turkey and Its Destiny*, vol. 2, 436–8; Clark, "Textile Manufacturing," 38; Karal, *Osmanlı Tarihi*, vol. 7, 255; Issawi, *Economic History*, 273.

133 Önsoy, *Sanayileşme Politikası*, 27; Sarc, *Sanayimiz*, 8–9; Tekeli & İlkin, "Nafia Programları," 141; Karal, *Osmanlı Tarihi*, vol. 7, 258; Quataert, *The Age*, 763–4, 901; Şevket Pamuk and Jeffrey G. Williamson, "Ottoman De-Industrialization," 10–14; Önsoy, *Sanayileşme Politikası*, 55; Issawi, *Middle East and North Africa*, 155–58; Pamuk, *Ottoman Empire and European*, 117–29.

> Today, we have only raw materials. In fact, the cotton and silk producer, and livestock farmer in our country work hard the whole year though only to undersell their produce to Europe. They buy the final product manufactured in their factories for tenfold of what they earned. That even the most basic tools come from abroad shows the backwardness of our homeland in science, workmanship, and industry.[134]

In 1891, apart from the gunpowder and tobacco factories, there were four state factories operating in Istanbul, engaged in tanning and manufacturing woollen and cotton yarn and cloth and fez at quite high production costs. By 1913, the empire was exporting eighty per cent of its production of raw cotton, but importing about the same percentage of its consumption of cotton thread and ninety per cent of its cotton textiles.[135] Despite hefty investment and the transnational transfer of industrial technology and expertise, the end results of the industrialisation efforts in the 1840s were, in fact, a relative decline and de-industrialisation for the empire. The arrival of the factory system and the textile technology in the Ottoman Empire was delayed by a century in the context of rapid integration into the world markets and the mid-century boom of the world economy. The next attempt at industrialisation would have to wait until the 1930s, after the Great Depression had given birth to the paradigm of a national economy.[136]

Starting already in the 1860s with the Young Ottomans' critique of the Porte, the conventional narratives of Ottoman economic history have characterised the nineteenth century as a period of political and economic decline. As we shall see by the end of this chapter, in the early republican period, the failed crash industrialisation programme was either completely ignored or it came to be a matter of mockery. The first director of the Bakırköy Factory, Fazlı Turga, criticised the Ottoman industrialisation efforts as "random and haphazard." The few cotton factories, he continued, were nothing but a "worn-out legacy."[137] With the onset of state-led industrialisation in the 1930s, the demonisation of the Tanzimat industrialisation efforts gained further ground as the Kemalists presented the Ottoman ruling elite as their constitutive other.

---

134 Karal, *Osmanlı Tarihi,* vol. 7, 256.

135 Issawi, *Economic History,* 275; A. Gündüz Ökçün, ed., *Osmanlı Sanayii 1913, 1915 Yılları Sanayi İstatistiki* (Ankara: Ankara Üniversitesi, 1970), 26.

136 Donald Quataert, *Ottoman Manufacturing in the Age of Industrial Revolution* (Cambridge: Cambridge University Press, 1993), 16; Pamuk, *Ottoman Empire and European*: 114, 119, 127.

137 "Bizde ve Dışarıda Pamuk ve Pamuklu Sanayii," *Feshane Mensucat Meslek Dergisi* 2, no. 2 (1949), 28–9.

8 The Bakırköy Factory in the Twentieth Century

Details on the history of the factory around the turn of the century mainly derive from one essay and a speech by the then director, Şefkati Türkekul (the reader will meet him again in the coming pages), at the centennial celebration of the factory. Türkekul knew a great deal about the factory's past, possibly because his father, District Governor Şemsettin Bey, also managed the factory between the time of the armistice and the establishment of the republic. In 1894, an earthquake hit the factory, destroying the chimney and cracking the walls. The factory ceased operations amid the calls to demolish the entire building. The factory director successfully resisted these calls; the factory building was repaired and production resumed again in October 1898.[138]

FIGURE 1 The weavery of the Bakırköy factory, c. 1920s
ALAGEYIK, "BAKIRKÖY BEZ FABRIKASININ," 81

By the beginning of the First World War, the Bakırköy Factory was the oldest of the nine cotton mills in operation. It had a total of 6,400 spindles, six thousand of which were in use, and one hundred weaving looms. Of the 3,024 workers in the cotton industry, Bakırköy employed 417 workers and produced 8.4 per cent and 14.9 per cent of cotton yarn and cloth, respectively.[139] During the war, the factory commenced double-shift operations and produced gun slings made of cloth due to the scarcity of leather. Behind this production was a foreman from Bursa, Nuh Bilal Efendi, who developed a foot pedal loom and wove slings that were of the same quality as those made in Germany. Toward the end of the war, food provision for workers started, which, according to Şefkati Türkekul, was a good managerial practice on the part of the factory director Major Ali Rıza Bey, who understood "the connection between production and

138 Altuğ, "Sümerbank Bakırköy," 30–1.
139 Eldem, *Osmanlı İmparatorluğu'nun İktisadi Şartları*, 131.

a worker's belly," and slaughtered three sheep on the factory site every day. The factory came under French occupation in 1918 for one and a half years, during which time production continued. The management building was lost to a fire in this period.[140]

In 1921, under the Ankara Government, another management transfer saw the factory come under the control of the General Directorate of Military Factories under the auspices of the Ministry of War. A three-year-long repair and renewal project entailing machinery modification and replacement followed. Production resumed once again on 15 September 1924 with an almost hundred per cent increase in yearly production from 370,000 metres to 600,000 metres. In 1925, management changed once again, this time to the Turkish Industry and Mining Bank (*Türk Sanayi ve Maadin Bankası*).[141] Over the next two years, the factory was electrified and it "got rid of" the German steam looms dating back to 1852. A separate weaving department equipped with sixty simple-technology looms was established in 1931, and English carder and roving machines were installed; the preparatory department was also extended. The factory pioneered modern machinery technology in the cotton industry, Türkekul claimed. When the first automatic weaving looms came to Turkey in 1927, they were tested at the factory. In 1931, Swiss twisting machines, and American warp and weft machines were installed. Modern bleaching and finishing machines were also used at the factory for the first time in 1933.[142] The impact of these renovations was substantial. Between 1932 and 1934, the factory's market sales increased from fifty-two to seventy per cent of its total production, with the rest of the products being sold to the state. The factory's market share increased from 0.92 to fourteen per cent.[143]

At the same time as these renovations and mechanical updates were going on, the factory underwent two more rounds of management transfer. The reader will find the reasons behind these multiple management transfers in the next chapter, but suffice to say here that they reflected the search for an economic policy and institutional restructuring during the republic's first decade. In 1933, the factory came under the management of the Industrial Office for a short while and on 11 July 1933, the factory finally reached its final destination

140 Altuğ, "Sümerbank Bakırköy," 30–1.

141 *Istanbul Ansiklopedisi*, vol. 4 (Istanbul: Koçu Yayınları, 1960), 1,904; Ömer Alageyik, "Bakırköy Bez Fabrikasının Kısa Tarihçesi," *Feshane Mensucat Meslek Dergisi* 1, no. 2 (1948), 81–2.

142 Turga, "Pamuk Dikiş İplikleri," 28–9.

143 Bilsay Kuruç, *Belgelerle Türkiye İktisat Politikası, 1933–1935*, vol. 2 (Ankara: Ankara Üniversitesi Yayınları, 1993), 263.

through its transfer to Sümerbank, the state holding that would manage the factory until its privatisation in 2004. At the time when Sümerbank took over the factory, it had 3,200 spindles and sixty weaving looms, produced 1,100 tonnes of yarn and seven million metres of cloth annually, while it employed 369 workers.[144]

Immediately after the takeover, Sümerbank adopted a reconstruction plan. Old buildings were demolished. Except for the base of the water tower, nothing from the built structure survived.[145] The new factory building was designed by the most prominent architect of the time, Sedat Hakkı Eldem, whose nostalgia for the demolished imperial residences of the nineteenth century we have noticed above. The site of the initial factory building of three or four floors was now the space between the newly built cotton warehouse (*ambar*) and the repair workshop. The new factory building had a total of 8,928 spindles, 320 weaving looms, and a large-capacity dyeing and finishing department. Five years later, in 1949, the factory was extended once again. By 1951, it had 39,000 spindles, and 445 weaving looms.[146]

At the opening ceremony of the new factory buildings on 13 August 1934, the first prime minister of the republic, İsmet İnönü, proudly noted the recent technical and technological improvements at the factories that the republican state had inherited from the empire. The Bakırköy Factory, he claimed, had a peculiarity among these factories:

> Next spring, Sümerbank factories will be the largest textile factories in the country with thirty thousand spindles. Comparatively speaking, the Bakırköy Factory might be a small enterprise. That being said, it is my pleasure to bring the peculiarities and the special value of the Bakırköy Factory to your attention. Among state and private factories, this factory is the one with the newest machinery. But, for our present day, the most precious fact about this factory is the following. It started as a small and primitive enterprise, it has been continuously expanded and improved to become a large factory. To plan or even to build a factory is easier compared with managing it. The real challenge is to take over the management of an old factory.[147]

144 Alageyik, “Mensucat Sanayi,” 18.
145 Köksal, “Istanbul'daki Endüstri Mirası,” 68.
146 Altuğ, “Sümerbank Bakırköy,” 30–1.
147 *Istanbul Ansiklopedisi*, vol. 4 (Istanbul: Koçu Yayınları, 1960), 1,904.

The challenge also applied to three other major factories inherited from the Ottoman Empire: Feshane for woollen textiles; Hereke for wool and silk; and Beykoz for leather and shoes. Together, these four factories were the physical symbols of a hundred-year-old industrial aspiration. Their modernisation was incorporated into a comprehensive five-year industrial plan in 1934, when, a century after the first, it was time for the second attempt at state-led industrialisation. Originally established against the background of the world-market integration of a nineteenth-century peripheral economy, they were re-born as modal spaces of Turkish national industrial modernity.

It was this national aspect that would dominate public opinion on factories and factory work in the following years. In Türkekul's account of the factory's history, we find the echoes of an almost fifty-year-old ideology of national economy that emerged in the Young Turk era. The persistence of Mehmet Şükrü Bey in keeping the factory open, the diligence and inventiveness of Nuh Bilal Efendi, and the benevolence of Major Ali Rıza Bey are all instances of the fitness and commitment of Turkish/Muslim elements for industry against the background of an industrial history full of foreign and ethnic/religious minority figures. Major Ali Rıza Bey, for example, was much loved by the workers, who called him "Father." Interestingly, as the reader will see in the upcoming pages, Türkekul himself enjoyed the same epithet during his directorship, pointing to continuity in managerial ideology and practice.

In his speech at Bakırköy's centenary celebration, Türkekul did not mention Ohannes Dadian by name. He recounted that the factory had been founded by "a citizen entrepreneur," and that Hurşit Ağa was its first director, acknowledging that the entrepreneur had done so much for the factory that "it would be fair to call him the founder." Sidelined in the factory's foundational history, the Armenian Ottoman inventor and entrepreneur only returned to the story when Türkekul proudly narrated the replacement of his Armenian foremen with Turkish men. Some of these had entered the factory school at the age of twelve and worked at the factory until 1920. The oldest worker at the time of the speech, that is, in 1950, was Hidayet Usta, who had spent fifty-seven "healthy and joyful years" at the factory. When asked about his time at the factory, Hidayet Usta, replied in a state of happy disbelief at the fact that he was sitting and eating together with the factory director, and even more incredibly with the "Pasha," the head of Sümerbank's board of directors, who held the rank of general. In the words of the journalist reporting on the celebration, it was a "family dinner table" of at least 1,500 "shining, happy, and proud people." In one of the stories shared at the table, a worker of thirty-five years told how a foreign foreman, a man "who did not carry the blood of our people" responded to the "Turkish workers' cries of hunger" after months of unpaid work during the French occupation. Pointing to the nearby Veliefendi meadow, the foreman replied: "You hungry? The meadow is there, go ahead!"[148]

FIGURE 2 Hidayet Usta at the factory celebration, 1950
COURTESY OF ERGİN AYGÖL

The centenary celebration encapsulated the republican structures of feeling around national industrial modernity. The hegemonic discourse sharply contrasted the failures of the Ottoman Empire with the accomplishments and vision of the Kemalist regime; and industrialisation was the most significant of these accomplishments. Ottoman industrialisation was mocked as a chronicle of ignorance, corruption, and folly. It was simply "a comedy," a wasted opportunity in the hands of "dishonest and treasonous men," wrote a journalist in 1939; "after learning the cost of the ridiculous, terrible history of industrialisation efforts in the 1840s, any patriotic Turk would be heartbroken for life."[149] Ottoman industrialisation was "shrouded in mystery," claimed an economics journal in 1942, but it is "now working wonders thanks to the technical and physical capacity of Turkish workers."[150] The local textile industry, which came down to a few broken looms after years of neglect, was now supplying local

148 Altuğ, "Sümerbank Bakırköy," 28–32.
149 Ali Rıza Seyfi, "İmparatorluk Devrinde Sanayileşme Komedisi," *Cumhuriyet*, 5 August 1939.
150 "Endüstri Hayatında Mühim Bir Dava: İşçi ve İçtimai Teşkilat," *İktisadi Yürüyüş* 6, no. 61–2 (1942), 11.

demand to a large extent, the general director of Sümerbank claimed in the same issue.[151] State factories are the embodiment of national will and strength, another author wrote, since they "saved us from our dependency on foreign manufacture."[152] Accelerated social and economic development was finally realising the historical potential of the Turkish nation, and the factories, especially the state-owned ones, were the carriers of that development.

In the next chapter, the reader will encounter the intricate interweaving of Kemalist nationalism with state-led industrialisation. The underlying narrative centred on *Turkish* workers producing with *Turkish* capital for the *Turkish* homeland. The failed Ottoman industrialisation efforts bequeathed a material infrastructure that included the Bakırköy Factory, an industrial culture in which foreign expertise played an important role, and an industrial geography that circumscribed the national industrial development agenda of the republic. In the words of a prominent Ottoman historian of the 1940s, the industrialisation efforts of the 1840s were "a distant preparation for the industrialisation efforts of today."[153] Equally as important, these efforts left behind a failed legacy that the republican elite would use as a rhetorical device to derive legitimacy for the displacement of the labour-capital conflict. It is to the politico-economic underpinnings of the second round of state-led industrialisation efforts that we turn in the coming pages.

---

151 Hulki Alisbah, "Sümerbank'ın Remzi," *İktisadi Yürüyüş* 6, no. 61–2 (1942), 5.

152 Selim Cavid, "Yapılacak ve Yapılmasını İstediğimiz Yeni Fabrikalar," *İktisadi Yürüyüş* 6, no. 61–2 (1942), 1.

153 Sarc, *Sanayimiz,* 17.

CHAPTER 2

A "Home-Grown Plant"[1]

State-Led Industrialisation between Ideology and Empiricism

> The new labour code is a regime law … With it, we are building a castle against the division of citizens along class lines … The code will clear away the clouds of class consciousness once and for all.[2]

∵

"The thing we need most is factories, factories, and more factories!" Ferid Bey, the finance minister of the Government of the Grand National Assembly, commonly known as the Ankara Government, cried out in 1921, in the midst of the Greco-Turkish War.[3] "We work hard to produce raw materials only to undersell them to foreigners, who then sell us the manufactured goods made with these materials … We get forty piasters for an *okka* of wool, and then get down on our knees to buy a metre of woollen cloth for 1,200 piasters." Ferid Bey's lamenting over Turkey's unfavourable balance of trade echoes the grand vizier Hayrettin Pasha's depiction of the Ottoman economy in 1876 (see Chapter 1). During the half a century separating these two statesmen, the empire had disintegrated into a number of states. Ferid Bey was the minister of a war government, the military successes of which increased hopes for a politically independent country. But without factories, Ferid Bey warned, "political independence is

1 I borrowed the phrase "home-grown plant" from William Hale, "Ideology and Economic Development in Turkey 1930–1945," *Bulletin British Society for Middle Eastern Studies* 7 (1980), 105.

2 Recep Peker, General Secretary of the Republican People's Party, speaking during parliamentary discussions on the labour code. See: TBMM Tutanak Dergisi (Records of the Grand National Assembly), "İş kanunu layihası ve Muvakkat encümen mazbatası" (1/162), 8 June 1936, Session V, Volume 12, Meeting no. 75, 83–84.

3 Following Istanbul's invasion by the Allies in March 1920, the Ankara government was established as the second Turkish government in effect led by Mustafa Kemal in opposition to the Istanbul government of Sultan Mehmed VI (Vahdeddin). By 1923, the duality was resolved with the promulgation of the Republic of Turkey.

 | DOI:10.1163/9789004687141_004

nothing but a butterfly that flies off leaving its shiny powder on your fingers."[4] Amid the background of political turmoil and military conflict, the idea that industrialisation was the only way to escape poverty and stagnation was gaining strength. Its realisation, however, would have to wait until the 1930s, when the problem of underdevelopment and a possible cure was thrust firmly onto the agenda of Kemalist politicians and economists. Against the background of this shift were two global developments. First, the crisis of world capitalism had weakened the grip of the core countries on the periphery. Second, the success of centrally planned Soviet industrialisation was influencing economic policy in various peripheral contexts. But Turkey was the first developing country outside the Soviet Union to make an industrial planning attempt, three decades before planned and directed industrialisation would gain ground in development agendas worldwide.[5]

In this chapter, I explain the politico-economic and policy determinants of state-led industrialisation. The particular path of industrialisation taken by Turkey was the outcome of the complex interaction between the world conjuncture, internal class structure, and political alliances. The policy change from an open economy in the 1920s to a mixed economy of protectionism and etatism in the 1930s was a double response to the Great Depression, on the one hand, and the political and economic crisis of the country, on the other. The republican rulers chose state-led industrialism as their developmental strategy in 1932 after fierce national debates in which foreign expertise played a significant role. Behind this choice was a combination of economic and extra-economic motives, such as achieving national strength and sovereignty, self-sustaining industrial growth, the end of rural poverty, and catch-up modernisation via industrialisation.

Disagreements on how to achieve these goals soared early and intensified with time. Turkish industrialisation unfolded as a highly politicised process, characterised by trade-offs among multiple state goals and an accompanying intra-elite conflict. The politics of foreign industrial expertise, the debate on the institutional framework of industrialisation, and the multiple failed

4 Adnan Giz, "Kurtuluş Savaşı Sırasında Ankara'dan Yükselen Ses," *Istanbul Sanayi Odası Dergisi* 38 (1969), 12–3.

5 Gunnar Myrdal, *Asian Drama: An Inquiry into the Poverty of Nations* (New York: Pantheon Books, 1972), 248–249; Korkut Boratav, "Kemalist Economic Policies and Étatism," in *Atatürk: Founder of a Modern State*, eds. Ali Kazancıgil and Ergun Özbudun (London: C. Hurst&Company, 1981), 175; Charles Issawi, "De-industrialization and Re-industrialization in the Middle East Since 1800," *International Journal of Middle Eastern Studies* 12, no. 4 (1980), 474.

attempts to enact a Turkish labour code were important manifestations of these divisions and conflicts. Although much ambivalence on the meaning and scope of etatism characterised these debates, state-led industrialisation and the populist nationalism it was embedded in served to deepen capitalist relations by securing the conditions of capital accumulation, including the repression of working-class opposition. In this chapter, I explain the macro processes on both the local and global level that shaped the political economy of the early republican period—as a prelude to our journey into the Bakırköy Factory.

1 From National Economy to Economic Nationalism

As a general rule, the development of manufacturing in peripheral economies is fuelled by the export of primary materials. This means that it is circumscribed by the interests of commercial capital. In Chapter 1, I explained how the unfavourable balance of trade and the lack of state capacity to protect local manufacturing hampered industrialisation in the Ottoman Empire. The last Ottoman attempt to bypass this arrested development was orchestrated during the Young Turk regime under the Committee of Union and Progress. The Ottoman bourgeoisie was a predominantly non-Muslim class that engaged mainly in commercial activity and enjoyed foreign protection.[6] Increasingly seen as the agent of an undetermined foreign power, the non-Muslim bourgeoisie came to be perceived as a threat to the very survival of the Ottoman state.[7] Between the Constitutional Revolution of 1908 and the First World War, a strong nationalist and corporatist industrial discourse gained ground. Within the paradigm of national economy, known as "*milli iktisat*" or "*devlet iktisadiyatı*," the Young Turk's policy of "Turkification" aimed to end foreign control of the Ottoman economy and create a national bourgeoisie through capital transfer from the non-Muslim to the Turkish-Muslim population.[8]

---

6 Korkut Boratav, *Türkiye İktisat Tarihi 1908–2009* (Istanbul: Imge, 2005), 23.

7 Tauraj Atabaki and Erik J. Zürcher, *Men of Order: Authoritarian Modernization Under Atatürk and Reza Shah* (London: I.B. Tauris, 2003), 2.

8 Feroz Ahmad, "*Vanguard of a Nascent Bourgeoisie: The Social and Economic Policy of Young Turks 1908–1918*, in *Türkiye'nin Sosyal ve Ekonomik Tarihi*, eds. Osman Okyar and Halil İnalcık, (Ankara: Meteksan, 1980), 329–350; Zafer Toprak, *Türkiye'de Milli İktisat: 1908–1918* (Ankara: Yurt Yayınları, 1982), 160–77; Haldun Gülalp, "Capitalism and the Modern Nation-State: Rethinking the Creation of the Turkish Republic," *Journal of Historical Sociology* 7 (1994), 15–170; M. Şükrü Hanioğlu, *A Brief History of the Late Ottoman Empire* (Princeton: Princeton University Press, 2008), 161.

The Muslim boycott of 1913 boosted the number of Muslim commercial pursuits to a certain extent, but the decisive turn came with World War I. The Young Turk government abolished capitulations and the privileged status of foreign firms, bringing the latter under Ottoman jurisdiction and tax legislation. The government introduced new customs tariffs to protect the infant industries and local products. It also enforced Turkish as the imperative language in all business correspondence.[9] To encourage local industrial development, the Young Turks eased land acquisitions and granted private investors customs tariff exemptions for importing raw materials and machinery. There was also a legal obligation that Ottoman products should be preferred even if they were as much as ten per cent more expensive than the imported equivalent.[10] According to the 1913 industrial census, which covered manufacturing located in a few industrial centres and included only those establishments employing more than three workers, there were only 269 establishments working with machines across the whole of Ottoman Turkey. Almost half of these were in the food and textile industries. The size of the industrial workforce was seventeen thousand.[11] In the end, these measures did not prove effective in boosting local private industrial investment. However, they had an equally, if not more, important effect on local industrial structure.

In 1915, Muslim-owned industrial enterprises made up fewer than twenty per cent of all industrial enterprises. Two years later, Muslim control over industrial enterprises had increased to more than fifty per cent.[12] Minorities furnished eighty-five per cent of the industrial workforce, meaning that their exodus in the following years would leave a difficult void to fill. After 1915, industrial activity was restricted due to military mobilisation and the Greek occupation of the relatively advanced Smyrna region. By the time of Ferid Bey's speech in 1921, Turkey "was reaping industrially the whirlwind, the seeds of which were sown by its former rulers."[13] Traditional craft production dominated the

---

9 Erik J. Zürcher, *Turkey: A Modern History* (London: I. B. Tauris, 2015), 125–137; Zafer Toprak, "National Economy and Ethnic Relations in Modern Turkey," in *State Formation and Ethnic Relations in the Middle East*, ed. Usuki Akira (Osaka: The Japan Center for Area Studies, 2001), 187–96.

10 Zvi Yehuda Hershlag, *Turkey: The Challenge of Growth* (Leiden: E.J. Brill, 1968), 52; Zürcher, *Turkey*, 126.

11 Hershlag, *The Challenge of Growth*, 52.

12 Toprak, *Türkiye'de Milli İktisat*, 268–270.

13 G. B. Ravndal (compiled by), *Turkey: An Economic Handbook* (unpublished, 1924), 347–349, 349; Records of the Department of State Relating to Internal Affairs of Turkey, Economic Matters, 2 June 1910—17 December 1929, Decimal File 867.50, National Archives and Record Administration (NARA), accessed 1 May 2020, https://go.gale.com/ps/retrieve.do?tabID=Manuscripts&resultListType=RESULT_LIST&searchResultsType

manufacturing sector, and two thirds of the capital held by manufacturing firms incorporated in the 1920s was of foreign origin.[14] In March 1922, Mustafa Kemal pointed to the free trade policies of the Tanzimat reformers as the culprit behind the government's relegation to the status of "the gendarmes of the foreign capital" and the empire to "a colony of foreigners."[15] The Young Turks may have failed in their attempt to remedy the underdevelopment of late Ottoman society, but the national economy paradigm they institutionalised would continue in the republic's economic policy.[16]

Turkey of the 1920s amounts to a near-perfect example of a dependent economy with minimal state intervention. Partly to secure international recognition, the new regime was forced to accept a free trade regime at the 1923 Lausanne Conference, with the guarantee that it would pay off approximately two thirds of the Ottoman debt.[17] The economy remained agriculture-based with the share of agriculture in the national income at fifty per cent and the share of the population engaging in agricultural production carried out by simple methods at eighty per cent.[18] The urbanisation rate was quite low: of a total population of thirteen million in 1927, only sixteen per cent was living in urban centres. Agricultural products made up the biggest share of the export trade, the final stage of which was monopolised by foreign merchants. Industrial production amounted to between ten and eleven per cent of the national income, the rest of which derived from service sector activities.[19]

Foreign capital quickly capitalised on the free market economy and played an important role in the encouragement and organisation of export-oriented agriculture through mechanisms such as trading ventures, merchant houses, banks, and direct participation in the distribution of credit. Foreign direct investment also increased with the liberalisation of the conditions of property ownership in January 1924. Between 1923 and 1929, foreign capital investment

=SingleTab&searchType=AdvancedSearchForm&currentPosition=1&docId=GALE%7CSC5111519615&docType=Manuscript&sort=Relevance&contentSegment=GDSC221&prodId=GDSC&contentSet=GALE%7CSC5111519615&searchId=R11&userGroupName=cumhurb&inPS=true&ps=1&cp=1.

14 Keyder, *The Definition of a Peripheral Economy: Turkey 1923–1929* (Cambridge: Cambridge University Press, 1981), 57.

15 Feroz Ahmad, *The Making of Modern Turkey* (London: Routledge, 1993), 93.

16 Kemal H. Karpat, *Turkey's Politics: The Transition to A Multi-Party System* (New Jersey: Princeton University Press, 1959), 84; Toprak, "National Economy," 187–188.

17 Boratav, "Kemalist Economic Policies," 168.

18 Gülten Kazgan, "Türk Ekonomisinde 1927–35 Depresyonu, Kapital Birikimi ve Örgütleşmeler," *Atatürk Döneminin Ekonomik ve Toplumsal Tarihiyle İlgili Sorunlar Sempozyumu* (Istanbul: IITIA, 1977), 236.

19 Kazgan, "Türk Ekonomisinde 1927–35 Depresyonu," 238.

in manufacturing corporations doubled the contributions of Turkish capital. Plus, certain foreign firms acquired monopoly rights to import and sell particular goods. To take another indicator, the state budget comprised only eight to nine per cent of the total national income, whereas the total capital of ninety-four foreign companies in 1924 amounted to one third.[20]

Mid-way into the decade, the state enacted a series of laws to further nationalise the economy. The abolition of tax concessions, the enforcement of correspondence between firms in Turkish, the obligation to employ Turkish personnel, and the nationalisation of foreign railway companies were among these legal changes.[21] The ethnoreligious composition of the labour force in the major economic sectors was rapidly changing in favour of Muslim workers.[22] On 11 June 1932, a new law specified the crafts and services that could only be done by Turkish citizens, giving foreigners one year to leave their jobs in these designated areas. In the banking sector, the number of deposits controlled by national and foreign banks changed in favour of the former. In the greater scheme of things, however, the laissez-faire policy reigned supreme, and the commercial bourgeoisie continued to benefit from the economic reconstruction of the 1920s.[23]

Political power was now based on an alliance between the military-bureaucratic and the socioeconomic elite. The former needed the latter's support for the top-down reforms, which it secured through protecting their class interests.[24] "The civilian and military bureaucracy," Yerasimos argued, "granted the urban bourgeoisie and the rural notables representation of the vital forces of the nation, thus turning over to their discretion workers and peasants."[25] At

20 Henry J. Barkey, *The State and The Industrialisation Crisis in Turkey* (New York: Routledge, 1990), 45; Ahmad, *The Making of Modern Turkey*, 94; Çağlar Keyder, *State and Class in Turkey: A Study in Capitalist Development* (London: Verso, 1987), 93–94; Keyder, *The Definition of a Peripheral Economy*, 59.

21 Kazgan, "Türk Ekonomisinde 1927–35 Depresyonu," 238.

22 Murat Koraltürk, *Erken Cumhuriyet Döneminde Ekonominin Türkleştirilmesi* (Istanbul: İletişim Yayınları, 2011), 240–242.

23 Haldun Derin, *Türkiye'de Devletçilik* (Istanbul: Çituri Biraderler, 1940), 25, 51; Feroz Ahmad, "The Progressive Republican Party, 1924–1925," in *Political Parties and Democracy in Turkey*, eds. Metin Heper and Jacob Landau (London: I. B. Tauris, 1991), 74; Keyder, *The Definition of a Peripheral Economy*, 69–71; Çağlar Keyder, "The Political Economy of Turkish Democracy," *New Left Review* 1, no. 115 (1979), 10; Kazgan, "Türk Ekonomisinde 1927–35 Depresyonu," 236.

24 Feroz Ahmad, *The Turkish Experiment in Democracy* (London: C. Hurst, 1977), 3; Keyder, *State and Class*, 82–83.

25 Stephane Yerasimos, "The Monoparty Period," in *Turkey in Transition: New Perspectives*, eds. Irvin C. Schick and Ertuğrul Ahmet Tonak (New York: Oxford University Press, 1987),

the 1923 Izmir Economic Congress, for example, the Istanbul Workers' Union, a union founded by an employers' association, was the entity representing workers. The congress accepted private initiative as the carrier of industrialisation.[26] Though the state maintained direct control of a number of monopolies in tobacco, alcohol, salt, matches, sugar, and petroleum, private capital was assigned the role of the main industrialising agency. The government established a publicly controlled but privately owned and financed savings bank, Business Bank (*İş Bankası*), as well as the Turkish Industry and Mining Bank (*Türk Sanayi ve Maadin Bankası*) to provide credit for industrial investments. During the industrialisation policy debates in the 1930s, the Business Bank became an influential lobbyist in favour of private interests and a mediator between business and government circles.[27]

In the political sphere of the 1920s, the government was busy with superstructural reformism and overcoming threats to territorial integrity, especially the 1925 Kurdish rebellion, a full-scale insurrection with religious and separatist overtones (see Chapter 6). In the aftermath of the violent repression of the rebellion, the government enacted the Law for the Maintenance of Order, endowing itself with powers to prohibit and abolish "any institution, behaviour, and publications which disrupt the country's social order, calm, security, and safety." This law laid the basis for the CHP's authoritarian rule that would eliminate all possible channels of opposition until the end of the 1940s. The single-party regime was now in full swing.[28]

2 Industrial Structure in the 1920s

The first industrial census of the republic was carried out in 1927, reporting a total of 256,855 workers employed in 65,245 industrial establishments, a third of which belonged to self-employed artisans. Each establishment had, on average, 3.9 workers, with seventy-nine per cent of all establishments employing three or fewer workers, and three per cent employing more than ten. Geographically, the larger manufacturers were located in the larger cities. For example, forty per cent of firms employing more than ten workers were based

---

76; İlkay Sunar, *State and Society in the Politics of Turkey's Development* (Ankara: Ankara University Faculty of Political Science, 1974), 74–5.

26 Yerasimos, "The Monoparty Period," 76.

27 Boratav, "Kemalist Economic Policies," 169.

28 Mete Tunçay, *Türkiye'de Sol Akımlar: 1908–1925*, vol. 1 (Istanbul: İletişim Yayınları, 2009), 187–101; Yerasimos, "The Monoparty Period," 84.

in either Istanbul or Izmir. The industrial workforce in these two cities also accounted for one fourth of the entire industrial workforce. In terms of sectoral concentration, enterprises in the textile and food sectors made up sixty per cent of the total. Due to low levels of industrial productivity, the country was dependent on imports and thus suffered from a chronic trade deficit and the accompanying devaluation of the Turkish lira.[29] In 1927, every fourth lira spent on manufactured goods was being spent on imports.[30]

The government amended the 1913 Law for the Encouragement of Industry (*Teşvik-i Sanayi Kanunu*) in 1927. The new law explicitly called for the building of "industrial plants for mass production with the assistance of advanced machines, tools, or mechanical equipment."[31] In the range of subventions and incentives it provided for new industrial establishments, the law, argues Boratav, is without parallel in the history of republican Turkey.[32] The government was now backing private industrial investment through customs duties and profit tax exemptions, provision of free land, a thirty per cent reduction in rail and sea shipping rates, monopoly rights, and other mechanisms. Within the first five years of the law's enactment, 1,473 firms had made use of these concessions, with fewer than a quarter of these companies predating 1923. The law was planned to remain in effect until 1942, giving private entrepreneurs fifteen years to increase their levels of capital accumulation.[33] With the Law for the Protection of Industry (*Sanayi Koruma Kanunu*) in 1929, the CHP enacted further protectionist policies.[34]

After 1930, the number of enterprises benefiting from the industrial encouragement law fell in number, but their scale grew, and the gross output per firm was 2.4 times the 1932 value by 1939.[35] In 1933, a total of 1,397 industrial

29 T.C. Ekonomi Bakanlığı, *Türkiye Milli Geliri* (Ankara: Başvekalet Matbaası, 1937), 98–9; Donald Everett Webster, *The Turkey of Atatürk: Social Process in the Turkish Reformation* (Philadelphia: The American Academy of Political and Social Science, 1939), 65–66; Keyder, *The Definition of a Peripheral Economy*, 50–1; Kazgan, "Türk Ekonomisinde 1927–35 Depresyonu," 237–8.

30 Osman Okyar, "The Concept of Etatism," *Economic Journal* 75, no. 297 (1965), 99.

31 Zafer Toprak, *Sümerbank* (Istanbul: Creative Yayıncılık, 1989), 24; Okyar, "The Concept of Etatism," 98; Hershlag, *The Challenge of Growth*, 52–5.

32 Boratav, "Kemalist Economic Policies," 169.

33 William Hale, *The Political and Economic Development of Modern Turkey* (London: Croom Helm, 1981), 42–3; Richard D. Robinson, *The First Turkish Republic* (Cambridge: Harward University, 1963), 105–106; *Türkiye'de Toplumsal ve Ekonomik Gelişmenin 50 Yılı* (Ankara: DIE Yayınları, 1973), 149.

34 Şevket Süreyya Aydemir, *İkinci Adam*, vol. 1 (Istanbul: Remzi Kitabevi, 1984), 360.

35 Keyder, *State and Class in Turkey*, 103. Of the 1,473 enterprises benefiting from the law in 1932, 651 were in sectors related to agriculture, animal raising, and hunting activities,

establishments employing a workforce of 64,926 workers were beneficiaries of the law. By 1934, the number of establishments had fallen further to 1,310, while the number of workers increased to 69,150.[36] Five years after the law's enactment, the average number of workers per enterprise was thirty-eight for qualifying firms. The striking difference in this metric compared with the 1927 figure for all enterprises suggests that the approved firms had come close to becoming modern factories.[37]

But the industrial scene was still far from "factory chimneys belching smoke, the whir of machines and long trains of box cars being loaded from factory or warehouse," in the words of Donald Everett Webster, an American sociologist. "A man sitting in his two-metre-square shop and turning the crank of a manual stocking loom" was considered an industrialist.[38] As for the "real factories," the situation was not much better. Ahmet Hamdi Başar, Mustafa Kemal's economic advisor during his 1930 national tour, described the factories he saw in Istanbul, the industrial capital of the country, as follows:

> Behind the protective custom tariff barriers, a primitive industry has emerged in the last few years. Take this nail factory built inside the ruins of a *medrese* [a school for Islamic instruction] for example. It turns iron cords into nails and sells them at many times the world prices. Moreover, because it is considered as national industry, it does not pay customs fees for the cords. Or take this other famous factory (!) under a booth squeezed in-between two vacant plots in Galata. [The owner] also imports duty-free iron cords as raw material, galvanises them, and sells at many times the world prices. Another one, a copper products factory, is nothing but an old stone house in our neighbourhood. Its sheet-iron chimney releases so much soot that the people in the neighbourhood cannot even open their windows. But they have no right to complain! Because these [factories] work for the salvation of the homeland. Their real owners may be this and that person but they are registered under Turkish owners who rarely visit the factory. Still, they are our industrial masters, our patrons![39]

---

while 351 were in the textile sector. The percentages are respectively, 44.3 per cent and 23.8 per cent; Derin, *Türkiye'de Devletçilik*, 84.

36 T.C. Ekonomi Bakanlığı, *Türkiye*, 100.

37 Keyder, *The Definition of a Peripheral Economy*, 58. It should also be noted that these firms were highly concentrated geographically, with forty-seven per cent located in Istanbul or Izmir.

38 Webster, *The Turkey of Atatürk*, 65.

39 Ahmet Hamdi Başar, *Atatürk'le Üç Ay ve 1930'dan Sonra Türkiye* (Istanbul: Tan Matbaası, 1945), 97.

Başar's sardonic account points to both the primitive state of industrial production and the continuing dominance of foreign industrial investors. About one third of the corporations established between 1920 and 1930 were partnerships entered into by Turks with foreign capital.[40] The newspapers were frantically reporting tax evasion attempts and the misuse of concessions by private industrialists.[41] While private industrial capital benefited from the protective environment, the state's direct involvement in production was limited to the operation of the four state factories inherited from the Ottoman state and the establishment of two sugar-processing plants to lighten to burden of sugar imports.[42] The Great Depression paralysed the country's already hampered industrial development.

3 The Search for a Post-depression Economic Policy

The Great Depression hit the Turkish economy with catastrophic force. The plummeting returns from the agricultural products, Turkey's primary exports, aggravated the trade balance deficit. The trade deficit reached fifty million dollars in 1929, a figure that clearly exposed the new regime's economic vulnerability. The ensuing currency exchange crisis and the devaluation of the Turkish lira caused bankruptcies in the commercial sector, highlighting its excessive dependency on foreign markets. Domestic trade also remained stagnant from 1929 to 1932. The crisis of the commercial bourgeoisie required new economic policies; 1930 and 1931 were marked by economic innovation and zealous debates on the role of the state in the economy. Both statesmen and the intelligentsia were increasingly giving voice to the need for at least some level of insulation from international markets to create an integrated national economy.[43]

---

40 Boratav, "Kemalist Economic Policies," 168.

41 "Suistimal İptidai Maddeler Üzerindeymiş," *Haber-Akşam Postası*, 14 January 1935; "Mevkuf Bir Fabrikatör," *Haber-Akşam Postası*, 15 January 1935; "Çürük Mal Yapanlar Çoğalmış," *Haber-Akşam Postası*, 14 December 1934; "İhtilaf: Sanayi Birliğile Maliye Anlaşamıyorlar," *Haber-Akşam Postası*, 21 December 1934; "Fabrikatörler Ökonomi Kurumunu Aldatmıya Calışmışlar," *Haber-Akşam Postası*, 25 December 1934.

42 S.C. Wyatt, "Turkey: The Economic Situation and the Five-Years Plan," *International Affairs* 13, no. 6 (1934), 835; John Parker and Charles Smith, *Modern Turkey* (London: Routledge, 1940), 113.

43 Mustafa Türkeş, "A Patriotic Leftist Development-Strategy Proposal in Turkey in the 1930s: The Case of the Kadro (Cadre) Movement," *International Journal of Middle East Studies* 33, no. 1 (2001), 91; William Hale, *The Traditional and The Modern in The Economy of Kemalist Turkey: The Experience of the 1920s* (London: Routledge, 1984), 166;

If the worldwide economic circumstances were not pressing enough, there were also more than purely economic considerations behind the Turkish government's policy choice to move away from an open economy. The CHP was coming under increasing criticism for its high taxes and deflationary policies, and its growing networks of corruption and nepotism. Added to these economic grievances were the outbursts of reactionary incidents such as in Menemen, as well as ethnic rebellion in the province of Ağrı.[44] The growing discontent resulted in the establishment of an opposition party that added the adjective "Free" before the ruling "Republican Party." Initially an *Ersatz* party designed by Mustafa Kemal himself to ease tensions, the party became a serious contender in the 1930 municipal elections, exposing the CHP's waning popular support and intensifying the struggle and debate over economic policy.[45] By the end of the decade, it was clear that the regime would not be able to succeed in forging central authority either economically or politically. The Kemalist leadership's strategy of increasing state control was as much a result of securing political stability as achieving economic development. A politically directed national economy therefore emerged in response to the economic problems created simultaneously by the Great Depression, at the global level, and by domestic developments in the Turkish political economy.

Initially, protectionism functioned as an economic policy instrument to combat dependence on foreign commercial capital in the context of escalating hostility toward foreign merchants speculating against the domestic currency. Until 1931, policy measures had concerned the control of foreign trade and exchange transactions, and did not include directly interventionist elements.[46] In December 1929, the government founded the Association for National Economy and Parsimony (*Milli İktisat ve Tasarruf Cemiyeti*) "to promote frugality, to reduce the consumption of commodities by encouraging the production and consumption of local products, and to promote the idea

---

Keyder, *State and Class*, 95–6; Oya Silier, *Türkiye'de Tarımsal Yapının Gelişimi: 1923–1938* (Istanbul: Boğaziçi Üniversitesi, 1981), 47–60; Hale, "Ideology and Economic Development," 100–17.

44 Umut Azak, *Islam and Secularism in Turkey: Kemalism, Religion and the Nation State* (London: I.B. Tauris, 2010), 21–44.

45 Walter F. Weiker, *Political Tutelage and Democracy in Turkey: The Free Party and Its Aftermath,* (Leiden: Brill, 1973), 96–116; Cem Emrence, *99 Günlük Muhalefet: Serbest Cumhuriyet Fırkası* (Istanbul: İletişim Yayınları, 2006), 49–77; Cemil Koçak, *Belgelerle İktidar ve Serbest Cumhuriyet Fırkası* (Istanbul: İletişim Yayınları, 2006), 584–614; Korkut Boratav, *Türkiye'de Devletçilik* (Ankara: İmge Kitabevi, 2017), 53–9, 97–8.

46 Boratav, "Kemalist Economic Policies," 171.

of economic self-sufficiency."[47] When the era of low tariffs, mandated by the Treaty of Lausanne, ended in 1929, tariffs were increased first from thirteen per cent to forty-six per cent, and then to over sixty per cent by the latter part of the 1930s.[48] In 1930, the government established a central bank to control national monetary policy, and introduced custom duties. Together, these two measures improved the trade balance, decreasing the volume of imports by forty-two per cent between 1928 and 1934.[49] Despite various disagreements, economic planning and protectionism were on the rise, but the extent of state intervention in the economy remained an open and heated debate, creating significant intra-elite conflict.

Turkey was not alone in its search for a new economic regime in the 1930s. Following the Great Depression, economic nationalism arose as a reaction to the reigning liberal doctrines of the previous half-century in East-Central Europe, South America, and the Middle East (particularly Iran).[50] Used for the first time in 1928, the term economic nationalism gained currency after the Depression.[51] Tainted by a dislike for foreign capital, the building blocks of economic nationalism were protectionism, autarky, and industrialism.[52] The first three elements had already been strengthening in Turkey. It was the last element, industrialism, and the state's role in it that created fissures among the ruling elite. The decades-long oscillation between the two developmental models of agriculture and industry was finally resolved in favour of the latter.[53]

---

47 Keyder, *State and Class*, 98; İlhan Tekeli and Selim İlkin, *1929 Dünya Buhranında Türkiye'nin İktisadi Politika Arayışları* (Ankara: Orta Doğu Teknik Üniversitesi, 1977), 92.

48 Şevket Pamuk, *Turkey's Response to the Great Depression in Comparative Perspective, 1929–1939* (San Domenico di Fiesole: European University Institute, 2000), 7–8.

49 Barkey, *The State and The Industrialisation*, 46; Stanford J. Shaw and Ezel Kural Shaw, *History of the Ottoman Empire and Modern Turkey-Reform, Revolution, and Republic: The Rise of Modern Turkey 1808–1975*, vol. 2 (Cambridge: Cambridge University Press, 1977), 390; İlhan Tekeli and Selim İlkin, *Uygulamaya Geçerken Türkiye'de Devletçiliğin Oluşumu* (Ankara: ODTÜ İdari İlimler Fakültesi, 1982), 35.

50 Henryk Szlajfer, ed., *Economic Nationalism in East-Central Europe and South America 1918–1939* (Geneva: Droz, 1990); Joel Wolfe, "Populism and Developmentalism," in *A Companion to Latin American History*, ed. Thomas H. Holloway (Oxford: Wiley-Blackwell, 2011), 348–349; Amin Banani, *The Modernization of Iran 1921–1941* (Stanford: Stanford University Press, 1961), 137–143; Barkey, *The State and The Industrialisation*, 4–5.

51 Michael A. Heilperin, *Studies in Economic Nationalism* (Geneva: Publications de L'Institut Universitaire de Hautes Etudes Internationales, 1960), 16.

52 Jan Kofman, "How to Define Economic Nationalism: A Critical Review of Some Old and New Standpoints," in *Economic Nationalism in East-Central Europe and South America 1918–1939*, ed. Henryk Szlajfer (Geneva: Droz, 1990), 52.

53 In a 1936 article in the official journal of the People's Houses, the community centres opened and operated by the CHP, Nusret Köymen referred to the local intellectuals who were advocating an agricultural development model as the "colonial intelligentsia."

As one of the earliest examples of a planned economy in late industrialisation, etatism had become the Turkish version of a wider trend of nationalist movements with a developmentalist agenda. As in other comparable nationalist regimes such as Mexico, Argentina, Egypt, Indonesia, Brazil, Thailand, and India, the Kemalist elite adopted a common agenda of state-led industrialisation, political modernisation, and a non-aligned foreign policy; they were pioneering post-colonial state strategies long before the dismantling of the colonial world after the Second World War.

In hindsight, state-led industrialisation could be seen as an inevitable economic policy choice for a regime in search of economic development and political stability. Yet, the implementation of etatism was a contentious political process. The majority of the disagreements on the definition of the term centred on the protection of the investment rights of private capital. Initially coined in France in the 1890s by protectionists and socialists, by the 1920s the term etatism had come to mean direct state intervention in economic life. In 1930s Turkey, definitions of etatism oscillated between "a preferable alternative to capitalism" to "the nursemaid for capitalist development." Often, the government elite preferred to reject both definitions, presenting etatism as a peculiar policy to address the country's specific problems.[54] As might be expected, the effort to dissociate etatism from socialism was much stronger. In 1954, Hanson described the ambivalence around the term as follows: "Turkish publicists are usually at some pains to emphasize that 'etatism' in this country is not the product of preconceived or 'doctrinaire' socialistic theories, but of certain practical necessities confronting the Government of the young Republic."[55] They repeatedly underlined this difference so as to reassure private capital that a state-led approach to industry would benefit the private sector in the long run. By 1935, private enterprise was positioned as the "basic idea" in the party programme and the "principle means" in *Civil Knowledge for the Citizen* (*Vatandaş İçin Medeni Bilgiler*), a reference book authored by the adopted daughter of Mustafa Kemal under his close supervision.

More often than not, the emphasis was on the pragmatic and practical qualities of etatism as a quick remedy for underdevelopment. In 1933, when international conferences were yet to find solutions for economic and disarmament issues, Mustafa Kemal argued that Turkey had to take its own measures and set

See: "Türkiye Evvela Sanayileşmeli mi, Yoksa Ziraatini mi İlerletmeli?" *Ülkü* 40, no. 7 (1936), 248–52.

54 Hale, *Modern Turkey*, 55–56; Hershlag, *The Challenge of Growth*, 125.

55 A. H. Hanson, *The Structure and Control of State Enterprises in Turkey* (Ankara: Public Administration Institute for Turkey and The Middle East, 1954), 6.

out its own path to development.[56] He repeated the exceptionalism argument in the preface to the second five-year industrial plan. William Hale summarised the official definition of etatism as "a home-grown plant" that "specifically evolved for Turkish conditions."[57] The contemporary economist Ömer Celâl Sarc doubted the possibility of a satisfactory definition of the term since its content had changed through its application.[58] In the end, Turkish etatism had more of a haphazard nature than involving a set of clearly designed and executed policy decisions.

From the very beginning, the government underlined its preference for a complementary, instead of oppositional, relationship between state and private investment. True, the industrialisation programme was inspired by German, Italian, and Soviet models, but it would not go so far as following a fascist or a collectivist ideology. Economic analysts looked up to Germany with admiration, especially with regard to its temporary protection of infant industries. Simultaneously, the success of Soviet industrialisation in the 1920s sparked serious debates around the state's ability to manage and transform the economy.[59] Still, the state's involvement in the economy was presented as a last pragmatic solution aimed at jump-starting industrialisation. The given rationale for heavy state intervention was that the state had to undertake what undercapitalised private actors could not. "Our statist policies are essentially based on private individual enterprise," Mustafa Kemal declared in 1931. However, he continued, the state would directly intervene in the economy "in order to bring welfare to the people and develop the nation as soon as possible."[60] A strong sense of urgency for development characterised both policy documents and public opinion, which, the liberal opposition protested, put the entire burden of national development onto the shoulders of one generation.[61]

Although empiricism guided the implementation of etatism, one principle remained constant: state intervention was a must to speed up development. But because the country lacked the technical know-how to jump-start development, it needed foreign assistance. Against the background of the chronic instability facing interwar international relations, disagreements within the

56 Bilsay Kuruç, *Belgelerle Türkiye İktisat Politikası, 1933–1935*, vol. 2 (Ankara: Ankara Üniversitesi Yayınları, 1993), 93.

57 Hale, "Ideology and Economic Development," 105.

58 Ömer Celal Sarc, "The Economic Policy of the New Turkey," *Middle East Journal* 2, no. 4 (1948), 434.

59 Toprak, *Türkiye'de Milli İktisat*, 29–34; Ahmad, "*Vanguard,*" 333.

60 *50 Yılda Türk Sanayii*, (Ankara: Sanayi ve Teknoloji Bakanlığı, 1973), 6.

61 Parker and Smith, *Modern Turkey*, 106; Hanson, *Structure*, 10; Cited in Aydemir, *İkinci Adam*, 372, 445; Hershlag, *The Challenge of Growth*, 71.

ruling elite on the scope and ultimate goal of etatism would complicate the question of whom to turn to for loans and technical know-how.

4 Etatism and the Politics of Foreign Expertise

The Turkish state sought the help of foreign experts in its search for a post-1929 economic policy that would depart from economic liberalism and set out toward a planned economy.[62] The two earliest foreign expert reports were written by a German financial expert, Karl Müller, who advised against establishing a central bank, and a French professor of economics, Charles Rist, who advocated for direct foreign financial control and advised against the nationalisation of the railways and ports and, in general, any state intervention in the economy. Both reports intensified the political infighting about the pace of industrialisation within the ruling bloc. In his opening speech for the Sivas railway in August 1930, Prime Minister İnönü criticised both foreign experts and the liberal opposition for failing to see the absolute necessity of nationalising the economy.[63] The CHP was determined to follow this line, he reassured, but with careful consideration to the interests of private capital, he chose his words to describe the new economic policy carefully: *moderate etatism*.[64] The following year, after Mustafa Kemal had positioned etatism as a party principle, it was written into the CHP's programme.[65] The disagreements over the meaning and scope of etatism, however, were far from over. There were two factions within the ruling party. The first camp argued for active state involvement and government regulation over private enterprise, and was led by the minister of economy, Mustafa Şeref Özkan. As a liberal-oriented interest group, the second camp argued in favour of limiting the state's role in the economy and preferred to define etatism as a transitionary phase to be followed by private industrial activity. Celal Bayar, the first general director of the Business

62 İlhan Tekeli and Selim İlkin, *Dr. Max von der Porten'in Türkiye'deki Çalışmaları ve İktisadi Devlet Teşekkülleri Sisteminin Oluşumu* (Istanbul: Friedrich Ebert Vakfı, 1992), 9.

63 Tekeli and İlkin, *1929 Dünya Buhranında*, 110–115, 140–154. The building and controlling of a railway network had been a priority for the government since 1923. Under foreign ownership, the network was oriented toward the requirements of foreign trade, and connected the areas producing primary commodities to the main export centres. See: Boratav, "Kemalist Economic Policies," 165. The development of a wider national railway network was a prerequisite for an integrated national market.

64 Bilsay Kuruç, *Belgelerle Türkiye İktisat Politikası 1929–1932*, vol. 1 (Ankara: Ankara Üniversitesi Siyasal Bilgiler Fakültesi Yayınları, 1988), 101.

65 *Atatürk'ün Söylev ve Demeçleri*, vol. I–III (Ankara: Türk Tarih Kurumu Basımevi, 1989), 295.

Bank, around which the private sector was constantly growing and increasing its political influence over, led this second group.[66]

The tension between the two factions crystallised over the investment plan for a paper factory. While the first camp wanted to establish the factory as a state enterprise, the second pushed for a private enterprise funded by the Business Bank. In the end, the state invested in the paper factory, but Mustafa Kemal resolved the dispute by replacing Özkan with Bayar as the economy minister. This bureaucratic change signalled a shift from a more radical etatism and extensive economic planning approach to a model involving a mixture of state and private investment.[67] By then, parliament had passed two new laws on the institutional arrangements for the implementation of the planned industrialisation. Accordingly, the Industrial Credit Bank (*Sanayi Kredi Bankası*) would provide credit for both state and private industries, and the State Industrial Office (*Devlet Sanayi Ofisi*) would manage the state enterprises.[68] The liberal faction in the CHP was heavily critical of this dual institutional structure. The law governing the Industrial Credit Bank abolished the customs exemptions for industrial imports that the private sector had enjoyed since the 1927 Law for the Encouragement of Industry. The bank, liberals further lamented, would end up mainly financing state industries. The Industrial Office was designed to permanently own and manage the state industries. This led a member of parliament who was a self-described etatist to ask if forced collectivisation would be the next step. Others joined him in his worries over Turkish etatism turning into a Bolshevik project.[69]

The performance of the Soviet planned economy had indeed impressed the Kemalist ruling elite. Moreover, Soviet support for the Turkish national resistance movement was fresh in the national memory. The two countries signed a Treaty of Friendship and Neutrality in 1925. In his December 1929 visit to Turkey, the Soviet vice foreign minister Lev M. Karakhan declared Soviet support for the Turkish economic struggle; he advised Turkish officials to adopt

66 Türkeş, "A Patriotic Leftist Development," 93; Korel Göymen, "Stages of Etatist Development in Turkey: The Interaction of Single-Party Politics and Economic Policy in the 'Etatist Decade,' 1930–1939," *Gelişme Dergisi* 10 (1976), 114; Boratav, *Türkiye'de Devletçilik*, 139–46.

67 Selim İlkin, "Birinci Sanayi Planının Hazırlanışında Sovyet Uzmanlarının Rolü," in *Cumhuriyetin Harcı 2-Köktenci Modernitenin Gelişimi,* eds. Selim İlkin and İlhan Tekeli (Istanbul: Bilgi, 2004), 201–238.

68 Bilsay Kuruç, *Mustafa Kemal Döneminde Ekonomi* (Istanbul: Bilgi Yayınevi, 1987), 91–94.

69 Tekeli and İlkin, *Uygulamaya Geçerken,* 149–58, 213.

a five-year plan and offered technical help.[70] By then, the Turkish statesmen and economic analysts were specifically in awe of the extraordinary growth of Soviet heavy industry and the technological development of its textile industry. Indeed, the interest was mutual. In 1932, Turkish industrialists accompanied the Turkish prime minister and foreign affairs minister during their visit to Moscow and Leningrad. The visit proved to be successful in initiating economic cooperation.[71] In the meantime, the American embassy in Ankara was vehemently warning the secretary of state about the "strings attached to the generosity" of the Soviet Union toward Turkey. The planned productive enterprises offered a market for a considerable amount of capital goods, the ambassador wrote, encouraging the American contracting firms to participate in the industrialisation of Turkey.[72]

One of Bayar's first moves as the minister of economy was turning to the United States for foreign expertise to counterbalance the predominance of the Soviet experts in economic policymaking.[73] By the end of 1932, he launched a search for six American experts, four experts in commerce and mining, an economic specialist to supervise the preparation of a detailed economic survey report, and a general economic advisor to implement the recommendations.[74]

---

70 Dilek Barlas, *Etatism and Diplomacy in Turkey: Economic and Foreign Policy Strategies in an Uncertain World, 1929–1939* (Leiden: Brill, 1998), 124–26.

71 Peter Sugar, "Economic and Political Modernization: Turkey," in *Political Modernization in Japan and Turkey*, eds. Robert E. Ward and Dankward. A. Rustow (Princeton: Princeton University Press, 1964), 166; Ali Nejat Ölçen, "1923–1938 Döneminde Birinci ve İkinci Sanayi Planları," *Atatürk Dönemi Ekonomi Politikası ve Türkiye'nin Ekonomik Gelişmesi Semineri* (Ankara: SBF Yayınları, 1982), 137–140; Hale, *Modern Turkey*, 56.

72 Letter from Robert P. Skinner to the United States Department of State (28 June 1932, Ankara), Records of the Department of State Relating to Internal Affairs of Turkey 1930–1944, Economic Matters, 30 June 1932—14 April 1938, Decimal File 867.50, NARA, accessed 29 April 2020, https://link.gale.com/apps/doc/SC5111457718/GDSC?u=cumhurb&sid=GDSC&xid=093827ec.

73 Ceren Kalfa, "Planlamada Sümerbank Modeline Geçiş," in *Türkiye Cumhuriyeti İdare Tarihi Araştırması*, eds. Birgül A. Güler et al. (Ankara: Ankara Üniversitesi, 2007), 416; Selim İlkin, "Birinci Sanayi Planı Döneminde A.B.D'li Uzmanlara Hazırlatılan 'Türkiye'nin İktisadi Bakımdan Umumi Bir Tetkiki' Adlı Rapor," *Atatürk Döneminde Türkiye Ekonomisi Semineri* (Istanbul: Yapı ve Kredi, 1982), 221–239.

74 Letter from Wallace Murray to Dr. Sumner Schlichter (25 February 1933), Records of the Department of State Relating to Internal Affairs of Turkey 1930–1944, Economic Matters, Turkey, Economic Adviser, 19 January 1933—8 April 1935, Decimal File 867.50A, NARA, accessed 28 April 2020, https://go.gale.com/ps/retrieve.do?tabID=Manuscripts&resultListType=RESULT_LIST&searchResultsType=SingleTab&searchType=AdvancedSearchForm&currentPosition=2&docId=GALE%7CSC5111457416&docType=Manuscript&sort=Relevance&contentSegment=GDSC221&prodId=GDSC&contentSet=GALE%7CSC5111457416&searchId=R5&userGroupName=cumhurb&inPS=true&ps=1&cp=2. Despite

Walter D. Hines wrote a report advocating an agricultural development policy, to the dissatisfaction of the pro-industrialists. "Foreign observers are more inclined to criticize this branch of the Government's program than any other," the American embassy reported in August 1934, "on the ground that too much is being undertaken at once and that there is not sufficient technical skill in the country to make all of these industries successful."[75] But the government was determined to continue. At the press conference for the first five-year plan earlier the same year, Bayar had referred to the proponents of an agricultural development model as "old-fashioned" thinkers who wanted to maintain international trade based on unequal exchange.[76] The Kemalists had made up their mind, they would break through the largely agrarian economic structure and pull the society toward an industrial future.

The Soviet experts and ruling elite agreed with the Kemalists. *Izvestia*, a daily newspaper that expressed the official view of the Soviet government, accused the European experts who were advocating an agricultural development strategy for Turkey of imperialism. Following the Turkish prime minister's 1932 visit to Moscow, a group of Soviet experts led by Professor Orlov came to Turkey for a preliminary study on the establishment of textile factories. Orlov's report concluded that the development of Turkish industry was not only possible, but also absolutely necessary.[77] On 21 January 1934 the two countries signed a protocol that granted Turkey Soviet industrial credit of eight million gold American dollars without interest, mechanical equipment, help with drawing

---

diligent efforts by the Division of Near Eastern affairs at the request of the Turkish Embassy in Washington, the latter position was not filled. On 5 May 1933, the Chief of Division wrote they have "found it much more difficult than we had expected to find qualified persons to suggest to the Turkish Ambassador for these positions, particularly for the position of General Economic adviser." By June 1933, the enthusiasm of the Turkish government seemed to have faded away. In September 1933, the Turkish ambassador replied to a letter indicating interest in the position that "[the Ministry of Economy] does not contemplate engaging the services of a specialist immediately." Eventually, in the fall of 1934, a refugee German industrial expert, Max von der Porten, was hired as the head consultant at the Ministry of Economy. I have written on the transfer of scientific management to Turkish textile and shoe factories by exilic German engineers here: "Experts, Exiles, and Textiles: German 'Rationalisierung' on 1930s Turkish Shop Floor," *International Review of Social History* 66, no. 2 (2021).

75 Letter from Robert P. Skinner to the United States Department of State (7 August 1934, Istanbul), Records of the Department of State Relating to Internal Affairs of Turkey 1933–1935, Economic Matters, Turkey, Economic Adviser, 19 January 1933—8 April 1935, Decimal File 867.50A, Decimal File 867.50A, NARA, accessed 29 April 2020, https://link.gale.com/apps/doc/SC5111457416/GDSC?u=cumhurb&sid=GDSC&xid=093827ec.

76 Ali Süreyya, "Niçin ve Nasıl Sanayi Kuruyoruz?" *Cumhuriyet*, 12 January 1934.

77 Barlas, *Etatism and Diplomacy*, 97; Tekeli and İlkin, *Uygulamaya Geçerken*, 158–64.

up industrial projects, setting up machinery, and training specialists, and other technical cooperation.[78] In 1935, two large pictures of Mustafa Kemal and Lenin faced each other on the canteen walls at the Kayseri Factory, and between them hung broad red streamers with an inscription in Turkish and Russian: "Long live the Turkish-Russian friendship."[79] A council of Soviet planning experts were involved in the preparations for the first five-year industrial plan in 1933. The basic principles of Turkey's development policy were now official: an industrial development plan in which the state would take the lead. The parliament approved the first five-year plan on 8 January 1934 and implemented it three months later on 17 April 1934.

5 The First Five-Year Industrial Plan

In his 1940 book on etatism, a contemporary bureaucrat described the policymaking atmosphere of the early 1930s as imbued with anti-capitalist sentiment.[80] The analysis of Turkish underdevelopment in the preface of the first five-year industrial plan is the strongest expression of this sentiment. Foreshadowing the basic premises of the *dependencia* school, the preface explains the historical conditions under which core countries underwent industrialisation at the expense of the periphery and defines the relation between the two categories as a political relation of dominance and an economic relation of dependence. By weakening the ties between the core and the periphery of the capitalist world economy, the crises wrought by the Great Depression presented a window of opportunity for underdeveloped nations to break free from this unequal exchange. Turkey needed to seize this opportunity quickly since the industrialised nations would reinstate the terms of the international division of labour once they recovered.[81]

The plan focused on manufacturing previously imported simple consumer goods for which internal markets and local raw materials existed and labour-intensive production methods could be employed. This import substitution

78 The visit received a lot of enthusiastic attention from the media. Pro-government newspapers such as *Akşam, Cumhuriyet, Hâkimiyet-i Milliye and Vakit* published extensively on the details of the visit and the agreement in late April and May 1932.

79 Lilo Linke, "Social Changes in Turkey," *International Affairs* 16, no. 4 (1937), 541.

80 Derin, *Türkiye'de Devletçilik*, 5.

81 Tekeli and İlkin, *Uygulamaya Geçerken*, 184–185; Korkut Boratav, "Büyük Dünya Bunalımı İçinde Türkiye'nin Sanayileşme ve Gelişme Sorunları: 1929–1939," in Tarihsel Gelişimi İçinde Türkiye, eds. Orhan Kurmuş et al. (Ankara: Makina Mühendisleri Odası, 1977), 4–5.

model of industrialisation was expected to improve the trade balance, provide an impetus to the development of an industrial base, and stimulate an internal market by boosting agricultural production and opening new areas of employment. To address the significantly different levels of economic development between the old industrial centres, that is, especially Istanbul and its hinterland, and to a lesser extent cities in western Anatolia such as Izmir and Bursa, the planned industrial investments were geographically dispersed to medium-sized urban centres along the existing railway networks. In the next chapter, we will delve into the politics of industrial site selection and their long-term effects on national development and working-class politics.

Being lighter, labour-intensive industries that did not require highly developed technology, textiles and leather formed the centrepieces of the plan. Together with mining, textiles constituted the biggest share in imports at the beginning of the 1930s. Accordingly, these two sectors received the biggest share in the total expected investment, at 50.7 and 26.9 per cent, respectively.[82] Cotton and woollen goods in 1932 made up thirty per cent of Turkey's total imports.[83] Within textiles, cotton received the biggest share, with 42.2 per cent of the total investment.[84] By the early 1930s, fifty-seven per cent of Turkey's cotton textiles were imported; by the end of the decade, local cotton production was suppling eighty per cent of the demand "primarily by production of cheaper goods from local low grade fibres."[85] In 1935, the mouthpiece of the regime summarised the industrialisation programme as the production of "three whites": flour, sugar, and cotton, and "three blacks": coal, iron, petroleum. The production of the blacks was slow, but the first two whites, the newspaper claimed, would be entirely produced locally, and the country would eventually be self-sufficient in the third.[86]

Despite the strongly worded preface, the plan amounted to nothing more than a detailed list of investment projects.[87] Furthermore, even without the complete fulfilment of the programme, the actual cost was more than double the initial estimate. It would eventually take fourteen years to complete the programme, because of war, on the one hand, and the lack of adequate

82 Percentages calculated using the data in Aydemir, *İkinci Adam*, 414–15.

83 Wyatt, "Five-Years Plan," 838.

84 Percentage calculated using the date in Derin, *Türkiye'de Devletçilik*, 94.

85 İlhan Tekeli and Selim İlkin, "War Economy of a Non-Belligerent Country: Cotton Textiles: From Production to Consumption," *Turcica* 22 (1988), 117; Hershlag, *The Challenge of Growth*, 102.

86 "Cumhuriyetin 12.nci Yılındaki Endüstri Armağanları," *Cumhuriyet*, 29 October 1935, 2.

87 Boratav, "Kemalist Economic Policies," 175.

planning machinery, on the other.[88] Work on the second five-year plan began as early as 1936, and in 1938 the plan, which focused on the development of intermediate and capital goods industries such as steel and machinery, was adopted. However, it was soon abandoned due to the difficulties in securing financial means for the first five-year plan and the threat of a new world war. In its stead, a four-year plan was approved in September 1938, but with the outbreak of the war, many planned investments had to be dropped.[89]

The Soviet Union was the main source of professional instruction, financial aid, and equipment during the execution of the first plan. In the mid-1930s, however, Turkish-Soviet relations started to deteriorate. The tensions escalated in 1936, when the Soviet Union refused to support the Turkish cause in the Montreux Convention, which gave Turkey control over the Bosporus and Dardanelles straits. For the second plan, Turkey turned increasingly to British advisers and firms. The United Kingdom granted Turkey credit of close to three million pounds sterling for the construction of an iron and steel works in Karabük. In 1938, further credit of 10 million pounds and 150 million Reichsmark were secured from the United Kingdom and Germany respectively for the purpose of increasing the country's capital equipment.[90]

The government established two new development banks to execute the industrial investments and manage state enterprises. Founded in 1933 as a public holding company, Sümerbank was responsible for the promotion and management of industry. Two years later, Etibank was founded to establish state control over mining and ore processing. The name choice for the two holdings asserted nationhood by referring to an imagined continuity between the pre-Ottoman Anatolian civilisations and the newly independent Turkish republic. The idea was rooted in the Turkish History Thesis, which based its claim to a national identity on excavating a pre-Ottoman past, situated Turks in Asia Minor at the outset of history, and fabricated ties with ancient tribes of Anatolia. The tension between archaism and futurism, Mary Matossian argues, is a common ambiguity in ideologies of delayed industrialisation because at the start line "the West is 'the new' and the native culture is 'the old'." The Turkish references to a remote and mythical past is but one example of glorifying an imagined "golden age," which Matossian compares to Mussolini's reinvention of Imperial Rome and Gandhi's urge to return to the age of "Rama

88 Tekeli and İlkin, *Uygulamaya Geçerken*, 179–91.

89 Hershlag, *The Challenge of Growth*, 81; Aydemir, *İkinci Adam*, 418–9; Tekeli and İlkin, *Uygulamaya Geçerken*, 198–199; Hanson, *Structure*, 12.

90 Hershlag, *The Challenge of Growth*, 84; E. R. Lingeman, *Turkey: Economic and Commercial Conditions in Turkey* (London: His Majesty's Stationery Office, 1948), 83.

Raj."[91] By naming the two industrial holdings after the claimed pre-Ottoman forebears, the Sumerians (*Sümerler*) and the Hittites (*Etiler*), the government effectively distanced the republican present from the bleak legacy of the Ottoman past.[92] The erasure of the Ottoman past from the historical narrative sat at ease with the (re)birth of a Turkish nation breaking free from the chains of underdevelopment.

The legislative intention behind the establishment of Sümerbank was to replace the dual institutional structure of the Industrial Credit Bank and State Industrial Office, which, the law's preamble argued, "instead of helping the development of national industry, [had the effect of] worrying the industrialists."[93] The new institutional arrangement was a response to the criticism of the liberal camp led by Bayar, and signalled a shift to a more moderate form of etatism, meaning the state would undertake only those investments that private capital *could not* afford. Besides establishing and managing state factories, Sümerbank would co-finance large industrial ventures with private capital, which was expected to flourish. The holding would also establish schools to train industrial personnel for both the state and private industrial sectors. A contemporary economics journal aptly summarised the function of Sümerbank as creating an industrial army for the national industrial development project.[94]

Sümerbank took over the financing, construction, and operation of such diverse production units as textiles (cotton and wool), steel, paper, rayon, ceramics, caustic soda and chlorine, and cement plants. By the end of the decade, Sümerbank's share in cotton production was thirty-five per cent (see Table 1). By 1943, the workforce at the Sümerbank factories amounted to 23,023, that is eight per cent of all workers employed in industrial enterprises employing five or more workers.[95]

---

91 Mary Motassian, "Ideologies of Delayed Industrialization: Some Tensions and Ambiguities," *Economic Development and Cultural Change* 6, no. 3 (1958), 223–4.

92 Sibel Bozdoğan, *Modernism and Nation Building: Turkish Architectural Culture in the Early Republic* (Singapore: University of Washington Press, 2001), 118; Hugh Seton-Watson, *Nations and States: An Enquiry into The Origins of Nations and The Politics of Nationalism* (London: Methuen & Co. Ltd., 1977), 259; Benedict Anderson, *Imagined Communities: Reflections on the Origin and Spread of Nationalism* (New York: Verso, 2016), 12.

93 Tekeli and İlkin, *Uygulamaya Geçerken*, 177; Boratav, *Türkiye'de Devletçilik*, 198.

94 Hanson, *Structure*, 29; "Sanayileşme Davamızı Tahakkuk Ettiren Büyük Milli Müessesemiz," *İktisadi Yürüyüş Sümerbank Fevkalade Sayısı*, no. 61–62 (1942), 3; Tekeli and İlkin, *Uygulamaya Geçerken*, 192–5.

95 *Başvekalet Umumi Murakebe Heyeti, Sümerbank 1943 Yılı Umumi Murakabe Heyeti Raporu* (Ankara: 1944), 20; Ahmet Makal, *Türkiye'de Tek Partili Dönemde Çalışma İlişkileri: 1920–1946* (Ankara: İmge Kitabevi, 1999), 307.

TABLE 1 The share of the Sümerbank in the volume of industrial output, 1939

Industry	Sümerbank's share in the volume of output (in %)
Cotton	35
Wool	60
Artificial silk	100
Leather	62
Shoes	90
Paper and cardboard	100
Cement	55
Coke	70
Iron	100
Superphosphates	100
Steel	80
Lubricating oils	80

SOURCE: HERSHLAG, *CHALLENGE*, 92

6 "A Classless, Fused Mass": Populism and Industrial Labour

For the young republic, the 1920s had been a decade of crises at both the national and the international levels. The following decade witnessed the solidification of state power and consolidation of the Kemalist regime, which social scientists described as "Kemalism par excellence", or "High Kemalism".[96] From 1931 onward, the Republican People's Party consolidated its monopoly of power, resulting eventually in the merger of the party with the state. Kemalism attained its most succinct definition in May 1931 when the CHP adopted six "fundamental and unchangeable principles" of republicanism—nationalism, populism, secularism, populism, revolutionism, and etatism—in its programme. On 5 February 1937, these principles were incorporated into the constitution.

96 Gülalp, "Capitalism and the Modern Nation-State," 171; Soner Çağaptay, "Reconfiguring the Turkish Nation in the 1930s," *Nationalism and Ethnic Politics* 8, No. 2, (2002), 68.

After etatism, populism was the most commonly invoked principle in economic policy. The republican rulers attributed Ottoman underdevelopment to foreign capital dependence, which benefited the corrupt imperial elite at the expense of the impoverished masses. In contrast, state-led industrialisation promised developmental benefits to the nation as a whole. To be distinguished from the type of populism that rests on a cross-class coalition of workers and industrialists such as in Latin America, the Kemalist populism of the 1930s either rejected the existence of class or "merged all social classes into a strong, 'impartial' state."[97] Kemalist populism would allegedly ensure that class interests could not infiltrate the Turkish state's constituency in general. Specifically, it would function as the antidote to the incipient threats of industrialisation. In 1936, one of the founding fathers of Turkish nationalism, Tekin Alp, an Ottoman Jew by birth who converted to Islam and advocated for the Turkification of minorities, sought to reassure those concerned about the dangers of an industrial future:

> [I]n the Kemalist regime, Nation and State form a single, indivisible, and inseparable whole. The spirit with which the whole nation, and particularly the elite which surrounds the leader is imbued ... constitutes a guarantee against any possible deviation or degeneration of etatism ... The Kemalist state cannot tolerate the implantation in Turkey of perpetual and fratricidal struggles between the two elements of national production, the employers and the workers.[98]

The fresh memory of national resistance and the continuity between the old military and new political cadres strengthened the claim to a supra-class state. The regime rose on the heels of an extraordinary string of military successes, and the higher echelons of the state were almost exclusively staffed by men who had taken a leading part in the War of Independence. To put it differently, the saviours of the nation yesterday were its rulers today.[99] The ruling party

97 Karpat, *Turkey's Politics*, 71.

98 Cited in Hale, *Ideology*, 105.

99 The strongest expression of this identification was the presentation of the Society for the Defence of the Rights of Thrace and Anatolia, the organisation that led the Independence War, as the predecessor of the CHP, and the acceptance of the Sivas Congress as the first party congress of the party. See: Hakkı Uyar, "Devletin İşçi Sınıfı ve Örgütlenme Girişimi: CHP İzmir İşçi ve Esnaf Cemiyetleri Birliği (1935)," *Tarih ve Toplum* 27, no. 157, (1997), 14.

thus had a specific character, as described by Mustafa Kemal shortly after the Free Party experiment turned into a disaster:

> As you know political parties are formed for narrow and specific reasons. For example, the merchants of Izmir may form a party to accomplish their own aims. Or there could be a party for farmers. There may be such narrow parties but our party is set up to achieve the aims of each class of the people without hurting the interests of any other.[100]

In state discourse, it was this narrative of exceptionalism that would insulate the party-state from the infiltration of any class interests. "Privileges and classes never existed in our case," claimed Prime Minister Şükrü Saraçoğlu: "We have been populist, are populist, and will remain populist. The fact that we have formed a single-party state is mainly based on this fundamental reality. We want no reign of court, of capital, or of classes. All we want is the sovereignty of the Turkish people!"[101]

It was the combination of their biographical stories, the epitome of which was the rise of Mustafa Kemal as the saviour of the nation, and their successful manoeuvring of collective memory and national sentiment that legitimised the ruling elite's self-presentation as the trustees of the people. This image aided the proponents of etatism in propagating nationalism as the dominant discourse of development and refuting the liberal critique of state intervention into the economy during the economic policy debates of the early 1930s. "The radical-reform nationalist," argues William Hale, "saw etatism as a permanent alternative to capitalism and ... linked its principles to the belief in social solidarism labelled as 'populism'."[102] The appeal to populism, however, was much wider than he recognised. The assumed unity between the Turkish state and the nation, and the idea of a "Turkish people" as a classless, fused mass underlined the entire official discourse and extended its hegemonic capacity to both the external and internal regulation of labour, as we shall see later in this book. During the time of rapid industrialisation, the state and employers resorted to

---

100 Cited in Feroz Ahmad, "The Development of Class-Consciousness in Republican Turkey, 1923–45," in *Workers and the Working Class in the Ottoman Empire and the Turkish Republic,* eds. Donald Quataert and Erik Jan Zürcher (London: Tauris Academic Studies, 1995), 90. In a publication of Association of Izmir Workers and Craftsmen in 1935, the CHP addressed the Turkish workers as follows: "There is no you and me, dear Turkish worker; there is only us!" (Uyar, "Devletin İşçi Sınıfı ve Örgütlenme Girişimi," 17).

101 Cited in Ayhan Aktar, *Varlık Vergisi ve Türkleştirme Politikaları*, (Istanbul: İletişim Yayınları, 2001), 142–3.

102 Hale, *Ideology,* 105.

these discourses to avoid what they described as the awfully familiar malaise of industrial societies.

A mission report of the International Labour Office from 1949 observed the peculiar—and definitely transitional, according to the writers—public opinion with respect to the labour question in the country:

> On the one hand, the sentiment of national unity which was generated by the independence movement and which played so large a part in assuring that movement's success is still a very real factor in Turkish public life. Class distinctions do not appear to be at all sharply defined ... On the other hand, there appears to exist in many circles a feeling of distrust toward "labour"—a feeling based rather on a knowledge (not always entirely accurate) of developments in other countries than on actual experience in Turkey.[103]

The Turkish industrialists lost sleep to intrusive concerns over the inherent political dangers of industrialisation. In parliamentary debates and public statements, bureaucrats often referred to horrific images of a Europe torn apart by class warfare.[104] In 1932, Vedat Nedim Tör, an economist and a bureaucrat, aptly summarised the state perspective on industrial society: "We want to transfer the advanced industrial techniques to our country, but we do not want these techniques to cause class warfare."[105] The leitmotif of the independence struggle had been sacrifice for the sake of national salvation; the same leitmotif was now being extended onto industrial workers. As we shall see in later chapters, the industrialists appealed to their patriotic duty and the necessity to make sacrifices for the nation. The document that formulated this appeal was the 1935 party programme, which described the solidarist view of society:

> It is one of our main principles to consider the people of the Turkish Republic, not as composed of different classes, but as a community divided into various professions according to the requirements of the division of labour for the individual and social life of the Turkish people ... The functioning of each of these groups is essential to the life

103 International Labour Office, "*Labour Problems in Turkey*," *Report of a Mission of the International Labour Office* (Geneva: ILO, 1950), 17.

104 TBMM Tutanak Dergisi (Records of the Grand National Assembly), "1937 yılı muvazenei umumiye kanunu layihası ve Bütçe encümeni mazbatası," (1/702), 28 May 1937, Session V, Volume 18, Meeting No. 67, 355–356.

105 Vedat Nedim, "Sınıflaşmamak ve İktisat Siyaseti," *Kadro* 1, no. 11 (1932), 17–21.

> and happiness of the others and of the community ... Every economic enterprise shall harmonize with united national work as well as with the general interest. This harmony is also the principle in the union of work between the employer and worker ... We are interested in the life and rights of the nationalist Turkish workers within the framework of these principles. The Labor Laws to be promulgated shall conform to these principles. ... No association shall be founded in Turkey with the purpose of propagating ideas of class distinction, or of class conflict ... We shall make a point of organizing the Turkish workers and members of different trades within the main existence of the nation, and in such a way as to render them useful and invigorating to it, in accordance with the attitude outlined in the party program.[106]

The programme also contained the blueprint for the labour code that would be enacted the following year. In an effort to ease concerns over a possible "poisoning of the Turkish worker" with ideas of class conflict, the party secretary, Recep Peker, announced a ban on strikes and lockouts. Congress participants replied with an enthusiastic "Bravo!" But, he added, the party would also not allow a capitalist to pressure a worker unfairly, because, after all, populism dictated that they were both sons of the country.[107]

In 1936, that is, four years after industrialisation became official economic policy, the ruling party formalised the industrial employment relations of a core workforce in large industries with an authoritarian labour code adapted from the Italian equivalent. In total, it had taken the Kemalist regime fifteen years to enact a labour code. This is a strikingly long period for a regime that had impressed both its own citizens and the international community with the speed of its superstructural and legislative reforms. As the developments leading to that formalisation of industrial relations demonstrate, the delay was due to the contentious class politics behind the making of etatist policy.

7 The Labour Code: Fifteen Years in the Making

"Aside from industry, transport, and banking," wrote Richard D. Robinson in 1963, "Turkish etatism likewise invaded the field of labour-management relations." The advancing of industrialisation gave rise to a growing necessity for

106 Webster, *The Turkey of Atatürk*, 308–17.

107 "Türkiye'de Sınıf Mücadelesi Olmayacak," *Haber-Akşam Postası*, 14 May 1935.

the codification and enforcement of basic labour regulations, which, in the absence of labour organisation, required "some sort of state administrative machinery."[108] Robinson's claim that etatism and its accompanying nationalist populist discourses shaped the labour code may be true, but the attempts to codify labour relations certainly go much further back than the beginning of etatism.

The first attempt at a labour code was during the war, shortly before the adoption of the first constitution of the republic in January 1921 under the Ankara Government. The attempt failed even before reaching the draft stage, and according to a contemporary journalist and trade unionist, Kemal Sülker, the pro-worker stance of the minister of economy, Mahmut Esat, cost him his seat.[109] Following a wave of strikes in 1924, the government presented a draft code to the parliament with a message underlining the need to "prevent conflicts between capital and labour."[110] But the feared conflict came in a different form. In 1925, the government bloodily suppressed the first large-scale nationalist rebellion by the Kurds, commonly referred to as the Sheikh Sa'id Uprising, declared martial law, and enacted the Law for the Maintenance of Order, granting itself sweeping powers. In the turmoil of the time, the attempt to enact labour legislation failed once again.

Although martial law suppressed all legal labour activity, it could not eliminate strikes and worker associations, and thus increased the pressure on the government to enact a labour code. When the third draft came in 1927, a newspaper covered the reaction of both employers and workers.[111] Employers strongly opposed the doubling of overtime pay, the obligation to give notice of contract termination to employees with at least three months of service, and the obligation to pay wages and medical expenses in the event of a work accident. Workers, organised under the Society for the Advancement of Turkish Workers (*Türk Amele Teali Cemiyeti*), prepared a list of what they wanted to see. In addition to the more predictable demands concerning the working day, minimum wages, overtime pay, and the protection of child workers, two of the demands would become points of contention throughout the following decades. First, they demanded the expansion of the definition of worker to include agricultural workers. Second, they objected the centrality of the individual

108 Robinson, *The First Turkish Republic*, 108–9.

109 Kemal Sülker, *100 Soruda Türkiye'de İşçi Hareketleri* (Istanbul: Gerçek Yayınları, 1978), 46–47.

110 Sumner Maurice Rosen, "Labor in Turkey," in *Labor in Developing Countries*, ed. Walter Galenson (Berkeley: University of California Press, 1962), 268.

111 Zafer Toprak, *Türkiye'de İşçi Sınıfı 1908–1946* (Istanbul: Tarih Vakfı, 2016), 380–388.

employment contract as the hub of employment rights, and demanded a trade union law. The third attempt at a labour code also fell through, and, as we shall see below, both of these demands remained unfulfilled.

The search for an economic policy direction delayed the codification of labour relations, while the increase in unemployment and wage losses following the Great Depression provided further momentum for labour unrest. The 1930 Public Health Law (*Umumi Hıfzıssıhha Kanunu*) stipulated rules for the protection of child, juvenile, and female workers, issued regulations concerning the health and safety of all workers, and introduced medical services in larger enterprises. The economic programme put forward by the minister of economy that same year, however, ignored labour issues, except to report on Turkish workers' complacency and the benefits of the low cost of living in the country. A new draft labour code came after the success of the oppositional Free Party caught the government off guard in 1930.[112]

The Free Party found unexpected support in the rich farming areas of western Anatolia and coastal towns such as Izmir and Samsun, where labour unrest was on the verge of taking a violent turn.[113] The government responded with repression, suppressing the strikes and closing down worker organisations. But it also promised to give special attention to labour issues, including by creating a labour code.[114] The draft labour code was ready by February 1931. Two other changes in the CHP's labour policy in this period included the search for suitable workers to become parliamentary representatives, and the establishment of party-controlled workers' associations; this was in perfect alignment with the allegedly class-conflict-free etatist development model.[115] Slowly but steadily, labour was becoming a political category, one that needed to be controlled and contained in the eyes of the ruling elite.

---

112 Samet Ağaoğlu, "Türkiye'de İş Kanunu Tarihçesi," *Ülkü* 7, no. 41 (1936), 330–336; Kemal Sülker, *Türkiye'de Grev Hakkı ve Grevler* (Istanbul: TÜSTAV, 2004), 153; Hakkı Tarık Us, "İş Kanunlarının Tarihçesi: Bu Kanunlarda Yusuf Akçora'nın Emeği," *Vakit* (*Yeni Gazete*), 22–28 June 1952; Samet Ağaoğlu and Selahattin Hüdaioğlu, *Türkiye'de İş Hukuku: İş Hukuku Tarihi*, vol. 1 (Istanbul: Merkez Basımevi, 1938), 102–3, 117–45; Selim İlkin, "Devletçilik Döneminin İlk Yıllarında İşçi Sorununa Yaklaşım ve 1932 İş Kanunu Tasarısı," *Türkiye İktisat Tarihi Üzerine Araştırmalar-Gelişme Dergisi* (1978), 251–3.

113 Boratav, "Kemalist Economic Policies," 173.

114 "Liman Şirketi Amelesi Grev İlan Ederek Fethi Paşa'yı Selamladı," *Cumhuriyet*, 7 September 1930; "İzmir'de Grevler: Vali Paşa'nın Beyanatı," *Vakit*, 11 September 1930; "Amelenin Parası Nasıl Yeniyor," *Son Posta*, 19 September 1930; "Progamın En Mühim Esasları Neler Olacak," *Vakit*, 26 September 1930.

115 Mesut Gülmez, "1932 İş Yasası Tasarısı ve İzmir İşçilerinin Görüş ve Dilekleri," *Amme İdaresi Dergisi* 18, no. 1 (1985), 103; İlkin, "İşçi Sorununa Yaklaşım," 262–8.

In its 1931 programme, the CHP rejected the idea of a class-based society and promised to defend the rights of the "nationalist Turkish worker" with a labour code based on the idea of harmony between employer and employee. By then, the draft code was circulating government offices with no sign of its fate in sight. In December 1931, former minister of economy Mahmut Esat criticised the ten-year delay in the making of a labour code. "Children who were born when the preparations started are now workers," he lamented, claiming that the republican regime may have almost achieved the modernisation of the country, but had failed in enacting a labour code.[116] The delay in labour legislation also presented a political danger, he continued, because Turkish workers had fallen prey to foreign propaganda, which labour protection would better fight against than state repression. Meanwhile, unemployment soared and labour unrest continued. Press reports from 1931 claimed that there were one hundred thousand unemployed in Istanbul, a city of eight hundred thousand people. In the first half of 1932, there were eighteen strikes in Istanbul alone. Complaints about the employment of foreign workers were also on the rise. In June 1932, the government responded with a law banning foreigners from certain professions.[117]

Two months before the submission of the draft labour code to parliament, a newspaper conducted a survey on workers' and employers' expectations for the labour legislation.[118] Workers wanted, first and foremost, the right to organise. Employers wanted an extension of the workday, arguing that the eight-hour working day harmed both capital and labour. Unlike their European counterparts, Turkish workers were mostly unskilled and very poor, and thus had to work longer hours to earn a living wage. Two additional employer demands comprised stipulations against skilled workers' deserting their workplace, and exemptions from employer contributions to social provisions. Last but not least, employers claimed that it would be a mistake to model the Turkish labour code on European versions; the best examples to follow were countries such as Bulgaria, Greece, and Romania.

When the draft came before the parliament in March 1932, employers found support in the liberal faction, the members of which were severely critical of the draft's pro-worker stance. Indeed, the draft positioned labour as social category rather than simply a fact of production, and stipulated the right to organise. Its opponents proposed instead the adoption of the 1927 Italian labour code, the *Carta del Lavoro*. Considered "the fundamental expression of

116 İlkin, "İşçi Sorununa Yaklaşım," 271–275, Kuruç, *Belgelerle Türkiye*, vol. 1, 206.

117 Ibid., 278.

118 Ibid., 276–7.

the nature of Fascist work and of the Fascist surpassing of class conflict," the Italian code promoted the principles of corporatism, banned strikes and lockouts, and would become a source of inspiration for legislators in several countries.[119] To counter these criticisms, the minister of economy, Mustafa Şeref Özkan, took advantage of the ongoing negotiations to join the International Labour Organization, and submitted the copies of the draft to the 16th Session of the International Labour Conference in April 1932. Alas, the positive international reception of the draft failed to ease tensions back home. Özkan was forced to resign in September of the same year, to be replaced by the leader of the liberal wing, Celal Bayar. In one of his first statements in office, Bayar assured the public that the government would enact a labour code before the end of the parliamentary year because it was "high time to think of the selfless and hardworking industrial workers who bear all sorts of hardship." In 1934, after two years of waiting, Özkan's draft was replaced by another draft that adopted a repressive hard-line approach.

Bayar also underlined the government's vision of harmony between capital and labour, but specified a new expectation for the code: to bring production costs down. From then on, the rationalisation of industrial production would be a hallmark of his time in office. Private industrial capitalists quickly seized the window of opportunity and lobbied for the annulment of the weekly rest-day to ease the economic whiplash. They based their claims on two sets of comparisons. First, they compared the high production costs of their newly established factories with the old and large state factories such as Defterdar, Hereke, and Bakırköy. Second, citing Japan as a favourable example, they argued that low wages and longer working hours was a way of enabling late industrialising countries to compete with European manufacturing.[120] Engineers and academics successfully objected by referring to contemporary experiments in Europe showing an inverse relationship between industrial fatigue and productivity.[121]

On the labour front, the government adopted a harsher approach to dealing with the continuing unrest. In Istanbul, the police began collecting fingerprints

119 Richard Bosworth, *Mussolini's Italy: Life Under the Dictatorship* (London: Penguin Books, 2005), 227; Matteo Pasetti, "The Fascist Labour Charter and Its Transnational Spread," in *Corporatism and Fascism: The Corporatist Wave in Europe*, ed. Antonio Costa Pinto (London: Routledge, 2017).

120 "Sekiz Saat mi, Dokuz mu? Sanayi Erbabı Dokuz Saatin Lüzumundan Bahsediyorlar," *Haber-Akşam Postası*, 15 November 1932.

121 "İş Saatleri," *Haber-Akşam Postası*, 21 November 1932; "Yeni İş Kanunu," *Haber-Akşam Postası*, 24 December 1932.

of workers. Following the strikes at the Eastern Railway and the Industrial Tramcar Company in 1928, the CHP closed down workers' associations. In 1933, an amendment to the Turkish penal code prohibited strikes and lockouts. On the eve of etatism, an authoritarian regime of industrial relations was de facto in effect; the labour code would have to wait three more years.[122] On 12 June 1936, the parliament enacted the labour code, which was described proudly by ex-general party secretary Recep Peker as "a regime law" that would "act as a thick wall against the division of citizens into classes."[123]

8 The 1936 Labour Code: A Regime Law

Enacted on 12 June 1936 as law number 3008, the 1936 Labour Code covered enterprises that technically employed ten or more workers on a daily basis, meaning it applied to only 180,000 workers. The code stipulated a number of protective measures concerning conditions of employment, such as hours of work, daily rest periods, night work, and the weekly rest. It also dealt with such matters as protection of wages, employment of women and juveniles, health and safety labour inspections, employment exchanges, and conciliation and arbitration. These protective measures did not remain in effect for long, however, because the government, under the powers conferred upon it by the National Defence Act of 1940, would go on to suspend their operation. The 1940 act overrode the regulations on working hours, permitted compulsory work and overtime, and prohibited workers from leaving their place of employment.

Even before the 1940 act, two stipulations severely limited the code's protective mandates. First, it applied only to establishments with more than ten workers, which served to exclude around three quarters of the industrial workforce employed in small workshops. In the 1940s, and increasingly after the war, workers outside the scope of the code began to demand its expansion. Second, by prohibiting strikes and lockouts and enforcing compulsory arbitration, the code effectively eliminated collective bargaining; it defined the principal means of industrial dispute resolution as the case-by-case enforcement of individual work agreements through compulsory conciliation and arbitration. The code retained the individual work contract, which the Code of Obligations

122 Keyder, *State and Class*, 104; İlkin, "İşçi Sorununa Yaklaşım," 281–7.

123 TBMM Tutanak Dergisi (Records of the Grand National Assembly), "İş kanunu layihası ve Muvakkat encümen mazbatası," (1/162), 8 June 1936, Session V, Volume 12, Meeting no. 75, 83–84.

(*Borçlar Kanunu*) of 1926 had introduced as one type of European form of contract, as the basis of employer-employee relations, and dealt only with individual rights. To secure adherence to legal requirements in the absence of collective agreements, it prescribed the terms of the contract as well as the penalties for violating these terms, imposed a variety of compulsory provisions, and established administrative techniques for supervising the terms of contracts. The motive behind the protection of the worker as an individual rather than as a collective group was to prevent the development of mass discontent, which the prime minister explicitly stated after the passing of the code: "The new Labour Code will sweep away the clouds which make possible the birth and life of class consciousness."[124]

The code laid down a compulsory arbitration procedure for the settlement of labour disputes, and defined the main elements of the adjustment procedure as the workers' representatives, the departmental officials, and the arbitration boards. In each workplace, there would be one to five workers' representatives depending on the size of the enterprise. In the first stage of a collective dispute adjustment, workers' representatives and departmental officials were tasked with securing a voluntary agreement between employers and workers. If they failed, the case would be brought before the arbitration board, the final decision of which was binding for both parties. Remarkably, the government had the power to extend a specific decision to others working in similar conditions.

The individual contract remained the exclusive instrument regulating the employment relationship in the absence of trade unions, but, interestingly, the code made no reference to trade unions. A historian of trade unions explains this silence as cautionary to preclude accusations of violating the ILO convention on freedom of association.[125] In fact, the government used other types of legislation to outlaw trade unions. The penal code declared activities aimed at "establishing the hegemony or domination of one social class over other social classes, or eliminating a social class or overthrowing any of the fundamental economic or social orders established within the country" illegal in 1936, but the final blow came in 1938 with the revised Associations Act, which banned all forms of class-based organisations, thus making it virtually impossible to form a trade union.

After fifteen years in the making, the spirit of the labour code reflected a congruence between etatism as economic policy and an authoritarian Kemalism as the ruling ideology. Scholars explained the interconnections between

---

124 Rosen, "Labor in Turkey," 269–270.

125 Mesut Gülmez, *1936 İş Yasası'nın Hazırlık Çalışmaları* (Istanbul: Istanbul Üniversitesi İktisat Fakültesi, 1986), 161.

economic policy and the changes in state form and ideology as the emergence of a "new policy" in which "a particular political mode extends itself to previously uncontrolled spheres of a society."[126] According to Oscar Weigert, a German expatriate who worked as labour advisor to the Turkish government and assisted in the drafting of the new labour legislation, the prohibition of strikes and lockouts amounted to nothing more than a mere sanctioning of the existing position. By emphasising the solidarity of all citizens and rejecting the idea of rival classes, the political programme of the new Turkey, he argued, already embodied the principle of securing of "a harmonious footing" between employers and workers. As a whole, the new labour legislation aimed at eliminating "proletarian pressure" and a class war, and "introducing a new element of stability in Turkish national life."[127] A rhetoric of mobilisation based on national identity effectively repressed politics around the inequalities that had been created in the course of a top-down developmentalist agenda.

The question to ask is how the new legal-institutional framework affected state and private industries. The prevailing contemporary opinion was that state factories had already been implementing the rights and the protective measures codified by the law.[128] In some cases, managers of state factories claimed that actual practice fared better than the legislation. State workers saw it otherwise. In the second part of the book, the reader will find their testimonies on the incomplete and problematic implementation of the protective legislation. Added to the implementation problems was the delay in the establishment of a state employment service and the submission of bills on social insurance. Although the code enforced their introduction within one year of its application, the government would not take action until after the war.[129]

The shift from the open economy of the 1920s to state-led industrialisation in the 1930s did not pose a threat for the private industrial sector. On the contrary, the Turkish state continued to encourage private capital and private interests. In addition to the 1927 Law for the Encouragement of Industry, private industrial employers benefited from protectionist policies such as favourable price and cost structures and import restrictions. Finally, the legal-institutional framework constructed by the state in the 1930s benefited

126 Keyder, "The Political Economy of Turkish Democracy," 14; Faruk Birtek, "The Rise and Fall of Etatism in Turkey, 1932–1950: The Uncertain Road in the Restructuring of a Semiperipheral Economy," *Review Fernand Braudel Center* 8, no. 1 (1985), 407.

127 Oscar Weigert, "The New Turkish Labour Code," *International Labour Review* 35, no. 6 (1937), 770, 774.

128 Aydemir, *İkinci Adam*, 396.

129 Webster, *The Turkey of Atatürk*, 252–8.

private industrialists by defining the individual contract as the sole basis of the relationship between employers and employees; it effectively blocked the channels for working-class collective action. The increase in the rate of accumulation during the etatist years was so high that, a prominent economic historian of Turkey argued, "by the beginning of the war the country had already passed the critical first threshold on the difficult road to industrialisation."[130] With the outbreak of World War II, workers lost much of the protections the code had provided for them. The final impetus to private capital accumulation came during the war years, when industrialists benefited from high inflation, scarcity, hoarding, and black markets.[131] In the postwar period, private capital spearheaded the import substitution industrialisation process.

Both the government and private industrialists referred to the relation between the two as a relation of complementarity. A well-known economic journal defined the relationship as one of "guidance," where state industry would help private industry to secure capital, technology, and workers.[132] In the pages of a textile engineering journal the relationship was described as one of between siblings, with state industry the elder brother.[133] In the words of a prominent bureaucrat and advocate of etatism, the task of state industries was "to set an example and create a tradition" in the fields of modern business organisation and management, full employment, and productivity, as well as to train technical and managerial personnel for private industries.[134] Indeed, many prominent managers of state factories were transferred to private factories, where wages were higher than the state sector.[135] Some became private industrialists themselves, as early as 1945.[136] By fostering the development of the internal market on the one hand, and industrial skills, infrastructure, and

---

130 Boratav, "Kemalist Economic Policies," 186.

131 Robert V. Kerwin, "Private Enterprise in Turkish Industrial Development," *Middle East Journal* 5, no. 1 (1951), 27; Alec Alexander, "Turkey," in *Economic Development: Analysis and Case Studies*, eds. Adamantios Pepelasis, Leon Mears, and Irma Adelman (New York: Harper & Brothers Publishers, 1961), 475; Şevket Pamuk, "Political Economy of Industrialization in Turkey," *Middle East Research and Information* 93 (1981), 26; Barkey, *The State and The Industrialisation*, 5; Wyatt, "Five-Years Plan," 833–834; Boratav, *Türkiye İktisat Tarihi*, 53–4; Boratav, "Kemalist Economic Policies,"178.

132 "Sanayileşme Davamızı Tahakkuk Ettiren Büyük Milli Müessesemiz," 52.

133 Tarık Aksın, "Yıllık Çalışma Programı," *Feshane Mensucat Meslek Dergisi* 7 (1953), 243.

134 Aydemir, *İkinci Adam*, 446.

135 James M. Barker, *The Economy of Turkey: An Analysis and Recommendations for A Development Program* (Baltimore: The Johns Hopkins Press, 1951), 117; Sabahaddin Zaim, *Bölge ve Şehir Planlaması Yönünden Istanbul Sanayi Bölgeleri* (Istanbul: Istanbul Üniversitesi Yayınları, 1971), 256.

136 Ömer Alageyik, "Büyük Acımız," *Mensucat Meslek Dergisi* 6 (1958), 165–6.

habits on the other, the state fostered the emergence of a native industrial entrepreneurial class.

By the end of the war, the intra-elite conflict became impossible to manage. The submission of the Land Reform Bill to parliament in 1945 crystallised the class interests within the ruling bloc. Celal Bayar, the leader of the liberal faction on etatism in the early 1930s, became the spokesperson for rapidly developing private business. He founded and led the Democrat Party, which made its first electoral challenge to the CHP in 1946. By 1947, the CHP had relaxed some of the etatist policies, and limited the establishment of state enterprises to fields where the private sector could not succeed on its own. It also unsuccessfully attempted to introduce a new five-year plan. The international politico-economic dynamics were changing fast. Turkey was coming under increasing foreign pressure, especially from the United States under the Truman Doctrine. In 1948, the CHP came up with a new formulation, "the new etatism," but by then the interwar winds of economic nationalism had already changed direction.[137] Etatism slowly faded out, but its legacy, in terms of both the industrial cadres it created and the social change it induced, would shape the course of subsequent developmental policies.

9 Conclusion

Having begun in the wake of a shattering crisis, Turkey's state-led industrialisation had a dual character. On the one hand, it could be argued to have developed as the natural culmination of the national economy paradigm. On the other hand, its adoption as an economic policy was the result of a long and fierce intra-elite conflict. Though the ambivalences around the concept and practice of etatism portrayed it more as an empirical project than an ideology, at its core was a capitalist project of industrialisation with a very clear vision of class relations.

For a regime that had built its legitimacy on the condemnation of the imperial past, the nineteenth-century Ottoman's failed attempt at industrialisation provided leverage to present the republican project of industrialisation as a supra-class nationalistic development plan. Labour protectionism was one of the most important elements of the narrative of contrast between the "semi-colonised Empire" and the "independent republic." Intrinsic to this was also

137 İlhan Tekeli and Selim İlkin, *Savaş Sonrası Ortamında 1947 Türkiye İktisadi Kalkınma Planı* (Ankara: ODTÜ Yayınları, 1974), 5–15.

the framing of protective legislation as a bestowal to workers by an enlightened state. In the official publication of the Ministry of Labour, the Turkish state's labour policy was defined as the product of a "humanitarian perspective."[138]

A nationalist historiography of development and a patriotic motive attributed to labour constituted the discursive building blocks of industrialisation. As would be expected from any nationalist context, this historiography was quite selective. It successfully erased from the official narrative of recent Turkish history the wave of strikes and labour unrest that took place between the beginning of the second constitutional period in 1908 until the mid-1930s (see Chapter 6). The result being that, in a trade union paper, we find an author comparing workers to women, the two social groups that obtained their rights without having to struggle for them like their European counterparts.[139] In state rhetoric, class strife and class struggle were part of a Western history that the young republic needed to avoid repeating at all costs. It was this fear that pushed the ruling elite to act as if it faced a large, militant, and organised industrial labour force, and subdue the language of class under language of nation. The resulting regime of labour regulation would have long-term consequences for the structure of industrial relations in Turkey.

---

138 Kadri Kemal Kop, "Yakın Tarihimizde İş ve İşçi Meseleleri," *Çalışma Vekâleti Dergisi*, no. 2 (1945), 69.

139 Kadıoğlu, "İşçilerimiz ve Kanunlarımız," *Türk İşçisi*, 28 December 1946.

CHAPTER 3

Smokestacks of "Atatürk's Minarets"

Industrialisation and the Politics of National Space

The setting is 1940s Istanbul. Early in the morning, Sait Faik, a leading short story writer, is walking inside the old, walled city. Passing through the poverty-ridden neighbourhoods on his way, he sees ramshackle city walls and fountains, Ottoman minarets and *medreses*: the remnants of a distant past that he wants to walk away from. But "the dangerous, story-like history" and its accompanying imagined soundscape of war, violence, and bigotry would not let him break loose. With the next step, he finds himself outside the city walls overlooking a completely different scenery. It is no longer dark or wrecked; neither it is poisonous like the ghosts of the past. Relieved to have broken free from the heart-wrenching hands of history, he exults with joy: "Oh, the factories! … How beautiful they look afar with their chimneys, windows, sirens, mingling people, coal, and soot!"[1]

On a winter's night in 1938, a clerk at the public works department was driving on the newly constructed "straight as a rope" road stretching from the train station to the newly opened state textile factory in Kayseri, a small town in central Anatolia. He experienced the drive almost like time travel; with each passing kilometre, he moved away from the lethargy of the underdeveloped empire to the contemporary dynamism of the republic. As he left behind the old town that was "getting ready to sleep in the eternal depth of darkness and silence," he began to feel pity for its "poverty and senility" and focused his gaze on the factory buildings that extended before his eyes "wide as a city in itself … under a flood of lights," filling the flat-lying plain with mechanical sounds and radiating "youth and national energy." Resembling a starry skyline, what amounted to the largest state industrial investment of interwar Turkey lured him in and filled his heart with a sense of national pride and duty.[2]

---

1 Sait Faik Abasıyanık, "Sevgilime Mektuplar," *Tüneldeki Çocuk* (Istanbul: Türkiye İş Bankası Kültür Yayınları, 2019), 22–3. It should be noted that the story continues with the horrendous working conditions Sait Faik observed in the factories shortly after the establishment of the Ministry of Labour in 1945.

2 Sahir Üzel, "Kayseri Fabrikası Günde 40,000 Metro İş Çıkarıyor," *Cumhuriyet*, 11 May 1936; Endüstri Hayatımızda İnkişaf (three-part article), *Erciyes Halkevi Dergisi*, March, April, June 1938.

An emotive terrain of industrial modernity united these two men, who were otherwise separated by hundreds of kilometres. The sight of factories fuelled narratives of collective historical memory and national identity: a relief from the burden of a dark, underdeveloped past and an enthusiasm for a modern future. By the mid-1930s, "the chimneys of civilisation rising in all corners of the homeland" would receive enthusiastic public attention as beacons of modernity.[3] Industrial iconography and narrative around the belching smokestacks of newly constructed factories proliferated. The factory, both its physical shell as well as its internal organisation, signified Western modernity for the republican elite, who saw secular and modern industrial buildings and their surroundings as a way out of tradition-bound Ottoman architecture and backwardness. Both the mainstream printed press and state-produced visual media praised factory design, construction, and the machinery as tangible displays of technical prowess. Factories provided a powerful physical correlative to the alleged social consensus on national development.

If we return to the two travellers and their shared affective terrain, we note a significant difference between them. The sights that so powerfully moved these men belonged to two completely different landscapes of industrialisation. Sait Faik was walking in the old imperial capital, which was also a historical centre of industrial activity. The clerk, by contrast, was driving across a vast, empty landscape in the heart of Anatolia that was undergoing industrial transformation. The historically uneven geographies of economic growth and urbanisation resulted from the Ottoman patterns of integration into the world market. These postimperial, uneven geographies represented a dire problem for the republican rulers, who had witnessed the territorial disintegration of the empire throughout their military and political careers. They now had to transform what was left of the empire into a bounded, integrated, and coherent national unit, in and through which a sustained process of economic and sociocultural development was to occur. This required, first and foremost, the rearranging of the socio-spatial organisation inherited from the earlier round of the capital accumulation regime that had been shaped by the control of foreign commercial capital. With the adoption of state-led industrialisation, industrial site selection emerged as a powerful instrument of spatial intervention. The construction of large factories in inland areas signalled a change in the spatial organisation of capital away from the logic of commercial capital to national industrial capital.

3 Selim Cavid, "Fabrikalarımız: Izmit Kâğıt Fabrikası," *İktisadi Yürüyüş* 6 (1940).

Against the backdrop of the politico-economic context in the previous chapter, in this chapter, I analyse state spatial strategies and their relationship to local, regional, and national industrial development. I build my analysis on two premises informed by economic geography. First, questions of the spatiality of industrial processes are integral to an understanding of nation-building and industrial modernity. Second, the historically uneven unfolding of capitalism creates varied local labour markets, working conditions, and cultures of organisation.[4] In early republican Turkey, the key spatial variability of labour market processes lay between the old industrial centre, that is, Istanbul and its hinterland, and the new industrial centres in Anatolia.

I begin by analysing the spatial articulations of development thinking in 1930s Turkey to discuss how space and spatial thinking underlined the blueprints and implementation of industrial planning. I argue that industrial site selection was a state strategy designed to achieve national consolidation and effective statehood. I then attend to plant-and regional-level labour market dynamics, including problems of labour supply, recruitment and retention, and working-class housing. My argument here is that it was local rather than national forces that played a more determining role in the labour market, especially with regard to its gender dynamics. The historically and spatially uneven development of capitalism produced considerably divergent outcomes in terms of labour recruitment and stability, as well as the conditions of labour reproduction.

1 Space, Ideology, and Industrial Site Selection

FIGURE 3 Poster in the special new year issue of Vatan, 1933

4 Andrew Herod, "Workers, Space, and Labor Geography," *International Labor and Working-Class History* 64 (2003).

In the special New Year issue of *Vatan* (Homeland) newspaper, a Santa Claus-like bearded Father Time figure holding a scythe engraved with the word *zaman* (time) tears off the year 1933 from the calendar to mark the beginning of a new year imbued with industrial imaginary. In the foreground, a steam train bearing the crescent and the star, the two figures of the Turkish flag, emerges amid a heavy steam cloud, invoking a sense of speed and power. A huge factory complex with nine tall smokestacks piercing the sky forms the backdrop. Symbolising the two most important state policies of the 1930s, the steam train and the large factory framed Turkey's industrial future.

The year 1933 also marked the tenth anniversary of the young republic. In its first decade, the state prioritised the nationalisation and extension of the railway network. The *Tenth Year March*, still a powerful part of Kemalist iconography today, celebrates the success of the republic's railway policy: "in ten years, we [the Turks] covered the motherland with an iron web of railroads." Setting railroads alongside war victories, the rousing patriotic song reproduces the hegemonic state narrative that presented the war on underdevelopment as the consequential next step in the war for independence.

Underdevelopment, however, was not evenly distributed. Above all else, the railway network inherited from the empire highlighted regional inequalities. Before 1923, foreign concessionaires had built the railway lines in accordance with their interest in developing market-oriented agriculture, an accumulation regime that resulted in "an evident inequality between the market-oriented western regions, the surplus-producing interior, and the subsistence-farming east, northeast, and southwest."[5] And because they belonged to different regional economies, the sub-networks remained unconnected. The disconnected railway lines reflected a disarticulated economy that cut the inner Anatolian regions off from the coastal areas that were producing primary products for the Western markets. The railway linked Istanbul, the Aegean coastal area, and the eastern Mediterranean, but did not serve central Anatolia (except for a few towns around Ankara), the Black Sea region, or the eastern provinces. At the ground-breaking ceremony for the largest industrial investment in central Anatolia in 1934, the prime minister called this "a typical colonial economy."[6] The flow of commodities between the vast cereal-growing regions of inner Anatolia and the consuming cities

5 Çağlar Keyder, *The Definition of a Peripheral Economy: Turkey 1923–1929* (Cambridge: Cambridge University Press, 1981), 29.

6 Bilsay Kuruç, *Belgelerle Türkiye İktisat Politikası, 1933–1935*, vol. 2 (Ankara: Ankara Üniversitesi Yayınları, 1993), 175.

was so limited that it was cheaper to feed the population of Istanbul from Iowa rather than Ankara and Konya.[7] In the eyes of the republican elite, the spatial integration of the country represented the transformation of what remained from the semi-colonised empire into a politically and economically independent nation-state.[8]

The lack of a national railway network also entailed extra-economic costs for nation-building. In his tellingly titled journal *New Man* (*Yeni Adam*), professor of education and prolific author İsmail Hakkı Baltacıoğlu explained the centrality of railway policy to the vision of national modernity in 1934:

> Railroads are much more than [an economic investment] ... To become a family, a nation, people need to have ties that pull them together. These include a common language, collective duties, spiritual bonds, and last but not least, shared goals and convictions. Such sharing can only happen if certain collective sensibilities are sharpened. What makes a nation is the liveliness of these ties and sensibilities. Yet mountains, seas, deserts, in short, distances, material obstacles stand in the way of establishing and maintaining such ties. What should we do? We should eliminate those natural obstacles, right? How? By overcoming the mountains, seas, and deserts! ... The only way to do this is to improve railroad and maritime transportation. If this is realized, those constituents of the nation that are of the same ancestry will be drawn closer and bound together more easily. This will impact collective projects positively, accelerate industrial growth, promote agricultural production, and increase commercial transactions. Out of this revitalisation a new generation, which we call "the new man," will be born. Nothing can bring the kind of mental transformation that the railroads can.[9]

---

7 Korkut Boratav, "Kemalist Economic Policies and Étatism," in *Atatürk: Founder of a Modern State*, eds. Ali Kazancıgil and Ergun Özbudun (London: C. Hurst & Company, 1981), 165.

8 The political motive behind the railway policy found its clearest expression in a confidential report prepared by the prime minister after touring eastern and southeastern Turkey in the wake of the 1925 Kurdish insurrection. Put into operation over the next few years, the Plan for Reforms in the East (*Şark Islahat Raporu*) underlined the role of the railway in securing territorial integrity and ethnic control. See: Saygı Öztürk, *İsmet Paşa'nın Kürt Raporu* (Istanbul: Doğan, 2007), 24, 59–60.

9 Cited in Zeynep Kezer, *Building Modern Turkey: State, Space and Ideology in the Early Republic* (Pittsburgh: University of Pittsburgh Press, 2015), 165.

Dating back to the same year as the first five-year plan, Baltacıoğlu's words capture the intricacies of high modernism's apogee: the mastery of nature, including human nature. As a whole, the plan and the framework in which it was implemented embody the faith in rapid social transformation and authoritative intervention that James Scott describes in *Seeing Like a State* as a characteristic feature of many twentieth-century attempts at social change. In its quest to make society "legible", and more administratively manageable, Scott argues that the state has to achieve a combination of three elements: the unrestrained use of the power of the modern state, a weakened civil society, and an aspiration for the administrative ordering of nature and society. The common ideology of "high modernism" that drives large-scale social engineering projects rests on this administrative approach to both humans and their environments. Mustafa Kemal himself, and other leading figures of the Kemalist modernisation project as a form of high modernism in its authoritarian variant, would perfectly blend into the crowd imagined by Scott to populate the Hall of Fame of high modernist figures, and their faith in and desire to achieve "a sweeping, rational engineering of all aspects of social life in order to improve the human condition."[10] Particularly fitting to our case is the myriad ways in which ideology is enshrined in the official practices of national state bureaucracies in accordance with Scott's analysis of nation-building and governance.

As the republican rulers searched for a way out of underdevelopment, a world-historical change in the way nation-states related to the social and economic structures of the society was under way. Beginning in the 1930s, Timothy Mitchell argues, the very notion of the economy underwent a transformation. Previously understood as how resources are managed and power exercised, the economy gained a new definition as the totality of the relations of production, distribution, and consumption within a given country. The emergent discourse of the economy as the "total process" fuelled the discourses of nation-making by providing a new way for the nation-state to represent itself and "imagine its existence as something natural, bounded and subject to political management."[11] State-led industrialisation in Turkey built on this conception of the nation as a bounded and integrated totality, combined with the accompanying faith in its potential and obligation to act like an economic collective pursuing a common goal. The infamous 1935 CHP programme and its formulations of etatism, which we have closely looked at in previous pages, dictated that all

10 James Scott, *Seeing Like a State: How Certain Schemes to Improve the Human Condition Have Failed* (London: Yale University Press, 1998), 88–9.

11 Timothy Mitchell, "Fixing the Economy," *Cultural Studies* 12 (1998), 84, 89–90; see also: Timothy Mitchell, "Rethinking Economy," *Geoforum* 39, no. 3 (2008).

industrial enterprises, state or private, "shall follow one another in such a way as to render the country as an industrial unit." The geographical dispersion of new industrial investment was the logical and practical result of this vision.

The spatial politics of the republic took concrete form in three policies that relocated the economic and political centre from western to central Anatolia: moving the capital from imperial Istanbul to Ankara, a small town roughly in the middle of the country; extending the railroad; and the construction of new state factories in medium-sized towns near the republic's new capital.[12] The territorial boundaries of the nation-state excluded the important old economic centres of the empire, disrupting the former regional economies. The linking up of the disconnected railway sub-networks in central Anatolia became a priority for the republican state in achieving an integrated economy and a unified national market.[13] Starting in the second half of the 1920s, the government expanded the railway network with the double-goal of creating a national market and transmitting the ideology of national modernity to all corners of the country. By the end of the next decade, all foreign controlled railways had been nationalised and most of the medium-sized provincial cities were interconnected.[14]

It was no coincidence that etatism saw its first official and public mention at the opening of the railway line that integrated the central Anatolian town of Sivas into the railway network in 1930. Taken together, railway policy and etatism embodied the young state's strategy for leaping over centuries of underdevelopment and kick-starting the Turkish economy along the highway of rapid industrialisation. The late development of the country had given rise to a feeling of backwardness and a sense of urgency that affected both the modes of setting economic goals and the ways chosen to achieve them. This anxiety about being late, the widespread desire to "compensate for centuries-long

12 İlhan Tekeli, "Atatürk Türkiye'sinde Kentsel Gelişme ve Kent Planlaması," *Arredamento Mimarlık* 10 (1998), 61–63.

13 *Çalışma Vekâleti* 24 (1947), 76; İhsan Bilgin, "Modernleşmenin ve Toplumsal Hareketliliğin Yörüngesinde Cumhuriyetin İmarı," in *75 Yılda Değişen Kent ve Mimarlık,* ed. Yıldız Sey (Istanbul: Tarih Vakfı Yayınları, 1998), 255–72; İlhan Tekeli, "Türkiye'de Cumhuriyet Döneminde Kentsel Gelişme ve Kent Planlaması," in *75 Yılda Değişen Kent ve Mimarlık,* ed. Yıldız Sey (Istanbul: Tarih Vakfı Yayınları, 1998).

14 *Çalışma Vekâleti* 24 (1947), 76; Peter Sugar, "Economic and Political Modernisation: Turkey," in *Political Modernisation in Japan and Turkey,* eds. Robert E. Ward and Dankward. A. Rustow (Princeton: Princeton University Press, 1964), 166; Stanford J. Shaw and Ezel Kural Shaw, *History of the Ottoman Empire and Modern Turkey-Reform, Revolution, and Republic: The Rise of Modern Turkey 1808–1975,* vol. 2 (Cambridge: Cambridge University Press, 1977), 395.

neglect" and to catch up with the West economically and culturally underlined the spatial organisation of the industrialisation effort.[15] "We are running on a short cut [toward industrialisation]," Bayar said in 1935, taking advantage of the fact that "we know everything about the roads walked by [industrialised] countries."[16]

The linking of industrialisation with the larger Kemalist project of nation-building and modernisation distinguishes early-republican industrial culture from preceding (or succeeding) periods and also informs the distinct character, design, and location of early-republican factories. Industrial design and layout communicated changing social expectations, progress, and power. Republican factories distinctively differed from the ornate late-Ottoman factories in terms of their construction material, size, and the prioritisation of efficiency.[17] To foreign visitors, "the silhouettes of elongated sheds, high chimneys, isolated columns" in the otherwise underdeveloped provincial towns looked like they were "set up there by mistake."[18] Having travelled the country from the Black Sea to the Syrian frontier in the south, and from Smyrna to the Russian frontier in the east, Linke wrote: "But nowhere, not even at Ankara, did I find the contrasts more sharply expressed, the past, the present and the future closer to each other, than at Kayseri." After the shabby buildings and poorly dressed crowds in the streets, the sight of the factory reminded her of the "fantastic constructions" set up for the 1936 British science fiction film *Things to Come*.[19] Where foreigners saw strangeness, the local elite saw potential for social and cultural transformation.

But Kemalists were hardly unique in their high expectations for the proliferation of factories. In the interwar period, the public romance with the industrial workplace increasingly celebrated the factory aesthetic based on the idea of order, on the promise of efficiency, and on technical virtuosity both in the

---

15 İsmet İnönü, "Fırkamızın Devletçilik Vasfı," *Kadro* 22 (1933).

16 Kuruç, *Belgelerle*, vol. 2, 269.

17 Sibel Bozdoğan, "Industrial Architecture and Nation-building in Turkey: A Historical Overview," in *Workplaces: The Transformation of Places of Production—Industrialisation and the Built Environment in the Islamic World*, ed. Mohammad al-Asad (Istanbul: Istanbul University Press, 2010), 27–30.

18 Lilo Linke, *Allah Dethroned: A Journey Through Modern Turkey* (London: Constable and Co., 1937), 301.

19 Lilo Linke, "Social Changes in Turkey," *International Affairs* 16, no. 4 (1937), 540–541. In their 1940 book *Modern Turkey*, John Parker and Charles Smith give a similar description of the city: "[T]he peasants drive in to market looking as though they came out of an illustrated Bible. Only a mile away, however, is the cotton mill—and in another direction factories assemble aeroplane." *Modern Turkey* (London: Routledge, 1940), 110.

West and the Soviet Union.[20] As the encapsulation of industrial modernity, factories embodied the most significant aspects of life associated with modernity and came to be seen as carriers of an inevitable linear progress from tradition to an urban, industrial modernity in the context of late industrialisation. Both the history and the myth of the factory signified a new ordering, not only of the working space and the working time, but also the reordering of communities, especially of the national kind.[21]

The expected impact of these industrial investments in the name of progress and development penetrated every aspect of the social, transforming the very modes of social life and cultural identities. In this regard, state-led industrialisation was at the same time a "civilizing mission" linked with the larger Kemalist project of nation-building and modernisation.[22] In the words of a contemporary prominent intellectual and bureaucrat, the extra-economic motivation behind "dispersing industrial establishments to the inlands, the remotest corners of the homeland" was to demonstrate a modern, civilised, and progressive living style to the locals.[23] The idealised images of an industrial Anatolia in official publications, argues historian of architecture Sibel Bozdoğan, were "nationalist statements on how land truly becomes 'patria' when transformed and tamed by industry."[24] This would not be an easy transformation, however, especially with regards to securing the labour force needed for the new factories.

2 Industrialising Anatolia

Aware of the connection between the evolution of a railroad system and the development of a national market, the republican rulers decided to build the new state factories on the railway lines. Policymakers took three factors into consideration in industrial site selection: their proximity to raw materials, the potential to develop underdeveloped regions, and national defence requirements.[25] In 1932, Soviet experts carried out investigative visits to Anatolian

20 Joshua B. Freeman, *Behemoth: A History of the Factory and the Making of the Modern World* (New York: W. W. Norton & Company, 2018), 118–68.

21 Kevin Hetherington, *The Badlands of Modernity: Heterotopia and Social Ordering* (London: Routledge, 1997), 110–1.

22 Catherine Alexander, "The Factory: Fabricating the State," *Journal of Material Culture* 5, no. 2 (2000), 180.

23 Şevket Süreyya Aydemir, *İkinci Adam,* vol. 1 (Istanbul: Remzi Kitabevi, 1984), 446.

24 Bozdoğan, "Industrial Architecture," 27.

25 İlhan Tekeli and Selim İlkin, *Uygulamaya Geçerken Türkiye'de Devletçiliğin Oluşumu* (Ankara: ODTÜ İdari İlimler Fakültesi, 1982), 190.

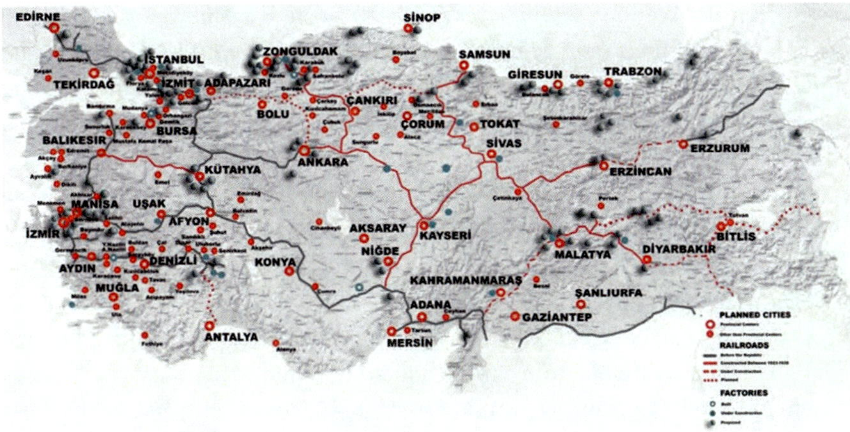

MAP 4 Railroad network, factories, and planned cities in Turkey in 1940
H. ÇAĞATAY KESKİNOK, "URBAN PLANNING EXPERIENCE OF TURKEY IN THE 1930S," *METU JFA* 27, NO. 2 (2010), 178

cities, and prepared detailed reports on the existing structure and the development possibilities of multiple industries.[26] They advised the establishment of two textile factories in Kayseri and Nazilli. These and two other textile factories in the first five-year plan were constructed along the major railroad lines and connected to either one of the two largest cotton-growing areas around Adana and Aydın plains.[27] Two sugar factories in Eskişehir and Turhal (1933) and a major new cement factory in Sivas (1942) were also built along railway lines. The iron and steel works of Karabük, the largest, and the most contentious, industrial investment, was built near the then recently nationalised coal mines of Zonguldak along the newly constructed Filyos-Zonguldak railway.

From this point on, state factories would play a significant role in republican urban planning, which, as a political practice of social transformation, displayed powerful physical markers of national modernity. In an accelerated manner during the 1930s, the urban space was fashioned along nationalist practices, performances, and symbols of nationhood. Urban planning schemes displayed a remarkable uniformity: lying tangent to the old town centres, the

26 The reports ("Türkiye Pamuk, Keten, Kendir, Kimya, Demir Sanayii hakkında Sovyet mütehassısları tarafından verilen raporlar") were published in Tekeli and İlkin, *Uygulamaya Geçerken*.

27 Selim İlkin, "Birinci Sanayi Planının Hazırlanışında Sovyet Uzmanlarının Rolü," ODTÜ Gelişim Dergisi 1979–1980 Özel Sayısı (1981), 271; Tekeli and İlkin, *Uygulamaya Geçerken*, 159–65, 190.

new Republic Avenue (*Cumhuriyet Caddesi*) hosted the new town hall and other state buildings, and Station Avenue (*İstasyon Caddesi*) connected the railway and the city centre. Modern-looking neighbourhoods extended along the axes of these avenues. State factories were located slightly outside the new centre, to which they were connected by the railway. Modelled after the company towns of the late nineteenth century, these factory complexes had all the elements of the simplified "garden-city" concept of the 1920s, a method of urban planning based on a planned town of limited size with broad streets and a spacious layout and surrounded by a green belt.[28]

As the physical encapsulation of Western modernity in the minds of industrial policymakers, the factory site embodied the unique benefits of urbanism and functioned as a training ground for armies of model citizens. In the early 1930s, Mustafa Kemal took a direct interest in the construction of a sugar factory in Eskişehir, a small town some 250 kilometres from Ankara. He chose a site close to a railway station not because of infrastructural logistics but because "[p]eople must see the factory."[29] The prime minister promised to the people of Bursa during the 1935 ground-breaking ceremony for the Merinos Wool Factory that the factory complex would function like a small town lighting up its surroundings.[30] Four years later, a journalist described the factory complex as "an industrial abode of the republican will, a masterpiece of the republic" that changed the cultural and social constitution of the entire city of Bursa.[31] "The factory and the city can no longer be thought of separately," a journalist wrote of the Kayseri Factory, for the former had changed the infrastructure as well as the economic and cultural life of the latter.[32] A French traveller similarly observed the modernising effects of these industrial settlements in 1937: "With a strong and well-cared road structure, green areas, sanitary neighbourhoods, well-organised water and electricity provisions, stadiums, and market places, these centres of settlement change the face of the old cities they are located

---

28 İhsan Bilgin, "Anadolu'da Modernleşme Sürecinde Konut ve Yerleşme," in *Tarihten Günümüze Anadolu'da Konut ve Yerleşme,* ed. Yıldız Sey (Istanbul: Tarih Vakfı Yayınları, 1996); Bilgin, "Toplumsal Hareketliliğin Yörüngesinde," 258; Sibel Bozdoğan, *Modernism and Nation Building: Turkish Architectural Culture in the Early Republic* (Seattle: University of Washington Press, 2002), 120.

29 Catherine Alexander, *Personal States: Making Connections between People and Bureaucracy in Turkey* (New York: Oxford University Press, 2002), 125.

30 Kuruç, *Belgelerle,* vol. 2, 372.

31 "Merinos Fabrikası Yeni Bir Hayat Uyandırdı," *Haber-Akşam Postası,* 25 December 1939.

32 S.C. Yazman, "Mensucat Endüstrimizin En Büyük Müessesesi: Kayseri Bez ve Dokuma Fabrikası," *İktisadi Yürüyüş* 61–62 (1942), 24–5.

in."[33] After the establishment of the state factories, the urban population of Bursa, Adana, Kayseri, Sivas, Izmit, Malatya, and Nazilli increased by between forty and one hundred per cent from 1927 to 1945.[34] The areas adjoining the factories became desirable places to live, as new neighbourhoods with a Sümer hairdresser here and a Sümer coffeehouse there emerged around the factory complexes.[35] Later in the century, these new neighbourhoods would turn into "privileged clusters," causing social tensions that would hinder the integration of these factory campuses with the city.[36] But even in the 1930s and 1940s, enthusiastic state propaganda and favourable press coverage on industrial site selection failed to convince everybody.

FIGURE 4 Preparations for the opening ceremony of the Nazilli Factory, 1937
COURTESY OF ILHAN ÖDEN

33 Cited in Ahmet İnsel, "Devletçiliğin Anatomisi," *Cumhuriyet Dönemi Türkiye Ansiklopedisi* 2 (Istanbul: İletişim Yayınları, 1984), 424.

34 Ahmet Özeken, "Türkiye Sanayiinde İşçiyi Barındırma Problemi," *Sosyal Siyaset Konferansları Dergisi,* no. 3 (1950), 111.

35 Özlem Arıtan, "Kapitalist/Sosyalist Modernleşme Modellerinin Erken Cumhuriyet Dönemi Mimarlığının Biçimlenişine Etkileri: Sümerbank KIT Yerleşkeleri Üzerinden Yeni Bir Anlamlandırma Denemesi" (PhD diss., Dokuz Eylül Üniversitesi, 2004), 101, 150.

36 İlhan Tekeli, "Endüstrinin Arazi Kullanımı Kararlarında Etken Olan Kurumsal Çerçeve," *Peyzaj Mimarlığı Özel Sayı* 6, no. 1 (1975), 48–9.

Foreign expert visitors to Turkey were heavily critical of the rationale behind the industrial site selection.[37] The Thornburg mission, for example, questioned the decision to locate factories "in places where supplementary occupations are needed because of more meagre resources for the sustenance of life than are usual even in Turkey." The disregard for labour supply, the authors claimed, evinced that the motive was "probably more political than social, and economic considerations have played little part in the choice."[38] In terms of planning for labour and raw material requirements, the iron and steel plant in Karabük was deemed to have been the worst mistake. An entire city had to be created to serve the various furnaces, mills, and shops of this "economic monstrosity."[39] Over-enthusiasm, inexperience, and a lack of statistics partly explained such failures, A.H. Hanson argued, but the main problem lay in the handling of the planning and its implementation.[40]

The politics of foreign expertise also played into the critique of industrial site selection. The Americans, for example, blamed the German and British advisors for "foisting such a white elephant on the Turkish people" in Karabük.[41] Zvi Yehuda Hershlag, an Israeli professor of economics, could partially justify the site selection but the "element of gigantomania in the striving for magnitude of the project," he argued, was causing erroneous considerations by the German and British advisers.[42] The Germans were also blamed by locals for machinery problems. In 1933, Germany and Turkey signed a comprehensive clearing agreement, which dictated that Turkey had to buy German goods in return for her exports. In 1939, Webster cited a Turkish engineer's complaints over how easy it had been for the German experts to convince the German-trained managers of state factories to buy machinery from Germany that they

37 John Parker and Charles Smith, *Modern Turkey* (London: George Routledge and Sons, Ltd., 1940), 108; E. R. Lingeman, *Turkey: Economic and Commercial Conditions in Turkey* (London: His Majesty's Stationery Office, 1948), 85; T.G.A. Muntz, *Turkey: Economic and Commercial Conditions in Turkey* (New York: Philosophical Library, 1951), 61; Alfred Bonne, *State and Economics in the Middle East* (London; Routledge, 1955), 282; Richard D. Robinson, *The First Turkish Republic* (Cambridge: Harvard University, 1963), 110–113; Morris Singer, *The Economic Advance of Turkey: 1938–1960* (Ankara: Turkish Economic Society Publications, 1977), 31–3.

38 Max Weston Thornburg, Graham Spry, and George Soule, *Turkey: An Economic Appraisal* (New York: The Twentieth Century Fund, 1949), 128.

39 Ibid., 108.

40 A. H. Hanson, *Public Enterprise and Economic Development* (London: Routledge, 1959), 121.

41 Thornburg et al., *Economic Appraisal,* 109.

42 Zvi Yehuda Hershlag, *Turkey: The Challenge of Growth* (Leiden: E.J. Brill, 1968), 105.

did not need.[43] The director of the Adana Cotton Factory reported in 1935 that the outdated English machinery from 1895 could only be replaced with German machinery because of the clearing agreement between Turkey and Germany. The agreement left Turkey in possession of German marks with which she could buy nothing but what the German government offered her. "Hence the German machinery," Linke wrote, "hence the German armaments there and in the Balkan countries."[44]

Almost a decade after the launch of state-led industrialisation, a Sümerbank inspection report explained the extra-economic rationale behind the establishment of state factories by way of a comparison between private and state enterprises. The private sector's geographical choices, the report argues, are based on economic calculations such as raw material supply and energy needs, whereas locations for state enterprises are chosen based on the long-term interests of the nation.[45] Beyond mere economic investments, state factories were social investments, in that they would function as the carriers of national social development: or, in the words of the prime minister, "moral and social institutions of culture and civilisation for our nationalist, republican country."[46]

In the post-WWII development literature, the efforts of new states to assert their authority over their territorial inheritance after gaining independence is a central theme. In analysing the "pursuit of effective nationstatehood" following decolonisation and the creation of new nations in Africa and Asia, for example, Gunnar Myrdal discusses development and its planning in relation to the processes of "national consolidation" and an "integrated national community." Rationality and productivity were the poster themes of national development plans. However, Myrdal also argues that development thinking and planning could not be merely reduced to a vision of economic growth. The new states were in search of "the new man or the modern man, the 'citizen of the new state'" with a set of values including efficiency, punctuality, diligence, orderliness, and preparedness for change.[47] In the modernising rhetoric of the 1930s, state factories were the trail blazers for the rapid economic development

43 Donald Everett Webster, *The Turkey of Atatürk: Social Process in the Turkish Reformation* (Philadelphia: The American Academy of Political and Social Science, 1939), 252.

44 Linke, *Allah Dethroned*, 265–75.

45 *Sümerbank 1943 Yılı Umumi Murakebe Heyeti Raporu* (Ankara: Başbakanlık Devlet Matbaası, 1944), 252.

46 "Ana Endüstriye Başladık," *Ulus*, 4 April 1937.

47 Gunnar Myrdal, *Asian Drama: An Inquiry into the Poverty of Nations* (New York: Pantheon Books, 1972), 32–34.

of the country and the springboards for a giant leap into a modern, industrial lifestyle.

The state factory directors were responsible for communicating this desire to "civilise" the factory workers and the rural population around the factories. In the stadium of the Kayseri Factory, the director, Mr Fazlı was demonstrating Swiss drill exercises to the workers and explaining to Linke the "civilising mission" he had taken upon himself:

> Perhaps you think it foolish to play football in this hot town. You are right. But I don't want it really for the sake of the sport. They'll be forced to wear shorts and show their naked knees, and that's what matters to me. Once they dare to appear in public like that, they've broken away from tradition and are free. That boy came to me last week and said: "My whole family makes fun of me and scolds me. But I won't give in." That's a fellow to my liking. I'm sure he'll be good at his work as well.[48]

The director of the Turhal Sugar Factory told Webster that one of his aims was to make sure that "every worker shall return to his village with an unshakable desire to live at a higher level." He was thrilled to see that the factory supplied workers with wages to clear their debt; but more importantly it gave them "a little education" and "the *élan* which has displaced the lethargy and hopelessness characteristic of Turhal before the factory was erected."[49] The opening up of the village economy played an important part in that "education."

3 Consuming Industrial Modernity: State Factories and the Rural-Urban Connection

An intricate connection between state factories and the rural economy emerged as one of the pillars of the first five-year plan. The Turkish state's industrialisation effort differed from state industrial investment strategies in other contexts such as India and Egypt, where the displacement of locals and the total disappearance of villages to make way for prestigious state factories ("Nehru's Temples") created long-term conflict between the locals and the state.[50] The construction of state factories on vacant land away from residential

48 Linke, *Allah Dethroned*, 307.

49 Webster, *The Turkey of Atatürk*, 143–144, 251.

50 Jonathan Parry, "The Sacrifices of Modernity in a Soviet-built Steel Town in Central India," in *On the Margins of* Religion, eds. Frances Pine and João Pina-Cabral

areas eliminated such conflicts over space. Furthermore, in choosing an industrial development plan over an agricultural one, the government adopted the strong language of interconnectedness between the two sectors. A successful agricultural policy depended on a sound industrial base, the minister for economic affairs declared in 1936.[51] The primacy of the textile sector in the state investment plans evinced this dependency. Textile manufacturing would contribute to the integration and expansion of a national market by increasing raw material production, on the one hand, and providing cheap commodities, on the other.

But the government's post-Depression policy of increasing cotton prices to protect the producers would clash with the industrialisation drive. In 1935, the economic affairs minister criticised the preference of private textile manufacturers for cheaper imported cotton, calling it anti-national because it would mean the return of the "colonial economy." Locally manufactured yarn was expensive, he admitted, but it was our nationalist duty to ensure that Turkish industry benefited Turkish agriculture.[52] At various official ceremonies on factory sites, government representatives emphasised the benefits that state factories would bring to the peasants. In Ereğli, the prime minister introduced the factory as a lucrative customer for cotton producers; in Turhal, he stressed that the population of eight close-by cities, including the villagers, would profit from the factory; in Nazilli, the minister for economic affairs said: "we establish industry to help agriculture"; in Kayseri, he claimed industrialisation would benefit the peasants by pushing up raw material prices.[53] At the 1935 groundbreaking ceremony in Nazilli, Bayar reminded the farmers in the audience how

---

(Berghahn: New York, 2008), 233–62; Jonathan Parry and Christian Strümpell, "On the Desecration of Nehru's 'Temples': Bhilai and Rourkela Compared," *Economic and Political Weekly* 43, no. 19 (2008); Christian Strümpell, "Law Against Displacement: The Juridification of Tribal Protest in Rourkela, Orissa," in *Law Against the State: Ethnographic Forays into Law's Transformations*, eds. Julia Eckert, Brian Donahoe, Christian Strümpell, and Zerrin Özlem Biner (Cambridge: Cambridge University Press, 2012), 202–27; Dina Makram-Ebeid, "Between God and State: Class, Precarity, and Cosmology on the Margins of an Egyptian Steel Town," in *Industrial Labor on the Margins of Capitalism*, eds. Chris Hann and Jonathan Parry (Berghahn: New York, 2018), 180–96.

51 Celal Bayar, "Celal Bayar'ın Endüstri Planımız Üzerinde Söylevi," *Ülkü* 7, no. 37 (1936), 9–11.

52 Kuruç, *Belgelerle*, vol. 2, 269.

53 State factories also joined this effort; in the 1970s, the Nazilli factory management placed billboards on the roadside assuring farmers an honest weighing of their cotton and instant cash payment ("Hakiki dara, peşin para!"). Cited in Çağatay Emre Doğan, "Nazilli Basma Fabrikası Yerleşimi: Tarihçe ve Yaşantı," in *Fabrika'da Barınmak: Erken Cumhuriyet Dönemi'nde Türkiye'de İşçi Konutları: Yaşam, Mekan ve Kent*, ed. Ali Cengizkan (Ankara: Arkadaş, 2009), 82.

they had complained about the low selling-prices of their produce during his previous visit in 1930. The region needed a factory, he had replied then, and that factory was now being built—with state money. He then asked the audience if they supported the etatist policy, and the crowd allegedly shouted: "We would give our lives for it!"[54]

State factories did indeed create regional economies around them. Investment in textile factories increased the Anatolian goat and sheep population, improved the quality of Turkish cotton, and encouraged better farm practices.[55] The average output of industrial crops increased from 500,000 tonnes per year between 1928 and 1935, to 1.2 million tonnes for 1936–1940, and to 1.8 million tonnes for 1946–1950.[56] For example, the Turhal Sugar Factory awarded beet contracts to eighteen thousand farmers, the majority of whom were engaged in subsistence farming. Between 1,300 and 1,400 local labourers were employed at the refinery during a three-month employment "campaign." Although wages were low, it enabled the locals to secure a debt-free winter. The refinery also created a substantial annual revenue for the state railway company.[57] State industries slowly opened up the closed village economy, dragging the peasantry into market relations.[58]

The industrial use of previously undervalued local agricultural products increased rural household incomes. But, according to the planners, the benefits that state industries would bring for the rural economy went beyond this. State industries would also cheapen consumer goods, creating "a healthy balance between Turkish citizens' income and expenditure."[59] Textiles, once again, had a special role here because they were the first and foremost commodity that would change the culture of the Turkish village. During his 1933 visits to Defterdar and Bakırköy, the prime minister set out his expectations for state textile factories: "I want cheap, really cheap clothes. The poor strata should not remain underclothed; we need to produce the cheapest clothes possible for

54 Kuruç, *Belgelerle,* vol. 2, 176, 235, 237, 349, 352.

55 "Bursa Merinosculuk İçin Merkez Olacak," *Haber-Akşam Postası*, 6 August 1934; Robinson, *The First Turkish*, 113.

56 William Hale, *The Political and Economic Development of Modern Turkey* (London: Croom Helm, 1981), 62.

57 Webster, *The Turkey of Atatürk,* 251; S.C. Wyatt, "Turkey: The Economic Situation and the Five-Years Plan," *International Affairs* 13, no. 6 (1934), 834–835.

58 Zafer Toprak, *Sümerbank* (Istanbul: Creative Yayıncılık, 1988), 7.

59 Kuruç, *Belgelerle,* vol. 2, 264.

our poor nation."[60] And cheap factory-woven cloth did indeed change village clothing.[61]

The government had established the Domestic Goods Bazaars in 1926 to sell the products of the Hereke Factory. The bazaars began to sell Sümerbank manufactures in 1933 despite protests from private merchants over the state becoming a merchant.[62] Sümerbank opened its own stores, first in Istanbul, and then in Ankara, Izmir, Mersin, and Adana. In 1942, there were twenty-three Sümerbank stores across the country. Before the war, domestic products could not compete with the cheaper imports, but war-induced import difficulties increased the demand for Sümerbank products. By the 1970s there were more than two hundred stores dispersed throughout the country.[63]

FIGURE 5 Poster for Sümerbank stores, c. 1940s
COURTESY OF SİBEL BOZDOĞAN

60 "Başvekil Hz. Sümer Bank Fabrikalarını Tetkik Ettiler," *Cumhuriyet,* 22 November 1933; "İki Buçuk Liraya Elbise," *Haber-Akşam Postası,* 6 August 1934.

61 Robinson, *The First Turkish,* 113–4.

62 Kuruç, *Belgelerle,* vol. 2, 262.

63 "Yerli Mallar Pazarları," *İktisadi Yürüyüş,* no. 61–62 (1942), 34–5; Emre Dölen, *Tekstil Tarihi* (Istanbul: Marmara Üniversitesi Teknik Eğitim Fakültesi Yayınları, 1992), 437–8.

As the circulation of state-manufactured goods expanded, an anti-import sentiment grew. In interwar Europe, the increasing circulation of American imports had begun to fuel a whole new economy of desire in the form of cinema, print advertising, rotary presses, and new consumer goods.[64] The end of the war further stimulated this economy by increasing the circulation of these commodities and cultural artefacts. In Turkey, this coincided with a change in monetary and trade policy. To qualify for International Monetary Fund membership and for participation in the Marshall Plan, the government initiated a major economic policy change involving devaluation and a set of foreign trade liberalisation measures. In 1946, the CHP devalued the lira by 54 per cent against the US dollar, seeking to gain a comparative advantage in terms of competitiveness before its entry into the Bretton Woods system. The government also abolished the drastic import restrictions that had been in effect since the 1930s to attain a favourable balance of trade. Devaluation, government officials claimed, would not only increase the value of the exports, it would also protect local manufacturing from imports.[65] The increasing trade deficit proved them wrong.

A language of economic nationalism began to charge the anxieties over the increasing availability of imports. These anxieties then quickly turned into a "struggle against luxury" that combined economic concerns and moral anxieties.[66] Luxury became a symbol of the social decadence of the elite, and was parodied as a sign of the class aspirations of working people. As a form of conspicuous consumption, the purchasing of luxury imports posed a serious threat to an imagined indigenous tradition and national economic policy. The republican elite often attributed the collapse of the Ottoman industries to consumer preferences for foreign products, and hoped that a nationalist discourse would eliminate this.[67] Disappointed middle-class writers urged industrial workers "to increase our local manufacturing … to protect our national pride," and investors to spend limited foreign currency reserves on "investing in industrial enterprises that would create employment" instead

64 Victoria de Grazia, "Beyond Time and Money," *International Labour and Working-Class History* 43 (1993), 27.

65 Yahya Sezai Tezel, *Cumhuriyet Döneminin İktisadi Tarihi (1923–1950)* (Istanbul: İş Bankası, 2015), 218–221.

66 "Lüksle Mücadele Davası," *Kadın Gazetesi,* 26 July 1948; İffet Halim Oruz, "Kadın Çorapları Mevzusuna Dair," *Kadın Gazetesi*, 27 June 1949.

67 Hüseyin Namık Orkun, "Milli Tarihimizde Fabrikalar ve İşçiler," *Çalışma* 1, no. 3 (1946), 84–5.

of importing luxuries.[68] Another author pointed to the "ridiculousness" of the fact that "foreign currency is spent on imported fabrics, nylon gewgaws ... when we have delightful woollen cloth produced locally."[69] The reader might remember the scene in Chapter 1 where the French director of an Ottoman state textile factory was eventually caught after presenting imported cloth as local wares to the Sultan for years. By the end of the 1930s, the reverse was the case. Sümerbank textiles were being sold as imports, an economics journal warned: "They sell them as English and French textiles ... Do not be deceived! These textiles bear the design of Turkish artisans, and are produced by Turkish workers under the supervision of Turkish engineers in Turkish factories."[70]

To foreign critics of planned industrialisation, the urban-rural or the industrial-agricultural relationship was all but smooth. The critics claimed that Turkey had chosen the wrong path to development, in that state-led industrialisation undermined agricultural growth, leaving eighty per cent of the population underemployed, underproducing, and underconsuming. According to economic liberal thinking, the primitive status of agriculture and insufficient private industrial investment hindered both the growth of national capital and the expansion of the domestic market. By the end of the 1940s, consumption levels in the country compared poorly even among low-income economies such as Portugal and Greece.[71] The authors of the 1949 American *Twentieth Century Fund* on Turkey highlighted the "curious fact" that "in an intensive drive for industrialisation and self-sufficiency, Turkey has not, within the twenty years since the programme was started, provided enough capacity to supply even the modest wants of its population." Out of a total population of twenty million, they claimed, seventeen million were insufficiently clothed. They observed a visible discrepancy between the urban industrial and rural agricultural economies:

> One sees on the skyline of Istanbul and other cities, in clear spaces between mosques and balconies, slender smoking chimneys of modern factories— "Atatürk's minarets." But these factories are mysteries to the peasants, traders and craftsmen who make up the great majority of

68 Müjgan Ağaoğlu, "Lüks ve İsraf Davamız," *Kadın Gazetesi*, 22 August 1948; Halide Nusret Zorlutuna, "Ev Ekonomisi," *Kadın Gazetesi*, 25 December 1950.

69 "Lüks Vergisi Bir Lükstür," *Kadın Gazetesi*, 13 December 1948.

70 Selim Cavid, "Feshane Fabrikasında Bir Tedkik," *İktisadi Yürüyüş* 1, no. 7 (1939), 9.

71 Hershlag, *The Challenge*, 290–91.

> the Turkish population ... The latest products of Western industrialism which they are designed to make—high speed, chromium plated and cellophane wrapped—are in many cases as alien to the life and the most elementary needs of the Turks as are the smoking "Atatürk's minarets" to the Mosque of Suleiman the magnificent.[72]

To these authors coming from the birthplace of mass consumption, consumption levels and patterns in Turkey were not compatible with an industrial development plan. The picture as seen through the eyes of the republican elite, however, was quite different. Upon hearing from a merchant that his best radio sales were in Kayseri, Ereğli, Nazilli, and Adana because the locals in these new industrial centres were accessing the radio for the first time at factory cafeterias, a journalist happily broke the news that "after so much waiting and hardship," a new lifestyle had arrived in the Anatolian villages. This was the same journalist that had decried Turkish cotton as having previously been seen as "only as worthy as a Negro's sweat," whereas by the end of the 1930s every turn of the spindle was eroding "part of our Asianness."[73] In distinguishing his country and his people from the horrible fates of the enslaved Africans and the colonised Asians, he alluded to the trope of a nation recovering its former glory; this summarised the republican faith and optimism in rapid development from an agrarian colonial economy to an independent industrial economy. But the industrialisation drive faced one big problem: where would the state factories find the required industrial workforce in a predominantly agricultural society?

4 National Planning versus Local Labour Markets

In the 1930s and 1940s, state-led industrialisation was experiencing chronic labour instability. To begin with, the political exigencies of nation-building after World War I played a part in reducing the labour supply. Turkey's population had been ravaged by consecutive wars, forced migrations and deportations, epidemics, and high infant mortality. The population in the republican territories fell from sixteen million in 1913 to thirteen million in 1923.[74] During

72 Thornburg et al., *Economic Appraisal*, 105–116.

73 Cemal Kutay, "Değişme," *Ulus*, 18 May 1939.

74 Cem Behar, *Osmanlı İmparatorluğu'nun ve Türkiye'nin Nüfusu 1500–1927* (Ankara: T.C. Başbakanlık Devlet İstatistik Enstitüsü, 1996).

the first two decades of the twentieth century, much of the Ottoman industrial labour force was removed by deportation and emigration. As late as 1915, Turkish workers made up only fifteen per cent of the industrial workforce.[75] Finally, the 1923 population exchange with Greece had led not only to the loss of an important source of cheap labour but also to the loss of artisanal skills especially in urban areas.[76]

The new nation-state sought to bolster its birth rate and population growth by pursuing aggressive pronatalist policies, and succeeded in growing the population from 13.5 million in 1927 to 18.5 million in 1945.[77] The urbanisation rate, however, remained low until the beginning of rural-urban migration in the 1950s.[78] The urban population increased from 2.2 million to 3.9 million between 1927 and 1950, whereas the rural population increased by almost 6 million. Almost eighty per cent of the labour force was still working in agriculture by 1950.[79] In 1941, the exiled urban planner Ernst Reuter wrote that the threat of urbanisation had not yet arrived in Turkey. There was even a slight decrease in the percentage of the population living in cities with more than ten thousand inhabitants between 1927 and 1940.[80] The scale of rural-urban migration was not comparable to nineteenth-century Europe or the interwar Soviet Union, a Turkish social scientist noted in 1950.[81] As late as 1955, only twenty-five per cent of the population lived in cities, with almost twenty per cent of

75 G. Bie Ravndal (compiled by), *Turkey: An Economic Handbook* (unpublished, 1924), 347; Records of the Department of State Relating to Internal Affairs of Turkey, Economic Matters, 2 June 1910—17 December 1929, Decimal File 867.50, NARA, accessed 1 May 2020, https://go.gale.com/ps/retrieve.do?tabID=Manuscripts&resultListType=RESULT_LIST&searchResultsType=SingleTab&searchType=AdvancedSearchForm&currentPosition=1&docId=GALE%7CSC5111519615&docType=Manuscript&sort=Relevance&contentSegment=GDSC221&prodId=GDSC&contentSet=GALE%7CSC5111519615&searchId=R11&userGroupName=cumhurb&inPS=true&ps=1&cp=1; Zafer Toprak, "National Economy and Ethnic Relations in Modern Turkey," in *State Formation and Ethnic Relations in the Middle East,* ed. Usuki Akira (Osaka: The Japan Center for Area Studies, 2001), 187–196.

76 Çağlar Keyder, *State and Class in Turkey: A Study in Capitalist Development* (London: Verso, 1987), 104; Erik J. Zürcher, *Turkey: A Modern History* (London: I. B. Tauris, 2015), 172.

77 Frederic C. Shorter, "Turkish Population in the Great Depression," *New Perspectives on Turkey* 23 (2000), 114.

78 Ömer Celal Sarc, *Türkiyede Şehirleşme Temayülleri* (Istanbul: İsmail Akgün Matbaası, 1949), 5.

79 Tezel, *Cumhuriyet Döneminin*, 134.

80 Ernst Reuter, "Türkiye'de Şehirlileşmenin Temayülleri," *Siyasi İlimler Mecmuası,* no. 126 (1941), 246.

81 Özeken, "İşçiyi Barındırma," 110.

city dwellers living in the country's five largest cities.[82] The urbanisation rate increased steadily thereafter, reaching 31.9 per cent in 1960.[83] Istanbul was and remained the most populated city: its population doubled between 1927 and 1960, and hit almost 1.5 million.[84]

In 1932, more than half of the industrial workforce in the country worked in Istanbul (28.4 per cent), Zonguldak (14.9 per cent), and Izmir (12.6 per cent).[85] As might be expected, labour instability brought with it heavier consequences for the newly opened factories near small Anatolian towns without a potential labour supply. Some of the new locations were in the middle of nowhere, sometimes even unknown to the administrators in the big cities. Until 1935, Karabük, for example, was a neighbourhood of thirteen households that did not even appear on the map. The hamlet emerged in administrative documents only after a railroad station was built nearby.[86] Kayseri was similarly unknown, with a young teacher from Istanbul becoming quite distraught during a desperate search for information on how to find his way after being assigned to a school there in 1925.[87] The population of the town centre had decreased from 56,000 in the early twentieth century to forty thousand in 1927 following to the forced migration of religious minorities. After the opening of the factory, it initially increased to forty-six thousand in 1935 before more than doubling in 1955.[88]

Much of the contemporary information on labour supply problems in the 1930s comes from travellers' accounts and scattered press coverage. One of the earliest visitors to the Anatolian state factories was the German journalist and social worker, Lilo Linke, who visited the Kayseri Factory during the time of its construction. Her vivid observations and conversations with the engineers and the factory manager portray an intriguing picture of the "labour problem":

82 *1955 Population Census of Turkey* (Ankara: Republic of Turkey, Prime Ministry, General Statistical Office, 1957), 9–10.

83 *Statistical Indicators: 1923–1990* (Ankara: Başbakanlık Devlet İstatistik Enstitüsü Yayınları, 1991), 8.

84 Michael N. Danielson and Ruşen Keleş, *The Politics of Rapid Urbanisation* (New York: Holmes & Meier, 1985), 56.

85 Kurthan Fişek, *Türkiye'de Kapitalizmin Gelişimi ve İşçi Sınıfı* (Istanbul: Doğan Yayınevi, 1969), 73.

86 Ziyaeddin Fahri Fındıkoğlu, "Karabük'ün Teşekkülü ve Bazı Demografik ve İktisadi Meseleler," *Istanbul Üniversitesi Sosyoloji Konferansları Dergisi*, no. 1 (1960), 2–3.

87 Cited in Kadir Dayıoğlu, *Kayseri'de Ticaret ve Sanayi* (Kayseri: Kayseri Büyükşehir Belediyesi Kültür Yayınları, 2019), 92.

88 Burak Asiliskender, "Modernleşme ve Konut; Cumhuriyet'in Sanayi Yatırımları ile Kayseri'de Mekansal ve Toplumsal Değişim" (PhD diss., Istanbul Teknik Üniversitesi, 2008), 81.

> Endless queues had lined up outside the temporary gates where wooden railings had been put up to hem in the human flood. A number of overseers were walking up and down to control the men. Most of the workers looked wild and uncouth, with faces burnt by the sun and clothes torn by age and hard work, but at the same time they showed a strangely timid expression. Peasants and casual workers, hitherto living without any regular order, sleeping in hovels or, during the summer months, out in the open with nothing but their soiled quilts to cover them, half animals in their dumbness and ignorance.[89]

A young engineer lamented the effort it took to discipline these workers. "In the beginning they were like a herd of stampeding animals," he said. The morning and evening controls of two thousand building workers would take two hours each time because the mostly illiterate men could not remember the numbers they had been assigned to use at the check-clocks. He reported partly solving the problem by sewing their numbers onto their jackets and having the overseers deal with the clocks. But the checks often turned violent, with workers, frustrated by the delay at the gates, attacking the overseers. The engineer fired the workers involved, which meant they lost any claim to their wages for that month. He defended himself by claiming that the men were "so used to kicks and blows that any corporal punishment wouldn't make the least impression on them." Dismissals worked; the control time was shortened by more than half.[90]

Unruly behaviour among migrant workers also complicated railway construction projects. The Austrian engineer supervising the *Simeryol* (Sivas-Malatya-Erzurum) railway line reported that "occasionally [a worker] grows wild and thrusts his knife into somebody else's belly." But thanks to the exhaustion from the ten-hour working day, workers did not "feel up to a great deal of nonsense" and spent their time in the military tents they shared with ten to fifteen others. Aware of the potential for conflict between migrants from different regions, the management kept them in separate tents.[91] Frequent ethnic conflicts were successfully manipulated to break worker solidarity in the Zonguldak mines, where the management relied on ethnic stereotypes to determine who would get a job and which job they would get.[92] At Karabük, assumed ethnic characteristics played a role in labour recruitment. Workers

89 Linke, *Allah Dethroned,* 303–4.
90 Linke, "Social Changes," 543–544.
91 Linke, *Allah Dethroned,* 188–9.
92 İrfan Yalçın, *Ölümün Ağzı* (Istanbul: Adam Yayınları, 1979).

from certain provinces were assigned to hot shops, for example, due to their "tolerance for hardship," while Laz workers were given assembly jobs because they were thought to be "agile and light on their feet."[93]

In Chapter 1, we saw the widespread use of unfree labour in Ottoman factories. The republican state also resorted to unfree forms of labour, mainly of two types. Chronologically, the first of these involved the labour-based prisons that emerged after the amendment of the penal code in 1936. Convict labour was initially used in agriculture, but in the 1940s it was extended to state factories and mining enterprises, where each working day counted as two days of imprisonment. Prison labourers earned daily wages and slept in dormitories instead of prison cells, which, according to Gerhard Kessler, made them the most obedient workers. By the end of the decade, the labour-based prisons incarcerated one third of the entire convict population, that is, seventeen thousand inmates.[94] In 1942, there were 150 women prisoners working at Kayseri Factory. These women were so content with their working conditions, an economics journal claimed, that they did not leave the factory even after their sentence expired.[95] Three years later, the number of women prisoners had increased to 190 at Kayseri. Karabük and Malatya factories had 523 and 292 convict workers, respectively, all of whom were male. The authors of a 1945 inspection report, however, did not share the enthusiasm of Kessler and the writer in the economics journal. They did not observe a willingness on the part of the convict workers to continue working at the factories after they had served their sentence. At Kayseri, for example, only eleven such women chose to stay on. Moreover, the inspectors objected the use of these "hard to rehabilitate" prisoners in the factories. To protect the respectability of industrial workers, they claimed, convict workers should better be employed in home-based industries.[96]

The state had also begun to use convict labour in mining operations in 1937. Their number increased considerably after the enactment of the National Defence Act on 18 January 1940. In addition to cancelling much of the recently enacted labour protective legislation, this law institutionalised a forced labour regime (*mükellefiyet*) in the Zonguldak coal basin. In 1942, the mines employed

93 Özeken, "İşçiyi Barındırma," 120.

94 Gerhard Kessler, "Zonguldak ve Karabükteki Çalışma Şartları," *İstanbul Üniversitesi İktisat ve İçtimaiyat Enstitüsü ayrı bası*, no. 11 (İstanbul: Kenan Matbası, 1949), 15; Ali Sipahi, "Convict Labor in Turkey, 1936–1953: A Capitalist Corporation in the State?" *International Labor and Working-Class History* 90, (2016), 246–7.

95 Yazman, "En Büyük Müessesesi," 25.

96 "İşletmede İnsan," 13.

fifty-eight thousand forced labourers, who toiled under the threat of physical torture and of harm to their families. The law remained in force until 1948 and it was formally abolished only in 1960. In 1948, there were fifteen thousand convict workers in the mines. These convicts worked side by side with free workers, and earned ninety per cent of the latter's wage. They would receive their payment at the end of their sentence.[97]

Due to the absence of a ready supply of local labour, state factories had to create a social and material infrastructure to attract workers to the new industrial centres.[98] The Soviet mission noted in 1932 that because Nazilli did not have any "free workers," which in this context meant dispossessed wage labourers, the two thousand workers needed by the factory had to be brought in from elsewhere. The experts then suggested areas for building worker houses.[99] The dependence on outside labour continued into the 1940s; by 1945, fewer than one third of state textile workers were being recruited from the local labour markets. Factory inspectors blamed this on industrial site selection as well as the inefficient employment policy. Because they depended on migrant workers, the new state factories spent a lot on worker accommodation, but a decade after their establishment, they could neither recruit locally nor retain the migrant workers.[100]

Visiting the Kayseri Factory shortly after it was opened, Webster was impressed by the athletics field (which, an engineer had earlier boasted to Linke, was an "an exact replica of the stadium at Cologne"), which included a football stadium, swimming pool, gymnasium equipment, riding track, and space for other pastimes. But there were only two thousand workers on the factory's payroll, fewer than half of what was estimated, and the factory operated on a single shift. Additional living quarters would be the only solution to increase the number on the payroll, Webster wrote. Single workers slept in dormitories, while some married men lived in poorly built company apartments because in the city there were few vacancies and almost no decent quarters available.[101] Until 1944, that is, when the price of agricultural products started

---

97 Kessler, "Zonguldak ve Karabük," 15; Theo Nichols and Erol Kahveci, "The Condition of Mine Labour in Turkey: Injuries to Miners in Zonguldak, 1942–90," *Middle Eastern Studies* 31, no. 2 (1995), 200–202; Nurşen Gürboğa, "Compulsory Mine Work: The Single-Party Regime and the Zonguldak Coalfield as a Site of Contention, 1940–1947," *International Review for Social History* 54 (2009), 123–4.

98 *Çalışma Vekâleti*, no. 24, (1947), 64.

99 Tekeli and İlkin, *Uygulamaya Geçerken*, E198.

100 "Sümerbank İşletmelerinde İşletmede İnsan ve İşçi Meseleleri," in *Sümerbank 1945 Senesi Faaliyet ve Hesap Devresine Ait İdare Meclisi Raporu, Bilanço, Kâr ve Zarar Hesabı* (Ankara: Başbakanlık Devlet Matbaası, 1946), 11.

101 Webster, *The Turkey of Atatürk*, 248–249; Linke, *Allah Dethroned*, 306.

to fall, six hundred weaving looms lay idle due to labour shortages.[102] In the Zonguldak mines, too, American experts blamed productivity problems on the absence of living facilities, which hindered the "building up of a skilled, experienced mining force."[103]

FIGURE 6 Machinery at the Kayseri factory, c. 1936
COURTESY OF SİBEL BOZDOĞAN

102 "Sümerbank 1945 Yılı Fabrika Raporları Yönetim Kurulu Kararı Ekleri," 1946, file 730 05 01 EK 1–11 16–11, Republic of Turkey Prime Ministry General Directory of State Archives.

103 Walker D. Hines, "Conclusions and Recommendations," *A General Economic Survey of Turkey, 1933–1934*, vol.1 (Ankara: Ekonomi Bakanlığı, 1934), 20.

Enervating shortages of skilled workers and high rates of labour turnover were the biggest concerns of the director of Kayseri Factory, who had to hire three thousand workers to maintain a steady workforce of two thousand. "His workers came from villages all over the countryside, attracted by stories about the pleasant working and living conditions at the new factory," Webster reported.[104] Leaving their homes for the first time in their lives, many workers "succumbed to homesickness." And then there was malaria. During the first summer at the factory, a mild epidemic rendered a large number of workers hysterical and caused a serious labour shortage.[105] About half of the workforce had malaria between 1942 and 1943 in Kayseri, the numbers halved after the factory took measures but in 1945 twenty-two per cent of the workforce still suffered from the disease.[106]

Among state enterprises, Nazilli had the highest labour turnover rate, mainly because the factory was built near a swamp, which remained undrained until 1944. Handweavers from the Denizli region went there to work in late 1937 and early 1938, but a malaria epidemic put a stop to this labour migration and the handweavers returned to their hometowns. To ease the labour shortage, workers from the Kayseri factory were transferred to Nazilli, but they did not stay there long either.[107] Later, recent migrants from Greek islands were also resettled in Nazilli in an attempt to solve the labour scarcity problem.[108] The son of one such migrant family, with a father from Bulgaria and mother from a Greek island, heard from his parents that one out of every four workers in the 1940s were foreign-born.[109] A Bakırköy weaver, whom the reader will come to know in great detail in the coming pages, left Nazilli Factory in 1938 because he could not bear the climate.[110] Peasants around Karabük described the site as a "terrible source of malaria," located as it was on the rice paddy fields at

104 Sahir Üzel, for example, reported seeing young peasants from the villages of Kayseri, Aksaray, Kilis, and Birecik in: "Kayseri Fabrikası," *Cumhuriyet*, 25 June 1935.

105 Webster, *The Turkey of Atatürk*, 250.

106 Can Nacar, "Our Lives were not as Valuable as an Animal: Workers in State-Run Industries in World War-II Turkey," *International Review of Social History* 54, no. 17 (2009), 160.

107 Haluk Cillov, *Denizli El Dokumacılığı Sanayi* (Istanbul: Istanbul Üniversitesi İktisat Fakültesi, 1949), 149.

108 "Sümerbank 1944 Senesi Faaliyet ve Hesap Devresine Ait İdare Meclisi Raporu, Bilanço, Kâr ve Zarar Hesabı," *Sümerbank 1944 Yılı Umumi Murakebe Heyeti Raporu* (Istanbul: Ankara Başbakanlık Devlet Matbaası, 1945), 8, Amb./Db.no: K.A./255.07.02.01.06.3251, Sümerbank Murakebe Raporu 1944; "Şehrimize Gelen Mülteciler Yerleştirildi," *Nazilli*, 19 October 1946.

109 İlhan Öden, interview by the author on 6 December 2022.

110 Interview with Ahmet Cansızoğlu by Yıldırım Koç, 1988, video recording *V1/51*, Trade Union Movement in Turkey Oral History Collection, IISH.

the intersection of two rivers.[111] In 1944, thousands of working hours were lost at the Iron and Steel Company to malaria; by the end of the decade, malaria was still one of the main factors influencing labour turnover in Karabük and Ereğli.[112] A Sümerbank engineer summarised the failed optimism of the 1930s in the following words:

> It was thought that simple word of mouth would be enough to secure the labour force for the newly built factories. This was not the case at all. At first, curiosity brought some workers to these factories. But, having close ties to agriculture, these sons of the country could not keep up with industrial discipline. The local labour supplies were not big enough anyway. Bringing workers from nearby and faraway cities, towns, and villages did not work either because of housing problems. Workers left the factories during harvest time. And then there was also malaria. Our factories faltered for a long time under these circumstances.[113]

But what about the handloomers who produced approximately one third of the cotton textiles in Turkey?[114] Could not the new state factories solve their labour problems by recruiting them? To a contemporary academic, the prospect of providing employment for struggling carpet weavers in and around Kayseri was one of the main reasons for choosing the town as the location of the largest state textile factory. As a local, cheap, and considerably skilled source of labour, these weavers were thought to be the "perfect workers" for the cotton industry.[115] During her visit to Malatya in 1935, Linke also assumed that handweavers would turn into factory hands:

> From a hut across the street came a strange clinking sound, and I went in to discover what it was. In a very small, dusky room six men were sitting, the lower part of their bodies buried in little holes cut out of the earthen floor. Simple hand-looms were standing before them, and mechanically, half asleep, they were weaving pieces of rough white cotton cloth. When

111 Fındıkoğlu, "Karabük'ün Teşekkülü," 8.

112 Ahmet Özeken, "Türkiye'de Sanayi İşçileri," *Sosyal Siyaset Konferansları Dergisi*, no. 1 (1948), 61–2.

113 Fahri Fuat Orsan, "Bir Fabrikanın Kurulacağı Yer Nasıl Seçilir?" *Mensucat Meslek Dergisi*, no. 2 (1951), 60–1.

114 Cillov, *Denizli El Dokumacılığı*, 19.

115 Ahmet Özeken, "Sanayi Tesis Yerleri Problemi ve Türkiye'nin Sınai Kalkınmasında Tesis Yeri Davası," *İstanbul Üniversitesi İktisat Fakültesi Mecmuası* 3, no. 3–4 (1942), 365–366.

> I entered, they turned their colourless faces up to me without speaking. The scene was a strange contrast to the exuberant life outside and as sad and depressing as if the men were weaving their own shrouds. It took them twelve hours to produce a piece of cloth ten or eleven yards in length and to earn a net sum of sixty piasters—something like two shillings. Three hundred of these weaving looms were still in existence at Ismet Pasha. Not for much longer, however. During the course of 1936 the foundation stone will be laid at Malatya for a huge state-owned cotton-factory, large enough to produce about a quarter of the total Turkish consumption. And the men who, today, slave in dark holes from morning till night, will a few years hence be turned into factory-workers, earning a minimum wage of sixty piasters in piece work during an eight-hour day. How will these peasant craftsmen react to the change? Whatever their feelings, they cannot alter the course of development. '*Atılan ok geri dönmez*—the arrow set flying cannot return.'[116]

At the ground-breaking ceremony in Nazilli, Bayar reassured the crowd that the factory would not take jobs away from the local weavers; on the contrary, it would supply high quality yarn to handloomers, help them with marketing their products, and provide them with jobs at the factory if they so wish. "Before too long," he continued, the factory would turn Nazilli into "a developed town."[117]

In view of the paucity of data on the background of factory workers in the 1930s and 1940s, it is difficult to know to what extent handloomers became factory hands. A contemporary academic claimed in 1948 that the Sümerbank factories had failed to attract the handloomers. Ninety per cent of handweavers in the Denizli region said they would prefer not to work at local factories.[118] The Thornburg mission similarly reported that the many thousands of handicraftsmen in the bazaar shops of the cities remained an untapped source of labour.[119] A 1949 International Labour Organization publication reported that the time gap between the disappearance of the old guild system and the development of modern industry impeded the adaptation of traditional skills to the methods of factory production.[120] The ongoing complaints on labour

---

116 Linke, *Allah Dethroned*, 203–4.

117 Kuruç, *Belgelerle*, vol. 2, 349.

118 Cillov, *Denizli El Dokumacılığı*, 149–50.

119 Thornburg et al., *Economic Appraisal*, 127.

120 International Labour Office, "*Labour Problems in Turkey*," *Report of a Mission of the International Labour Office* (Geneva: ILO, 1950), 10, 14.

instability and the persistent lack of skilled labour in the 1950s supports this claim. In Istanbul, a survey conducted among a hundred workers found no prior artisanal experience in the early 1950s.[121] According to a 1958 United Nations report, the considerable increase in employment in medium and large-scale industry between 1927 and 1954 was a result of rapid population growth rather than manufacturing establishments' drawing labour from agriculture and small-scale industry.[122] But what about that other cheap labour supply used globally in textile manufacturing?

5 "But Where Are the Heroic Turkish Women?"

When we last met the Public Works Department clerk at the beginning of this chapter, the starry, sky-like appearance of the Kayseri Factory had lured him in and filled his heart with national pride and sense of duty. But something disrupted this picture-perfect image of the Turkish state factory: Why could the factory, which had only a ten per cent female workforce as opposed to the required ninety per cent, not attract the women of Kayseri? Spinners were mostly male in this Anatolian factory, he wrote, although spinning "of course does not befit men." The factory manager complained to him that Kayseri women chose to work on their handlooms at home instead of working at the factory. The clerk could not understand why women who were already spinning at home in the hinterland of the factory looked crossed-eyed at factory work. Why, he asked, were the heroic Turkish women who had fought and worked side by side with men, first, in the Independence War and, then, in the republican revolutions, running away from their national duty at the factory? Some argued the problem was men's bigotry while others blamed women for looking down on factory work; and there were those claiming low wages kept spinning women at home. Our factory-loving author was not convinced. To him, the reason that women did not come to the factory, "the homely place of labour and honour," was because the "high ideal of the factory" was still not understood by the people.[123]

---

121 Ziyaeddin Fahri Fındıkoğlu, "Türkiye'de Sınai Sosyoloji Araştırmaları 3," *Mensucat Meslek Dergisi* no. 12 (1954), 7, 228.

122 United Nations, Department of Economic and Social Affairs, *The Development of Manufacturing Industry in Egypt, Israel and Turkey* (New York: United Nations, 1958), 29.

123 Sahir Üzel, "Kayseri Fabrikası Günde 40,000 Metro İş Çıkarıyor," *Cumhuriyet*, 11 May 1936. For a detailed analysis of the relationship between state discourses and shop floor control over women's industrial labour in the 1930s and 40s, see Görkem Akgöz, "Between State Feminism and Work Intensification: Gendered Labour Control Regimes in Turkish Textile and Tobacco Industries, " in *Power at Work: A Global Perspective on Control and Resistance*, eds. Marcel van der Linden and Nicole Mayer-Ahuja (Oldenbourg: De Gruyter, 2023), 99-134.

At the same time as the factory acquired a potent social imagery in interwar Turkey that was cast in both economic and cultural terms, another equally (or possibly even more) powerful signifier of modernity was gaining ground. The secular republic represented nothing short of an all-out attack on existing social institutions relating to the status of women, making their legal and social status the banner of Kemalist development narratives.[124] A central feature of the nascent state's self-identification was to distance itself from its Ottoman legacy. References to a remote and mythical past glorified as a golden age were common currency within Turkish intellectual circles of the period, with women playing the forefront role in this glorification.[125] In her 1930 *Turkey Faces West* treatise published in the United States, a prominent national heroine figure, the novelist and feminist Halide Edib, called for a "cleansing" of Turkish culture from foreign elements. The inferior position of women was a result of Byzantine and Persian, as well as Islamic, influences, she claimed; the "genuine" nomadic culture of Anatolia "would delight the soul of the western feminist in some respects ... [because] women are on an equal footing with men in every respect."[126] This narrative would lose none of its appeal among middle-class women and men alike in the coming decades. By the end of the 1940s, a female author writing for a middle-class feminist newspaper portrayed the republican regime as a morning full of light and joyful excitement for women, who had just woken up from a centuries-old suffocating night. By recognising women's right to work, the republic, she claimed, saved women from the dishonour of being mere toys for men.[127] The condemnation of certain aspects of Ottoman patriarchy associated mainly with religious bigotry

124 Yeşim Arat, "From Emancipation to Liberation: The Changing Role of Women in Turkey's Public Realm," *Journal of International Affairs* 54, no. 1 (2000), 107–123; Yeşim Arat, "Nation Building and Feminism in Early Republican Turkey," in *Turkey's Engagement with Modernity: Conflict and Change in the Twentieth Century,* eds. Celia Kerslake, Kerem Öktem, and Philip Robins (London: Palgrave Macmillan, 2010), 39; Deniz Kandiyoti, "Emancipated but Unliberated? Reflections on the Turkish Case," *Feminist Studies* 13, no. 2 (1987), 317–338; Deniz Kandiyoti, "The End of Empire: Islam, Nationalism and Women in Turkey," in *Women, Islam and the State,* ed. Deniz Kandiyoti (Philadelphia: Temple University Press, 1991), 22–47; Binnaz Toprak, "Emancipated But Unliberated Women in Turkey: The Impact of Islam," in *Women, Family and Social Change in Turkey,* ed. Ferhunde Özbay (Bangkok: UNESCO, 1990), 39–50; Jenny B. White, "State Feminism, Modernisation, and the Turkish Republican Woman," *NWSA Journal* 15, no. 3 (2003), 145–159.

125 Mary Motassian, "Ideologies of Delayed Industrialisation: Some Tensions and Ambiguities," *Economic Development and Cultural Change* 6, no. 3 (1958), 223–224.

126 Halide Edib Adıvar, *Turkey Faces West: A Turkish View of Recent Changes and Their Origin* (New Haven: Yale University Press, 1930), 6.

127 Şükûfe Nihal, "Cumhuriyette Kadın," *Kadın Gazetesi,* 17 October 1947.

became part of official state ideology, making celebratory images of women in public life central to the iconography of the new regime. A series of legal reforms concerning women's legal and civil status were undertaken in the 1920s and 1930s. These included the replacement of the Islamic civil code with the Swiss secular code, the abolition of polygamy, the recognition of women's right to vote, and a nationwide campaign for girls' education.[128]

Comparisons between the gendered oppression women suffered under the Ottoman imperial rule and their emancipation in the republic filled the pages of the mainstream media and fuelled state and middle-class intellectual discourses. These comparisons celebrated the republican present as a historical moment, with women in Turkey first encountering modernity through their entry into modern forms of labour, including factory work. The mixed-gender industrial workspaces and recreational facilities significantly reinforced the republic's secularisation agenda and strengthened its claim to a new positioning of the state vis-à-vis women. As key spaces for a modern and secular state in the making, factories could be seen as a sort of Westernised cultural representation of the world with women at the forefront.

Despite Üzel's and many other republican elite claims, factory work was not a novelty for women in Turkey. In a similar way to the historical trends in Western Europe, female industrial employment emerged as a result of the transfer of home production to factories in the Ottoman Empire, making textiles the single most important industry. Historically, the employment of women and children in textile production worldwide has been higher than in other industries. Although slightly lower than the global average, this was the case in the Turkish textile industry as well.[129] Women had worked in factories in Rumelia since the 1840s. In Ottoman Salonica, the heart of the tobacco sector, for example, young Jewish girls constituted an important part of the workforce, particularly in the textile and tobacco industries.[130] By the 1860s, silk

128 Until the 1980s, these reforms had been presented as a set of top-down policies enacted by an enlightened leader, resulting in an amnesia on women's struggles in the late empire and the early republic. Feminists increasingly problematised this historiography by bringing women's writing and organising to the forefront. See, for example, Serpil Çakır, *Osmanlı Kadın Hareketi* (Istanbul: Metis Yayınları, 1993) and Yaprak Zihnioğlu, *Kadınsız İnkılap* (Istanbul: Metis Yayınları, 2003).

129 Sabahaddin Zaim, *Istanbul Mensucat Sanayiinin Bünyesi ve Ücretler* (Istanbul: Istanbul Üniversitesi İktisat Fakültesi, 1956), 134.

130 Donald Quataert, "The Social History of Labour in the Ottoman Empire," in *The Social History of Labour in the Middle East,* ed. Ellis Jay Goldberg (Boulder: Westview Press, 1966), 27; Donald Quataert, "The Workers of Salonica," in *The Workers and the Working Class in the Ottoman Empire and Turkish Republic 1839–1950*, eds. Donald Quataert and

factories in Bursa employed both Muslim and non-Muslim women.[131] By the end of the century, approximately three thousand workers, primarily women and children, worked in tobacco factories.[132] In Anatolia, Izmir and Istanbul were the two major sites of cigarette production, and factories in these cities had an almost fifty per cent female workforce.[133] A women's publication from the 1910s reported a massive female labour force in the textile sector working in miserable conditions.[134] The textile and food processing industries were the two main industries with the highest levels of female employment, but with time, women took up industrial jobs in other sectors as well. For example, in 1897, 121 of a total of 201 workers at the Istanbul Match Factory were women and young girls.[135] According to the 1913–1915 industrial census, almost one third of the total industrial workforce across the empire was female.[136]

In terms of ethnic composition, Muslim women made up a small part of the total female workforce. The Régie Française des Tabacs tobacco factory in Istanbul did not employ Muslim women in 1914, for example,[137] and when it finally did, male and female cigarette makers and packers worked in separate rooms.[138] In 1912, in response to reports of sexual abuse in tobacco workshops in Aydın, "the local government stipulated that women tobacco workers were to be hired only with the permission of their guardians, employed in separate rooms, and paid their wages by female accountants."[139] With the First World War, the number of Muslim women on the shop floors started to increase.[140]

Erik Jan Zürcher (London and New York: Tauris Academic Studies in Association with the International Institute of Social history, Amsterdam, 1995), 66.

131 Michael Palairet, *Balkan Ekonomileri, 1800–1914: Kalkınmasız Evrim,* trans. Ayse Edirne (Istanbul: Sabancı Üniversitesi Yayınevi, 2000), 324–325; Oya Sencer, *Türkiye'de İşçi Sınıfı, Doğuşu ve Yapısı* (Istanbul: Habora Kitabevi Yayınları, 1969), 93–4.

132 Can Nacar, "Labour Activism and the State in the Ottoman Tobacco Industry," *International Journal of Middle East Studies* 46, no. 3 (2014), 535.

133 Gündüz Ökçün, *Osmanlı Sanayi İstatistikleri: 1913–1915* (Istanbul: Hil Yayınları, 1984).

134 Serpil Çakır, *Osmanlı Kadın Hareketi* (Istanbul: Metis Yayınevi, 1994).

135 Donald Quataert, "Women Households and Textile Manufacturing 1800–1914," in *The Modern Middle East,* eds. Albert Hourani et al. (London: I.B. Tauris, 1993), 255–270; Lütfü Erişçi, *Türkiye'de İşçi Sınıfının Tarihi* (*özet olarak*) (Ankara: Kebikeç, 1997), 7.

136 Ahmet Makal, "Türkiye'de Kadın Emeğinin Tarihsel Kökenleri: 1920–1960," in *Geçmişten Günümüze Türkiye'de Kadın Emeği,* eds. Ahmet Makal and Gülay Toksoz (Ankara: Ankara Üniversitesi Yayınevi, 2012), 42.

137 Tiğinçe Oktar, *Osmanlı Toplumunda Kadının Çalışma Yaşamı: Osmanlı Kadınları Çalıştırma Cemiyet-i İslamiyesi* (Istanbul: Bilim Teknik, 1998), 179.

138 "The Ottoman Tobacco Industry," *Journal of the Society of Arts* 42, no. 2,173 (1894), 733–734.

139 Nacar, "*Labour Activism,*" 537.

140 A.J. Sussitzki, "Ethnic Division of Labour," in *The Economic History of the Middle East (1800–1914),* ed. Charles Issawi (Chicago: The University of Chicago Press, 1966), 120.

Of the eight thousand workers at the Imperial Military Factory, Feshane, in 1917, five thousand were women and children. "[This is] a complete revolution," wrote the editor of *Frankfurter Zeitung* upon seeing men and women working together at this factory, "caused by the necessities of the war." Female labour at this factory, as well as everywhere else, had become indispensable.[141] Though he did not comment on the religious composition of the workers, the demographic change suggests an increasing presence of Muslim women on the shop floor. This increase accelerated after the 1923 population exchange with Greece. Worker statistics from the 1930s and 1940s do not specify the ethnic and religious identities of workers. However, given the demographic change explained above and women's increasing presence in the public sphere under Kemalist modernism, it would be safe to say that the majority of women in factories in the 1930s and 1940s were Muslim.

An alternative characterisation of Ottoman women's industrial labour was a depiction of women's suffering under foreign control. The republic had finally freed the Turkish women from the *kafes* (lit., cage, referring to the latticed windows that blocked passers-by from seeing into Ottoman homes), and brought her "by the side of the machinery."[142]

FIGURE 7 Comparison of women's industrial work under the Ottoman Empire and the Turkish Republic, 1949
HÜRBILEK, 15 JAN. 1949

141 Alexander Giesen, "National, Economic and Cultural Work in the New Turkey," 5 December 1917, Records of the Department of State Relating to Internal Affairs of Turkey, Economic Matters, 2 June 1910—17 December 1929, Decimal File 867.50, NARA, accessed 1 May 2020, https://go.gale.com/ps/retrieve.do?tabID=Manuscripts&resultListType=RESULT_LIST&searchResultsType=SingleTab&searchType=AdvancedSearchForm&currentPosition=1&docId=GALE%7CSC5111519615&docType=Manuscript&sort=Relevance&contentSegment=GDSC221&prodId=GDSC&contentSet=GALE%7CSC5111519615&searchId=R11&userGroupName=cumhurb&inPS=true&ps=1&cp=1.

142 Üzel, "Kayseri Fabrikası," 1935.

Stories of New Year's parties organised by factory girls, pianos and gramophones played and listened to by women on the shop floor filled the pages of mainstream and women's papers. As such, depictions of women's presence on the shop floor often included a comparison with the "dark, old times" (see Figure 7). In the Ministry of Labour journal, one author compared women's conditions of work in the Ottoman factories with those in the republican factories:

> The factory whistles were blown before sunrise to call the workers in [he uses 'amele', a degrading term for worker]. The female worker emerged from her warm bed, left behind her home unattended, packed her daily food—that is, only cheese and olives—and rushed to the factory. At sunset, she came back home exhausted and weary. Her nails fell off because she had to put them in boiling water, her body was exhausted after a twelve-hour working day, but she would not find anybody to listen even if she complained. The war changed everything ... In the past, women working at these so-called factories that were managed by foreigners would leave their young kids with their neighbours and the older ones on the street. Today, working mothers at the Cibali Tobacco Factory, for example, leave their children in the care of a doctor and nanny in a clean nursery next to the factory ... The colonialist minded [non-Turkish employers] did not treat workers humanely.[143]

Despite the celebratory rhetoric on women's industrial labour and many years of insistent efforts on the part of both the state and industrialists, the number of factory women did not rise to the desired levels, even long after state-led industrialisation had taken off in Turkey. According to the first republican industrial census in 1927, 23.7 per cent of workers older than fourteen were women; the percentage increased to 35.7 per cent for workers under fourteen.[144] By the early 1930s, women made up a quarter of all workers. The number of women in industrial employment increased from 32,474 in 1927 to 129,076 in 1935.[145] By

143 Osman Şevki Uludağ, "İş ve İşçi," *Çalışma Vekâleti*, no. 1 (1945).

144 Feroz Ahmad, "The Development of Class Consciousness in Republican Turkey, 1923–45," in *The Workers and the Working Class in the Ottoman Empire and Turkish Republic 1839–1950*, eds. Donald Quataert and Erik Jan Zürcher (London and New York: Tauris Academic Studies in association with the International Institute of Social History, Amsterdam, 1995), 78; Makal, "Türkiye'de Kadın Emeğinin," 47; *İstatistik Yıllığı 1931–1932* (Istanbul: Başbakanlık İstatistik Genel Müdürlüğü, 1932), 216.

145 Safaeddin Karanakçı, "Tarlada Çalışan Kadının Himayesi," *Çalışma Vekâleti* no. 5 (1946), 25.

1945, women made up 26.3 per cent of Sümerbank workers, with almost ninety per cent of these women working at state textile factories. More than one third of the Sümerbank female labour force was under eighteen and 64.5 per cent were either single or widowed.[146]

Left to their own means, state factories would struggle to secure the labour force they needed. Anecdotal evidence shows that female workers at the new state factories lived in the hinterland of these factories, and factory work was completely alien to them. The first step in female labour control was thus to bring women to the factories. The availability of a specific group of workers in the social space of the labour market is determined by, among other things, the social constructions of the group's identity. During her visit to the Kayseri Factory, Linke noted a managerial strategy—developed in response to local community characteristics— to manipulate that social construction. The region, she argued, was the most conservative in the whole country and the local women were "shocked at the very idea of working side by side with men though they were living in dire poverty and could well do with a few piasters." To break the women's resistance to factory work, the ambitious factory director devised a strategy of employing girls "while they were too young to be spoilt by their mothers" to familiarise them with the mixed-gender world of the factory. A number of girls had already been enlisted during the time of the factory's construction, and they were kept "in a kind of kindergarten" where they played. They were a little older than twelve, Linke was told, but they looked younger, "like half-starved mice." The factory director compared their living conditions with the homes they had come from, while setting out his plans for the girls once the factory started operation:

> Dirty hovels where they had neither air nor light and worked from morning to night. Here they'll be properly looked after. I'll get two forewomen from Russia to train and mother them. They'll have decent meals, the sports grounds as a playing-field, clean dresses and a doctor to watch over their health. You won't be able to recognize them two years hence.[147]

When Linke approached an orphan girl who had unwillingly worked at a tobacco factory in Istanbul before she moved in with her aunt in Kayseri, and asked her if she liked the factory, "her eyes lit up, her face lost its expression

---

146 "Sümerbank İşletmelerinde İşletmede İnsan ve İşçi Meseleleri 1945 Yılı Umumi Murakebe Heyeti Raporu," Archival Collection of the Republic of Turkey Prime Ministry Supreme Audit Board. Amb./Db.No: K.A./255.07.02.01.7462, 8.

147 Linke, *Allah Dethroned*, 312.

of grown-up self-composure." She was especially happy because the factory director had told her she could live in one of the new boarding houses built for the girl-workers.[148] The clerk happily noted girls aged between ten and fifteen working at stations above head-height.[149] The factory director boasted of not leaving these juveniles "to loaf in corrupting company," Webster reported, and regarded factory work as a favour to them and a benefit to the society.[150]

In many cases, local children waited at the factory garden to be chosen for recruitment by the foremen.[151] Young local girls would be accompanied by an adult worker during their walk from home to the factory. One of them, Muazzez, told me how she hated the commute. Muazzez left the factory in 1953 when she turned twenty, after almost seven years of work. She could have qualified for insurance compensation if she had just worked another two months, but she could not face walking to and from work three kilometres each way, every day, in the freezing cold. An expression of contempt flashed across her face when she recalled the mud they had to walk through and the white frost the girls brought in on their hair and eye lashes.[152]

In terms of women's industrial employment, Istanbul also showed marked differences from the new Anatolian industrial centres. According to the 1934 statistics, female workers were concentrated in the two industrial centres of Istanbul and Bursa.[153] Hundreds of women and children would beg small textile factories for work at very low wages for twelve hours a day.[154] A 1946 publication by the Ministry of Labour reported an increase in the number of female workers in Istanbul from 14,350 to 46,538 between 1935 and 1943. Although the enlistment of men played an important role in this increase, the ministry argued, this could not be entirely attributed to wartime conditions. Employers preferred female labour in industries such as textiles since "the female hand is more dexterous, and the female wage is cheaper." Women who were "trying to get out of poverty" became "a factor of production" and they did not seem to want to leave employment. Since rapid industrial development required a wider use of female labour, the increase was expected to continue, especially for the big industrial centres like Istanbul.[155]

148 Ibid., 311.

149 Üzel, "Kayseri Fabrikası," 1935.

150 Webster, *The Turkey of Atatürk*, 250.

151 Sebahat Yürekli, interview by the author on 4 June 2019.

152 Muazzez Atalay, interview by the author on 4 June 2019.

153 "Sanayi İstatistiği," *Haber-Akşam Postası*, 31 January 1934.

154 "Sanayi Hayatımızda Amelenin Vaziyeti," *Cumhuriyet*, 19 January 1932.

155 "Çalışma Hayatımızda Çocuklu Kadınlar ve Kreş İhtiyacı," *Çalışma Bakanlığı: İlk Yılı ve İlk Hedefleri* (Ankara: T.C. Çalışma Bakanlığı Yayınları, 1946), 85–8.

FIGURE 8 Women and men at the Feshane factory spinnery, c. 1930–1940s
TAHA TOROS ARCHIVE, FILE NO. 88

FIGURE 9 Workers at the Bakırköy spinnery, 1950
COURTESY OF ERGİN AYGÖL

The changing structure of the textile sector, however, would contradict this expectation. In 1927, women made up forty-nine per cent of workers in textile enterprises employing more than four workers in Istanbul. But women's share in total textile employment dropped to 29.5 per cent in 1950 and thirty-four per cent in 1952. This decrease, Sabahaddin Zaim argued in his 1956 dissertation on Istanbul's textile industry, was the result of a disproportionate increase in the number of male workers. Between 1927 and 1952, the total number of workers increased by seventy-five per cent while the number of male workers increased by 233 per cent. Behind this discrepancy was an important change in the composition of the textile industry. Before state-led industrialisation, the most developed textile industries in Istanbul had been silk, hosiery, and knitting, which were traditionally female. After 1934, male workers became the majority in the state-owned wool and cotton weaving enterprises. Following the enlistments during the war and the rapid development of the private sector after the war, the demand for female labour increased, pushing the percentage of women in the textile industry above forty per cent in 1954.[156]

Though statistics comparing workers' province of residence and province of birth are not available for the 1930s, it would be safe to assume that the majority of women working in Istanbul's factories already lived in the city before their employment for two reasons. First, large migratory flows to major urban centres started only around the mid-1950s.[157] Second, the available archival information on the migration history of workers at two state factories in Istanbul points to migration centred on single males in the 1930s and 1940s. In a context of constant labour shortages, the demand for female industrial labour was partly due to the absence of a disadvantaged migrant group. The demand for female industrial labour persisted after the war, presenting an interesting contrast with the efforts to send factory women back home across Europe and North America.

6 Local Industrial Labour Market in Istanbul

In decisions on industrial site selection in early-1930s Turkey, an engineer argued, the cost of labour was not an important factor since it did not vary much throughout the country. The two most important factors were the

156 Zaim, *Istanbul Mensucat Sanayiinin*, 136–8. For a detailed analysis of postwar policies on women's industrial labour see Görkem Akgöz, "Metaphorical Machines or Mindless Consumers: Young Working-Class Femininity in Early Post-War Turkey," *International Labor and Working-Class History* 104 (2023), 32–54.

157 United Nations, *Egypt, Israel and Turkey*, 11; Richard D. Robinson, "Turkey's Agrarian Revolution and the Problem of Urbanisation," *Public Opinion Quarterly* 22 (1958), 399–401.

availability of labour and housing.[158] If it was not for the extra-economic considerations, the most apt locations for new state industries would be the old industrial centres.[159] As we have seen in Chapter 1, the imperial capital and its hinterland, together with cities in western Anatolia such as Izmir and Bursa, constituted the industrial heartland of the country. In 1915, Istanbul housed fifty-five per cent of industry; Izmir followed with twenty-two per cent.[160] By the beginning of the 1930s, these concentrated urbanisation and industrialisation patterns remained intact. According to the 1932 statistics, thirty-four per cent of a total of 1,087 factories were in Istanbul; Izmir and Bursa followed Istanbul with 16.7 and 10.7 per cent respectively.[161] By 1938, that is, after the opening of state factories in the Anatolian towns, these figures had fallen only slightly. Together, the Marmara and Aegean areas hosted 71.1 per cent of all industry. In the textile sector, eighty-six per cent of all industrial activity was being carried out in the Marmara region.[162] Because they continued to attract the bulk of private investment, the share of Istanbul and Izmir in manufacturing employment increased from twenty-six per cent in 1927 to thirty-three per cent in 1950, during the postwar period.[163]

In Istanbul, the number of industrial workers and artisans increased from 42,582 in 1927 to 93,897 in 1935.[164] "Istanbul has become a city of artisans and workers," a newspaper article claimed, drawing on the trope of the "parasitic Ottoman social structure": "In the past, stuck-up men with gold-framed glasses and silver walking sticks made up the majority of our city's residents. But now, ninety-five per cent of our townsmen are artisans, workers, or at best lower-ranking civil servants. Workshops occupy the sites where once stood manor houses and waterside mansions. Istanbul is no more a city of parasites."[165] Another group whose visibility in the city was increasing was

158 Orsan, "Kurulacağı Yer," 60–61.

159 An important exception was the paper factory in Izmit. To choose the best industrial site for this expensive investment, the government requested the help of British industrial experts. After comparing Izmit, which lies in the hinterland of Istanbul, with the small Anatolian town of Ereğli (Konya), the experts' recommendation was to take advantage of the ready labour supply in Izmit to secure the required labour force more easily and to save on housing provision costs. See: Özeken, "Sanayi Tesis Yerleri," 362.

160 Ökçün, *1913–1915*, 14.

161 "Sanayi Hayatı: Fabrikalar Hakkında Bir İstatistik," *Haber-Akşam Postası*, 25 January 1934.

162 Erdal Yavuz, "The State of the Industrial Workforce, 1923–40," in *Workers and the Working Class in the Ottoman Empire and the Turkish Republic*, eds. Donald Quataert and Erik Jan Zürcher (London: I.B. Tauris, 1995), 97–8.

163 United Nations, *Egypt, Israel and Turkey*, 59.

164 T.C. Ekonomi Bakanlığı, *Türkiye Milli Geliri* (Ankara: Başvekalet Matbaası, 1937), 102.

165 "Istanbul, Esnaf ve İşçi Şehri Oldu," *Haber-Akşam Postası*, 22 August 1934.

the unemployed.[166] In Anatolian villages, newspapers reported, "the hearsay is that new factories in Istanbul are in desperate need of workers." Many of these immigrants ended up unemployed in the city.[167] The city municipality had been planning to establish an employment bureau in 1935, but this did not materialize until after the war.[168] The labour market was left unregulated to a great extent. Despite having the largest labour pool in the country, labour turnover rates were high in Istanbul as well.[169] But, for Istanbul's industrial employers, including the state, the problem was not so much the inadequacy of the labour supply as the problem of labour instability—of keeping the workers at the factories for long enough.

"Despite the efforts to build new industrial cities," a trade union journalist wrote in 1947, "the number of workers in Istanbul equalled the total number of workers [in the new industrial centres]." The city was comparable to Manchester and other industrial centres across the world in terms of worker concentration in urban population, he ambitiously claimed. The two sides of the Golden Horn hosted hundreds of factories and shipyards, and thus had the highest labour density in the city. Factory workers densely populated close-by neighbourhoods, such as Eyüp, Balat, Fener, Hasköy, and Kasımpaşa. Galata followed in terms of labour concentration. Workers were dispersed across various parts of the city with considerable concentration in Zeytinburnu, Yeşilköy, and Bakırköy.[170]

The 1930 Public Health Law defined three categories of industrial establishments based on their distance from residential areas, but rapid urban growth rendered this classification and the regulations based on it redundant. While the state was building new factories in Anatolia, private capital preferred to invest in and around Istanbul. In the 1940s, twenty-three new factories were built in the city. The locations of these new industries laid the foundations for the Bakırköy, Kazlıçeşme, Topkapı-Sağmalcılar, Rami-Topçular, and Bomonti industrial zones. The geographic distribution of the seventy-one new textile establishments in the 1950s strengthened this pattern of industrial geography.[171]

166 "İşsizler: Vilayete Müracaat Edenlerden Vesika İstenecek," *Haber-Akşam Postası*, 9 March 1932; "İşsizliğe Karşı Belediye Yeni Teşkilat Yapmak İstiyor," *Haber-Akşam Postası*, 6 August 1932; "Istanbula İş Bulmak İçin Gelenler," *Haber-Akşam Postası*, 21 November 1932; "İş Bulmak İçin Belediye Bu Sene Bir İş Bürosu Açıyor," *Haber-Akşam Postası*, 14 June 1934.

167 "İşçi Bürosu," *Haber-Akşam Postası*, 17 June 1934.

168 "İş Bulmak" *Haber-Akşam Postası*, 9 February 1935.

169 ILO, "Labour Problems in Turkey," 216; Özeken, "İşçiyi Barındırma," 106.

170 Süreyya Oral, "Istanbul'da İşçi Yatakları," *Türk İşçisi*, 15 February 1947.

171 Erol Tümertekin, *Istanbul Sanayiinde Kuruluş Yeri* (Istanbul: Istanbul Üniversitesi Coğrafya Enstitüsü Yayınları, 1972), 27–28; Seyfettin Simdek, "Yurtta Mensucat Hareketleri," *Mensucat Meslek Dergisi* no. 9 (1958), 349.

Among these industrial centres, Bakırköy held a distinct place because this is where the largest factories were located. Historically, the two old imperial textile factories, that is, the Bakırköy Factory and the Yedikule Spinnery played a part in the emergence of a working-class neighbourhood.[172] In 1934, Hungarian experts considered Feshane, Bakırköy, and Gemlik as suitable construction sites for an artificial silk factory. They chose Bakırköy for its water sources and the availability of skilled and experienced labour.[173] After the war, Bakırköy, Zeytinburnu, and Kazlıçeşme were informally designated industrial zones because the land was flat and close to the sea, had an abundance of water sources, and a large labour supply, which reduced employers' labour transport and housing provision costs. In the late 1940s, immigrants from the Balkans began to settle in Bakırköy, adding to the already high urban concentration.[174] In the workers' files from the 1950s, I have frequently seen former Ottoman Balkan cities listed as a worker's place of birth. Between 1945 and 1960, migrant workers from Thrace and Anatolia settled in the district, taking the population to above 100,000.[175] In the late 1940s, the Bakırköy Factory recruited workers from the district for the Kayseri Factory.[176] By 1961, 11.6 per cent of large industrial enterprises in Istanbul were located in Bakırköy, and 32.2 per cent of these enterprises manufactured textiles.[177] Industrial overconcentration was controlled to some extent through the designation of industrial zones, but concerns over urban congestion and squatter settlements would intensify in the 1950s and 1960s.[178]

In 1953, a contemporary sociologist conducted a survey among industrial workers in Eyüp, where, he argued, "the genuine worker-type lived." Eyüp workers, most of whom were employed at Defterdar, were highly unionised. His findings could be generalised to Bakırköy, since both neighbourhoods had been home to state textile factories. The Defterdar (Feshane) Factory, which

172 Sabahaddin Zaim, *Bölge ve Şehir Planlaması Yönünden Istanbul Sanayi Bölgeleri* (Istanbul: Istanbul Üniversitesi Yayınları, 1971), 241–2.

173 Özeken, "Sanayi Tesis Yerleri," 363.

174 "Dünden Bugüne," *Istanbul Ansiklopedisi*, vol. 7 (Istanbul: Tarih Vakfı Yurt Yayınları, 1995), 557.

175 *Istanbul Ansiklopedisi*, vol. 4 (Istanbul: Koçu Yayınları, 1960), 1,893–1,897.

176 "Bakırköy Bez Fabrikası Müdürlüğünden," *Türk İşçisi*, 8 February 1947.

177 Zaim, *Istanbul Sanayi Bölgeleri*, 166, 174.

178 Charles W.M. Hart, *Zeytinburnu Gecekondu Bölgesi* (Istanbul: Istanbul Ticaret Odası, 1969); Kemal H. Karpat, *The Gecekondu: Rural Migration and Urbanisation* (Cambridge: Cambridge University Press, 1976); İlhan Tekeli, *Gecekondulu, Dolmuşlu, İşportalı Şehir* (Istanbul: Cem Yayınevi, 1976); In February 1960, Yaşar Kemal, a prominent Turkish novelist, published a ten-piece journalistic inquiry on gecekondu's in *Cumhuriyet*.

had been located in Eyüp since 1839, had recruited workers from the local labour market since its inception. Sixty per cent of the factory's workforce lived within walking distance of the factory; twenty per cent travelled by public transport, and the rest had to change at least once and travelled a maximum of one hour each way.[179] In many cases, generations from the same family were employed. Chain migration and settling in Istanbul following compulsory military service in the city were the two mechanisms through which outside labour joined the Defterdar workforce. Fındıkoğlu found that these workers did not retain any rural ties; they completely adopted the culture of industrial labour and passed it down generation to generation. In the pages of the Ministry of Labour's journal, an author argued that a factory labourer working on the side of the Golden Horn for a daily wage of 250 piasters would not accept work in a small Anatolian town even for 450 piasters a day.[180] In the 1950s, private industrialists increasingly invested in the area to make use of the available labour supply.[181]

7 Conclusion

For a war-torn, underdeveloped, and young state like Turkey, state-led industrialisation had a dual function. Economically, the crisis of capitalism and the rise of economic nationalism in the interwar period provided a window of opportunity to catch up with Western industrialisation. Politically, etatism was a project of socio-spatial integration designed and commanded by a ruling elite that had witnessed the territorial disintegration of an empire. Besides vast ethnic, linguistic, and religious differences, regional economic and social inequalities in postimperial Turkey were produced by peripheral integration into the world economy. It was in this context that the ordering of national space emerged as an indication of both sovereignty and progress. Together with a nationalised and expanded railway network, factories were seen as state instruments to transform the disparate postimperial land into an integrated national unit. They were planned as channels for disseminating the new ideas of the republic and the means of connection between centre and periphery.

---

179 Ziyaeddin Fahri Fındıkoğlu, *Defterdar Fabrikası Hakkında Bir Tatbiki Sınai Sosyoloji Denemesi* (Istanbul: Türkiye Harsi ve Araştırmalar Derneği Yayını, 1955), 30.

180 Celal Dinçer, "Endüstri İşçisinin Kalkınması," *Çalışma Vekâleti*, no. 21 (1947), 10.

181 Ziyaeddin Fahri Fındıkoğlu, "Türkiye'de Sınai Sosyoloji Araştırmaları 1-2-3-Defterdar Fabrikası," *Feshane Mensucat Meslek Dergisi* no. 3, 6, 12, (1954).

Although the institutional and discursive bases of central industrial planning operated on a national scale, it was the local labour market dynamics that determined the successful operation of the new state factories. In this chapter, I moved away from an aggregate analysis of state industries to reveal the inherent spatiality of industrial relations and labour markets, including their gender dynamics. I argued that a textured, spatialised understanding of state-led industrialisation is key to understanding the local dynamics of a national development project. I have shown that the main line of distinction in the spatial unfolding of state-led industrialisation was between the old industrial centres and the new industrial sites. This line has produced considerable variations in labour supply, recruitment, retention, and reproduction. The fact that workers were dispersed in widely separated plants also affected the development of trade unionism in the second half of the 1940s.

The newly built factories were designated as modal spaces of Western industrial modernity in Anatolia. In terms of their scale and symbolic value, they overshadowed the old Istanbul factories. Yet, beyond these differences lay a significant similarity. The operation of state factories would present an alternative to a "Western" style of industrialisation characterised by a long and arduous history of class conflict, a model that was utterly detested by the ruling elite of the new republic. They shared a widespread optimism that the Western experience of industrialisation could be used as a model for economic change without its accompanying social turmoil or even class divisions.

This chapter concludes the first part of this book, comprising a historical and spatial analysis of industrialisation in Turkey starting from the 1840s. I have discussed the failed nineteenth-century attempts at industrial development in the context of Ottoman peripheral integration and the political uses of this failure by the republican ruling elite. I went on to explain the political economy of postimperial Turkey and argued that, under the influence of competing world powers and in the short window of opportunity that opened after the Great Depression, state-led industrialisation emerged as a capitalist development strategy. Finally, I discussed the spatiality of planned industrialisation in relation to nation-building and the local dynamics of industrial labour.

In the second part of the book, I depart from this macro-scale political economy approach. By reducing the scale of the historical analysis, I will redirect the reader's gaze toward the dense textures of workers' everyday lives, social relationships, and political agency. How workers experienced the simultaneous processes of nation-building and industrialisation will be the guiding question throughout the next three chapters. I now kindly ask the reader to follow me into the Bakırköy Factory to silence the loud and powerful external voices of this ambitious national development project, and pay attention to the nitty-gritty of everyday life and the micro-physics of power on the shop floor.

PART 2

CHAPTER 4

The View from the Factory

State-Led Industrialisation as Myth and Ceremony

Among all the people who Lilo Linke met during her tour of Turkey in 1935, Bay [Mr] Fazlı was arguably the person who enchanted her most. This "tall, slender man [with] a pair of amazingly blue eyes" looked like a "*Herrenmensch*" to her, "the type of man which [Germans] always dream of as their master and which they rarely find." Fazlı Turga was a veteran of the Balkan War, an engineer with a European degree, and a devoted member of the industrialist front in his country. When Linke met him, he was the head of the Kayseri *Kombinat* as the factory was called referring to the industrial business conglomerations in the Soviet Union. As the largest industrial investment of the period, the factory was regarded as the poster project of state-led industrialisation. Before he was chosen for this most prestigious position, his abilities were put to the test when he was appointed as the director of "an old, almost bankrupt factory in Istanbul."[1] He passed with flying colours. The year before he met Linke, at the opening ceremony of the new building of that old factory, he had received praise from the prime minister for proving that he deserved to be trusted with "the people's capital."[2]

That old factory was none other than the Bakırköy Factory. It was an example of the republic's "new industrial mentality," in the words of the minister for economic affairs.[3] The two main components of that mentality were the principle of rational work and industrial labour as patriotic service. Together, they shaped the discourse on national industrial modernity in the 1930s and 1940s. To achieve the first, the government sought the help of, first, foreign, and then, increasingly local industrial experts. The factory reports penned by these experts portrayed quite a different industrial world to the one presented by the ruling elite. To achieve the second, the state elite interpellated industrial workers as "dutiful republican citizens." They could not have found a better

1 Lilo Linke, *Allah Dethroned: A Journey Through Modern Turkey* (London: Constable and Co., 1937).

2 "Büyük Kaybımız: Fazlı Turga," *Feshane Mensucat Meslek Dergisi*, no. 7 (1954), 1–2; "Bakırköy Bez Fabrikasının Yeni Daireleri Dün Açıldı," *Akşam*, 14 August 1934.

3 Bilsay Kuruç, *Belgelerle Türkiye İktisat Politikası, 1933–1935*, vol. 2 (Ankara: Ankara Üniversitesi Yayınları, 1993), 269.

DOI:10.1163/9789004687141_006

stage than a rundown Ottoman factory to contrast the darkness of the past against their promise of an enlightened modernity. In a newspaper article that was by no means particularly unusual, a reporter narrated how he had been touched by the benevolence of the state elite toward industrial workers when the prime minister put his hands on the shoulders of the Bakırköy workers with the "compassion of a father." The prime minister referred to emotion as well as technical literacy in setting the tone for the Turkish state's approach to industrial relations:

> Each worker should think of the most efficient way of using their machine, not only based on knowledge but also on a desire that is like a burning passion. These factories are important for they give a new direction to our economy; they are places for only those who are knowledgeable, hardworking, and eager … Entering through the factory gate on their first day of service, every civil servant and worker should feel this deep in their hearts.[4]

Having covered the historical and spatial underpinnings of planned state-led industrialisation in the previous three chapters, I now focus on the "traditional" realm of working-class politics: shop-floor industrial relations. In attending to social relations between labour and capital at the point of production, I explore the broad patterns of economic development that existed for working people where they worked and lived.[5] In this and the following two chapters, my focus is on the interactions between the "politics in production," that is, the relations of cooperation and conflict, persuasion, and coercion between capital and labour on the shop floor, and the "politics of production," that is, the interventions of the state, employers', and workers' organisations, as well as third parties such as the International Labour Organization, that influence this balance of power, more or less, from the outside.[6]

In this experience-near level of analysis, I take issue with the prevailing view of state workers' working and living conditions in the 1930s and 1940s.

---

4 "Başvekil Hz. Sümer Bank Fabrikalarını Tetkik Ettiler," *Cumhuriyet,* 22 November 1933; "Yeni Daireleri," *Akşam*; *Istanbul Ansiklopedisi,* vol. 4 (Istanbul: Koçu Yayınları, 1960), 1,904.

5 Ira Katznelson, "Working-Class Formation: Constructing Cases and Comparisons," in *Working-Class Formation: Nineteenth-Century Patterns in Western Europe and the United States*, eds. Ira Katznelson and Aristide R. Zolberg (Princeton: Princeton University Press, 1986), 15–7.

6 Michael Burawoy, "Between the Labor Process and the State: The Changing Face of Factory Regimes under Advanced Capitalism," *American Sociological Review* 48, no. 5 (1983), 587; Michael Burawoy, *The Politics of Production: Factory Regimes under Capitalism and Socialism* (London: Verso, 1985), 7–8.

Characterised by an overreliance on secondary and state-produced material, studies on the working class in this period have portrayed these workers as a relatively well-off and obedient social cluster. As would be expected from the type of archival material they are based on, these studies provide a detailed account of state actions, and largely ignore the worker's experience. This experience is multi-faceted and complex; it encompasses the lives of workers both inside and outside the factory, starting from the moment they apply for work, their experience of the labour process, the labour control regimes, and their housing conditions. To explore the ways workers related and adapted to their work situation, I rely on workers' files and the interviews I conducted. For information on the actual work process, I use foreign expert and state inspection reports. Together, these sources reveal that shop-floor industrial relations substantively diverged from the central plan and entailed a considerable resistance to the efforts to rationalise the production process. Starting from the physical conditions of production, I set out the administrative structure of the Bakırköy Factory, the employment and wage policy, labour control strategies, social provisions, and the housing problems faced by the workers. Where possible, I also bring in different actors in the workplace social relations and explore their social position and mentality.

I make three interrelated arguments in this chapter. First, behind the celebrated transformation of this old, rundown Ottoman factory into a modern mass production site lay a failed attempt at rationalisation and a set of repressive shop-floor management practices. Second, behind the regime's proud presentation of industrial relations lay high labour exploitation. Third, behind the assumed docility and passivity of workers lay isolated and individualised worker resistance.

1 "It Looks Like One of Those Famous American Factories!"

Following the expansion of ideas of scientific management and manufacturing self-sufficiency, the first two decades of the twentieth century witnessed a shift in factory design principles. The physical space of the factory was no longer seen as "a passive shell simply to house machines, tools, and workers"; it was a part of the production technology itself. The purpose-built factory design was expected to respond to the pull of mass production by functioning as an architectural machine that would combat the problems standing in the way of efficiency. Here we see the wooden and brick multi-storey buildings of the nineteenth century give way to single-storey reinforced concrete structures that allowed for bigger uninterrupted spaces to avoid the cost of hoisting materials.[7]

Turkish reformers were keeping a close eye on the industrial and engineering achievements of the West. Visuals of industrial architecture and design filled the pages of the journal *Sanayii* (Industry) in 1918. In the 1930s, futuristic images of factory buildings and machinery adorned the front covers of popular magazines. With the onset of etatism, photographs of Turkish factories gradually replaced the images of Western industrial architecture. The drawings and models of the new factories were featured in the pages of *La Turquie Kemaliste* (a propaganda periodical published by the internal affairs ministry), the professional journal *Arkitekt,* and the mainstream newspapers.[8] The reconstruction and expansion of the old Ottoman factories resulted in a dramatic transformation in their size, technological structure, and productive capacity. The use of the "latest technology and design principles" in these physical renewal processes were praised as a sign of the republic's successful efforts to catch up with Western industrial design and technology. Looms featuring the latest technology were installed at Hereke and Feshane, new departments were added to the Beykoz Leather and Shoe Factory, but it was the Bakırköy Factory that was the location for "the first significant step in planned industrialisation."[9]

In May 1933, a visiting journalist observed the contrast between the old and rundown factory building and the new machines that had been gradually installed since 1925.[10] A couple of months later, the prime minister also was struck by the sight of the brand-new machinery that had been placed in the century-old building. "The young and active director Fazlı Bey," the reporter covering the visit wrote, had done his best to rejuvenate an old building that looked like "a hunchbacked elderly man." The volume of production had increased by two-to threefold and the production costs had gone down thanks to his "expertise, effort, and business acumen," which, as we learn a few lines later, included the introduction of the night shift. Production variety had also expanded: in addition to canvas and plain cotton cloth, the factory

7 Lindy Biggs, *The Rational Factory: Architecture, Technology and Work in America's Age of Mass Production* (Baltimore: The Johns Hopkins University Press, 2002), 2; Joshua B. Freeman, *Behemoth: A History of the Factory and the Making of the Modern World* (New York: W. W. Norton & Company, 2018), 139; Gillian Darley, *Factory* (London: Reaktion Books, 2004), 118.

8 Sibel Bozdoğan, *Modernism and Nation Building: Turkish Architectural Culture in the Early Republic* (Seattle: University of Washington Press, 2002), 115–124.

9 "1,5 Milyon Metreden 5,5 Milyon Metreye," *Haber Akşam Postası,* 5 July 1934; "Paşabahçedeki Fabrika Modern bir Hale Getiriliyor," *Cumhuriyet,* 11 May 1936; "Sanayi Planının Tahakkukuna Doğru," *Milliyet,* 14 August 1934.

10 "Bakırköy Bez Fabrikası," *Cumhuriyet,* 13 May 1933.

FIGURE 10 Cover of the official publication La Turquie Kemaliste, late 1930s
COURTESY OF SİBEL BOZDOĞAN

was producing batiste cloth, linen canvas, muslin, apparel cloth, and home textiles.[11]

In the press coverage of the factory's and its manager's performance, faith in technology was strong. For example, the reader was assured that the new machines were capable of doing the same job with just 380 or 400 workers instead of the previous 1,600 or 1,800. The bad news was that, with its existing structure, the factory had reached the physical limits of its productivity, making it imperative to renovate it as soon as possible.[12] But the government

11 "Başvekil Hz. Sümer Bank Fabrikalarını Tetkik Ettiler," *Cumhuriyet*, 22 November 1933.

12 "Fabrikalarımız," *Haber Akşam Postası*, 14 February 1934; "Bakırköy Bez Fabrikası," *Haber Akşam Postası*, 11 May 1936; "Yeni Daireleri," *Akşam*; Hans Landau, *Kayseri, Ereğli, Nazilli, Merinos Fabrikaları Hakkında* (n.p., 1938), 12; *Sümerbank 1939 Yılı Umumi Murakebe Heyeti Raporu* (Ankara: Titaş Basımevi, 1940), 5, Archival Collection of the Republic of Turkey Prime Ministry Supreme Audit Board. Amb./Db.No: K.A./ 255.07.02.01.06.3227; "Bakırköy Bez Fabrikası," *Cumhuriyet*, 13 May 1933; "Başvekil Hz.," *Cumhuriyet*.

FIGURE 11 The old factory building at the back and the construction site at the front, 1934
COURTESY OF EMRE ÖNCÜ

FIGURE 12 Construction of the main production building, 1934
COURTESY OF EMRE ÖNCÜ

FIGURE 13 Construction site, 1934
COURTESY OF EMRE ÖNCÜ

FIGURE 14 Bakırköy neighbourhood, 1934
COURTESY OF EMRE ÖNCÜ

actually had bigger plans for the factory. Besides renovating the factory premises, Sümerbank was to invest in the construction of a new adjacent building.

Construction started in the summer of 1933. The coverage of the construction and the opening of the new building, unfortunately, does not detail the plans for the factory premises. There are some bits and pieces of information available on the changes that were made. For example, the old main building was not demolished, but transformed into a dining hall. And the new building had a "dormitory" (*yurt*) for the female workers' children, and a shower area for workers. The extended capacity would require the employment of 1,200 workers at the peak of the factory's production. The factory was now completely modernised, setting an example for all Turkish factories.[13]

The opening ceremony for the new factory building in August 1934 aimed to showcase Turkey's industrial vision. The new building was hailed as the physical manifestation of the regime's success in catching up with Western technological modernity. Besides a large group of bureaucrats, English journalists and the Soviet commercial representative were also in attendance. The prime minister arrived on the presidential yacht at the factory pier, where he was met by Mr Fazlı. The director gave him and his entourage a one-and-an-half-hour tour starting from the entrance gate where the workers would go in, taking in each department, and ending at a second gate where the finished goods would come out. The crowd was impressed, as was a later visitor, who described the factory as "a perfectly modern factory on the coast of the beautiful Marmara Sea." Another visitor spoke for many a reformer with a burning industrial desire when he wrote that the factory "looks like one of those famous American factories which took cows from one end and churned out sausages from the other."[14]

13 "Bez Fabrikası," *Haber Akşam Postası*, 2 August 1934; "Yeni Daireleri," *Akşam*; "Sanayileşme Yolunda Yeni Bir Adım," *Cumhuriyet*, 14 August 1934.

14 Abidin Daver, "Devlet Fabrikalarında Sosyal Yardımlar," *Türk İşçisi*, 12 Nisan 1947; Salahattin Güngör, "97 Yıl Önce Kurulan Bir Fabrika," *Türk İşçisi*, 22 February 1947.

FIGURE 15 The front of the factory overlooking the train tracks, 1940s
COURTESY OF TURGAY TUNA

FIGURE 16 The back of the factory, 1949
COURTESY OF TURGAY TUNA

Technological investment continued throughout the decade. New machinery increased the number of spins from 3,000 to 8,928 and looms from 60 to 320. By 1940, the factory's operations superintendent could boast that "there is not even a single old machine, they are all of the latest model" at the factory. The factory worked very well, he claimed, because besides the workers and the engineers, the technology was top quality. Management increased the spinning capacity once again in 1943 to ease the scarcity of yarn that had been exacerbated by the war. At the end of the decade, another extension increased the number of spins almost fourfold and the number of looms by half.[15]

FIGURE 17 The construction of the new production building, 1934
COURTESY OF EMRE ÖNCÜ

15 Selim Cavid, "Bakırköy Bez Fabrikası," *İktisadi Yürüyüş,* no. 3 (1940), 12; *Istanbul Ansiklopedisi* 4, 1905; "Yakın ve Orta Doğu Bölge Toplantısına Sunulan Türk Raporu," *Çalışma Vekâleti Dergisi,* no. 24 (1947), 76; Fazlı Turga, "Bizde ve Dışarda Pamuk ve Pamuklu Sanayi XI," *Feshane Mensucat Dergisi,* no. 3 (1949), 45.

FIGURE 18 Workers bringing in new machinery to the new production building, 1934
COURTESY OF EMRE ÖNCÜ

FIGURE 19 Factory Director explaining the new machinery to Prime Minister, 1933

Despite the enthusiasm for the latest industrial technology and design, the factory's productivity remained low. As did the productivity of the other state factories. The initial hope that these factories would easily adjust to the markets quickly gave way to distress over their financial crises and, eventually, to a loss of faith in central planning among industrialists. "Industry is planned at the desk," wrote an author in a textile engineering journal, but "it is performed on the shop floor." No matter how noble the social and national goals behind industrialisation were, they were not enough to achieve industrial efficiency. Industry could only rise on the shoulders of a trained industrial cadre operating on the basis of rational organisation, and state textile factories, including the Bakırköy Factory, lacked both.[16]

But old habits die hard. The contrast between the new machinery and the old factory building was not the only, or even the most important, incongruence at work at the factory. Production also was bottlenecked by a curious blend of modern technologies and traditional working methods. At the same time as the latest industrial design and technology were being imported, traditional modes of social organisation continued to exert a powerful hold in the factories. Numerous foreign experts called for urgent measures to reorganise production and to implement scientific labour control methods, as we shall see below, but their suggestions largely fell on deaf ears. Local industrial experts had joined them by the beginning of the 1940s. A report written by the Sümerbank General Directorate for the Ministry of Economy admitted that the holding relied on constructing new buildings and enlarging the existing ones to increase production instead of focusing on rationalising the operation and management of the factories.[17] Factory establishment costs were extremely high as a result of the necessary technological and physical investment, claimed the German head advisor to the minister for economic affairs. In both state and private factories, industrial managers relied on the newest technology and design coupled with high mechanisation to compensate for the lack of skilled workers.[18] Especially in the early years of state-led industrialisation, another foreign expert argued, Sümerbank increased capital investment in an attempt to bring down production costs rather attending to the problems of

16 Abdülkadir Gözen, "Bizde Devletçilik ve Devlet Endüstrisi," *Feshane Mensucat Meslek Dergisi*, no. 1 (1949), 11.

17 Sümerbank Genel Umumi Müdürlük, "İktisat Vekâleti Yüksek Makamına," *Sümerbank Genel Müdürlüğü Personel Servisi Genel Müdürlük Kadroları, 1933–1940* (Sümer Holding Archives), 17 April 1940, 1.

18 Max von der Porten, "Devlet ve Hususi Sınai İşletmelerin Kontrolü ve Islahı," 1939, Register K.A./255.07.02.01.06.1056.

administration and management, or training workers to be more efficient.[19] Local and foreign experts alike agreed on the primacy of achieving administrative rationality and systematic labour control. Since the vision of productivity was based, first and foremost, on an effective managerial command and control system, I now move on to an exploration of the organisational structure of Sümerbank and its effect on factory performance.

2 Organisational Structure and Managerial Personnel

Although the government was tremendously proud of the new economic policy and its main organ of "rational" implementation, Sümerbank, there were increasing concerns about its organisational structure from the very beginning of the first five-year plan. Writing in the context of growing public disapproval over economic planning in the mid-1950s, A.H. Hanson identified the problem as a lack of "the machinery capable of translating the will to plan into the practice of planning, to train the personnel required for the job, and to give them the freedom of action that they need."[20] His formulation captures the essence of the debates on administrative efficiency, for it encompasses the regulation of relations at different levels between central management and the factories, as well as the competence of the managerial rank and the legal status of factories as financially autonomous, economically integrated production organisations.

It is obvious from the foreign expert reports that the operation of Turkish state factories in the 1930s was trapped between the rock of centralised planning and the hard place of the shop floor. "Turkish planning was a hit-or-miss affair," wrote Hanson; there was a considerable gap between formal planning and practical execution.[21] For the German experts writing on state textile factories, rationalisation in administration was a prerequisite for the full exploitation of technological knowledge in mass production. Accordingly, problems associated with decision-making and implementation were given extensive coverage in the reports by the experts, who all reiterated the need to streamline national economic development and central planning, as well as for

19 James M. Barker, *The Economy of Turkey: An Analysis and Recommendations for A Development Program* (Baltimore: The Johns Hopkins Press, 1951), 115, 153.

20 "Sümerbank Sanayiimizin Hamisi ve Pişdarıdır," *Cumhuriyet*, 29 July 1933; A. H. Hanson, *The Structure and Control of State Enterprises in Turkey* (Ankara: Public Administration Institute for Turkey and The Middle East, 1954), 13.

21 A. H. Hanson, *Public Enterprise and Economic Development* (London: Routledge, 1959), 121.

effective execution and inspection. The reports also hint at a chasm between the official definition and actual practice of central planning and management during those formative years of Turkish etatism, which validates our analysis of planning and centralisation as an open-ended process rather than top-down implementation. This analysis could also be read as a corrective to the tendency of historians to mistake management objectives for what actually happened inside the workplace. The blueprints of the plan—as they were presented in the laws on state enterprises, parliamentary discussions, and other official documents—belonged somewhat uneasily somewhere between the decision-making process and everyday practice. As such, the reports perfectly exemplify the "piecemeal, uncoordinated and empiricist" character of much management policymaking and execution, and reveal the contentions and conflicts within central planning.[22]

Various reports noted that state factories suffered from a lack of trained clerical staff and, consequently, from a lack of attention to the establishment of systematic financial and production accounting methods. Experts complained bitterly about the inadequacy of financial accounting practices for the task of managing the growing complexity of production. Statistical records were either not kept or not used for shop-floor operational management, financial control was limited to expenditure, data on various costs were not kept or were gathered only irregularly, managers had little economic awareness or profit consciousness, job descriptions were not available, and standards of capacity and faculties were not set, particularly for executive jobs, and the principle of "the right man in the right place" was not followed.

At the Bakırköy Factory, job assignment and task division at the managerial level was a serious problem. The archive and sales department of the factory compared much worse to other state factories, making cost calculations extremely difficult.[23] Workshop managers' lack of interest in reducing waste, given the much-complained-about general overhead costs, struck a foreign expert in 1937. The large amount of waste in the Bakırköy cotton mill, he wrote, remained unaddressed mainly because of accounting errors, the elimination of which he identified as the first step toward a general reorganisation of

22 Richard Coopey and Alan McKinlay, "Power Without Knowledge? Foucault and Fordism, c. 1900–50," *Labor History* 51, no. 1 (2010), 107, 114, 125; M. Rose & B. Jones, "Managerial Strategy and Trade Union Responses to Work Reorganisation Schemes at Establishment Level," in *Job Redesign: Critical Perspectives on the Labour Process,* eds. David Knights, Hugh Willmott, and David Collinson (Brookfield: Gower, 1985), 99.

23 Hösli, *Bakırköy Bez Fabrikası Hakkında Rapor*, 1943. Archival Collection of the Republic of Turkey Prime Ministry Supreme Audit Board. Amb./Db.No: K.A./255.07.02.01.06.1241.

production: "It allows you to calculate the actual cost of your product and lays the basis for the second step. This second step is rationalisation, that is, the totality of all the measures taken to reduce the cost." He drew detailed comparisons between the operational and labour costs of German factories and those of the Bakırköy and Beykoz factories, and although he found that the labour costs were considerably lower in Turkey, the general overheads differed greatly due to a combination of accounting mistakes and lack of effort. The flow of production was hindered by the lack of coordination between the various departments of the factory; if production speed was to be increased, greater coordination and systemisation would be required.[24]

Solutions to these problems could not be found at the factory level, however. The overcentralisation of decision-making and the lack of enterprise autonomy presented an impediment to productive efficiency. The excessive level of centralisation and the bureaucratic rigidity left factory managers with little authority, with even the most minor of decisions being made by head office. For example, Sümerbank controlled the hiring and distribution of personnel, even in the lower echelons of factory administration. Von der Porten explained the problem in 1937 as follows: Sümerbank factories did not have a legal entity; they functioned as the branches of the holding without the autonomy to determine their own budgets. The aggregated Sümerbank budget concealed individual factory performance, killed the sensitive gauge of profit and loss, and hindered the development of competitive spirit and ambition. But the same factories found themselves in competition with each other when it came to, for example, the purchasing of raw materials such as cotton. This structure put a heavy burden on factory directors because they had too much responsibility but too little power. The solution was to manage these factories without curbing their business autonomy and to rationalise their management starting from the top level. In practical terms, this meant coordinating the operations of factories across the same sector, and establishing an administrative council at each factory to ease the burden of the factory directors.[25]

---

24 Ewald Sachsenberg, "Bakırköy Bez Fabrikası Organizasyonu Hakkında," 1937, Register K.A./255.07.02.01.06.1139.

25 United Nations Department of Economic and Social Affairs, *The Development of Manufacturing Industry in Egypt, Israel and Turkey* (New York, 1958), 55; Von der Porten, "Devlet ve Hususi Sınai İşletmelerin Kontrolü ve Islahı"; "Denizyollarile Akay ve Fabrikalar Nizamnamesi," *Haber Akşam Postası*, 20 November 1935; Max von der Porten, *Devlet Sermayeli Müesseseler Raporu*, 1937. Archival Collection of the Republic of Turkey Prime Ministry Supreme Audit Board. Amb./Db.No: K.A./255.07.02.01.06.1125; Barker, *The Economy of Turkey*, 153.

Five years into the plan, Sümerbank underwent an administrative reorganisation aimed at rationalising production and financial operations under the auspices of a new law seeking to standardise the operations of state factories. In theory, the law granted enterprises financial and administrative autonomy by giving them a juridical personality and limited liability. In practice, however, the administrative structure became even more confusing. The autonomy of the factories had already been eroded due to government-induced price controls with the advent of the war, and the law now virtually eliminated establishment autonomy, perpetuating an excessive measure of centralisation in the management of factories. The overall direction of state factories was assigned to a General Economic Commission chaired by the prime minister and composed of representatives from the ministries, members of special committees of the National Assembly, and the directors of state and other banks. This administrative structure increased the degree of political interference in factory management, rendering them "prey to inefficiency, excessive red tape, and the demands of political patronage." A young employee at one of the state factories summarised the new work culture as follows: "What's the use of an engineer working for a politician? If the answer matters, he tells you what it is. If it doesn't, he doesn't care, he doesn't want to know it."[26] The system continued to evolve, often in an ad hoc manner, through the interaction between planned policies and reactions to the unforeseen consequences of those policies.[27]

Each state factory was run by a director and an administrative council, composed of the director himself, two assistant directors, and three representatives from among the officials and employees of the factory. The administrative council would prepare the yearly work programmes and send them to the Sümerbank General Directorate for approval. The council would also appoint the departmental superintendents. Factory employees, including minor clerical staff, were hired and dismissed by the central office of the holding company.

---

26 Hanson, *Structure*, 20–26; Barker, *The Economy of Turkey*, 153–156; Osman Okyar, "The Concept of Etatism," *The Economic Journal* 75, no. 297 (1965), 101–102; Max Weston Thornburg, Graham Spry, and George Soule, *Turkey: An Economic Appraisal* (New York: The Twentieth Century Fund, 1949), 203.

27 *Sümerbank 1939 Yılı Umumi Murakebe Heyeti Raporu*, 7; "Sümerbank İplik ve Dokuma Fabrikaları Müessesesi 1941 Yılı Raporu," *1941 Yılı Umumi Murakebe Heyeti Sümerbank Raporu* (Ankara: Alaaddin Kıral Basımevi, 1942), 5–6; "Sümerbank Bakırköy Sanayii Müessesesinin 1949 Yılı Raporu," *Başbakanlık Umumi Murakebe Heyeti 1949 Yılı Raporları* (Ankara: Başbakanlık Devlet Matbaası, 1950), 1–2; "Sümerbank İplik ve Dokuma Fabrikaları Müessesesi 1948 Yılı Raporu," *Sümerbank 1948 Senesi Faaliyet ve Hesap Devresine Ait İdare Meclisi Raporu, Bilanço, Kâr ve Zarar Hesabı* (Izmit: Selüloz Basımevi, 1949), 4.

The factory manager was directly accountable to the general management. His two assistant directors were separately responsible for administrative and technical duties. The administrative assistant director had jurisdiction over the departments of commerce, correspondence and records, health activities, internal services, food and assistance, accounting, supply and warehouse, and personnel. The production departments and the laboratory operated under the technical assistant director's management. In 1945, Sümerbank enterprises, including the iron and steel and paper factories, employed 309 engineers, 328 technicians, 400 head foremen, and 264 foremen for a total number of 28,346 workers. The number of workers in the production departments per engineer, technician, and head foreman or foreman were 60, 71, and 35 respectively.[28]

Who were the managers of those state factories? What class background and education did they have? What was it like to be the manager of a Turkish state factory? In the absence of research on the bureaucratic and managerial cadre manning the state factories, we have to rely on anecdotal observations and the biographical information in the obituary notices published in textile engineering journals. These sources suggest that the young engineers of the republic had studied in Europe, especially in German-speaking Europe, since German political and economic thought had already penetrated the Ottoman Empire by the late nineteenth century. Fazlı Turga, for example, had studied at the Textilfachschule in Brünn during World War I.[29] But according to Linke, "a good many of his theories came from Russia," where he, together with other Turkish engineers and mechanics, had spent several months before coming to Kayseri. The training, he told Linke, was more than technical; they were "taught to educate and lead their fellow-workers without thinking themselves their bosses." He enthusiastically explained his management goal as follows:

> What I want more than anything else is a real comradeship, the feeling that we are all one family from the director down to the last apprentice. It ought to be possible since here in Turkey the State is the most important entrepreneur. The few existing capitalists don't really matter, and in

28 Hanson, *Structure*, 23–24; Barker, *The Economy of Turkey*, 156; "Sümerbank İşletmelerinde İşletmede İnsan ve İşçi Meseleleri," *Sümerbank 1945 Senesi Faaliyet ve Hesap Devresine Ait İdare Meclisi Raporu, Bilanço, Kâr ve Zarar Hesabı* (Ankara: Başbakanlık Devlet Matbaası, 1946), 5.

29 Linke, *Allah Dethroned*, 309; Darina Martykanova, *Reconstructing Ottoman Engineers: Archaeology of a Profession (1789–1914)* (Lungarno Pacinotti: Pisa University Press, 2012), 97, 167; Selim Cavid, "Feshane Fabrikasında Bir Tedkik," *İktisadi Yürüyüş*, no. 1 (1939), 9; Selim Cavid, "Fabrikalarımız: Izmit Kağıt Fabrikası," *İktisadi Yürüyüş*, no. 6 (1940), 7, 21; "Büyük Kaybımız," *Mensucat*, 1–2.

> any case, they, too, are controlled by the State. If we take care from the outset not to create an exploited proletariat, if we make our workers feel that this factory belongs to the state and, therefore, to themselves, and if we really keep all the doors open to them to advance—why shouldn't we succeed?[30]

Around the same time as Linke, Webster was visiting the sugar factory in Turhal, whose director, Muammer Tuksavul, another European-educated engineer, challenged the bureaucratic management of state factories. Tuksavul had no tolerance for red tape, Webster wrote; to him, "efficiency is more important than formalities—production than meaningless checks and audits." But he was also "no worshiper of success in the narrow economic or political sense"; he was more interested in the human by-products of industrialisation, the "civilising" effect of the state factories. Especially in the early years of state-led industrialisation, factory managers impressed their foreign visitors with their agility and self-confidence. Managers were not simply cogs in the machine; when the system was in the process of formation, their behaviour modified the way in which the system operated. In Webster's words, they typified "the best of the generation next following the innovators of 1908 and 1923," and they personified "the new optimism of the Devrim (revolution)."[31]

This optimism and managerial autonomy seem to have been lost in later years as state factories came under increasing scrutiny for their administrative and productive competence. By the end of the 1940s, factory directors and departmental superintendents at state factories worked under "a crippled personnel and wage policy" that undermined scientific labour controls and kept productivity low.[32] To contemporary observers, state factory managers had an interest in keeping the wages as low as possible in order to garner favour with the higher echelons of central industrial management. In 1956, an industrial journalist and later a trade unionist praised the then director of the Bakırköy Factory for not following the steps of his predecessors in "trying to get in his superiors' good books by paying his workers low wages," and for fully understanding the direct connection between wage rates, promotion rules, and productivity.[33]

30 Linke, *Allah Dethroned*, 307–8.

31 Donald Everett Webster, *The Turkey of Atatürk: Social Process in the Turkish Reformation* (Philadelphia: The American Academy of Political and Social Science, 1939), 143–4.

32 Ahmet Ali Özeken, "Türkiye'de Sanayi İşçileri," *Sosyal Siyaset Konferansları Dergisi*, no. 1 (1949), 64; Thornburg et al., *Economic Appraisal*, 130.

33 Kemal Sülker, "Fabrika Müdürleri Arasında Yerleşmeye Başlayan Zihniyet," *Gece Postası*, 3 April 1956.

The entrepreneurial, solution-oriented manager of the early years was now a "bureaucratic" manager, but the altruistic character of the managerial attitude with a deep faith in the Kemalist revolution survived. A "heart-to-heart talk" between the factory director and the workers at the factory in 1950 demonstrates this continuity in managerial values, which were very much premised on the idea that the factory was the prime locus for moulding a good citizen and a good society. Addressing a worker who had accidentally damaged machinery for a second time, the director, Şefkati Türkekul, encapsulated the workings of the nationalist ideology on the shop floor: "This factory is our home, our source of livelihood. Who will protect it if we don't? [Our state] invested a whole lot in this factory. We should take care of it the way we take care of our own home."[34] Let's now turn to the rules of entrance and residence in this "home-like" factory.

3 Recruiting and Promoting

In almost every worker file I examined, the first document was an employment form (*İşe Giriş Çıkış Pusulası*) prepared by the personnel department. The form requested a wide range of information, from personal details to qualifications, previous work experience, and preferred job at the factory. While this suggested a careful recruitment process, the forms were rarely filled out completely and often created more confusion than clarity. On most forms, the worker was specified as "new," meaning they had no previous industrial experience; the job preference section would be left empty, and if it was provided, the specified job would always match the one assigned.

In 1934, a German industrial expert, Bauer, reported that the lack of scientific methodology in worker and foreman selection and task allocation was the primary impediment to rationalisation efforts at the factory. The notes on a conversation between Bauer and the director of the Bakırköy Factory, Fazlı Turga, nicely illustrate the gap between the theories of the central planners and the realities of the men on the shop floor. The two engineers talked enthusiastically about the importance to productivity of well-trained workers. Here, it is interesting to speculate whether, during his talk with the factory director, Bauer mentioned anything about the German debates. Or, perhaps Turga was already following them. Unfortunately for us, the reports are silent on such social transactions and Bauer's own notes end with reference to a promise

34 Muzaffer Daysal, "Bakırköy Bez Fabrikasında," *Hürbilek*, 7 April 1950.

he made to Turga to provide further information on vocational training. The information supplied by Bauer would then need to be adapted to the conditions of the shop floor by means of psychotechnical devices to measure the intelligence and dexterity of the workers. Unfortunately, again, the archive does not allow us to follow up on the two men's conversation. All we do know is that Bauer's and Turga's optimistic plans did not materialise, at least not before the beginning of the 1950s, as we can infer from the labour minister's and textile engineers' complaints about the lack of psychotechnical studies in Turkish industry.[35]

Always in need of labourers, especially skilled ones, state textile factories had a fairly loose recruitment policy. Dismissals were rare and even workers who disappeared without notice were recruited again. There were two main reasons behind the inefficiency of recruitment policy. The first was administrative inefficiency and managerial incompetence. The second hinderance to the development of an efficient recruitment policy was a structural one that could not be easily solved with managerial competence, for it concerned the structure of the labour market itself.

There was a personnel department in charge of the employment policy at each state factory, but they proved to be inefficient in their operations. "Those who direct labour," an industrial expert wrote, "have usually been preoccupied with technology and rarely know the workers' jobs."[36] From the foremen to the directors, inspectors reported in 1943, "all supervisors are busy in their offices instead of supervising workers."[37] In the absence of skill evaluations and sufficient vocational training, job were assigned randomly according to the labour needs of the different shops of the factory. To industrial experts, both local and foreign, low productivity was to a large extent a reflection of weak management starting from the point of recruitment.

Historically, the creation of personnel departments was a response to the failure of informal methods of hiring to handle the demands of large firms. The centralisation and standardisation of recruitment meant that employment policy was treated as an end in itself. In many industrial contexts, the

35 Bauer, *Bakırköy Fabrikası İğleri Hakkında*, (n.p., 1934); Sadi Irmak, "Yeni Kanunlarımız," *Çalışma Dergisi* 1, no. 3 (1946), 1–2; "Türk Raporu," *Çalışma Vekâleti Dergisi*, no. 62; "Prodüktivite ve Memleketimizde Prodüktiviteyi Artırmağa Matuf Tedbirler," *Çalışma Vekâleti Dergisi* 1, no. 2 (1953), 6, 38–50.

36 Barker, *The Economy of Turkey*, 117.

37 W.O. Wegenstein and G.W. Käser, "Management and Organisation of the Turkish State Monopolies," *Başvekalet Umumi Murakebe Heyeti Kitaplığı*, no. 222 (1958), 4, 20–1; *Sümerbank 1943 Yılı Umumi Murakebe Heyeti Raporu* (Ankara: Başbakanlık Devlet Matbaası, 1944).

formalisation of recruitment was also an attempt to curb the authority of the foremen in the fields of both hiring and promoting. The decasualisation of employment came to be seen increasingly as a prerequisite for more stable labour relations as it served to maintain employee morale and wellbeing. The bureaucratisation of employment, as it came to be known, was a long and complex process marked by struggles on and beyond the shop floor.[38]

A close examination of the Bakırköy workers' files reveals that, despite the existence of a personnel department, the foreman had considerable power over recruitment and promotion decisions. In the newly built state factories, the foreman's control over employment began literally at the factory gates. In the interviews I conducted with workers from Ereğli and Nazilli factories, stories of local children waiting at the factory gates to be chosen for recruitment by the foremen came up repeatedly.[39] A 1945 inspection report strongly criticised this practice and cited it as evidence for the urgent need for a national employment bureau.[40] State factories were left to their own devices to secure a stable workforce until the second half of the 1940s. In 1947, the Ministry of Labour declared that the Turkish state would deal with the employment problem as a public service.[41] The Employment and Recruitment Agency was established in 1946, but skills shortages, which I address in detail below, hampered effective placement services. The mostly unskilled applicants refused to accept factory work because of the low remuneration.[42] And those who took it, as we shall see, tended to leave the factories after only a couple of months.

Stories of recruitment and promotion at the Bakırköy Factory portray a chaotic decision-making and execution process. Despite the formal administrative organisation of the factory, the whole system of appointment, remuneration, and promotion was hardly in accordance with the concept of a bureaucratic organisation. The information I gathered from the workers' files, interviews with workers, and the press coverage of state factories points to what Meyer and Rowan called the "ceremonial façade." According to this perspective, the highly institutionalised, rationalised, and seemingly impersonal prescriptions create the image of an organisational practice based on objective and legitimate rules that restrict the discretion of any individual participant. But

38 Sanford M. Jacoby, *Employing Bureaucracy: Managers, Unions, and the Transformation of Work in the 20th Century* (London: Routledge, 1985), 5–6.

39 Sebahat Yürekli, interview by the author, 4 June 2019.

40 "İşletmede İnsan," 17.

41 "Yurdun En Büyük İşçi Sendikası Kömür Havzasında Kuruldu," *Türk İşçisi*, 12 April 1947.

42 Sait Kesler, "Çalışma Bakanlığının Büyük Hizmeti: Kalifiye İşçi Kursları," *Türk İşçisi*, 28 June 1947.

the actual operating activities are decoupled from this formal bureaucratic structure.[43]

Despite the pretence of a centralised bureaucratic management, the organisation of work at the Bakırköy Factory depended largely on the local labour market and changed from shop to shop within a given factory depending on the technological and production structure. Data from the workers' files illustrate that there was no central factory control over wage and labour organisation. Promotion was by seniority and wage levels were also scaled almost exclusively by seniority. But both were characterised by irregularities. Criteria for promotion were vague and, in practice, inequitable. When a worker asked for a pay rise, decision-making went through the foreman to the departmental superintendent, who scribbled brief notes in the margins of their petitions. These notes were impressionistic and vague comments rather than clear and standard rules, and they showed that the foreman's authority was almost invariably upheld. The absence or ineffectual enforcement of promotion plans strengthened further the foreman's authority. When a former worker was rehired, his accumulated seniority was often erased, a practice that adversely affected pay levels since a pay rise was formally tied to an unbroken service record. The worker needed the foreman's support in proving their seniority. The inclusion of prior service was one of the main demands made by workers to the Ministry of Labour shortly after it was established in 1945.[44]

As noted in Chapter 3, the industrial labour market of the 1930s and 1940s was a market of movement characterised by high rates of mobility. Throughout the period, a permanent and skilled industrial labour force was conspicuously lacking and high rates of labour turnover were of great concern to industrialists. Since workers changed jobs easily and frequently, market pressures played a decisive role in shaping employers' strategies and practices with regard to the utilisation of labour power. As we have seen in the story of Hidayet Usta, the ceremony at which the factory director recognised an aged employee's years of faithful service was poignant precisely because it was so unusual. While there was no shortage of unskilled labour in Istanbul, scarcities appeared quickly and progressively as one went up the scale. Skilled workers were hard to find and to keep. This situation continued into the 1940s and was exacerbated by

43 John W. Meyer and Brian Rowan, "Institutionalized Organisations: Formal Structure as Myth and Ceremony," *American Journal of Sociology* 83, no. 2 (1977), 341–343.

44 Şefik Ungun, "Hayat Pahalılığı Karşısında Devlet İşletmelerinde İşçi Ücretleri ve Sosyal Yardımlar," *Feshane Mensucat Meslek Dergisi* 2, no. 6 (1949), 94; "İş ve İşçi Hayatı Bakımından Önemli Toplantılar," *Türk İşçisi,* 3 May 1947.

the war.[45] "Even half-trained men were in demand because of the general scarcity of skilled labour," reported experts in 1949. "As soon as men are prepared for higher types of operations, they gravitate to better paying jobs at lower levels outside the plants where they received their training."[46]

The shortage of skilled labour and the absence of skill evaluation meant that task assignment at the Bakırköy Factory was random to a large extent. But there was an important exception to this general pattern: gender segregation of jobs. A weaver described the gender composition of the factory workforce in the 1940s as follows:

> There were a lot of women; a lot at the spinnery, not that many at the weavery, only a few, [but] the spinners were mostly women. In the dressing [department] there were no women, [they were] all men. In the warp [department] there were women, I mean those who bring the thread back when it is broken, and you tie it to the warp beam, and it keeps going again. Later it got automatic, it stopped when it [the thread] broke, and you find the tip and tie it.[47]

A comparison of spinning and weaving by a German industrial expert offers a glimpse into how such stereotyping worked on the Turkish shop floor. Spinning is much easier than operating weaving looms, von der Porten wrote; in fact, it was so easy that virtually anybody could master it. More to the point, if spinning were to be mechanised, all preparatory work would be done automatically, which would leave no room for mistakes. The only skill needed would then be to tie the ends of the broken yarn as quickly as possible and with the minimum loss of material. Apart from that, the productivity of the spinning workshop depended on the availability and quality of raw materials, the quality of the spinning machines, the spindle gauge, and the technical knowledge of the managing engineer. Echoing the dominant gender stereotyping of jobs in Germany, von der Porten concluded that since the task required no intellect, women—or better still, girls—should be employed in the spinning shop. By contrast, he claimed, both the quality of cloth and productivity depended on the weaver's skill.[48] Unsurprisingly, therefore, weaving

45 Raufi Manyas, "İş, İşçi, İşsizlik," *İktisadi Yürüyüş* no. 2 (1940), 9; "Türk Raporu," 61.

46 Thornburg et. Al., *Economic Appraisal*, 129–30.

47 Asım Kocabaş, interview by the author, 3 August 2009.

48 Mary Nolan, *Visions of Modernity: American Business and the Modernisation of Germany* (Oxford: Oxford University Press, 1994), 96; Max von der Porten, "Kayseri Fabrikası İplik ve Dokuma Daireleri Hakkında," 1939, Register K.A./255.07.02.01.06.1114.

in Turkish textile factories was almost exclusively a job for men. Weavers were considered skilled and sought-after workers, and as such, they enjoyed a considerable degree of structural bargaining power. We will see how that played out in industrial bargaining and trade-union membership in the next two chapters.

FIGURE 20 Women at the spindlers at the Bakırköy Factory, 1950s
IISH KEMAL SÜLKER PAPERS, BG A63/94

In 1945, there were 291 women working at the weavery of the Bakırköy Factory. They made up thirty-five per cent of the weavery workforce, and worked mainly in the preparation process and as weavers' helpers. In the spinnery, 225 out of 377 workers were women or girls. As a whole, woman made up thirty-eight per cent of the 1,500 workers at the factory.[49] During his 1934 visit to the factory, the prime minister was impressed by the number of women on the shop floor. He referred to the oft-cited "nimble female fingers" and the "refined female taste" tropes to explain why female labour was so important for the textile industry.[50] In 1940, an engineer from the Bakırköy Factory proudly claimed

49 Sümerbank Genel Müdürlük Yüksek Katına, "Fabrikalarımızın 1945 Senesi Faaliyetleri, Neticeleri ve Tahlilleri," 9 February 1946, file 730 05 01 EK 1–11 16–111, Republic of Turkey Prime Ministry General Directory of State Archives, 29.

50 Kuruç, *Belgelerle*, vol. 2, 227.

that the majority of the workforce comprised women and girls.[51] The fact that women made up twenty-six per cent of the state textile workforce by 1945 supports my argument in the previous chapter regarding the higher female labour participation rate in Istanbul.[52] Women's presence in all industrial workplaces covered by the labour code was even lower, at seventeen per cent.[53]

The picture was the opposite for child labour. In 1945, workers under eighteen made up thirty per cent of the workforce at state textile factories. The percentage of children under fourteen was six per cent. Factory inspectors noted the unfavourable comparison between the use of child labour in the Turkish textile industry with the Western European and American textile industries, and cited the high Turkish figure as one of the reasons behind labour instability and low skill levels in the state textile industry.[54]

The lack of skilled labour resulted in labour hoarding at the Bakırköy and other state textile factories. According to a 1945 inspection report, the actual size of the Bakırköy workforce was fifty-one per cent higher than a normal workforce of one thousand workers. Two years later, the factory director complained that the fourfold increase in the factory's workforce after Sümerbank had taken over did not bring a corresponding increase in production. In the face of high labour costs in production, the practice came under increasing criticism, but it was inevitable according to an inspection report from 1942. Lack of skills and a high level of absenteeism obliged state factories to employ backup workers.[55] In 1939, a German industrial expert compared the performance of Turkish and German weavers: "There are factories [in Germany] where a weaver attends sixteen looms; we would be happy if a weaver attended eight looms because today, on average, a weaver attends only six. Both the volume and quality of production at every stage of weaving depends on the weaver."[56] To state inspectors, labour hoarding was normal because of "the infancy of [the Turkish] industry." As late as 1971, only 9.7 per cent of all textile workers employed in large enterprises in Istanbul were skilled.[57]

---

51 Cavid, "Bakırköy Bez Fabrikası," 12.

52 "İşletmede İnsan," 8–10.

53 *Çalışma Vekâleti Dergisi*, no. 24 (1947), 88.

54 "İşletmede İnsan," 10.

55 Sümerbank Genel Müdürlük Yüksek Katına, "Fabrikalarımızın," 29; "97 Yıl Önce Kurulan Fabrika," *Türk İşçisi* (1947); "*Sümerbank 1942 Yılı Umumi Murakebe Heyeti* Raporu," *Sümerbank 1942 Senesi Faaliyet ve Hesap Devresine Ait İdare Meclisi Raporu, Bilanço, Kâr ve Zarar Hesabı* (Ankara, 1943), 160, Amb./Db.No: K.A./230.1/338.4, Prime Ministry Supreme Auditory Board Archives.

56 Von der Porten, "Kayseri Fabrikası İplik ve Dokuma Daireleri Hakkında".

57 "İşletmede İnsan," 4; Sabahaddin Zaim, *Bölge ve Şehir Planlaması Yönünden Istanbul Sanayi Bölgeleri* (Istanbul: Istanbul Üniversitesi Yayınları, 1971), 269.

The loose recruitment policy at the Bakırköy Factory was the combined result of managerial incompetence and the labour market structure. Bureaucratic employment practices, such as formal recruitment and selection, promotion and career structures, and job evaluation and seniority systems were not institutionalised. Standardised procedures for dealing with employees and an internal labour market providing substantial opportunities for employees within the organisation did not exist at the factory. As we shall see below, labour turnover and mobility were to some extent the cost of this. Industrial experts continued to expose the costs and other deleterious consequences of the lack of any standardisation of job requirements, promotion ladders, and merit-rating systems. They insistently called for more systematic employment relations including elaborate training programmes and policies on pay retention, as well as promotion. As we shall see later in this chapter, the persistent turnover of labour increasingly came under the spotlight as a direct result of the problematic employment policy of the 1940s. But the lack of an inexperienced working class is not the only factor that negatively affects the transfer of industrial knowledge and practice. For the transfer to achieve its "theoretical" productivity, managerial experience and skill were also a prerequisite.[58]

4 Wages: Policy, Payment Systems, and Valorisation

Experts writing on industrial workers in Turkey in the 1930s and 1940s were in unanimous agreement on two points: wages were low, and labour costs in production were high. The rates of remuneration across the country were a reflection of the country's poverty, reported the International Labour Organization in 1949. Most workers lived at a bare subsistence level, and many below it. Any increase in wage rates was swallowed up by the increase in the cost of living; money wages were far too low even to cover a minimum standard of living.[59] It is perhaps partly due to this overall bleak picture that several historians argued that state workers were privileged in terms of their wage levels.[60] All other

58 Alain Lipietz, *Mirages and Miracles: The Crisis in Global Fordism* (New York: Verso, 1987), 61.

59 International Labour Office, *"Labour Problems in Turkey," Report of a Mission of the International Labour Office* (Geneva: ILO, 1950), 16; Thornburg et. al., *Economic Appraisal*, 130.

60 Korkut Boratav, *100 Soruda Gelir Dağılımı* (Istanbul: Gerçek Yayınları, 1969), 162; Ahmet İnsel, *Düzen ve Kalkınma Kıskacında Türkiye, Kalkınma Sürecinde Devletin Rolü* (Istanbul: Ayrıntı Yayınları, 1996), 228–229; Ahmet İnsel, "Devletçiliğin Anatomisi," *Cumhuriyet Dönemi Türkiye Ansiklopedisi*, vol. 2 (Istanbul: İletişim Yayınları, 1984), 422; Yıldırım Koç, *Türkiye'de İşçi Sınıfı ve Sendikacılık Tarihi: Olaylar-Değerlendirmeler*

issues notwithstanding, there are two data-related problems with such conclusions. First, the skewed aggregate data conceals the wide variation in wages within and between state factories. Second, there were considerable discrepancies between the formal wage policy and its implementation.

Criticism over Sümerbank's lack of a consistent wage policy started as early as 1936. The absence of a clear and accessible system of remuneration hindered the formation of a stable labour force. The incompetence in bookkeeping and the inability to present a clear structure of wage rates created dramatically different results, not only among state factories but within a single factory as well. As a result, significant wage discrepancies both within and across factories abounded. In 1945, there was a more than two hundred per cent difference between the average hourly wages in the Isparta and Defterdar factories.[61] A parliamentary discussion in 1943 problematised inconsistent wage scales at state textiles for causing unfair wage differences between unskilled and skilled workers that favoured the former group.[62] By the end of the decade, because they did not have a consistent and effort-based wage policy, state factories were increasingly losing their workers to private factories, where task assignment based on skill evaluation and vocational training was gaining ground.[63] A contemporary sociologist put it succinctly in 1954 that "until very recently" wage levels at state factories were determined on the basis of "social justice and moral deliberation."[64]

(Ankara: Türkiye Yol-İş Sendikası Yayınları, 1996), 30; M. Şehmuz Güzel, "1940'larda İşgücünün (İşçilerin) Özellikleri," *Mülkiyeliler Birliği Dergisi*, no. 119 (1940), 18–22.

61 Bereznitsky, *Kayseri Bez Fabrikası Hakkında* (n.p., 1936); "Sümerbank Birleşik Pamuk İpliği ve Dokuma Fabrikaları Müessesesi 1939 Yılı Umumi Murakebe Heyeti Raporu, 37," *Sümerbank 1939 Yılı Umumi Murakebe Heyeti Raporu* (Ankara: Titaş Basımevi, 1940), 39, Amb./Db.No: K.A./ 255.07.02.01.06.3227, Prime Ministry Supreme Auditory Board Archives; Hösli, *Ereğli Bez Fabrikası Hakkında Rapor* (n.p., 1940); Hösli, *Nazilli Bez Fabrikası Hakkında Rapor*; Hösli, *Merinos Fabrikası Hakkında Rapor* (n.p., 1943); "Sümerbank 1942 Senesi Faaliyet ve Hesap Devresine Ait İdare Meclisi Raporu, Bilanço, Kâr ve Zarar Hesabı," *Sümerbank 1942 Yılı Umumi Murakebe Heyeti Raporu* (Ankara: Başvekalet Devlet Matbaası, 1943), 23; Sümerbank Genel Müdürlük Yüksek Katına, "Fabrikalarımızın," 31; Sabahaddin Zaim, "Türkiye Mensucat Sanayiinde Ücretler," *Sosyal Siyaset Konferansları*, Sekizinci Kitap (1956), 37–8; "Sümerbank İplik ve Dokuma Fabrikaları Müessesesi 1948 Yılı Raporu," 33–4.

62 *3460 Sayılı Kanuna Bağlı Devlet Ekonomi Kurumlarının 1943 Yılı İşlemleriyle Bilanço ve Kâr ve Zarar Hesaplarını İnceleyen Genel Kurul Tutanağı* (Ankara: Başbakanlık Devlet Matbaası, 1945).

63 Suat Aray, "İktisadi Devlet Teşekkülleri Ücret Rejimi," 1951, Register K.A./255.07.02.01.06.1119, Prime Ministry Supreme Auditory Board Archives.

64 Ziyaeddin Fahri Fındıkoğlu, "Türkiye'de Sınai Sosyoloji Araştırmaları 1-Defterdar Fabrikası," *Feshane Mensucat Meslek Dergisi* 2, no. 12 (1954), 393.

The foreman was an important factor in this process of deliberation. He played an important role in this industrial wage structure, which was nothing more than a hotchpotch of inconsistencies and inequities. On a petition for a pay raise, the foreman's evaluation of the worker would be decisive, making the worker's economic success dependent on their personal relationship with their foreman and the foreman's arbitrary exercise of power. As a result, different individuals doing the same job were often paid very different rates. Rate variation within and across departments was common. At Bakırköy, especially in the 1940s, workers often filed petitions addressing the inequities in intraplant rate structures, suggesting that these relative differences were as important to workers as their absolute wage levels.

The wage scales were inflexible and not updated according to changes in the workforce. When a worker was transferred from one state textile factory to another to work in the exact same role, they suffered a wage cut if the corresponding wage scale was not available. Having been transferred from Nazilli to Bakırköy in 1951, Ahmet lost fifteen per cent of his hourly wage, for example.[65] Kamil also suffered from a loss of wages after starting to work at Bakırköy. His salary at Bakırköy in 1947 was sixteen per cent lower than his previous salary at another state textile factory in 1944. İbrahim, a highly skilled worker, had earned seventy-five piasters an hour at the Ereğli Factory. When he started working at the Bakırköy Factory in 1949, he was given a starting hourly wage of fifty-five piasters during his six-month trial period. He confronted the factory director after the six months had passed. His wage was not raised and he demanded to be tested again.[66]

In his 2007 book on workers in the early republican period, Ahmet Makal made a set of wage calculations comparing state and private factories, and concluded that state workers had not distinctly suffered from the torments of industrialisation.[67] My findings show otherwise. First, the data on wages at the Bakırköy Factory in inspection reports show that the average daily wage at Bakırköy was seventeen per cent lower than Makal's figure for state textile factories in Istanbul.[68] Second, data from the worker files also show lower wages.

65 Personnel file of Ahmet Ergün.

66 Personnel files of Ahmet Cansızoğlu and Kamil Uygun; Daysal, "Bakırköy Bez Fabrikasında."

67 Ahmet Makal, *Ameleden İşçiye: Erken Cumhuriyet Dönemi Emek Tarihi Çalışmaları* (Istanbul: İletişim Yayınları, 2007), 159.

68 "Sümerbank İplik ve Dokuma Fabrikaları Müessesesi 1945 Yılı Raporu," *Sümerbank 1945 Senesi Faaliyet ve Hesap Devresine Ait İdare Meclisi Raporu, Bilanço, Kâr ve Zarar Hesabı* (Ankara: Başbakanlık Devlet Matbaası, 1946), 32; Ahmet Makal, *Ameleden İşçiye*, 132–133;

For example, a worker from the dyeing workshop made eighteen piasters an hour in 1943; that is, 198 piasters a day if he worked eleven hours as stipulated by the National Defence Act (more on this below). His hourly wage had increased by only seven piasters since 1936, although according to Makal's calculations, nominal wages almost doubled between 1938 and 1943. Between 1945 and 1948, Cemil was also trying very hard to make ends meet. He left the factory twice; the first time to work at a private factory in Istanbul (although he did not mention this when he was leaving) and the second time because he and his wife could not live on his wages even though they did not have children. When he came back in 1948, his hourly wage was still twenty-five piasters.

After ten years at the factory, a weaver, Mehmet, was earning twenty-five piasters an hour in 1947, which, he wrote, was "not enough even for one person, let alone a family." In 1942, his monthly wage had been 140 liras; five years later, he was making only fifty-two liras per month. He decided to file a petition after having to sell furniture to buy food for his family. Mehmet's file reveals a very important point regarding the way that wage data was kept. Mehmet actually earned twenty-five piasters an hour, but his hourly wage was recorded as thirty-five piasters. The factory wage cards did not break down the wage figures, but we can safely assume that the higher figure was his wage before taxation, and that Mehmet was paying twenty-eight per cent tax. A 1945 report gave the average hourly wages in the Bakırköy weavery and spinnery as 37.7 piasters and 33.3 piasters.[69] In their petitions, workers claimed to earn around twenty per cent less than these figures.

Later in this chapter and in the next two chapters, I introduce a variety of cases where Bakırköy workers describe their extremely hard living conditions. In most cases, their demands for a wage increase are rejected because they are found not to meet the necessary conditions. These conditions, however, are never clearly defined and, in many cases, workers work for the same wage for years.

Given the low remuneration, the high labour costs in production could be attributed to low labour productivity. The German industrial experts writing on state textile factories in the 1930s had two main solutions to this, namely, vocational training and the piece-work system. The second was already being

---

Makal based his calculations on the wage data published by Zaim in 1956. See: Sabahaddin Zaim, *Istanbul Mensucat Sanayiinin Bünyesi ve Ücretler* (Istanbul: Istanbul Üniversitesi İktisat Fakültesi Yayını, 1956).

69 Sümerbank Genel Müdürlük Yüksek Katına, "Fabrikalarımızın," 30. The lira contains 100 piasters.

implemented to some extent at state factories by the mid-1930s, but because industrial engineers believed that most employment and labour-relations problems could be solved through a properly devised incentive wage, they pressed for its wider and better use. In 1936, von der Porten wrote: "Piece rate is a better wage system for a mechanised factory like Bakırköy, where the labour movement has little effect, and hard work and attention are of the utmost importance for productivity." Piece-rate payment would increase the production incentive while simultaneously improving shop-floor control, which was a burning problem at the factory, as we shall see below. Another foreign expert, Klopfer, agreed, adding that because state textile factories were highly mechanised, the priority was to reduce unproductive machine time. Based on his observations in American factories, he proposed an incentive pay system based on saving this time. The method was simple enough to be understood by "the simplest of the workers," he wrote, but it would be most beneficial when used with skilled workers. There was only one group of workers who would not have an interest in this payment system: the girls, "because they are obliged to give their earnings away to their families anyway."[70]

At state factories, carefully determined and implemented piece-rate schemes were rare, while examples of faulty calculations and inconsistencies abound in the reports. For example, at Bakırköy, the ten per cent difference between planned and actual labour costs in 1937 was partly due to mistakes in the determination of wage norms.[71] Sources are curiously silent on norm determination except for a 1939 inspection report, which mentions that the piece rates at cotton textile factories were fixed by Sümerbank based on the "characteristics" of each factory. What these characteristics were, or how they played out for the Bakırköy Factory, we cannot know.[72] The factory's weaving shop operated under "best practice" rules, with workers paid according to the number of shuttles they made instead of the weight or length of the fabric weaved, for that would have led to unfairly higher wages for those weaving coarser yarn or wider wefts.

Best practice in the spinning shop, however, was an entirely different matter, and two German experts were surprised by the situation they found there

70 Von der Porten, "Feshane ve Hereke Fabrikaları Tetkiklerine Dair," 1936, Register K.A./255.07.02.01.06.1285; Hösli, *Bakırköy Bez Fabrikası Hakkında Rapor*; Klopfer, *Sümerbank Memur ve Amelelerine Prim ve İkramiye Esasları hak*, (n.p., 1941).

71 Sachsenberg, "Bakırköy Bez Fabrikası Organizasyonu Hakkında".

72 "Sümerbank Birleşik Pamuk İpliği ve Dokuma Fabrikaları Müessesesi 1939 Yılı Umumi Murakebe Heyeti Raporu," 37.

on different occasions.[73] "They think they are implementing piece rates," wrote von der Porten, "by paying the male and female workers according to the hank they produce." He compared the counters attached to the machines to a goods-vehicle tachometer. Just as the tachometer counting the rotations of the wheels could not indicate the weight of cargo transported, a counter counting the rotation of the spindles could not indicate the amount of yarn spun. Not only that, the counters continued to rotate even when the yarn was broken, leaving the spindles running idle, a recurrent problem. Sachsenberg reported the same problem both with spinning machines and drawing frames a year later. All the same, it appears that von der Porten's warning was not taken seriously. During his visit, von der Porten's critical eye observed experiments with different pay systems and noted an incident that hints at the intricacies of the decision-making process in centrally planned production. A shop-floor engineer objected to von der Porten's suggestion that workers be paid for the yarn they spun rather than the rotations of the spindles. The engineer argued that this would adversely affect the quality of spun yarn. Von der Porten noted that after protracted discussions, the director of Sümerbank's Istanbul office, Muhip Bey, intervened on behalf of the factory engineer and insisted that the current practice was wholly fair and accurate.

What, then, was the experience of labour in this encounter with technology and regulations? Much like any other piece-rate shop floor, the Bakırköy workers did not confront these imposed conditions of labour as passive objects. Asım told me how weavers actively sought to manipulate the piece rate, a strategy Michael Burawoy called "making out" and defined as a conscious collective worker effort to restrict the amount of work to a jointly regulated upper limit.[74] Here is how and why Asım and his fellow workers did it:

> In a piece-rate system, you are paid as much as you work. If you don't work at all, you get nothing. But there is something else, you see, when you do more than the rate, they do not pay you accordingly, because it would be a lot of money. Then you are actually not paid accordingly when you work hard … If you work hard, [later] you get fifty per cent of what you normally earn. So, I slowed down the job … For example, how much did I use to earn? [his wife interrupts: one hundred and twenty liras] They were supposed to pay one hundred and eighty liras, they never

73 Sachsenberg, "Bakırköy Bez Fabrikası Organizasyonu Hakkında"; Max von der Porten, "Bakırköy Bez Fabrikası Hakkında," 1936, Register K.A./255.07.02.01.06.1285.

74 Burawoy, *Politics of Production*, 131.

> paid that much. I mean there is the foreman who follows you, he keeps an eye on you, but we were all alert. We slowed down the pace, the foreman could not tell. He never paid me the right amount, why would I wear myself out? Others did the same.[75]

Workers controlled their production to take advantage of the progressive income tax as well. Daily wages below eighty piasters were not taxed, between eighty and 120 piasters, workers were taxed on the forty piasters only. Above 120 piasters a day, the full amount was taxed. A 1939 inspection report on state cotton factories reported that workers manipulated the piece rate accordingly.[76] But this did not diminish the faith in the piece-rate system. Inspection reports from later years complained of the slow and problematic implementation of piece-rate payments in spinning compared with weaving shops, suggesting that gender continued to play an important role in skill evaluation and labour remuneration.

In 1939, for example, of the 7,789 workers at four cotton textile factories (Nazilli, Kayseri, Ereğli, and Bakırköy), 4,303 were paid piece rates and worked mostly in weaving preparation and weaving shops.[77] While many spinners at the Kayseri Factory were earning hourly wages, all weavers were on piece rate.[78] In 1943, 583 out of 869 weavers at Bakırköy were on piece rate.[79] In 1945, 821 workers, that is, fifty-four per cent of the workforce at Bakırköy, worked on piece rate.[80]

A group of employees, however, happily remained untouched by the piece rate until 1949. In a petition addressed to the municipal branch of the Republican People's Party in July 1949, thirty-two foremen and head foremen from the Bakırköy Factory protested the implementation of the piece rate wage system.[81] "We have devoted our lives to the factory," they wrote, "we expected

75 Kocabaş, interview.

76 "Sümerbank Birleşik Pamuk İpliği ve Dokuma Fabrikaları Müessesesi 1939 Yılı Umumi Murakebe Heyeti Raporu," 39.

77 "Sümerbank Birleşik Pamuk İpliği ve Dokuma Fabrikaları Müessesesi 1939 Yılı Umumi Murakebe Heyeti Raporu," 37.

78 Von der Porten, "Kayseri Fabrikası İplik ve Dokuma Daireleri Hakkında."

79 "Sümerbank 1942 Yılı Umumi Murakebe Heyeti Raporu," 162.

80 "Fabrikalarımızın 1945 Senesi Faaliyetleri, Neticeleri ve Tahlilleri," 9 February 1946, file 730 05 01 EK 1–11 16–111, Republic of Turkey Prime Ministry General Directory of State Archives, 29.

81 "C.H.P. İlçe İdare Kurulu Başkanlığına," Correspondence between 22 July 1949 and 10 March 1950, file 490.01.1444.23.1, Republic of Turkey Prime Ministry General Directory of State Archives.

appreciation and affection from the management; instead, our devotion has been totally disregarded." Piece rates, they claimed, would not only jeopardize their future; it would also demoralise them and thus damage productivity. Two important points arise from the replies to this petition. First is the anxious urge among the party members to help the foremen. "Lately, trust in us among workers has increased," one member wrote, implying growing competition with the opposition party, and argued, "it is important especially now to pay attention to this demand." Second, the business minister, in his response, strongly defended the piece rate as the more rational and advanced wage system, citing its recent implementation at the Bakırköy spinnery as proof. The foremen, the minister claimed, feared that the piece rate would reveal their indifference to work and decrease their salaries. The petition was declined, and the implementation went through, suggesting the emergence of a new managerial style that would limit the authority of the foreman on the shop floor. For the period under discussion here, however, their authority remained unchallenged.

5 Wages and the Working Day during the War

The earliest information on the length and organisation of the working day at the Bakırköy Factory is found in a critical report by von der Porten in 1936 on the two work shifts of eleven hours each. The factory engineers seemed to him to be either unaware of, or indifferent to, the low work efficiency during the night shift. Due to a lack of labour controls, it was extremely difficult to measure the amount of work being done, and so he based his calculations on electricity consumption. The figures he arrived at were indeed striking. While electricity consumption at night should have represented twenty-seven per cent of the month's consumption, it was only eleven per cent. The figure was even lower for the month of August, when efficiency was at its lowest. Despite these calculations, the factory engineers refused to shorten the working day, for the factory was under great pressure to meet the work programme. A reduction in production could not be risked. Von der Porten insisted that implementing two work shifts of eight hours instead of eleven would not damage production. In the end, he managed to convince the engineers to experiment with a few looms and compare the results.[82]

82 Max von der Porten, "Bakırköy Bez Fabrikası Hakkında."

Von der Porten's main goal was to reduce the production costs, in this case, by saving on energy, and, in general, by tightening labour controls. Nowhere in his reports did he refer to the hardships, night shifts, or long hours of work enforced upon workers.[83] Likewise, the connection between the length of the working day and worker wellbeing got no mention in other documents from the early years of state factories. In fact, the 1936 Labour Code had limited the working day to eight hours and the working week to forty-eight hours, allowing three hours of overtime work for a maximum of ninety days a year and providing extra remuneration for overtime work. A weekly rest day was introduced for employees at state offices and industrial enterprises in 1925, and it was increased to thirty-six hours starting from Saturday noon in 1935.[84] But, in practice the working day was extended beyond these limits. In a 1939 report, again by von der Porten, he mentions the practical reduction of the working day to eight hours the previous year. Factories were ordered to rearrange their hourly wages to avoid possible wage losses. But for workers on piece rate no such measurement was taken. This, von der Porten warned in 1939, would alienate workers on piece rate.[85] And it did at the Bakırköy Factory. Mustafa described his situation in powerful words when the working day at the Bakırköy weavery was shortened to eight hours (for a certain amount of time, as we shall see below): "I am in a terrible situation for this reason. I have been put off with the promise of an increase so far which caused my damnification. Taking my current situation into consideration, I would kindly ask for an increase in my hourly wage with utmost respect."[86]

The practice did not last long. The enactment of the National Defence Act on 18 January 1940 overturned the 1936 Labour Code's protective provisions.[87] Maximum hours of work were prolonged from eight to eleven in the day.[88] The eleven-hour working day was still common by the end of the 1940s.[89] When

---

83 I have written elsewhere about the transfer of the German version of scientific management, *Rationalisierung*, to Turkish state factories in the 1930s and how it lost its emphasis on the "humanisation" of work during this transfer. See: "Experts, Exiles, and Textiles: German 'Rationalisierung' on 1930s Turkish Shop Floor," *International Review of Social History* 66, no. 2 (2021).

84 Sait Dilik, "Atatürk Döneminde Sosyal Politika," *Ankara Üniversitesi SBF Dergisi* 40, no. 1 (1985), 97.

85 Von der Porten, "Kayseri Fabrikası İplik ve Dokuma Daireleri Hakkında."

86 Personnel file of Mustafa Arap.

87 Nusret Ekin, "Türkiye'de Endüstri İlişkilerinin Gelişimi ve 1936 İş Kanunu," *Sosyal Siyaset Konferansları Dergisi*, no. 35–36 (1986), 33–51.

88 Makal, *Ameleden İşçiye*, 196.

89 Rebi Barkın, "Heder Olan İş Saatleri," *Hürbilek*, 19 June 1948; ILO, "Labour Problems in Turkey," 18.

I asked Asım, a retired worker from Bakırköy, if he ever worked eleven hours a day after he came back from the army in 1943, he responded with laughter and a hand gesture that said: plenty. He also noted that management would force workers to punch their cards at the end of the eighth hour on the days that they worked for eleven hours in order not to pay the overtime remuneration. Asım explained how this administrative infraction affected the accord workers and those paid hourly differently: "For the accord workers it is the same thing [i.e., they still got the pay according to how much they produced]. For those paid hourly, it was twelve to thirteen hours of work [for eight hours' payment]."[90] Another worker, Ahmet, also reported having worked for twelve hours a day before he left for the army in 1943.[91]

At the Bakırköy Factory, the war conditions exacerbated problems of production integration between shops. In 1942, because the spinnery could not keep up with the weavery, the factory had to buy yarn from the Kayseri and Nazilli factories.[92] Workers at the spinnery worked day and night to supply enough yarn to the weavers and to end the factory's dependence on other state textile factories.[93] In 1942, the prime minister explained the cotton supply crisis as follows: "The handlooms are increasing at a surprising rate. Those who possess four looms in their homes easily become rich ... They can live very well by reselling the yarn they buy from the state at a low price [and sell] to people at four or five times the original price."[94] Cotton yarn shortages and the low-quality yarn bought from state factories decreased the productivity of prominent private factories as well.[95] At the four state-owned cotton factories, the lower quality warp yarn, which would break easily, reduced automatic loom productivity to the extent that even the best weaver could attend to fewer than eight looms. Production efficiency in these factories was barely above ffity per cent in 1940.[96] Labour hoarding was further increasing the labour costs in production, but, as discussed above, at this point it was considered inevitable.

---

90 Kocabaş, interview.

91 Interview with Ahmet Cansızoğlu by Yıldırım Koç, 1988, video recording *V1/51*, Trade Union Movement in Turkey Oral History Collection.

92 Hösli, *Bakırköy Bez Fabrikası Hakkında Rapor*, 6.

93 Sümerbank Genel Müdürlük Yüksek Katına, "Fabrikalarımızın," 12.

94 Cited in Kemal H. Karpat, *Turkey's Politics: The Transition to a Multi-Party System* (New Jersey: Princeton University Press, 2016), 90.

95 *İktisadi Yürüyüş*, no. 4 (1940), 16.

96 "Sümerbank Birleşik Pamuk İpliği ve Dokuma Fabrikaları Müessesesi 1940 Yılı Raporu," *Sümerbank 1940 Senesi Faaliyet ve Hesap Devresine Ait İdare Meclisi Raporu, Bilanço, Kâr ve Zarar Hesabı*, 17, 25.

Although mobilisation and difficulties in procuring equipment and spare parts from abroad hampered industrialisation during the war, the profits of the state textile factories increased from just over nine per cent of the capital invested in 1940 to forty-seven per cent in 1945. Between 1942 and 1943, the Bakırköy Factory also increased its profits almost fourfold despite the increase in production costs due to more expensive raw materials, higher wages, and the expansion of the workforce. The factory directors boasted that the state factories had fulfilled the yearly production programmes.[97] But there was a twist. Four years into the war, an industrial engineer from Hungary, Hösli, compiled a detailed report on the Bakırköy Factory and revealed a very interesting picture of changes on the shop floor. He made two main points.

First, the work programmes had been prepared in such a way as to allow for low levels of production efficiency. The figures may have matched up, but this did not mean that state factories were operating at "normal productivity levels."[98] The increase in production was actually the result of work intensification. From 1942 to 1943, increase in productivity lagged behind the increase in the utilisation rate. For example, the weavery had an almost one hundred per cent rate of use, but only sixty-eight per cent productivity was achieved. Second, average wages increased at the factory but so did the total hours of work. The increase in production was thus a direct result of work intensification, and it was achieved at the expense of wearing down the workers. Having been forced to work on holidays, many workers left the factory due to exhaustion, he noted. Together, labour scarcity and poor machine maintenance accounted for more than ninety per cent of the unproductive time on the shop floor.[99]

To put a human face to all these figures, let us now hear from Asım on his experience of this work intensification. When he mentioned in passing during our conversation that he was called to work on religious holidays, I confronted him for not refusing, and he got angry: "One cannot say I am not coming. It just does not work, you have to deal with the head foreman, it does not work ... We had to go. There is no such thing as a religious festivity for you [i.e., the worker] ... you go to the factory on the religious festival and get paid according to the output leve." I then asked him whether work on official holidays was remunerated extra, and got yet another agitated response: "What overtime pay are you talking about? ... Who cares about your rest time? The guys tell you to

97 United Nations, *Egypt, Israel and Turkey*, 17–18; United Nations, *Review of Economic Conditions in the Middle East 1951–1952* (New York, 1953), 36.

98 Hösli, *Bakırköy Bez Fabrikası Hakkında Rapor*, 2, 16; "Fabrikalarımızın 1945 Senesi Faaliyetleri, Neticeleri ve Tahlilleri," 9 February 1946, file 730 05 01 EK 1–11 16–111, Republic of Turkey Prime Ministry General Directory of State Archives.

99 Hösli, *Bakırköy*, 10–19.

come. I went on Sundays, there was nobody else than me, the factory was not working. It was Sunday but we went anyway because the weavery was lagging behind."

The weavers worked hard and long, and they did everything in their power to make it bearable. Their structural bargaining power helped them to an extent, but they, and the other Bakırköy workers, had a strong adversary on the shop floor.

6 Labour Discipline

Following the managerial revolution of the late nineteenth and early twentieth centuries, the work of "the skilled engineer … as pacemaker and technical supervisor" rendered the foreman's determination of job tasks, skill levels, and appropriate pay redundant.[100] The foreign expert reports on Turkish state textile factories were written by these very engineers, and their calls for technical control fell on deaf ears except for one aspect: the gradual replacement of time-based payment with incentive payment systems. Apart from that, labour control was "simple" or "hierarchical," meaning that workers were under the direct supervision of the foreman. The slow and problematic implementation of incentive wage systems coupled with the failure to adopt bureaucratic and technical forms of control was to a large extent compensated by disciplinary measures and foreman pressure.

But who were the foremen at the state textile factories? What kind of authority did they have and how did they use it? The foreman's discretionary power was at work to a large extent in the allocation of tasks and determination of the skill levels required to realize those tasks. He assigned skill levels and tasks to workers, ensured that the appropriate equipment was in working order,

100 John Foster, *Class Struggle and the Industrial Revolution* (London: Routledge, 1974), 227. For the change in the foreman's role and status, see especially the following contemporary publications: "Foremen and superintendents," *Scientific American* 22, no. 6 (1870); Allen Rogers, "The Technically Trained Foreman," *Scientific American* 105, no. 12 (1911); Hollis Godfrey, "The Foreman," *The Annals of the American Academy of Political and Social Science* 85 (1919); Benjamin E. Mallary, "The Foreman-His Training and Education," *The Annals of the American Academy of Political and Social Science* 91 (1920); Louis Ruthenburg, "Training the foremen of a manufacturing organisation," *SAE Transactions* 20 (1925); William F. Whyte and Burleigh B. Gardner, "Facing the foreman's problems," *Applied Anthropology* 4, no. 2 (1945); Kenneth K. Kolker, "The Changing Status of the Foreman," *Bulletin of the Business Historical Society* 22, no. 3 (1948); Donald E. Wray, "Marginal Men of Industry: The Foremen," *American Journal of Sociology* 54, no. 4

evaluated the performance of the workers, and reported any workers that violated labour discipline to the higher management of the factory. The power of the foreman was defined as follows in the file of a Bakırköy worker: "The whole department will continue to operate as before, under the total control and responsibility of the foremen." In another file, the superintendent of the weaving department warned a foreman about his unit's poor performance and threatened that he would not give this unit any further jobs unless production was increased.[101]

We do not have records on the background and mobility of foremen or the process by which they were recruited. In the 1930s, there was no formal specialised education: at Kayseri, Linke remarked on the hasty training of two dozen foremen "who had just reached the first stage of manhood."[102] The anecdotal evidence from Istanbul factories suggest that it took at least some years of practice on the shop floor to become a foreman. They were mainly "yesterday's workers," as Lewis Siegelbaum termed the Soviet foremen of the 1930s, who commanded respect on the shop floor mainly through their skill, experience, and age.[103] In 1943, Hösli held the foremen at the Bakırköy Factory responsible for the poor technical conditions of production. Because the foremen are not trained properly, he wrote, labour control is inadequate. The foremen employed rule-of-thumb methods to use machines and train workers. Sümerbank tried to organise in-service training for its foremen in the following years, but by the end of the decade, foreman training was still insufficient.[104]

Although the foreman was essential to the maintenance of discipline on the shop floor, he was not part of the management. The collar line was a significant boundary on the shop floor. The reader will remember Hidayet Usta's surprise and delight at eating at the same table with the engineers and managers. At the Kayseri Factory, Turga embarked on what Linke called "an experiment in democracy" by instituting a weekly tea party to enable the foremen

(1949); Sidney C. Sufrin, "Foremen and Their Social Adjustment," *Industrial and Labor Relations Review* 4, no. 3 (1951); Robert G. Scigliano, "Trade-Unionism and the Industrial Foreman," *The Journal of Business* 27, no. 4 (1954).

101 Personnel files of Mehmet Hetman and Ahmet Çelenoğlu.

102 Linke, *Allah Dethroned*, 306.

103 Lewis H. Siegelbaum, "Masters of the Shop Floor: Foremen and Soviet Industrialisation," in *Stalinism: Its Nature and Aftermath, eds.* Nick Lampert and Gábor T. Rittersporn (London: Palgrave Macmillan, 1992), 176.

104 Sümerbank Genel Müdürlük, "Sümerbank Sanayiinin İhtiyacı Olan Elemanı Yetiştirme Planı Hakkında," 26 February 1946, file 730 05 01 EK 1–11 16–111, Republic of Turkey Prime Ministry General Directory of State Archives; *Çalışma Vekâleti Dergisi*, no. 24 (1947), 70; Barker, *The Economy of Turkey*, 116–7.

and engineers to fraternise. After a few weeks, the engineers protested, claiming that this was undermining their authority over the foremen and workers. The director was disappointed with the reaction of the engineers, which Linke attributed to their impatience and ambition to climb the bureaucratic ladder at the expense of losing contact with the working men on the shop floor.[105]

An incident at the Bakırköy Factory that was reported in the trade union newspaper reveals the extent of this disconnect between the foreman and engineer. When the operations superintendent scolded the head foreman for some broken windows in the weavery, the head foreman reminded him of the workers' multiple requests to open the windows. The weavery was unbearably hot and humid, the head foreman explained, and because the management did nothing, some workers resorted to purposefully breaking the windows. He agreed to pay for them from his pocket. But the superintendent was not content; he called the police on the head foreman and the vice foreman, and humiliated the two men. Within the same week, a second incident on the shop floor set another foreman in direct conflict with an engineer. The engineer of the repair workshop had made a habit of taking spare parts for his car from the factory. When the foreman warned him that upper management was aware of the situation but refused to help him, the engineer slapped and swore at the foreman.[106]

We can see that the foremen were clearly distinguished from the management, but they were also not perceived as one of their own by the workers. Hüseyin and İsmail explain why. Decisions on wage increases were made by the head foreman, although, as I mentioned above, any raise would also have to be approved by the upper echelons of the factory management. Skill, and consequently wage, valorisation is an intrinsic mechanism of labour control and the foremen at Bakırköy made extensive use of this mechanism. The wages were paid by the head foreman with the assistance of the other foremen, we learn from a weaver's file.[107] To Hüseyin, the head foreman of his department was an employer who had "contempt for the workers." In the twenty-six years they worked together, Hüseyin did not once hear him say "you are doing well." On the shop floor, he never greeted the workers, which Hüseyin interpreted as a sign of their different social status. Both he and İsmail told me that the majority of the workers supported the worker representative candidates who

105 Linke, *Allah Dethroned*, 309.

106 "Bakırköy Bez Fabrikası Basit Bir Hadiseyi Ne Maksatla Polise Aksettirdi?" and "Bir Hadise Daha," *Hürbilek*, 19 June 1948.

107 Personnel file of Ahmet Çelenoğlu.

had been endorsed by the trade unions after 1947, and these candidates were not foremen. Hüseyin explained that "we could only tell our problems to those like us, not to those who are higher in status."[108]

The factory was run by the iron hand and arbitrary justice of the foreman, who continued to be the prime regulator of work efforts on the shop floor. The foreman applied elements of the "drive system," such as close supervision, abuse, profanity, and threats, to maintain or increase effort levels.[109] Physical violence also took place. A rare petition by a female worker, Emine, sheds light on the misconduct by foremen at the Bakırköy Factory. When she showed up late to work due to familial responsibilities, the foreman furiously shouted at her. Unable to decipher his words, Emine asked him to repeat what he had said. The incident escalated quickly, with the foreman raising his hand to hit her, only to be stopped by the head foreman. "I am a married woman with children," Emine wrote, "I come to work to feed my children, not to be beaten by the foremen!"[110] Hüseyin also reported verbal and physical abuse by his head foreman.

Workers were fined for violating disciplinary rules, with the personnel department deducting the specified amount from their paycheques. I have found a total of 117 receipts for fines dating from 1941 to 1951 just in the sample of workers' files that I had access to. Based on my interviews and the foreign expert reports, it would not be unreasonable to assume that the absence of receipts for fines prior to 1941 is merely down to poor record keeping. Another interesting point about the distribution of fines over time lends further support to this speculation. Fines increased considerably after 1947, that is, when trade unionism started, suggesting that the factory management felt the need for more accurate record keeping at this time.

Violations over labour discipline covered a wide variety of offences, such as lateness, absenteeism, the misuse of equipment, slackened effort, and insubordination. Together, lateness and absenteeism made up for more than half of the fines imposed. The second most common reason for a fine was poor performance, which is defined as "neglect" or "doing the job wrong" in the receipts, and made up almost forty per cent of all fines. Insubordination ranks third in the list. Finally, two workers were fined for damaging machinery. The gender composition of the fines presents an interesting picture, in that, although women did not even make up one quarter of the sample, they

108 Hüseyin Yılmaz, interview by the author, 4 August 2009.

109 Jacoby, *Employing Bureaucracy*, 17.

110 "Gece Postası Gazetesi Yazı İşleri Müdürlüğü Yüksek Makamına," 10 July 1955, Kemal Sülker Papers, Folder no. 402, IISH.

received more than thirty-five per cent of all fines. The most common reasons for fining women were, again, lateness, absenteeism, and poor performance. One woman was fined for sleeping in the toilet during work time.

But widespread fines and strict foreman authority did not solve the problem of unproductive time; the shop floor remained a disorganised mess. Tighter and continuous control were the sole remedy, wrote state inspectors in 1945; foreign experts were also calling for technical control. As von der Porten put it, state factories needed to adopt the principle of the rational organisation of the labour process, that is, work should drive the worker, and not the other way around.[111] But there was another major impediment to higher productivity: workers' technical illiteracy and poor machine maintenance.

7 Technical Relations and Workers' Skills

When Fazlı Turga was proudly showing his new factory machinery to the prime minister in 1934, his enthusiasm was met with concern. "I asked him about worker training and machine maintenance," the prime minister told the crowd that had gathered for the opening of the new factory building, because "worker training is an important part of our new industrial life."[112] Perhaps he had read the inspection report on the Bakırköy Factory written the same year by Bauer, who had bitterly complained about the lack of control over machine maintenance and cleaning. His report was exceptionally technical in that he mainly focused on machine cleaning, maintenance, and workshop ventilation and how this affected yarn quality. He made simple suggestions to eliminate production stoppages resulting from technical failures, such as placing a signboard with instructions on the machines for the foremen to follow when changing the bobbins. In the end, technical reorganisation is no more than a partial solution, he wrote; the real answer to the many problems can be found in the establishment of a control mechanism to compare the productivity of each machine and worker.

In the following years, both foreign experts and Sümerbank inspectors exhaustively cover the reasons and solutions for the "technological idiosyncrasies" of the production process, giving detailed information on the state of the

111 "Fabrikalarımızın 1945 Senesi Faaliyetleri, Neticeleri ve Tahlilleri," 9 February 1946, file 730 05 01 EK 1–11 16–111, Republic of Turkey Prime Ministry General Directory of State Archives; Max von der Porten, "Beykoz Deri ve Kundura Fabrikasında Memur ve Ameleden Ne Gibi Tasarruflar Yapılabileceği Hakkında," 1939, Register K.A./ 255.07.02.01.06.1075.

112 "Sanayileşme Yolunda," *Cumhuriyet*.

machinery and the appropriate technological investment that was needed.[113] The problems with the machinery at the Bakırköy Factory could be categorised into two types. One was a lack of investment in new machines and/or inadequate maintenance; the other was the inefficient use of existing machinery. In 1936, von der Porten reported that a lack of maintenance had rendered the old spinning machines and weaving looms useless. The factory manager had demanded that new machines be purchased, but, once again, foreign experts had advised against a reliance on technological investment. Change should be slower, von der Porten wrote, and the emphasis should be on scientific labour control. For the old weaving looms, the situation was different. Of the 340 looms, sixty were old and completely unusable.[114] The reader will recall the Turkish engineer who bragged that there was not a single old machine left in the factory by 1940. But, according to a state inspection report from the same year, the old looms were still in use. Comparing the four cotton textile factories (that is, Ereğli, Kayseri, Nazilli, and Bakırköy) in 1939 and 1940, the authors of the report found that unproductive machine time was the highest at the Bakırköy weavery. Maintenance was still ignored, to the point of posing a risk of industrial accidents. Between 1937 and 1940 the number of work accidents in industrial workplaces almost doubled, reaching 8,620.[115]

During his time as director of the Kayseri Factory, Fazlı Turga had a conversation with Webster over machine breakages. The problem was so severe that the replacement of broken parts made up twenty per cent of annual first costs. Although a shocking figure for foreign observers, it was seen as normal by the director, whose biggest concern was the rate of labour turnover. But the two problems were directly related. Machine maintenance was a problem because practically the entire workforce were novices, with even half-trained workers leaving the large factories for more skilled operations and better paying jobs at lower-level plants.[116]

In 1943, Hösli attributed the extremely poor condition of the machines in the Bakırköy spinnery to a lack of labour control. The managerial mentality,

113 Chris Ward, "Languages of Trade or a Language of Class? Work Culture in Russian Cotton Mills in the 1920s," in *Making Workers Soviet: Power, Class, and Identity*, eds. Lewis H. Siegelbaum and Ronald Gregory Suny (New York: İthaca, 1994), 194–219.

114 Max Von der Porten, *Bakırköy Bez Fabrikası Hakkında* (n.p., 1936).

115 Von der Porten, *Bakırköy Bez Fabrikası Hakkında*; "Sümerbank Birleşik Pamuk İpliği ve Dokuma Fabrikaları Müessesesi 1940 Yılı Raporu," 17–27; Samet Ağaoğlu, "İş İstatistikleri IV," *İktisadi Yürüyüş*, no. 65 (1942), 14; Samet Ağaoğlu, "İş İstatistikleri V," *İktisadi Yürüyüş*, no. 66–67 (1942), 42.

116 Webster, *The Turkey of Atatürk*, 250; Thornburg et al., *Economic Appraisal*, 129–130.

he argued, was focused on getting the most out of the machines, as well as the workers, instead of maintaining them in good condition.[117] Calling this managerial approach "the anxiety to increase production" two years later, Sümerbank inspectors warned that not only would it increase machine wear and tear, but it would also damage product quality.[118] The maintenance and repair costs were indeed extremely high. A message scrolled on the factory wall reminded workers of the centrality of the machines to their livelihood: "Worker Citizen! You earn your bread by working at the machine, take good care of your machine!"[119] But, inadequately trained and technically illiterate workers did not know how. Stoppages due to technical problems were common and, quite naturally, adversely affected the morale of the piece-rate workers. Machine utilisation was very low; more often than not, part of the available equipment would be lying idle. Similar to other industrial contexts, mechanisation hardly ever meant an increase in output when those assigned to the machines had little training in their use.[120]

Von der Porten advised setting up a factory school for foreign textile technicians to teach young workers how to maintain and repair the machinery. If workers could keep their own machines running, they would not be dependent on technicians, which, in turn, meant they would be encouraged to work harder thanks to the wage incentive.[121] In fact, a vocational training plan had already been put together in 1934, the first year of the first five-year plan. The plan provided for apprentice courses and schools for technicians and engineers. In 1938, vocational training courses at industrial enterprises and mines employing more than a hundred workers on a daily basis were made compulsory by law. But, although workers were fined to the amount of half of their daily wage for missing a session and fired after five missed days in a month, attendance remained low and graduation rates remained under fifty per cent throughout the late 1940s and early 1950s for three reasons. First, classes were held after working hours. In 1949, the Bakırköy management fined Cemil one fifth of his daily wage for not attending the foreman training course. The receipt for the fine took an exceptional tone, in that the writer explicitly expressed

---

117 Hösli, *Bakırköy*, 19.

118 "Sümerbank İplik ve Dokuma Fabrikaları Müessesesi 1945 Yılı Raporu."

119 Salahattin Güngör, "97 Yıl Önce."

120 Sümerbank Genel Müdürlük Yüksek Katına, "Fabrikalarımızın," 30–35; Hiroaki Kuromiya, "The Commander and the Rank and File: Managing the Soviet Coal-Mining Industry, 1928–33," in *Social Dimensions of Soviet Industrialisation,* eds. William G. Rosenberg and Lewis H. Siegelbaum (Bloomington: Indiana University Press, 1993), 152.

121 Von der Porten, "Feshane ve Hereke Fabrikaları Tetkiklerine Dair."

his disbelief at Cemil's behaviour: "You are supposed to be most enthusiastic and diligent and not miss this opportunity provided by the factory for you."[122] Second, the employer was responsible for the training costs and there was no obligation for the worker to pay this back through continued service. In many cases, workers left their workplaces for better pay during or after the training. Last but not least, the law did not stipulate a pay rise for workers who had completed training. The minimal difference in wages between unskilled and skilled workers discouraged young unskilled workers from attending courses that lasted much longer than their European counterparts. In the absence of a clear policy, worker training remained uncoordinated, piecemeal, and, as a result, ineffective.[123]

8 Unweaving Leaving

The better records available for the 1930s and 1940s show continuing high levels of turnover in the state textile sector. But the aggregate figures on labour turnover concealed the specific reasons for workers not showing up on the shop floor.[124] Relying mainly on state-produced documents, several labour historians approached the labour turnover question from the perspective of the employer, leaving the workers' perspective out of the analysis. The dominant explanation in the literature is the persistence of workers' rural ties, that is, an incomplete proletarianisation, which has been termed variously an "obstructed transitional stage," a "[lack of] classical types of class divisions," a "class formation as an incomplete process," and an "underdeveloped class structure."[125] I argue that there were two other equally, if not more, important factors behind the high turnover rates: the wage policy and the repressive shop floor industrial relations at state textile factories.

---

122 Personnel file of Cemil Kotman.

123 "Produktivite ve Memleketimizde Produktiviteyi Artırmağa Matuf Tedbirler," *Çalışma Vekâleti Dergisi* 1, no. 2 (1953), 38–50.

124 Nusret Ekin, "Memleketimizde İşçi Devri Mevzuunda Yapılan Araştırmalar ve Ortaya Koydukları Neticeler," *Sosyal Siyaset Konferansları Dokuzuncu, Onuncu, Onbirinci Kitap* (Istanbul, 1960), 123–192.

125 Walker Hines et al., *Türkiye"nin İktisadi Bakımdan Umumi Bir Tetkiki, 1933–1934* (Ankara: Mehmed İhsan Matbaası, 1936), 238; Makal, *Ameleden İşçiye*, 121; Oya Silier, *Türkiye'de Tarımsal Yapının Gelişimi (1923–1938)* (Istanbul: Boğaziçi Üniversitesi İdari Bilimler Fakültesi Yayınları, 1981), 95; Kazgan, on the other hand, argues that from the mid-1930s onward, the process of impoverishment started in the countryside, giving way to loosening ties with the land: Gülten Kazgan, *Tarım ve Gelişme* (Istanbul: Fakülteler

In what follows, I introduce new archival material that helps us to understand the high turnover rate as a worker response to their working and living conditions. Workers cited a variety of reasons in their petitions to explain—and sometimes to explain away—their reasons for leaving. In many cases, they were not truthful, which, as we shall see, elucidates at least partly why the aggregate data is not reliable. Through a close reading of these petitions and the notes scribbled on them, I construct a dynamic account of the negotiation process concerning the leaving and re-recruiting practices at the Bakırköy Factory.

A 1945 report on the Sümerbank workers' conditions confirms the first impressions I had when examining the workers' files. The turnover resulting from low remuneration or unjust wage setting may not have been attributed in the statistics to poor management of labour or the lack of a consistent wage policy, but the official reasons for leaving given by workers did reveal a problem of poor labour discipline. The inspectors found that a reason for leaving was not specified in more than eighty per cent of a total number of 17,243 cases in the state textile sector. In the remainder of the cases, the most commonly cited reason was agricultural labour duties, at 9.2 per cent. Wage-related complaints ranked second and made up 4.4 per cent of all cases. A lack of housing and military conscription each made up 2.5 per cent of the total cases. The authors were of the opinion that reasons other than agricultural labour were in fact more common than these figures suggested.[126]

Some years later, another expert disputed the singling out of workers' continuing rural ties as the main reason behind the unstable and low-skilled labour force by referring to other factors such as low renumeration and workers' distaste for repetitious, monotonous jobs and being confined indoors all day. Workers tended to leave factories mostly in the summer, a fact that factory managers usually attributed to the agricultural work cycle. But this was only part of the reason, the expert claimed; workers were also making use of seasonal jobs, such as in construction, to compensate for the low wages offered by factories. They did not care for the stability of factory work, because they needed to secure the livelihood of their families first and foremost.[127] A number of expert reports pointed to low remuneration, housing problems, and a lack of

---

Matbaası, 1977), 273; Sabyasachi Bhattacharya, "Introduction," in *India's Labouring Poor: Historical Studies c.1600–2000*, eds. Rana Behal and Marcel van der Linden (New Delhi: Cambridge University Press India, 2007), 18.

126 "İşletmede İnsan," 19.

127 Suat Aray, "Sanayi İşletmelerinde İşçi Hareketleri ve Bunların Zirai Sebeplerle İlgileri," 1950, Register K.A./255.07.02.01.06.1153, Prime Ministry Supreme Auditory Board Archives.

skill (which meant low remuneration) as the reasons behind the high turnover rates.[128]

In 1945, Sümerbank inspectors broke down the data on turnover at state textile factories into several categories including sex, marital status, age, origin of birth, and seniority.[129] They used the following findings to make recommendations on worker recruitment and retention policies. The turnover rate for women was proportionate with their percentage make-up of the workforce; in other words, the data did not support the claim that women were particularly transient workers who tended to leave employment after a few years of service.[130] Supporting evidence for this would come in later reports, and in 1948, recruiting more women was cited as one possible solution to the labour turnover problem.[131] Married workers were far more stable than unmarried workers; the message was clear, the authors concluded: married workers should be prioritised in recruitment and single workers should be encouraged to marry. Children made up twenty-six per cent of the state textile workforce but accounted for more than fifty per cent of the turnover, which caused a major backlash in terms of worker training. The second age category with the highest turnover rate was workers aged between nineteen and thirty, at over twenty-five per cent. As would be expected, labour migration played an important role in turnover, and the rate was higher among non-local workers. The data confirmed the need to recruit from the local labour market.

The vast majority of all switching occurred during the first year of employment. Almost seventy per cent were workers with less than one year of seniority. A scientific approach in recruitment was a must, concluded the inspectors; psychotechnical methods and skill assessments were badly needed. Because skill levels were not classified, the inspectors used wages as a proxy to divide

128 "Sümerbank 1942 Senesi Faaliyet ve Hesap Devresine Ait İdare Meclisi Raporu, Bilanço, Kâr ve Zarar Hesabı," *Sümerbank 1942 Yılı Umumi Murakebe Heyeti Raporu* (Ankara: Başvekalet Devlet Matbaası, 1943), 23; Bereznitsky, *Kayseri Bez Fabrikası Hakkında*; Hösli, *Nazilli Bez Fabrikası Hakkında Rapor*; Hösli, *Merinos Fabrikası Hakkında Rapor* (n.p., 1943); ILO, "Labour Problems in Turkey," 216.

129 "İşletmede İnsan," 14–8.

130 For example, Yüksel Akkaya argues: "Women worked until they got married. Since they married at an early age, their length of employment was relatively short and this hindered the development of class consciousness." See: Yüksel Akkaya, "Türkiye'de İşçi Sınıfı ve Sendikacılık 1 (Kısa özet)," *Praksis*, no. 5 (2002), 135.

131 "Sümerbank İplik ve Dokuma Fabrikaları Müessesesi 1948 Yılı Raporu," *Sümerbank 1948 Senesi Faaliyet ve Hesap Devresine Ait İdare Meclisi Raporu, Bilanço, Kâr ve Zarar Hesabı* (Izmit: Selüloz Basımevi, 1949), Archival Collection of the Republic of Turkey Prime Ministry Supreme Audit Board. Amb./Db. No: K.A./ 255.07.02.01.06.3272, 30–1.

state textile workers into four wage groups. Group A workers earned less than one hundred piasters a day and were mostly children, whereas Group D workers were foremen earning between 400 and 720 piasters a day. Groups B and C accounted for more than eighty per cent of turnover. Foremen were quite stable, making up a mere 1.5 per cent of all turnover, while Group A workers accounted for seventeen per cent of total cases. Finally, the low starting wages for new recruits suggested that they were mainly unskilled or semi-skilled labourers, which also meant that the high turnover rates were causing severe skill shortages for state factories. This pushed up training costs and had a disruptive effect on the labour force as a result of a great number of workers coming and going.

Notwithstanding the data problems, this report represents the most detailed analysis of the dynamics of labour turnover that was available in the state textile industry at the time. The breakdown of the data adds nuance to a much-discussed but little-understood phenomenon. Still, because the inspectors were relying on aggregate data from all textile factories, they could not differentiate between the old Istanbul and the new Anatolian factories. In 1947, the Ministry of Labour reported that temporary industrial labour migration was much higher at the newly constructed inland factories.[132]

Among the cotton mills, the Bakırköy Factory came after Adana, Nazilli, and Kayseri in terms of labour turnover, but it still had a ninety-two per cent turnover rate. The main difference was that, in Istanbul, the high turnover rate did not translate into labour shortages, while the Anatolian factories were finding it extremely difficult to recruit new workers to replace those leaving. In 1945, only the Bakırköy spinnery and the Bünyan Factory had enough workers to operate on three daily shifts, while at the Kayseri Factory, for example, labour shortages had left six hundred looms lying idle. The inspectors claimed that, in the majority of the cases, workers were leaving one state factory for another, lending further justification to the criticism that Sümerbank's wage policy displayed great inconsistency among state textile factories. Striking proof of this can be found in the stark contrast between the two big state textile factories in Istanbul. Compared with the ninety-two per cent turnover rate at Bakırköy, the rate was only fifty-eight per cent at the Defterdar Factory. We would, then, not be surprised to learn that the Defterdar Factory paid the highest hourly wage. While the average hourly wage at state textile factories was between thirty and thirty-five piasters in 1945, it was thirty-eight piasters at Bakırköy and forty-four piasters at Defterdar.[133]

132 *Çalışma Vekâleti Dergisi*, no. 24 (1947), 64.

133 Sümerbank Genel Müdürlük Yüksek Katına, "Fabrikalarımızı," 30.

At the Bakırköy Factory, the workforce expanded by fifty per cent between 1940 and 1943, and the turnover rate increased from seventy-five to 96.5 per cent. In 1943, Hösli broke down the labour turnover data for the Bakırköy Factory and found three parallel trends to the 1945 analysis on the entire state textile sector.[134] First, the turnover rate for men was higher than for women. Second, workers on hourly pay changed jobs more than workers on piece rate. Third, turnover was higher in the weavery than in the other departments, which Hösli attributed to the work there being heavy and the hours being long. At the Nazilli Factory, for example, turnover rates in the weavery and spinnery were 176 and 100 per cent, respectively.[135] In the next section, I substantiate these findings and bring the workers' perspective into the picture by analysing the relevant documents in the workers' files. I argue that, as a symptom of an instable labour market, labour turnover was determined by the different job opportunities that were available for skilled and unskilled labourers.

9 How Long Does the Harvest Season Last?

Before we delve into the reasons given by the Bakırköy workers for leaving during the harvest season, we should understand that agricultural labour duties were seen as a legitimate reason for leaving by the factory management and factory inspectors. Murat's case is a good example. He requested to quit in 1944, that is, when labour turnover was at its highest due to the war, because he had received a letter "saying that my family is sick and my harvest is left unattended on the field." As usual, the petition went through the head foreman, who, in this case, supported Murat, for he was "a very hardworking worker but has to leave to go to his village." Murat left in August, and came back seven months later. In May 1948, Süleyman filed a similar petition. This was the second time that he had requested leave. In 1944, he had quit due to low pay. After four years as a construction worker in Istanbul, he had returned to the factory by the end of 1947, but five months later, he requested leave again: "I respectfully ask your permission and orders to terminate my contract since I will go to my village for the harvest." Once again, the note by the head foreman was supportive: "Since he has no family in the village, it is okay for him to leave." It was not until almost three years later that he would come back for the third time, and he would work at the factory until his retirement in 1969.

134 Hösli, *Bakırköy Bez Fabrikası Hakkında Rapor*, 12.

135 Hösli, *Nazilli Bez Fabrikası Hakkında Rapor* (1943), n.p.

At a first glance, these petitions appear to be simple formalistic texts informing the management about the reasons for the worker's leave. But, when the two aforementioned workers' petitions are read alongside the other documents in their files, they reveal three things. First, they both quit more than once. Second, their employment histories do not follow the rhythms of the agricultural season. Third, the support for their request shows that agricultural duties were seen as a legitimate reason for leaving the factory. All of this suggests that workers used agricultural duties as an excuse to take extended periods of unpaid leave. Both workers were re-employed without problem, even when returning three years after leaving to take care of the yearly harvest. İsmail, for example, also received the same treatment when he asked for temporary leave of twenty days in June 1948 to attend the harvest, and came back to the factory afterward.[136]

Workers would quit for family responsibilities too. Yakup, for example, found his family in a desperate state in a remote northern Anatolian village while he was on leave, and did not return to the factory in spite of eleven years of service. He filed a petition in 1950 to demand an indemnity payment for his service, a few months after the labour code had been amended to the effect that workers with more than three years of service would be paid fifteen days of wages for every year they worked.[137] Şükriye sought termination of her employment to take care of her sick mother in her village, but she came back to work a month later. The following year, she left for her village again, and came back seven months later. She left and returned a third time without filing a petition. The interesting thing was that each time she returned, she would submit a request to be moved from the maintenance department, where she worked on an hourly wage, to another department. Upon her final return, her demand was accepted. She was finally working on piece rate and stayed at the factory until her retirement.

Ali also left twice to attend to his sick parents. Ali had worked at the factory since 1940 with many interruptions. The first time he left after a fight with his foreman, and we will read more on this in the next chapter. He returned seven years later before being asked to leave only four months later. A further four months later, he was re-employed, and he worked seven months before being asked to leave again. A month later, he was back for yet another time, asking to be recruited to his old job at the weft machines. His prior indiscipline was

---

136 Personnel files of Murat Özcan, Süleyman Yapıcı, and İsmail Menenlioğlu.

137 *Düstur 3, Tertip*, v. 31, November 1949-October 1950. Ankara: Başbakanlık Devlet Matbaası, 1950, 713.

mentioned in the notes to his petition, but eventually Ali was re-employed once more. As these examples show, workers would use their return as a negotiating tool wherever possible.

These stories of Yakup, Şükriye, and Ali show that workers' decisions to leave were not always economically motivated; they were also due to social expectations and family responsibilities. The persistence of their rural ties did not always imply continuing agricultural activity, as is too easily assumed. It did, however, imply a burden of reproductive and care labour in a context where the state failed to provide for the sick and elderly. It has also been argued in a separate context that such visits had a social function. "The phenomenon of absenteeism—the visit back home—was not only economically necessary for the workers' survival," Chitra Joshi wrote with respect to Kanpur textile workers; "it was the only relief from the drudgery of work and unhealthy conditions of city life and an occasion for family reunion, enjoyment and participation in festivities."[138] The difficulty associated with becoming permanent urban residents, both financially and psychologically, could have played a role in workers' choosing to keep their family ties intact.

10 The Reasons Behind Discontinuity

In most cases, it is impossible to know what workers did while they were gone. But in Aslan's case, we do know. Aslan was one of the many workers fired for absenteeism from the Sümerbank factories. In 1945 alone, 3,241 workers were fired for this particular reason. The employment history of Aslan not only shows the extent of indiscipline on the shop floor, it also reveals the limits to the tolerance showed by the factory management toward experienced and skilled workers. When he was fired in April 1943 because of discontinuity, Aslan had been working at the Bakırköy Factory on and off for eight years. According to his file, he had either quit or been fired at least four times. The following month, he wrote a petition explaining the reason behind his absenteeism:

> I could not come to work about a month ago. Suddenly, by coincidence, I ran into a relative of mine from my hometown. Since he was very sick, I had to go all the way to Manisa with him. I had planned to come back immediately to start working. But I had to deal with housing matters.

138 Chitra Joshi, "Kanpur Textile Labour: Some Structural Features of Formative Years," *Economic and Political Weekly* 16, no. 44/46 (1981), 1,823.

> I spent fifteen days thinking I would come back either today or tomorrow. I respectfully ask your forgiveness for my mistake and your high orders and guidance to let me return to my job.

Aslan signed the petition: "laborious weaver at your factory, Aslan." Both his foreman and the weavery superintendent opposed his re-employment, according to the notes they added to his petition. Aslan did win in the end, and he was re-employed, only to be fired for absenteeism a month later. Six months later, he was back at Bakırköy. Aslan's story shows us two things. First, as a skilled weaver, Aslan did not even bother to give a legitimate excuse for his absence; unemployment was not a threat for him. Second, during the six months he was away, Aslan worked at the other state textile factory in Istanbul, Defterdar, despite his troubled employment history at Bakırköy.

Aslan did not give his true motive for leaving and coming back in his petition, but information from a 1943 inspection suggests a possible explanation. The inspectors compared the wages at the Bakırköy and Defterdar factories in 1940 and found that average wages were the same at that time. The following year, the average wage at Bakırköy slightly decreased, while it increased almost eight per cent at Defterdar. By 1943, Bakırköy workers were earning thirteen per cent less than Defterdar workers.[139] Cemil's employment history at Bakırköy resembles Aslan's in that he was also fired for absenteeism multiple times. In 1945, he wrote that he had to leave due to family responsibilities. When he came back almost two years later, it became clear that he had been working at a private glassware factory in Istanbul. Aslan and Cemil exemplified what factory inspectors had observed in 1943: whenever the opportunity to work elsewhere arose, state workers did not hesitate to leave their factories. Workers on piece rate left because they could not reach the output rates due to low-quality raw materials and damaged machinery. Unable to save on their low wages, factory work lost its appeal for many state workers.[140]

The employment histories I have cited were by no means exceptional. Work on the shop floor was highly casual; voluntary quitting or firing for absenteeism was usually followed by re-employment. Rates of persistence were quite low. In 1942, only thirteen per cent of the workers had worked at the factory more than five years.[141] Engineers in administrative positions within the factories

139 "Sümerbank 1942 Yılı Umumi Murakebe Heyeti Raporu," 34.

140 "Sümerbank 1943 Umumi Murakebe Heyeti Raporu," Archival Collection of the Republic of Turkey Prime Ministry Supreme Audit Board. Amb./Db. No: K.A./255.07.02.01.06.3246, 49.

141 Hösli, *Bakırköy Bez Fabrikası Hakkında Rapor*, 13.

found that their powers were limited, and this was partly as a result of the endemic skill shortages, which enabled workers to exercise a certain degree of independence.[142]

What does this newly found evidence teach us about labour turnover at Bakırköy? High turnover rates in the West, where there was an established industrial workforce, Makal argues, were a result of harsh working conditions. By contrast, in early republican Turkey, he attributes this mainly to continuing rural ties. If labour turnover was a response to working conditions, it should have been eliminated by the industrial welfare provisions.[143] The employment histories of Bakırköy workers and the factory reports by industrial experts, however, prove that quitting was a form of resistance to the rigours of factory life.

Industrial experts were increasingly pointing to the arduous working conditions and the inadequacy of material incentives offered to workers as the main reasons behind the high labour turnover. In the absence of worker organisation or the craft control of the labour process, Bakırköy workers seeking better wages or better working conditions had no alternative but to quit. By way of comparison, in his analysis of the extraordinarily high labour turnover in American industry in the 1910s, Sanford M. Jabocy cited two contemporaries, Samuel Gompers, a cigar maker and a key figure in American labour history, and a government official, both of whom used the word "strike" to define the situation. A "vast striking back of individuals in desperation," said Gompers, "a vast disorganized protest"; the official went for the term "individualistic strike."[144] The suspiciously long harvest seasons, the sequential ordering of wage demands and quitting, the negotiations on task and wage allocation upon return, and working at other industrial establishments during leave; these are all fragments from the lives of Bakırköy workers, fragments showing that turnover was a direct response to many of the problems they faced in their day-to-day operations such as close supervision, foreman abuse, and wretched working conditions. "Voting with their feet," as Wally Seccombe termed it, was the only available option for them in the face of growing intensity of work, poor remuneration, lack of training and promotion opportunities, as well as bullying in the workplace.[145]

In the factory reports of the 1940s, productivity and scientific management increasingly sought to address turnover. Industrial experts were concerned

---

142 Aray, "Sanayi İşletmelerinde İşçi Hareketleri ve Bunların Zirai Sebeplerle İlgileri," 14.

143 Makal, *Ameleden İşçiye*, 53.

144 Jacoby, *Employing Bureaucracy*, 24, 90.

145 Wally Seccombe, *Weathering the Storm: Working-Class Families from the Industrial Revolution to the Fertility Decline* (London: Verso, 1995), 92.

about constant changes in the workforce undermining vocational training efforts and impeding the implementation of even the simplest incentive wage system, which would "increase the enthusiasm for work."[146] A lower turnover rate would help to stabilise worker efforts, and it would give management time to build a corps of loyal employees. Anything that could retain workers at the state factories came to be seen as part of the solution to the turnover problem. Among these, the provision of social welfare gained wider appeal for two main reasons. First, raising monetary wages would increase the already high labour costs in production. Second, non-monetary wages were believed to be an efficient method of labour control. For the state, industrial welfare provision brought the extra benefit of a much-needed self-representation: the benevolent and worker-friendly state. This image gained wider currency in the heated national political context of the postwar era, as we shall see in the following chapters. But before that, we should look at the emergence and development of industrial welfare policy at the workplace level.

11 Industrial Welfare Policy

The interwar period witnessed the emergence of a management ethos that increasingly focused on the human aspect of labour. Having mastered the direct connection between greater control over labour and maximisation of profit under the American influences of Taylorism and Fordism, a growing number of industrial experts believed that they would have to take more positive steps if they were to win workers' cooperation and loyalty.[147] In the United States, the Hawthorne studies conducted by Elton Mayo and colleagues at Western Electric's plant in Chicago between 1924 and 1932 demonstrated the importance of social incentives and management intervention in employee motivation. In the United Kingdom, the "management movement" took a turn for welfarist inflection and underlined the obligation to care for their workers' wellbeing.[148] The German scientific management tradition diverged from Taylorist practices

146 Hösli, *Bakırköy Bez Fabrikası Hakkında Rapor*; Özeken, "Sanayi İşçileri," 64.

147 Mayo, E., *The Human Problems of an Industrial Civilisation* (New York: MacMillan, 1933); Mayo, E., *The Social Problems of an Industrial Civilisation* (London: Routledge & Kegan Paul, 1949).

148 Daniel Ussishkin, "The 'Will to Work': Industrial Management and the Question of Conduct in Inter-war Britain," in *Brave New World: Imperial and Democratic Nation-building in Britain between the Wars*, eds. Laura Beers and Geraint Thomas (London: University of London Press, 2011), 91–108, 93.

by advocating for the reconciliation of scientific management with "humanizing" industrial life under the term *menschliche Rationalisierung*.[149] Last but not least, the Soviet managerial practice approached industrial welfare as a prerequisite for raising productivity, on the one hand, and the banner of socialist modernism, on the other.[150] Common to all these industrial contexts was the move away from a crude, economistic view of labour productivity to one that linked workers' wellbeing and morale to workplace efficiency.

Industrial welfare provision has been one of the most popular topics among labour, economic, and political historians writing on early republican Turkey. As with other contexts of late and state-led industrialisation, historians have tended to view such policies as instruments in a broader policy of co-option or incorporation and repression of labour. The political conclusion in these analyses is obvious: By providing social benefits, the state managed to hinder the development of working-class consciousness.[151] Recent historiography on social welfare, however, has challenged this reductionist view by analysing social welfare as a process shaped by diverse national and broader transnational forces.[152] In his analysis of the Beveridge Plan, which had a powerful effect on postwar Turkish labour policy as we shall see in the next chapter, Göran Therborn warns against the treatment of state welfare policies as the manifestation of a clear and static political strategy. These policies are neither "an expression of supra-class benevolence nor a shrewd ruse of the ruling class [but] a manifestation of the inevitably contradictory and conflictual character of class rule."[153] The case in hand perfectly illustrates this complexity.

---

149 Karsten Uhl, *Humane Rationalisierung? Die Raumordnung der Fabrik im Fordistischen Jahrhundert* (Bielefeld: Transkript Verlag, 2014), 149-50; Nolan, *Visions of Modernity*, 84; Mary Nolan, "Das Deutsche Institut für Technische Arbeitsschulung und die Schaffung des: Neuen Arbeiters," in *Rationale Beziehungen? Geschlechterverhältnisse im Rationalisierungsprozess*, eds. Dagmar Reese, Eve Rosenhaft, Carola Sachse, and Tilla Siegel (Frankfurt am Main: Sührkamp, 1993), 189–221.

150 Stephen Kotkin, "Modern Times: The Soviet Union and The Interwar Conjunction," *Kritika: Explorations in Russian and Eurasian History* 2, no. 1 (2001), 146–7.

151 Koç, *Olaylar-Değerlendirmeler*, 30; Boratav, *Gelir Dağılımı*, 162.

152 Paulo Drinot, *The Allure of Labor: Workers, Race, and the Making of the Peruvian State* (Durham: Duke University Press, 2011), 193–196; Stephen Kotkin, *Magnetic Mountain: Stalinism as a Civilisation* (Oakland: University of California Press, 1997), 19–20; Yiğit Akın, "Erken Cumhuriyet Dönemi Emek Tarihçiliğine Katkı: Yeni Yaklaşımlar, Yeni Kaynaklar," *Tarih ve Toplum*, no. 2 (2005), 73–111; Can Nacar, "Working Class in Turkey during the World War II Period: Between Social Policies and Everyday Experiences" (master's thesis, Boğaziçi University, 2004); Murat Metinsoy, *İkinci Dünya Savaşı'nda Türkiye: Savaş ve Gündelik Yaşam* (Istanbul: Homer, 2007), 273–58.

153 Göran Therborn, *What does the Ruling Class do When it Rules? State Apparatuses and State Power under Feudalism, Capitalism and Socialism?* (London: New Left Books, 1978), 240.

In the Turkish context, there were three intertwined factors behind the expansion of industrial welfare in the 1940s, and especially after the war. The first was a preference for a form of non-monetary wage compensation to retain state workers. The implementation of factory-level social provisions was seen as the best way of increasing the wellbeing of workers without adding to direct labour costs. The second factor concerned the lack of effective labour control. Non-monetary improvements gave employers more control over workers than they would have had with higher wages because, with welfare programmes, it was the employers who decided how the money was spent. Welfare provisions made the employee into a better, more reliable worker. Last but not least was the hope that industrial welfare would increase productivity and disseminate a modern industrial lifestyle.

Despite extreme work intensification during the war years, labour costs in textile production stayed substantially higher than the norm. While total labour expenditure at state textile factories was thirty per cent more than the European average, labour productivity was only between thirty to sixty per cent of that at European textile factories.[154] In his report on the Bakırköy Factory, after documenting the "extremely high labour cost," Hösli proposed that hourly wages should be kept under thirty piasters and that the factory should increase non-monetary wages as well as welfare spending.

In fact, this was already the trend. Between 1941 and 1943, monthly monetary wages per worker increased from 29.43 liras to 61.32 liras, while non-monetary wages increased by more than ten times and amounted to 10.86 liras, that is, one sixth of the corresponding monetary wages. At Bakırköy, non-monetary wages comprised food and clothing only; housing and sales of cheaper food items (*ucuz gıda maddeleri*) were not provided. Welfare costs per worker also increased from 1.10 to 1.79 liras, and they included factory dispensary and medical treatment costs, sickness and work accident payments, and sports facilities. Overall, the monthly expenditure per worker increased by almost 2.5 times during 1943.[155]

Sümerbank factories initially provided a limited range and extent of factory-based social services. Though the labour code set a deadline of one year for the establishment of a state insurance scheme to cover industrial accidents and illness, maternity, retirement, unemployment, and sickness benefits, nothing was done to implement this until the end of the war.[156] Before the war,

154 Hösli, *Bakırköy Bez Fabrikası Hakkında Rapor*, 15; Özeken, "Sanayi İşçileri," 62.

155 Hösli, *Bakırköy Bez Fabrikası Hakkında Rapor*, 14.

156 Turan Yazgan, *Türkiye'de Sosyal Güvenlik Sistemi* (Istanbul: İktisadi Araştırmalar Vakfı, 1969), 15.

social welfare was provided at the factory level in a piecemeal fashion, and, as such, there were huge disparities between factories (more on this below). The provision of various amenities like lunchrooms and landscaped grounds, as well as the organisation of extra-work activities, such as company athletics, were enthusiastically reported in the newspapers and inspection reports alike. The recreational facilities at factory sites not only improved the morale of the workforce, they also functioned to carry the "modern, civilised, and progressive lifestyle" to the far corners of the country, thereby recasting not only the worker but also the locals around the factory site in a middle-class mould.[157] Especially in the lesser developed regions where the new factories were built and where there was a lack of general infrastructure for consumption, political, and leisure activities, the factory infrastructure played a prominent role as a symbol of cultural progress. But these documents failed to mention a small detail: these offerings proved inadequate in luring the workers into the factory and, more importantly, retaining them. A report on the social organisation of Sümerbank in 1940 argued for the need to change the managerial attitude at the state factories:

> Today, it is a must to provide the Turkish workers with not only material but also intellectual and moral sustenance; to endow them with the spiritual foundations and goals that the society and the regime are based on. And this can only be achieved by establishing institutions of moral education (such as schools, conferences, theatre, educational, and disciplinary institutions) that would transform workers into efficient and civilised members of society.[158]

The response of the economic affairs minister to these suggestions was absolutely positive. Boosting workers' morale was now a priority, and recreational facilities would be used to trigger the "joy of work" among state workers.[159] A prominent economics journal defined the joy of work as a prerequisite for a stable workforce and worker productivity the following year, and praised the

157 Şevket Süreyya Aydemir, *İkinci Adam Birinci Cilt,* vol. 1 (Istanbul: Remzi Yayınevi, 1984), 447; "Sümerbank Birleşik Pamuk İpliği ve Dokuma Fabrikaları Müessesesi 1939 Yılı Umumi Murakebe Heyeti Raporu."

158 "Sümerbank Fabrikaları İçtimai Teşkilat 1940 Yılı Raporu," *Sümerbank 1940 Senesi Faaliyet ve Hesap Devresine Ait İdare Meclisi Raporu, Bilanço, Kâr ve Zarar Hesabı* (Ankara: TBMM Matbaası, 1941), 27–8.

159 *Sümerbank'ın 1940 yılı Muamelatile Bilanço, Kâr ve Zarar Hesaplarının Tetkikine Dair Olan Umumi Murakebe Heyeti Raporu Hakkında İktisat Vekâleti Mütaelası,* 10.

sports facilities, conference halls, and cinemas at the Sümerbank factories.[160] Yet these documents also overlooked another minor detail: workers had to sign a statement agreeing to pay for these facilities. In 1948, Cemil was still paying a monthly fee of fifteen piasters for the cinema and fifty-four piasters for the sports club at the Bakırköy Factory, even though he had left the factory the year before because of the low pay.

12 Industrial Welfare Provision during the War

The wellbeing of workers was now directly linked to business results, and nutrition in the workplace became one of the cornerstones of this renewed emphasis on the social standard of industrial workers. The first effort to systematise social provisions involved food provision in 1941. Worker malnutrition had been a widely reported problem, which the war further exacerbated.[161] But in the face of soaring labour turnover, food provision was more a business urgency than a sense of social responsibility. As James Vernon has demonstrated, engineers had declared the industrial canteen "a sound business method of increasing the efficiency and productivity of the worker," for it improved the health and physical condition of the workers and reduced absences, broken time, and the tendency to alcoholism. The canteens also gradually emerged as tools of vital importance in producing sociable citizens by conferring a set of values, such as respectability, sobriety, punctuality, and cleanliness through their architecture, furnishings, and service.[162] The factory canteens functioned "as a prism of overlapping discourses and practices that connect work and home, individual productivity and social welfare, profit and health."[163]

In the 1930s, workers had been left to their own devices, a 1940 inspection report on the social organisation of state factories claimed. As a result, state workers had developed some peculiar eating habits. Some had to get by on

160 "Endüstri Hayatında Mühim Bir Dava: İşçi ve İçtimai Teşkilat," *İktisadi Yürüyüş* Sümerbank Fevkalade Sayısı, no. 61–2, (1942), 11–2.

161 Ungun, "Hayat Pahalılığı," 94.

162 James Vernon, *Hunger: A Modern History* (Cambridge: Harvard University Press, 2007), 160–80.

163 Frank Trentmann, "Beyond Consumerism: New Historical Perspectives on Consumption," *Journal of Contemporary History* 39, no. 3 (2004), 373–401; Rory Archer and Goran Musić, "Not All Canteens Are Created Equal: Food Provision for Yugoslav Blue-Collar Workers in Late Socialism," in *Brotherhood and Unity at the Kitchen Table? Cooking, Cuisine and Food Culture in Socialist Yugoslavia,* eds. Ruža Fotiadis, Vladimir Ivanović, and Radina Vučetić (Zagreb: Srednja Europa, 2020), 75–95.

one meal a day consisting of a few olives, a little bit of cheese, and some leek, and they generally lacked the physical strength to work. Another report added that, because of cultural habits, even those who had the financial means were not in the habit of having regular, nutritious meals.[164] This led the Ministry of Economy to announce in 1941 that the provision of food with sufficient calories was the most important sanitation measure to be taken by state enterprises.[165] In June 1941, factory directors had a meeting at the Nazilli Factory and decided to provide a hot meal to satisfy the assumed needs of workers involved in challenging physical work and living on low incomes. At first, workers earning up to 160 piasters a day would receive food free of charge, and the rest would pay the production costs. The upper wage limit was soon raised to 200 piasters, and Sümerbank began to examine the possibility of lifting the wage cap completely. Inspectors reporting on working conditions underlined the importance of a subsidised factory meal for workers whose living standards were falling precipitously from year to year, and argued that food provision would be more effective than wage increases in bettering the conditions of workers.[166]

In practice, hot meal provision varied enormously across state factories. Inspection reports reveal a great diversity of approaches taken by factories in providing for the nutrition of their workers. On average, the caloric value of the hot meal was between 1,000 and 1,500 calories—well below the limit then believed to be apt for an industrial worker, which was four thousand calories—and worker complaints on the quality of the food abounded.[167] The wage cap was lifted in March 1945, and the food quality was improved to 1,500 to 1,800 calories, including 450 grammes of bread. The differential practices in food provision were also having a negative effect on workers' morale and

164 "Sümerbank Fabrikaları İçtimai Teşkilat 1940 Yılı Raporu," 22–3; *Sümerbank Fabrikalarının İşçi Meseleleri ve İçtimai Teşkilatı Hakkında Rapor (1941)*, 38. Archival Collection of the Republic of Turkey Prime Ministry Supreme Audit Board. Amb./Db.No: K.A./ 255.07.02.01.06.3236.

165 "Sümerbank Fabrikaları İçtimai Teşkilat 1940 Yılı Raporu," 22–3; "Sümerbank'ın 1940 yılı Muamelatile Bilanço, Kâr ve Zarar Hesaplarının Tetkikine Dair Olan Umumi Murakebe Heyeti Raporu Hakkında İktisat Vekâleti Mütaelası," *1941 Yılı Umumi Murakebe Heyeti Sümerbank Raporu* (Ankara: Alaaddin Kıral Basımevi, 1942), 9.

166 "1941 Yılı Umumi Murakebe Heyeti Sümerbank Raporu," 29; "Umumi Murakebe Heyeti Sümerbank Fabrikalarının İşçi Meseleleri ve İçtimai Teşkilatı 1941 Yılı Raporu Hakkında Mütalaalar," *1941 Yılı Umumi Murakebe Heyeti Sümerbank Raporu* (Ankara: Alaaddin Kıral Basımevi, 1942), 26; *Sümerbank Fabrikalarının İşçi Meseleleri ve İçtimai Teşkilatı Hakkında Rapor* (1941), 39–41.

167 *Sümerbank Fabrikalarının İşçi Meseleleri ve İçtimai Teşkilatı Hakkında Rapor* (1941), *39–41;* Can Nacar, "Our Lives were not as Valuable as an Animal: Workers in State-Run Industries in World War-II Turkey," *International Review of Social History* 54, no. 17 (2009), 157–8.

productivity, inspectors noted. Factories began selling a second hot meal to put a stop to workers' unsanitary cooking practices at their places of accommodation. Food provision was now cited as evidence of the value that the state ascribed to its workers.[168]

Food provision at state factories gave rise to further heated debates in parliament on the social character of the state. A member of parliament lamented that the factories were turning into alms houses; others advocated the implementation of factory social services because Turkish state factories needed to be "places of compassion" to secure worker commitment. The disagreement spilled over into other realms of social welfare, such as educational opportunities for working-class children. At stake was not only the material wellbeing of the working classes; parliament feared the infiltration of socialist ideas. The minister for economic affairs assured his parliamentary colleagues that food provision addressed both productivity concerns and political fears; Turkish workers were slowly becoming "knowledgeable and alert about matters that interest them," and "they are acquiring their rights."[169]

At the Bakırköy Factory, the category *table d'hôte* made its first appearance in the remuneration tables in 1938. Referring to a meal offered at a fixed price and with few if any choices, the word suggests that all workers had to pay for food on the shop floor until 1941. In September 1938, Mehmet earned 17.39 liras a month before taxes, 1.52 liras of which he spent on the *table d'hôte*. In other words, 8.74 per cent per cent of his earnings before taxes were spent on food consumed at the factory.[170] Earning almost thirty per cent less than Mehmet, Yakup paid 1.68 liras for his factory-provided food in January 1940. Although his earnings fell over the course of the year, his food expenses went up, bringing the percentage of his income spent on food to fifteen per cent.[171] An analysis of the remuneration tables of different workers shows that, despite the differences in wage levels, the cost of food as a percentage of monthly earnings was never below eight per cent.

After 1941, food expenses were increasingly met by the factory. Canteen spending per worker at the Bakırköy Factory increased from 0.77 liras in 1941 to 3.16 liras in 1942, and to 9.90 liras in 1943.[172] The threefold increase between 1942

168 *Sümerbank 1944 Yılı Umumi Murakebe Heyeti Raporu* (Ankara: Başbakanlık Devlet Matbaası, 1945), 6, 41.

169 *3460 Sayılı Kanuna Bağlı İktisadi Teşekküllerin 1940 Yılı Bilançoları ile Kâr ve Zarar Hesaplarını Tetkik Eden Umumi Murakebe Heyet Zaptı*, vol. 3 (Ankara: TBMM Matbaası, 1942), 137–43.

170 Personnel file of Mehmet Ak.

171 Personnel file of Yakup Davulcu.

172 Hösli, *Bakırköy Bez Fabrikası Hakkında Rapor.*

and 1943 resulted from the expansion of free food to the lower wage groups, as well as the sharp increase in food prices. During the same period, the monthly social expenses per worker at the factory increased first from 1.87 liras to 5.23 liras, and then to 12.76 liras. To put it differently, this meant that food expenses were making up more than forty per cent, sixty per cent, and seventy-seven per cent of all non-monetary wages.[173] According to a 1944 report, among all state textile factories, the Bakırköy Factory spent the least on social welfare programmes.[174]

At the 1941 meeting, Sümerbank also decided to provide clothing for its workers in two different forms. The first was the provision of work clothes. Between June 1941 and 1942, 14,114 pieces of protective gear, including wooden sabots and gloves, were given to workers whose work involved acidic and high temperature materials. The second form was selling materials produced at Sümerbank factories to workers at production cost. These included shoes, garments, undershirts, woollen socks, leather shirts, and underwear. In June 1941, the "Local Products Bazaar," the sales agent of Sümerbank, started selling these materials to workers' families at a low cost.[175] The "clothing policy," as it was termed by the Ministry of Economy, followed an eligibility rule known as "continuous service" to reduce labour turnover. For example, three criteria were assigned to the sale of cheap fabric: marital status, work discipline, and length of service. Married workers were given priority to meet the clothing needs of their household members. Workers without a record of absenteeism could buy a variety of fabrics to make both clothing and household textiles. At the Bakırköy Factory, careful records were kept and notes on absenteeism were jotted down. Workers with six months of service were given enough fabric to make one garment, those with one year of service received forty metres of fabric, those with three years of service received enough fabric for a coat, and those with six years of service were given a blanket.[176] Yet, three years after the launch of the clothing provisions, the workers' clothing situation had barely improved. Workers lacked work gear such as boots, protective glasses, and gloves; some were so poor that they came to work barefoot and suffered from lice.[177]

173 Hösli, *Bakırköy Bez Fabrikası Hakkında Rapor*, 44.

174 "İplik ve Dokuma Fabrikaları Müessesi 1944 Yılı Umumi Murakebe Heyeti Raporu," *Sümerbank 1944 Yılı Umumi Murakebe Heyeti Raporu*.

175 *1941 Yılı Umumi Murakebe Heyeti Sümerbank Raporu*, 29–30.

176 "Endüstri Hayatında," *İktisadi Yürüyüş*; *1941 Yılı Umumi Murakebe Heyeti Sümerbank Raporu*, 30.

177 *Sümerbank 1944 Yılı Umumi Murakebe Heyeti Raporu*, 40.

Before 1942, Bakırköy workers' files made no mention of clothing provision. In 1942 and 1943, the factory was spending 0.52 liras and 0.96 liras on clothing per worker, respectively, and these expenses made up 9.9 and 7.5 per cent of the total social expenditure per worker.[178] These provisions were carefully recorded in the personnel files of each Bakırköy worker, with the date, the type, and the amount of provision specified. In some cases, short notes, for example "for giving birth" or "with petition," were added to the descriptions.

The social expenses at the factory were composed mainly of the hot meal, clothing, sports facilities, and medical treatment. The first two categories made up more than seventy per cent of total social expenses in 1942; the following year, their share increased to more than eighty-five per cent. Sickness was quite common among workers; medical treatment expenses made more than ten per cent of the total. Sickness pay was the bare minimum. And lastly, the sports facilities amounted to one to two per cent of total social expenses. That was it, Hösli wrote; workers' social needs were far from being adequately addressed.[179]

Despite the high-minded rhetoric that accompanied social provision, the amount spent was hardly enough to have a widespread effect on workers' loyalty or economic security. Through industrial welfare provision, the state aimed to achieve labour stability, with the ultimate goal of solving the productivity crisis at state textile factories. Three years in, factory inspectors admitted that social provision was proving insufficient in terms of labour retention.[180] Besides the widening recognition of the direct connection between meeting the social and material needs of workers and productivity, industrial welfare provision was also a response to the reality of the low-wage labour market. Especially during the war years, wage rates lagged behind the increase in the cost of living.

With these allowances in kind, the state aimed to mitigate the decline in levels of remuneration.[181] Industrial welfare provision in early republican Turkey should be understood as part of the historical increase in the cost of labour power since the mid-nineteenth century that took the form of benefits and services provided by the state. The trend is endemic to capitalism, as Seccombe argues, "due to the radical deficiencies of the wage form as a means of funding

178 Hösli, *Bakırköy Bez Fabrikası Hakkında Rapor.*

179 Hösli, *Bakırköy Bez Fabrikası Hakkında Rapor*, 44.

180 *Sümerbank 1944 Yılı Umumi Murakebe Heyeti Raporu*, 45.

181 International Labour Office, "*Labour Problems in Turkey*," *Report of a Mission of the International Labour Office* (Geneva: ILO, 1950), 16; Thornburg et. Al., *Economic Appraisal*, 131.

the long-term reproduction of labour-power."[182] The provisions were partly an intervention on the part of the capitalist state to stabilise and reinforce the system. As such, it is important to see their controlling and system-maintenance functions without neglecting the real benefits they provided. For the Bakırköy workers, these benefits were much less than thought previously. And especially in one crucial component of the reproduction of labour power, they were completely left to their own fate and they quite literally took the matter in their own hands.

13 Working-Class Housing in Early Republican Istanbul

When Gerhard Kessler, an exiled German economist and social policy expert arrived in Istanbul in 1933, he could not help but compare the housing conditions in the city with various European cities including London, Berlin, Vienna, Riga, and Bucharest. "I have seen no other city," he wrote, "with such poor housing conditions."[183] In her memoirs, tobacco worker and later trade unionist Zehra Kosova gives as much space to the dreadful housing problem as to the extreme precarity and wretchedly hazardous working conditions. Terrified of the long commute to the factory, Nazlı, the main protagonist in the prominent journalist and political activist Suat Derviş's 1936 social realist novel *This is the Novel of Things that Actually Happen*, compares her shaking body and knocking knees to Jesus carrying the cross on his way to his crucifixion.[184]

The situation was aggravated with the onset of the war, and especially after 1942 with the slowing down of the construction sector. By the end of the 1940s, there were estimated to be fifty thousand people without accommodation in Istanbul. In other words, one out of every sixteen people living in Istanbul did not have a proper home. Kessler estimated that half of them were sharing rundown houses with other families and lived in overcrowded dwellings under the threat of tuberculosis. A local social policy expert attributed the fifty thousand annual deaths from tuberculosis to poor sanitary conditions and overcrowding in working-class homes. The other half were forced to take the matter in their own hands by building their own dwellings, the *gecekondu* (lit., night-built).

182 Seccombe, *Weathering The Storm*, 16–7.

183 Gerhard Kessler, "Istanbul'da Mesken Darlığı, Mesken Sefaleti, Mesken İnşaatı," *Arkitekt* 18, no. 209 (1949), 131–133.

184 Zehra Kosova, *Ben İşçiyim* (Istanbul: İletişim Yayınları, 1996); Suat Derviş, *Bu Roman Olan Şeylerin Romanıdır* (Istanbul: İthaki, 1936), 33.

In 1940, there were 1,669 simple sheds (*baraka*) in the city. During the war years, these were transformed into *gecekondus*, squatter dwellings that came in quite a wide variety of forms. By the end of the decade, Kessler claimed there were around five thousand *gecekondus* in Istanbul. An article published in the Ministry of Labour's journal put the number between nine and fourteen thousand. Referring to the location of the settlements just outside the old city walls, a communist satire magazine described the allegedly thirty-five thousand inhabitants of the *gecekondus* as an army of "the dispossessed and labourers" that were besieging the Byzantium Empire five hundred years after the original conquest.[185] Among this army were the protagonists of this book, the Bakırköy Factory workers.

FIGURE 21 A street with rundown houses in Bakırköy, 1930s

Already at the beginning of planned industrialisation, the housing problem was on the state's agenda. By 1939, all new factories were providing some level and form of housing for their workers; a useful first step, the inspectors wrote, but nowhere near enough. At the Nazilli and Kayseri factories, the problem

185 Gerhard Kessler, "Istanbul'da Mesken Darlığı," 133; Cahit Talas, "Mesken Davamız," *Ankara Üniversitesi SBF Dergisi* 10, no. 1 (1955), 2; İlhan Tekeli, *Türkiye'de Yaşamda ve Yazında Konut Sorununun Gelişimi* (Ankara: T.C. Başbakanlık Toplu Konut İdaresi Başkanlığı, 1996), 45; Halit Ünal, "Mesken Davası," *Çalışma Vekâleti Dergisi* 1, no. 3 (1953), 25–33; "Gecekondular," *Nuh'un Gemisi*, no. 6 (1949), 3.

was most urgent, they continued. The following year, only 7.1 per cent of state workers were benefitting from housing provisions, and these were mostly single workers sheltered in workers' barracks. The living conditions at these barracks were described as follows: "They were full of lice, beds and bed sheets were dirty, rooms were covered with dust and trash, and bedsteads had bedbugs." Only at Nazilli and Kayseri were married foremen given houses. By 1944, still only ten per cent of Sümerbank workers were benefiting from housing provision. The percentage was between seventy to eighty per cent for Etibank workers, because the practice of compulsory work at the remotely situated mines ruled out commuting as an option. The combined figures on state housing provision concealed the severity of the problem for textile workers. Report after report underlined the housing problem and its damaging effect on industrial productivity.[186]

In 1947, the Ministry of Labour labelled the government's effort to solve the housing problem an "attempt to have a skilled workforce." Writing in a trade union publication the following year, the head of the CHP's Workers Bureau, a department designed to control the trade union movement, lamented over the waste of precious work time and worker energy during long commutes. His chosen example was a Bakırköy worker living in Eyüp.[187] Various authors in the labour press agreed that solving the problem of workers' accommodation would not only push the wages down, it would also boost worker morale and, in turn, work effort.[188]

The aggregate data on housing hid yet another important difference: the difference between housing provision for the old and the new textile factories. In the same way as the emergence of company towns in other industrial contexts, geographical isolation was a factor determining the extent and content of welfare provision. Housing provision was born out of the economic necessity of attracting labour to undeveloped areas.[189] In 1939, reports began to

---

186 *Sümerbank Birleşik Pamuk İpliği ve Dokuma Fabrikaları Müessesesi 1939 Yılı Umumi Murakebe Heyeti Raporu,* 42; "Sümerbank Fabrikaları İçtimai Teşkilat 1940 Yılı Raporu," 20; *Sümerbank 1944 Yılı Umumi Murakebe Heyeti Raporu,* 40–2; Aydemir, Ş. Süreyya, Bülent Büktaş, Fazlı Turga, and Turgut Akkaş, *Devlet Endüstrisinde Çalışan Personelin İşletmeler Civarına Yerleştirme Şekilleri Hakkında* (1945), Archival Collection of the Republic of Turkey Prime Ministry Supreme Audit Board. Amb./Db.No: K.A./255.07.02.01.06.1163.

187 Barkın, "Heder Olan İş Saatleri."

188 "Yurdun En Büyük İşçi Sendikası Kömür Havzasında Kuruldu," *Türk İşçisi,* 12 April 1947; Rahmi Alp "İşçi Teminati," *Türk İşçisi,* 5 July 1947; Koyulhisarlioğlu, "Mesken Meselesi," *Türk İşçisi,* 16 August 1947.

189 Jacoby, *Employing Bureaucracy,* 40.

mention that the old factories were being left behind in social expenses in general, and in housing provision, in particular.[190] The following year, Sümerbank had planned the construction of housing for workers in its Anatolian factories. The houses would be distributed on a priority basis, with skilled workers and households with more than one state worker taking precedence. The only construction planned for the Bakırköy Factory was a workers' barracks for migrant workers.[191] In 1945, the three old factories in Istanbul, that is the Bakırköy, Defterdar, and Beykoz factories, provided no housing for their workers except for the barracks for single workers. Among the textile factories, Kayseri, Nazilli, and Hereke were the top providers, but even at Kayseri, only twenty-two per cent of workers were given housing; the percentage was slightly higher at Nazilli. The housing situation was better at the Karabük Iron and Steel Factory. "It would be a great progress," Kessler wrote in 1949, "if we could bring up the working and living conditions in Istanbul, the biggest industrial city of our country, to the level of Karabük."[192]

In 1945, four inspectors, including the former director of the Bakırköy Factory, Fazlı Turga, estimated the number of houses that were urgently needed for each textile factory. They calculated that civil servants and workers at Bakırköy needed 153 and 750 houses, respectively. In addition, a barracks to accommodate fifty single workers was needed. The numbers, the inspectors warned, were based on the number of workers in work programmes, which was eight hundred workers for Bakırköy in 1945. The actual number of workers, however, was almost double. The situation was dire because compared with the seven per cent in Europe, Turkish workers spent twenty-five per cent of their monthly income on housing expenses.[193] The following years did not see the construction of these houses, while reports continued to advise an expansionary housing policy. An International Labour Organization report on Turkey at the end of the decade describes the housing conditions as "universally recognised to be deplorable." It underlined the close connection between decent and healthy housing, and the attainment of labour stability and efficiency.[194] Left to their own devices during the time between these two reports,

190 *Sümerbank 1939 Yılı Umumi Murakebe Heyeti Raporu*, 18; *Sümerbank 1941 Yılı Umumi Murakebe Heyeti Raporu*, 4, Archival Collection of the Republic of Turkey Prime Ministry Supreme Audit Board. Amb./Db.No: K.A./255.07.02.01.06.3236.

191 "Endüstri Hayatında," *İktisadi Yürüyüş*.

192 Gerhard Kessler, "*Zonguldak ve Karabükteki Çalışma Şartları*," Istanbul Üniversitesi İktisat ve İçtimaiyat Enstitüsü ayrı bası, no. 11 (Istanbul: Kenan Matbası, 1949), 31–2.

193 *Aydemir et al.*, "Devlet Endüstrisinde."

194 ILO, *Labour Problems in Turkey*, 16.

state workers in Istanbul had come up with a self-made solution to the housing problem.

14 The Move to *Gecekondus*

Workers' housing in Istanbul had been a problem since the beginning of state-led industrialisation. During his 1933 visit to the Bakırköy Factory, the prime minister specifically asked Bay Fazlı if the factory had lodgings for female workers who commuted long distances.[195] In 1934, the emergence of new working-class neighbourhoods in Yedikule and Zeytinburnu received press attention. Populated by factory workers as well as small business owners, the narrow and muddy streets and the dark and sunless houses of these neighbourhoods were under constant threat of fire and plague.[196] By the 1940s, rents were increasing faster than wages, pushing the working poor to find their own solution to the housing problem.[197] In the meantime, the population of Zeytinburnu was growing at a higher rate than other parts of the city. By the end of the decade, Zeytinburnu was the largest and most densely populated *gecekondu* area of Istanbul, and its residents established the first *gecekondu* dwellers' organisation in 1948.[198] By the beginning of the 1960s, there were five *gecekondu* neighbourhoods in Zeytinburnu, with more than forty per cent of residents working at factories.[199]

The connection between housing and public health, as well as working-class morality, was being increasingly viewed as both a medical and political issue in the scholarly surveys, unpublished official reports, and newspapers of the decade. Growing discontent with the government brought worker housing to the agenda of the 1947 party convention, at the end of which the provision

195 "Başvekil Hz.," *Cumhuriyet*.

196 "İşçi Mahallesi," *Haber Akşam Postası*, 20 March 1934.

197 Necip T. Tesal, *Milli Korunma Mevzuatı ve Kiralar Hakkında* (1952), Archival Collection of the Republic of Turkey Prime Ministry Supreme Audit Board. Amb./Db.No:K.A./ 255.07.02.01.06.1287.

198 "Zeytinburnu Çimento Fabrikasında Toplulukla İş Uyuşmazlığı Kesin Olarak Kotarıldı," *Türk İşçisi*, 16 August 1947; Charles W. M. Hart, *Zeytinburnu Gecekondu Bölgesi*, trans. Nephan Saran (Istanbul: Istanbul Ticaret Odası Yayınları, 1969); Ruşen Keleş, *Urbanisation in Turkey* (New York: Ford Foundation, 1971), 84; İlhan Tekeli, *Türkiye'de Yaşamda ve Yazında Konut Sorununun Gelişimi* (Ankara: T.C. Başbakanlık Toplu Konut İdaresi Başkanlığı, 1996), 45.

199 Hart, *Zeytinburnu*, 67: Kemal Sülker, "Valinin 35000 Gecekondu Arasında Yaptığı Tetkikler," *Gece Postası*, 3 November 1949.

of social housing made it onto the party programme.[200] In 1948, the head of the Workers Bureau of the CHP described the situation in a trade union newspaper as follows: "Housing is such a severe problem for the workers and the poor that homeless families build a shed wherever they find a piece of vacant land." The sight of a handful of *gecekondus* by the side of the railway connecting Europe to the city via Bakırköy had become thousands of people "living like wild animals." These settlements had quickly expanded because the state tolerated them. In the coffeehouse across from the Bakırköy Factory, he heard workers saying that if they acted together, "they could confiscate property that did not belong to them." These workers laboured day and night to earn more; their wives and daughters sold their gold jewellery, their pots and pans, and even their beds and duvets to collect the money needed to pay for water and transport costs, and for the bribes they had to give to the watchmen and the police.[201] A 1948 party report on industrial workers defined the housing problem as one of the most pressing agenda items for the government, and pointed to the *gecekondus* as evidence. "There is no guarantee," the report warned the government, "that those who built sheds on state and even private land will not go so far as to claim ownership over other things."[202]

The ruling elite was right to worry about the potential radicalisation of the housing struggle since the language of class was now being articulated through the politics of residence. Angry at the metaphors likening workers' *gecekondus* to palaces, an author described the living conditions in the following satirical spirit:

> They call it the Light Palace, but it is lit by a gas lamp
> On the door it reads "The Palace of Abundance," but it is only beans cooking inside
> The rooms of this "Spacious Palace" are but the size of a coffin
> Faces sulk and tuberculosis abound in this "Joyful Palace of Health"[203]

The application form to work at the Bakırköy Factory asked for the address and the ownership status of workers' houses. Until the mid-1940s, the majority of

200 Barış Alp Özden, "Health, Morality and Housing: The Politics of Working-Class Housing in Turkey," *New Perspectives on Turkey* 49 (2013), 91–120.

201 Rebi Barkın, "Gecekonduların Durumu," *Hürbilek*, 17 April 1948.

202 "Partimizin Meslek Teşekkülleriyle Münasebet ve Temasları Hakkında Umumi Mütalaa," in "CHP Genel İdare Kurulu'nun İşçi Raporunun Divan'da Görüşüleceği," file 490.453.1867.6, Republic of Turkey Prime Ministry General Directory of State Archives, 5.

203 Munip Koçoğlu, "Gecekondunun Sefaletini Bir Sarayın Rehaverinde Dile Getirmek İmkansızdır," *İşçi Hakkı*, 15 November 1951, 2.

the workers who answered these questions lived in nearby neighbourhoods such as Yenimahalle, Kartaltepe, Osmaniye, Zeytinlik, Cevizlik, Yeniköy, and Sakızağacı. Only one worker was an owner-occupier, one lived in a hostel, and another one stayed at a coffeehouse, the rest were tenants. In 1946, an increasing number of workers began to give their address as Zeytinburnu, some even specified it, "Zeytinburnu Gecekondu-Sümer Mahallesi," evincing that the area was populated densely enough by the Bakırköy workers to take its name from Sümerbank.[204] There was also a Sümer mosque in the neighbourhood, which, as I learnt from the mosque's imam back then in the 1950s, İbrahim Sevme, had been built by the residents themselves, including Bakırköy workers. The imam witnessed factory workers carrying cheap construction materials on horse carts during the night to build their tiny houses. Another witness described the materials as sometimes nothing more than planks of wood and flattened tin containers.[205] Dwellers often had to repair damage. In 1948, a Bakırköy weaver asked for four days' leave to repair the collapsed wall of his *gecekondu*.[206]

"The majority of workers live in *gecekondus*," claimed the head workers' representative of the factory in 1951 during a conflict with a wood dealer. The representatives had come to an agreement to buy wood for the factory workers, but the delivery was delayed by more than a month. Winter was at the door, which meant transportation would be almost impossible due to the road situation in the squatter settlements, he explained.[207] But the lack of infrastructure was hardly the only problem in the neighbourhood. Hüseyin told me why he and his wife had decided to stay away from the *gecekondu* settlement in 1949, preferring to share accommodation with his brother in Osmaniye. Throughout our conversation, he repeated how difficult it was to live on his wage. When I asked him if they had difficulty paying the rent, he responded: "Of course we did. The maximum I earned, including the bonuses, was forty-nine liras a month; calculate it, seven and a half hours a day [on hourly wage of thirty-eight piasters], and I paid twenty liras for rent … It did not even have a toilet inside. I paid half of my earnings on rent." When asked if there was a housing shortage, he immediately notes the *gecekondu* area: "There was. Everywhere

---

204 Although the name was already in use in the late 1940s, it was not the official name of the neighbourhood until the 1950s. Sümer Neighbourhood should not be confused with the Sümer Houses (*Sümer Evleri*), which were two-storey houses built by the workers' cooperatives later in the 1950s in Kartaltepe.

205 İbrahim Sevme, telephone interview by the author, 1 March 2009; Faik Akçay, *Zeytinburnu: Gerçek Yönleriyle Bir Gecekondu Kenti* (Istanbul: Çelikcilt Matbaası, 1974), 13.

206 Personnel file of Hayri Önen.

207 "Bakırköy İşçileri," *İşçi Hakkı*, 11 October 1951.

was *gecekondu*. Zeytinburnu and so on were all built then." Why then did he not move there? "I was going to move but my wife did not agree. I got married in 1949 and my wife wanted to stay in Osmaniye. [Because] we did not witness but they beat people up, they cut off [women's] arms to steal their jewellery; terrible things happened there; it was not for everybody to live in *gecekondu* … only those brave ones at the factory, who were ready to accept everything, went there." Foreman Ahmet and his wife also made an attempt by the end of the 1940s to build a house in Zeytinburnu after their army officer neighbour offered them protection by privates under his command. The two neighbours picked a site, to which they transported lumber for the house foundations. However, when they arrived to find the lumber burnt the next morning, they decided to stay away from the area.[208]

For Ali, living in a *gecekondu* was not a matter of brevity. On the contrary, it was a matter of desperation. In 1950, Ali asked for the factory director's permission to take half of his hot meal to his eight children. "We live in a *gecekondu*," he said, "I can't eat knowing that they don't have enough." The director refused, claiming that the main purpose of the hot meal was to increase the work effort.[209] It would be hard to find any other archival evidence to better summarise the managerial perspective on industrial welfare measures.

15 Conclusion

The decision to renovate the Bakırköy Factory was taken in 1933, the decennial year of the Republic of Turkey. The enthusiasm around the new factory building enhanced the celebratory and proud tone of the times in three different ways. First, as the first step in centrally planned industrialisation, the project signified the beginning of a new developmental paradigm. Second, the new factory building fulfilled the industrial imagery that portrayed large factories as markers of national greatness and the advance of civilisation. True, the new factories constructed in the later years were larger in size, but as the comparison with the American slaughterhouse—the industrial workplace that Henry Ford argues the idea of the assembly line was taken from—suggests, the renovated textile plant realised the ideal of the factory as a huge, integrated machine. Finally, the new, large factory materialised the ideal of rebuilding the country's physical and human infrastructure. Together with the nationalised

208 Ergin Aygöl (Ahmet's son), interview by the author, online, 15 February 2022.
209 Daysal, "Bakırköy Bez Fabrikasında."

and expanded railway network, the large factory symbolised the transcendence of Ottoman underdevelopment, both physically and mentally. The contrast between the old, run-down building and the new machinery was finally resolved, clearing away all the physical impediments to productivity. And the factory was ready to lead the way into the "new industrial mentality," that is, a combination of rational work and patriotic labour.

Through a micro-level study of industrial relations, I have shown that behind the ceremonial façade of a scientifically managed, worker-friendly industry, there hides a strictly authoritarian world of labour. Despite claims to a rationalisation of labour through more efficient organisation and modern work techniques, the internal organisation of the factory was a long way from bureaucratised protections and procedures such as standardised job requirements, promotion ladders, merit-rating systems, and rules concerning discipline and dismissal. These protections would emerge slowly but steadily after the 1950s, and have been projected backward onto the 1930s and 1940s by historians and the general public alike. In the 1930s and 1940s, productivity was sought mainly through technological investment and work intensification. An atmosphere of humiliation, harassment, and individual beatings suffused the worksite. Worker effort was maintained through close supervision and pressure.

In Istanbul, the main problem for factory directors was not so much the inadequacy of the labour supply but the problem of labour retention. Labour turnover was a response to inequitable payment systems and low remuneration, on the one hand, and harsh and arbitrary discipline, on the other. When the maintenance of effort and discipline was further obstructed because of wartime labour shortages, carrots were introduced in addition to sticks. Industrial welfare schemes gradually expanded after 1941, partly in line with transnational responses to the rise of the social and the labour question. Their workplace-level implementation, however, fostered various inequalities within and between factories. For state workers in Istanbul, the main line of distinction was housing. As state-led industrialisation turned Istanbul to a city of cramped housing conditions, state workers were left completely to their own devices. They became the first dwellers of *gecekondu*s, the most visible manifestations of the structural transformations Turkey went through in the post-WWII period.

The momentum gained by industrial production during the war years did not improve the working and living conditions of state workers. By the end of the war, discontent with the CHP's economic policies was growing at the same time as the global winds of change were signalling a bigger role for the state in industrial relations. The CHP quickly responded through institutional and legal arrangements, hoping to secure the support of the working classes.

Its major mistake was to underestimate the political capacity of the industrial workers. In its 1947 report for the International Labour Organization's Near and Middle East meeting, the then recently established Turkish Ministry of Labour proudly claimed that "as a general rule, workers are more knowledgeable about and enthusiastic for their work than for their rights."[210] In the next chapter, I continue my analysis of the micro-politics of shop-floor industrial relations to show how the increasing tension between the undercurrent of isolated and individualised worker resistance and CHP's proud presentation of industrial relations would shape the course of class politics in Turkey. After attending to state administrative structures, managers, foreign experts, and middle-class intellectuals, in the following pages, we will tune in to changes in the self-understanding and self-perception among Bakırköy workers in the face of the labour control regime that was being imposed upon them.

---

210 "Türk Raporu," 60.

CHAPTER 5

Voices from the Shop Floor

Politics, Law, and Workplace Industrial Relations

> [T]he historian who encounters such letters as these, and then turns back to the licensed press or to the papers of the great, has a sense of double vision. On the surface all is consensus, deference, accommodation; the dependants petition abjectly for favour; every hind is touching his forelock ... Then, from an anonymous and obscure level, there leaps to view for a moment violent Jacobite or Levelling abuse. We should take neither the obeisances nor the imprecations as indications of final truth; both could flow from the would now seem, Richard Cobb tells us, that half the valets of pre-Revolutionary Paris, who followed the nobility servilely through the suave salons, were nourishing in their reveries anticipations of the guillotine falling upon the white and powdered necks about them. But, if the guillotine had never been set up, the reveries of these valets would remain unknown. And historians would be able to write of the deference, or even consensus, of the ancien régime.[1]

∴

On 18 November 1945, the last day of the Muslim Festival of Sacrifice (*Eid-al-Adha*), the Bakırköy Factory was hosting a large group of bureaucrats for the opening ceremony of the new factory hospital, canteen, and performance hall. In the words of a prominent journalist, who was also a former member of the parliament, the new constructions would complete the social welfare aspect of the already architecturally and technically modern factory. The Bakırköy Factory was once again setting an example for Turkish factories:

1 Edward Palmer Thompson, "The Crime of Anonymity," in *Albion's Fatal Tree: Crime and Society in Eighteenth-Century England,* eds. Douglas Hay, Peter Linebaugh, John G. Rule, E. P. Thompson, and Cal Winslow (London: Verso, 2011), 306–307.

DOI:10.1163/9789004687141_007

> The state, in its own factories, takes care of the health and wellbeing of its workers and civil servants; it takes care of their nutrition, social education, and recreation. In one word, the state provides the workers with all the necessities of a civilised life and thus precludes class war, which has turned the Western world upside down. The reigning mentality [in state factories] is not to exploit but to prosper the workers. [That is why] the worker finds a heaven at [state] factories, not hell, and thus commits to them.[2]

Two discourses, one national and the other global, overlap in this celebratory portrayal published a few months after the war ended. The first, and by now familiar, is the Kemalist developmentalist discourse, which presented state factories as spaces of national modernity. The second, a strengthening global discourse, points at industrial welfare as the most effective weapon against class struggle, after the upheavals of the war pushed the "social question" to the forefront and increasingly brought the state into the lives of labour.

Readers looking at the front page of the same newspaper must have been puzzled by what happened at another state factory that very same day. As the celebrations continued at Bakırköy, some ten kilometres away, angry workers were storming the canteen of the tobacco warehouse in Beşiktaş. The incident started with a worker complaining about the quality of the food, and it quickly escalated when the factory director slapped the worker, causing turmoil in the canteen. The director pulled out his gun, kicked another worker who tried to grab it, and ran away to lock himself in his office. The situation escalated further to the point that the police, when they arrived, decided to fire gunshots in the air to clear the factory entrance. The police detained all three hundred and fifty workers, arresting eight of them in the end.[3]

There could hardly be a better example of the contrast between the official presentation of industrial relations and the actual restlessness on the shop floor than these two pieces of news. The immediate postwar period emerged as a catalytic moment in the history of labour in Turkey. It was shaped by the interplay between the crisis of the one-party regime and the rise of the international welfare discourse that transformed the labour question into a social question. A new labour regime emerged from the interactions between the two. In this chapter, I examine the rise and development of this labour regime at two levels: at the level of political and legal changes, and at the level of

2 Abidin Daver, "Bakırköy Fabrikasında," *Cumhuriyet*, 19 November 1945.

3 "350 İşçinin Çıkardığı Bir Hadise," *Cumhuriyet*, 19 November 1945.

workers' experiences of these changes through a micro-historical approach. How did the changes in the institutions of job regulation external to the workplace affect relationships and bargaining on the shop floor? This is the question that guides this chapter as I weave together biographical snapshots of Bakırköy workers' experiences of industrial work with the wider processes of politico-economic development.

My main source material for this chapter will be the petitions filed by the Bakırköy workers. In social history, petitions have been accepted as a peculiarly rich kind of documentary source. Two factors render them even more precious for the study of industrial relations in 1940s Turkey. First, in a context characterised by the absence of either trade unions (until 1946) or an effective and independent arbitration system, petitioning emerged as the predominant form of industrial bargaining. Second, in the absence of historical material left behind by workers, their petitions offer precious insights into workers' aspirations and the ideological categories through which they interpreted their own experiences and formulated their goals. As a major mechanism for grievance redressal, petitions are a window into the workers' acquiescence in and compliance with workplace rules, as well as their attempts to modify these rules in order to constrain the exercise of managerial control.

But it was not only workers who penned petitions at the factory. Managers also petitioned, and often scribbled notes on workers' petitions, revealing various kinds of exchanges on the shop floor. These documents voice rank-and-file workers' and managers' experiences in that they document their lives on the shop floor as well as their visions of a just world of industrial relations. Their conversational aspects allow us to reconstruct the procedures of mediation, repression, acceptance, and resistance in operation on the shop floor. In certain cases, correspondence between factory management and the higher authorities brings the state into the picture, exposing the wider interactions among the industrial policymakers, management, and workers.

In treating workers' petitions as representations of "actions in structured situations," I argue that Bakırköy workers quickly seized the opportunities presented by the changes in the external regulation of labour.[4] My close reading of the petitions compiled by workers in the 1940s reveals that their self-perception and self-representation changed dramatically over time. Despite the repressive nature of industrial relations, workers turned the shop floor into a bargaining ground and devised strategies to resist managerial attempts to

4 Carola Lipp and Lothar Krempel, "Petitions and the Social Context of Political Mobilisation in the Revolution of 1848/49: A Microhistorical Actor-Centred Network Analysis," *International Review of Social History* 46, no. S9 (2001), 153.

increase control both inside and outside the factory. The image of the helpless, complicit worker that prevails in the literature on this period does not square with the material I present in this chapter. The postwar political liberalisation, as well as the changes in the external regulation of labour, tilted the balance of shop-floor power in favour of the workers. Such fluid circumstances widened the possibilities for shop-floor bargaining and improved workers' ability to impose restrictive practices to limit managerial freedom of action in the workplace.

In the course of the 1940s, petitions increasingly came to rely on certain principles of legitimisation derived from elements of class consciousness. They displayed a heightened sense of worker identity, as workers became aware of their role in the production process as well as their rights as citizens, identifying themselves positively as workers belonging to the broader labouring community. The development of a culture that asserted ideas of workers' rights within society at large and within the workplace in particular would become discernible by the end of the decade.

1 The War at the Workplace

Despite her vital strategic location, Turkey managed to remain neutral during the greater part of the Second World War.[5] The country was thus saved from physical destruction but not from economic devastation. Between 1940 and 1945, Turkey's gross domestic product (GDP) decreased by an average of 6.9 per cent per annum. By the end of the war, GDP was down to its 1934 level, with GDP per capita thirty-eight per cent below the 1939 figure.[6] In 1944, a special party commission on the cost of living and profiteering compared the twenty-five per cent increase in the cost of living in some war-waging countries with the almost five hundred per cent increase seen in Turkey, blaming the wholesalers and those whose "only connection to the homeland is through their stomach."[7] The war left in its wake a poverty-stricken peasantry and industrial working class alongside a bourgeoisie that had reinforced its ranks by profiteering under wartime policies. In the face of the ever-rising prices and the spread of hoarding, wrote the then head of the provincial treasury of Istanbul,

5 Turkey was obliged to declare war on Germany and Japan on 23 February 1945 in order to secure a seat at the Conference on World Organisation.

6 William Hale, "Ideology and Economic Development in Turkey 1930–1945," *Bulletin British Society for Middle Eastern Studies* 7 (1980), 109.

7 Cited in Korkut Boratav, *Türkiye'de Devletçilik* (Ankara: İmge Kitabevi, 2017), 296–297.

the impoverished masses were gritting their teeth against the business class in general and the war-rich in particular.[8] A prominent member of the latter group, Vehbi Koç, had won a railway construction tender just before the start of the war. He wrote in his memoirs how the government had saved him from near-bankruptcy in 1942: "We started the construction in spring 1939, and the war began in September. Prices were increasing; the price of a kilo of wheat was ten piasters when we started, and the daily wages were one lira. Two years later, a kilo of wheat was one lira, and the wages were four."[9] Koç's wartime lobbying efforts paid off: the prime minister tripled the contract price, rescuing the wealth of what would become Turkey's richest family.

In the absence of trade unions or a worker-based political party, industrial workers had no lobbying power. The war aggravated working conditions by extending the working day and bringing real wages down by fifty-five per cent between 1938 and 1945.[10] The ad hoc, piecemeal benefits under wartime exigencies were nowhere near enough to prevent the pauperisation of industrial workers. Consumer prices tripled between 1938 and 1946, while wages increased by only twenty-five per cent.[11] In Istanbul, where the cost-of-living index had increased by 3.5 times between 1938 and 1943, the decrease in real wages in the textile sector was around fifty per cent overall.[12] In the two state-owned textile factories, Bakırköy and Defterdar, where wages fared slightly better than those in the private sector, workers demanded better wage. In 1942, the Defterdar Factory management reported worker complaints to Sümerbank and argued that state workers should also benefit from the wartime wage protections that civil servants were receiving. The General Directorate agreed and wages at the factory increased between ten and sixty per cent.[13]

The Bakırköy Factory management, however, did not implement such an initiative. And it was perhaps for this reason that a worker from the dyeing department decided to take the matter into his own hands. In 1943, Mehmet bypassed the factory management and petitioned directly to the Sümerbank General Directorate. He described how the rising cost of living was affecting his family:

8 Faik Ökte, *Varlık Vergisi Faciası* (Istanbul: Nebioğlu Yayınevi, 1951), 38.

9 Gürel Tüzün, ed., *Vehbi Koç Anlatıyor: Bir Derleme* (Istanbul: Yapı Kredi, 2018), 88.

10 Korkut Boratav, *Türkiye İktisat Tarihi 1908–1985* (Ankara: İmge Kitabevi, 2003), 88–90.

11 "Hayat Pahalılığı ve Dar Gelirliler," *Cumhuriyet*, 31 July 1946.

12 Sabahaddin Zaim, *Istanbul Mensucat Sanayiinin Bünyesi ve Ücretler* (Istanbul: Istanbul Üniversitesi İktisat Fakültesi Yayını, 1956), 279–282.

13 Ziyaeddin Fahri Fındıkoğlu, "Türkiye'de Sınai Sosyoloji Araştırmaları 1-Defterdar Fabrikası," *Feshane Mensucat Meslek Dergisi* 2, no. 12 (1954), 26.

> This person in destitution has worked at the Bakırköy Cloth Factory for seven years and dared to take refuge in your Higher Office as a worker who has always gained the approval of his superiors. [While] many of my friends benefited from wage increases, this destitute labourer did not. I am in extreme poverty; especially the latest increase in the cost of living has suffocated me. I kindly ask you, with my eternal respect, to order those concerned to give me an increase and prevent me from being damnified.

I will shortly address Mehmet's curious linguistic shifts between the first-person pronoun and "this person in destitution." But let us now focus on the possible reasons behind his choice of addressee. The first clue can be found in an earlier petition Mehmet wrote after his discharge from the army in 1942:

> [Your] servant is one of your workers who worked for five years. Eleven months ago, I went to the military to carry out my national duty and have recently been discharged. I beg with respect for the sake of humanity that your servant, who has a wife and children, is re-hired so that I am not aggrieved on this winter day and saved from extreme poverty.

Although the state guaranteed that workers would be rehired after military service, the note on Mehmet's petition from the personnel department stated that he had to wait until there was an opening. Two facts make this brief remark rather curious. First, Mehmet was a worker with an extraordinary length of experience in a highly mobile labour market. Second, the war had aggravated the already high labour turnover rates. The year Mehmet came back from his military service, the Bakırköy Factory management was searching for workers in Izmir, an Aegaen city some five hundred kilometres away from Istanbul.[14] But, again the same year, a weaver, also named Mehmet, was laid off a few days after he was rehired upon his return from the military, despite his superiors' favourable opinion of him. If it were not for this second weaver leaving the factory, Mehmet would have joined Istanbul's army of unemployed. In 1943, due to the extension, the factory needed new recruits, especially weavers, but even increased wages and benefits could not attract skilled workers.[15] Job advertisements claimed that a hardworking weaver could earn up to seven hundred piasters a day with the additional benefits of a free hot meal and a

14 Can Nacar, "Our Lives Were Not as Valuable as an Animal: Workers in State-Run Industries in WorldWar-II Turkey," *International Review of Social History* 54, no. 17 (2009), 151.

15 "İşçi Buhranı: Tecrübeli Dokumacı Aranıyor," *Haber-Akşam Postası*, 28 September 1943.

loaf of bread, and an additional ten per cent monthly bonus for presenteeism.[16] Only a few months earlier, the same newspaper had published advertisements by job-seeking weavers, claiming to be experienced and skilled, looking for employment. People with secondary or even high-school diplomas were looking for work at factories in Istanbul.[17]

What does this paradoxical information imply? First, the lack of coordination in the national labour market had given way to the contradictory coexistence of labourers moving around the country in search of employment, with factories searching for labour far away from their location. During the parliamentary discussions on the establishment of the Employment and Recruitment Agency in 1946, industrial policymakers acknowledged the delay in labour market regulation, documenting the high cost of non-intervention.[18] Second, the ensuing problems of high labour turnover, coupled with the lack of vocational training, created a labour market in which experienced and skilled workers were scarce, while unskilled workers abounded. Third, state factories were recruiting and laying off workers in response to wartime fluctuations in production caused by a lack of raw materials and variations in demand. By the end of the war, labour hoarding was a serious problem at state factories. News of possible layoffs were already circulating by the end of 1945.[19] But the layoffs at state factories had to end the following year because the continuing shortage of imported textile raw materials was aggravating unemployment.[20] In 1947, Sümerbank came up with another solution, the details of which we will read from the workers' petitions below.

Having found himself in this chaotic labour market after his return from the military in January 1942, Mehmet the dye worker had to beg to be rehired at fifteen piasters an hour. His wage was less than one quarter of the weaver's wage proclaimed by factory management and roughly seventy per cent of the average wage at an Istanbul state textile factory cited by a prominent historian of industrial relations.[21] Ten months later, he received a twenty per cent increase, but as we have seen in his 1943 petition quoted above, this did not improve his situation, which he described as "extreme poverty."

16 "Dokuma İşçisi Aranıyor," *Cumhuriyet,* 27 September 1943.

17 "İş ve İşçi Arayanlar," *Haber-Akşam Postası,* 29 March 1943; "İş Bulma Yurdu: İş İçin Yurda Yüzlerce Genç Müracaat Etti," *Cumhuriyet,* 26 May 1942.

18 "Çalışma Bakanlığının Hazırladığı Kanunlar," *Cumhuriyet*, 15 January 1946.

19 "Sümerbank Fabrikalarındaki İşçilerin Durumu," *Cumhuriyet,* 30 November 1945.

20 "İş Kazaları ve Analık Sigortalarının Tatbikatı," *Cumhuriyet,* 1 July 1946; "Memlekette İşsizlik Gittikçe Artıyor mu?" *Cumhuriyet,* 22 August 1946.

21 Ahmet Makal, *Ameleden İşçiye: Erken Cumhuriyet Dönemi Emek Tarihi Çalışmaları* (Istanbul: İletişim Yayınları, 2007), 132.

Disappointed with the factory management, first over not being rehired, and then, over not receiving the wage increase that other workers had, Mehmet appealed to the Sümerbank General Directorate relying on three arguments. He first referred to his seniority at the factory, knowing that his seven years of service was exceptional for the highly mobile labour market. Two years after his petition, the technician of his department would call him "a very old and hardworking" worker. He went on to cite this managerial approval, a precondition for wage increases at state factories as I have shown in the previous chapter. Last but not least, he objected to the unfavourable comparison between his wage and those of his fellow workers. Data from other workers' files supported his claim. To take two examples, in January 1943, another worker in the dyeing department, Mehmet's senior by only a year, was earning an hourly rate of thirty piasters, while a weaver who had worked at the factory since 1928 earned twenty-five piasters an hour. These figures support two arguments I made in the previous chapter. First, contrary to factory management's claims, wages did not reflect seniority. Second, considerable wage differentials existed between different production departments as well as within the same production department.

Mehmet's account of wage determination points to the tensions between the allegedly bureaucratic industrial relations structure and the piecemeal and informal regimes of labour control on the shop floor. That he petitioned the Sümerbank General Directorate suggests that he was both aware of and perturbed by the "ceremonial façade" at the factory.[22] In its reply to the General Directorate, the factory management defended its supposed bureaucratic organisation by referring to formal rules of wage determination. Mehmet had already received a wage increase within the last six months, it was reported; he would have to wait. Neither the previous delay in his wage promotion nor his complaint on wage differentials got a mention. The management had fended off Mehmet's bargaining effort without much difficulty.

We now turn to the story of the second Mehmet. Although Mehmet the dyer's story suggested that factory management ignored petitions written in a pleading tone and would strictly follow the bureaucratic rules, Mehmet the weaver's story proved otherwise. The first time we encountered Mehmet, he had just returned from his military service. He had been rehired but was laid

22 I have written on this in detail in chapter 4. The concept denotes the discrepancy between the image created by the seemingly highly institutionalised, rationalised, and impersonal prescriptions and the actual operating activities based on managers' discrete power. See: John W. Meyer and Brian Rowan, "Institutionalized Organisations: Formal Structure as Myth and Ceremony," *American Journal of Sociology* 83, no. 2 (1977), 341–343.

off only a few days later. His luck turned when another weaver left the factory and he was rehired once again. By the time we meet him a second time in 1947, he has been working at the factory for five years and is living in dire poverty:

> Although I used to work as a weaver for ten years at your factory, I was assigned to the electricity department on a low wage upon my return from the military and five months ago I got my old position. At present, I receive a daily wage of two liras, which is not enough for one person, let alone an entire family. In the last round of [biweekly] payments, a cleaner got thirty-five liras, whereas I got only twenty-five liras. In 1942, I used to earn 140 liras on average a month whereas now I only earn fifty-two liras. I have endured the situation and have kept working [at this wage] although I had to sell some furniture. I expect from your high conscience to increase my wage in accordance with my expertise and to save me from this terrible financial situation before I am obliged to sell the bed I sleep on.

Similar to Mehmet the dyer, Mehmet the weaver's first reference was to his qualities as a hardworking and disciplined worker. He cited his immediate return to the factory after military service and his acceptance of lower pay as twofold proof of his commitment to the factory. The similarities continue with the comparison in wages with other workers. From this point on, however, a remarkable difference emerges. In contrast to Mehmet the dyer, Mehmet the weaver is not begging, neither is he referring to himself as "this person in destitution" or "your servant." Instead, he refers to his expertise, which, he claims, should be taken into consideration in determining his wage level. Aware that his wage did not reflect his experience and skills, his tone was one of exasperation. Finally, in the final sentence, where he clearly formulated his demand, Mehmet presented himself as a worker who "expects" rather than "dared to take refuge in."

The management added four notes to Mehmet's petition. Probably written by his foreman, the first confirmed that Mehmet was indeed hardworking and supported his demand for a wage increase of five piasters. The second, by another administrator, reconfirmed this. The third, probably penned by the chief of the personnel department, provided information on his employment and wage history. His last wage increase had been in December 1946, which meant he would normally have to wait until June 1947. By September, Mehmet had still not received a raise and he had quite simply had enough:

> I have worked at the bobbin department as an assistant foreman for ten years. My hourly wage is thirty piasters. Although on 10 June 1947, both the production unit and the management ordered an increase in my wage, I did not see any results. Since it is impossible for me to support my family of four with fifty-two liras a month, I kindly request your permission to close my account.

To understand what Mehmet meant by it being impossible to support his family, it would suffice to say that in 1946, Mehmet would have had to spend 34.6 per cent of his monthly wage to buy two loaves of bread a day.[23] Once again, his department chief noted that Mehmet was indeed a hardworking and disciplined worker and should therefore be given an increase of five piasters an hour. The management approved the raise almost a month later but registered it as a consequence of Mehmet's hard work. Mehmet's struggle disappeared forever into the official records that were presented to the state inspectors.

Grievances over wages were also erased in another way. Employment histories of Süleyman and Cemil demonstrate how official records distorted workers' reasons for leaving. Only three months after he started working at the dyeing department in December 1943, Süleyman was ready to leave even though he had a one-year-old child. In his petition to the chief of his department, Süleyman requested the termination of his employment due to increasing financial difficulties caused by the rising cost of living. To his foreman, Süleyman was one of those disposable workers, of which "no inconvenience would be caused by his immediate leave." Three years later, in 1947, Süleyman was back in the factory. But this time, he was hired as a construction worker on a lower wage than he had earned in 1943. In the absence of any institutionalised social protection or workers' self-help organisation, Süleyman had no choice but to accept this demotion. Five months later, he left the factory again, claiming he needed to attend the harvest in his village. But two years later, he was back in the factory for the last and final time.

In 1941, Cemil's employment as an apprentice weaver was terminated because of absenteeism after only three months. During his second time at the factory in 1945, he resigned after five months of employment to go back to his village for family reasons. When he returned in July 1947, however, he submitted an employment certificate showing that he had been working at a private glassware factory. He, like Süleyman, was demoted to a wage that was less than what he had been earning in 1945. After four months of work, he wrote: "I am

23 Haluk Yılmaz, "Hayat Pahalılığı ve Dar Gelirliler," *Cumhuriyet*, 31 July 1946.

obliged to resign since I cannot make a living for my family with the wage that I am earning." The foreman's note was brief and concise: "Since a replacement has been found, he may leave today."

The employment histories of these two "disposable workers" raises questions about the validity of the commonplace assumption that high labour turnover resulted from workers' strong rural ties. Both workers cited agricultural work as their reason for leaving. But when we follow up on their work histories, it turns out that they actually left in search of better-paying factory jobs. But because agricultural duties were considered a legitimate reason—managers often noted remarks such as "he may leave because he needs to do the harvest"—and because employees were able to return to their jobs at state factories if they had left for such duties, workers also used it in official correspondence.

The petitions I have cited so far are fragments taken from an industrial world that is quite different from the one portrayed in state documents and media. In a context where the working classes lacked the tools to either make their voices heard at the time of their struggle or to archive it for historians to learn in posterity, workers adopted a powerless and deferential language in their petitions. If taken out of context, they could read more like petitions by subjects to a sovereign ruler. The deferential third-person self-references such as "this person in destitution" or "your servant," the emphasis on poverty and desperation, and the appeal to the management's benevolence, which echoes the idea of the state as a "benevolent father" (*devlet baba*), all suggest that a strictly hierarchical structure of labour-management relations prevailed at the factory. In their use of words such as "benevolence" and "despair," the workers mostly stayed away from the discourse of rights and obligations. But things would not stay like this for long. An undercurrent of change that would challenge both industrial policymakers and managers was on the way.

2 Postwar Changes in the External Regulation of Labour

"Istanbul is honoured to host this conference," wrote the first labour minister of the Republic of Turkey, Sadi Irmak, in November 1947, referring to the first International Labour Organization Regional Meeting for the Near and Middle East.[24] Originally planned to take place in Cairo, the meeting was relocated to Istanbul after Egypt was hit by a cholera outbreak in September. The timing

24 The piece was first published in a newspaper and then republished in the official Ministry of Labour journal: Sadi Irmak, "Istanbul Çalışma Konferansı," *Çalışma Vekâleti*

could hardly be better for the government, since it was struggling to prove its commitment to the postwar international order while also reconsolidating its rule in the face of a "seething undercurrent of popular hostility."[25] The newly founded ministry proudly reported back on the country's participation in the International Labour Organization, which, together with a wave of legislation and institutional arrangements concerning labour regulation, signalled the emergence of a new labour regime.[26] A gradual institutionalisation and extension of social insurance, increasing labour market regulation, and the legalisation of trade unions would change the face of industrial relations.

At the national level, the period when the party-state was less exposed to democratic pressures and in less immediate need of a legitimising authority had ended. In the first two decades of its rule, the CHP had mainly resorted to repression as a way of mediating the exploitation and domination of the working class.[27] The broader transnational social politics of the immediate postwar years, however, dictated the handling of the labour question in more hegemonic terms. Simple repression was becoming an inadequate solution and had to be supplemented by active government efforts to secure the consent of the masses. "The worker of our time does not want charity but rights," wrote a prominent sociologist who also worked as a consultant for the Ministry of Labour, "we should provide these rights [before workers] demand them peacefully or through strikes."[28] At the heart of the change in governmental labour policies

Dergisi, no. 24 (1947), 91–92. Irmak had stepped down from his ministerial position in September 1947.

25 Orhan Tuna, "Türkiye'de Sendikacılık ve Sendikalarımız," *Sosyal Siyaset Konferansları Dergisi*, no. 20 (1969), 256; M. Şehmus Güzel, "Çalışma Bakanlığının Kuruluşu-Çalışma Hayatında İngiliz Etkisi," *Tarih ve Toplum* 9, no. 50 (1988), 53; Cahit Talas, *Türkiye'nin Açıklamalı Sosyal Politika Tarihi* (Ankara: Bilgi Yayınevi, 1992), 125; Feroz Ahmad, *The Making of Modern Turkey* (New York: Routledge, 1993), 105.

26 The postwar years were marked by parliamentary ratifications of the International Labour Organization Conventions. By the end of the war, Turkey had ratified only one ILO convention (the Underground Work (Women) Convention of 1935) during the time of her membership since 1932. Within the first year of the ministry's establishment, the government ratified three ILO conventions: The Weekly Rest Convention of 1921, the Fee-Charging Employment Agencies Convention of 1933, and the Workmen's Compensation (Occupational Diseases) Convention of 1934. See: "Çalışma Meclisi Raporu," *Çalışma Vekâleti Dergisi*, no. 17 (1947), 64–81; "Milletlerarası Çalışma Konferansında Başdelegemiz Türk Görüşün Açıkladı," *Türk İşçisi*, 5 July 1947; Esat Tekeli, "Çalışma Konferansında Türkiye," *Çalışma Vekâleti Dergisi*, no. 20 (1947), 1–2; "Milletlerarası Çalışma Konferansında Türkiye (Bir Radyo Konusması)," *Çalışma Vekâleti Dergisi*, no. 22 (1947), 40–44; "Dünya Basınında Akisler," *Çalışma Vekâleti Dergisi*, no. 22 (1947), 46–49.

27 Göran Therborn, *What Does the Ruling Class Do When It Rules? State Apparatuses and State Power under Feudalism, Capitalism and Socialism* (London: New Left Books, 1978), 181.

28 Ziyaeddin Fahri Fındıkoğlu, "Türk İçtimai Siyasetinin İlk Zaferi," *İş*, no. 60 (*1946*), 2–5.

was the establishment of the Ministry of Labour in June 1945. The ministry replaced the Labour Department, which had been created under the auspices of the Ministry of Economy with the 1936 Labour Code.[29] The government went on to build an employment-based social insurance system for the urban working population. By creating new means of managing class conflict through institutionalised yet severely restricted and sectionally limited labour protections and limitations on organisational rights and strikes, the CHP's postwar labour policy aimed to secure the loyalty of the working classes. In a span of six months, it prepared a draft bill on industrial accidents, occupational diseases, and maternity insurance, and established the Workers' Insurance Institution (*İşçi Sigortaları Kurumu*) and Employment and Recruitment Agency (*İş ve İşçi Bulma Kurumu*). The government also repealed the prohibition of associations and alliances based on social class. However, after trade unions with connections to the newly founded socialist parties mushroomed, it proclaimed a state of emergency in December 1946, and liquidated the two socialist parties as well as the trade unions. A new trade union law was enacted in February 1947. The reader will learn more about this in detail in the next chapter.

At the global level, the debate on industrial welfare emerged as a political issue in the context of the postwar crisis. Global trends in social politics had already begun to influence debates on labour protections during the war years, but it was the postwar political crisis that created the conditions for legislation. In 1943, two years before becoming the first labour minister, Sadi Irmak had introduced the British government-commissioned 1942 Report of the Inter-Departmental Committee on Social Insurance and Allied Services, better known as the Beveridge Report, to a Turkish audience. Irmak aptly summarised the spirit of the age in this piece by writing that the war had moved social solidarity from the realm of philanthropy to the realm of the state's duties.[30] During the visit of a British mission to the newly established Ministry of Labour in 1945, he openly cited British social policy as the example the Turkish state sought to follow.[31] A collection of Beveridge's wartime essays and addresses was translated into Turkish accompanied by a strongly worded preface claiming that liberalism's time was over and that all nations now needed to jump on the wagon of state involvement in the economy.[32] The

29 Ahmet Makal, *Türkiye'de Tek Partili Dönemde Çalışma İlişkileri: 1920–1946* (Ankara: İmge Kitabevi, 1999), 468; Talas, *Sosyal Politika Tarihi*, 125.

30 Sadi Irmak, "Beveridge Planına Göre Sosyal Dayanışma," *Çalışma Vekâleti Dergisi*, no. 1 (1945), 24–25.

31 "Çalışma Bakanlığı Nasıl Çalışacak," *Cumhuriyet*, 6 July 1945.

32 Muammer Kurtay, "İçtimai Emniyetin Temelleri," *Çalışma Vekâleti Dergisi*, no. 16 (1947), 64.

bill on the establishment of the Ministry of Labour explicitly recognised the impact of the international atmosphere on Turkish lawmakers by referring to the 1944 Philadelphia Conference of the International Labour Organization, which envisaged the "progressive application" of universal labour standards to all parts of the world, as well as the social principles underlined in the Charter of the United Nations.[33] Similarly, parliamentary discussions on the social insurance bill referred to the stipulations of the 1936 Labour Code as well as the International Labour Organization's 1925 Workmen's Compensation (Accidents) Convention and its international applications.[34]

But it was not only the narrative of the good example that energised these changes. Preoccupied with industrial progress but distrustful of the disruptive power of organised labour, Turkish industrial policymakers turned to an expansion of social intervention and labour regulation in order to increase industrial productivity and secure working-class cooperation. In their presentation of the new legislation, they linked social security to the scientific management of industrial work. In the discussions on the social insurance bill, the chair of the CHP's labour department underlined that social insurance was not a philanthropic act but a measure to increase productivity.[35] "Protecting workers against risk," wrote the labour minister, is a prerequisite for improved work rhythm and efficiency.[36] In 1947, a journalist praised the harmony between the workers and the machines at the Bakırköy Factory. Behind the labour discipline at this model factory, he wrote, was not managerial supervision but workers' love for their jobs because "the management took care of all their needs."[37] The factory director also attributed increasing productivity to industrial welfare measures, citing the shrinkage in the workforce from 1,600 in 1944 to 1,090 in 1947.[38]

33 TBMM Tutanak Dergisi (Records of the Grand National Assembly), "Çalışma Bakanlığı Kuruluş ve Görevleri Hakkında Kanun Tasarısı ve Ekonomi ve Bütçe Komisyonları Raporları" (1/508), 26 November 1945, Session VII, Volume 21, Meeting no. 3, 52.

34 TBMM Tutanak Dergisi (Records of the Grand National Assembly), "İş Kazaları ile Mesleki Hastalıklar ve Analık Sigortaları Hakkında Kanun Tasarısı ve Geçici Komisyon Raporu," (1/316), 13 June 1945, Session VII, Volume 18, Meeting no. 2, 257–258.

35 TBMM Tutanak Dergisi (Records of the Grand National Assembly), "İş kazaları ile Mesleki Hastalıklar ve Analık Sigortaları Hakkında Kanun Tasarısı ve Geçici Komisyon Raporu," (1/316), 15 June 1945, Session VII, Volume 18, Meeting no. 2, 270.

36 Sadi Irmak, "İşçi Sigortaları Kurumu Genel Kurul Toplantısı," *Çalışma Vekâleti Dergisi*, no. 4 (1946), 51–54.

37 Süreyya Oral, "Bakırköy Bez Fabrikasında Çalışan İşçilerin Hayatı," *Türk İşçisi*, 1 March 1947.

38 Salahattin Güngör, "97 Yıl Önce Kurulan Bir Fabrika," *Türk İşçisi*, 22 February 1947.

FIGURE 22 Ground-breaking ceremony for the new social buildings of the Bakırköy Factory, c. 1948
COURTESY OF ERGİN AYGÖL

Accompanying the search for industrial productivity was the anxiety and fear of working-class politics. Worldwide postwar labour unrest was stoking the already widespread fear of the radicalisation of industrial workers among politicians, bureaucrats, and capitalists. In his piece on the aforementioned International Labour Organization meeting, Irmak referred to insurrectionary labour actions across Western Europe, specifically the May Day massacre in Italy and the wave of strikes in France, arguing that it was now more urgent than ever to reconcile personal liberty with social security, individual prosperity with social justice.[39] But labour unrest was engulfing the colonial and semi-colonial countries, too.[40] Right under Irmak's notes on the International

39 Sadi Irmak, "Istanbul Çalışma Konferansı," *Çalışma Vekâleti Dergisi*, no. 24 (1947), 92. In his 1947 novel, *Grev* (Strike), the prominent social realist author Orhan Kemal portrays the reactions of the factory owner, the police commissar, the governor, and the prosecutor in the face of spontaneous strike action at a textile factory. To calm the factory owner and his son, the governor repeats: "God forbid, what would we do if [Turkish] workers behaved like those in Europe?" Upon receiving the news of the strike, the prosecutor furiously reacts: "[Strikers] think they are in Italy or France, bastards!" See: Orhan Kemal, *Grev* (Istanbul: Everest, 2007), 1–13.

40 Jan Breman, "The Formal Sector: An Introductory Review," in *The Worlds of Indian Industrial Labour*, eds. Jonathan P. Parry, Jan Breman, and Karin Kapadia (New

Labour Organization meeting, the prominent sociologist quoted above argued that "a broad social policy is the best tool to save the Near East from the crisis the West has found itself in … and to stop the sneaky intrusions being prepared behind the iron curtain."[41] In the words of the exiled economist and social historian Gerhard Kessler, social policy was an instrument to avoid the "mistakes" made in the West.[42] Once again, as in the debates on state-led industrialisation in the early 1930s, the hegemonic trope of the new labour regime was "the peculiarities of our homeland." The references to international developments were selective. Similar to other industrial contexts, the new social policy direction did not take the form of diffusion, but rather of adaptation based on the interplay between transnational ideas and local historical contexts to result in a nationally specific labour regime.[43]

The reader will recall the dire conditions produced by the combination of transnational and national dynamics at the beginning of the 1930s. The situation the CHP found itself in by the end of the war was similar, in that it had to simultaneously handle a regime crisis at home while repositioning the country within the new international order. In the face of the eroded legitimacy of single-party rule at home and efforts to build a stronger alliance with the West, the bureaucratic elite hoped that the transition to multi-party politics would deflect any threats to their rule.[44] At the same time, internal divisions within

---

Delhi: Sage Publications, 1999), 30–31; Beverly Silver, *Forces of Labor: Workers' Movements and Globalisation Since 1870* (Cambridge: Cambridge University Press, 2003), 125–128; Vivek Chibber, "From Class Compromise to Class Accommodation: Labor's Incorporation into the Indian Political Economy," in *Social Movements and Poverty in India: Poverty, Power and Politics, eds.* Mary Falased Katzenstein and Raka Ray (*New York: Rowman* and Littlefield Publishers, 2005), 38–39; Ravi Ahuja, "Produce or Perish: The Crisis of the Late 1940s and the Place of Labour in Post-Colonial India," *Modern Asian Studies* 54, no. 4 (2020).

41 Ziyaeddin Fahri Fındıkoğlu, "Türkiye'de İçtimai Siyaset," *Çalışma Vekâleti Dergisi, no. 24 (1947), 95.*

42 Gerhard Kessler, "İşçi Hareketlerinin Hedefleri ve Yolları," *Çalışma Vekâleti Dergisi*, no. 16 (1947), 5.

43 Tehyun Ma, "A Chinese Beveridge Plan: The Discourse of Social Security and the Post-War Reconstruction of China," *European Journal of East Asian Studies* 11, no. 2 (2012); Ravi Ahuja, "A Beveridge Plan for India? Social Insurance and the Making of the 'Formal Sector'," *International Review of Social History* 64, no. 2 (2019), 220–221; Daniel Beland, Gregory P. Marchildon, Michele Mioni, and Klaus Petersen, "Translating Social Policy Ideas: The Beveridge Report, Transnational Diffusion, and Post-War Welfare State Development in Canada, Denmark and France," *Social Policy and Administration* 56, no. 2 (2022).

44 Cem Eroğul, *Demokrat Parti: Tarihi ve İdeolojisi* (Ankara: İmge Kitabevi, 1990), 30–31, 46–48; Taner Timur, *Türkiye'de Çok Partili Hayata Geçiş* (Istanbul: İletişim Yayınları, 1991), 18–27, 38–50, 61–63; Ahmad, *The Making of Modern Turkey*, 108; Boratav, *Türkiye İktisat Tarihi*, 91.

the party intensified and finally peaked with the enactment of the Land Reform Bill after heated debate in 1945. It was under these circumstances that the Democrat Party was established on 6 January 1946, representing the interests of private capital, which had benefited enormously from the war economy and was now becoming more assertive.[45] In the first multi-party elections in July 1946, the new party won sixty-four of the 465 seats. "A clear sign of the resentfulness and disillusion that workers developed against our party," reported a member of parliament. The majority of industrial workers, he continued, worked for wages way below the minimum subsistence level, and they were bitter toward the government. He advised the CHP leader to prioritise industrial workers, a social group that constituted an important electorate. "If workers feel that they have a place in society and a role in the development of the country," he continued, "they will more placidly endure their conditions of life."[46] A 1947 presidential decree described the Democrat Party as a loyal opposition party, "loyalty" here denoting adherence to the principles of Kemalist modernisation. But partisan polarisation escalated and the 1950 general election resulted in the defeat of the CHP. The CHP failed to win back the hearts of the electorate, including the industrial workers. The rest of this chapter draws on the accounts of two individual workers, Mümin and Mustafa, whose stories demonstrate the effects of these political changes on the shop floor.

3 Questions of Distribution: Mümin versus Management

When Mümin was hired as a maintenance worker in 1938, he was twenty-eight years old with prior industrial work experience. His file portrayed an ideal worker, with no record of absenteeism or any fines. Between 1945 and 1952, he received multiple non-monetary benefits distributed on the basis of seniority and labour discipline. One afternoon in 1949, he was given five hours' paid leave because he had "worked too much." Despite his untainted record, Mümin often had to wait more than a year for a wage rise. Between 1941 and the end of the war, his hourly wage increased from eighteen piasters to thirty

45 Kemal Karpat, *Turkey's Politics: The Transition to a Multi-Party System* (Princeton: Princeton University Press, 1959), 300–301; Osman Okyar, "The Concept of Etatism," *Economic Journal* 75, no. 297 (1965), 106.

46 Fazıl Şerafettin Bürge, "Partimizin Meslek Teşekkülleriyle Münasebet ve Temasları Hakkında Umumi Mütalaa," in "CHP Genel İdare Kurulu'nun İşçi Raporunun Divan'da Görüşüleceği," file 490.453.1867.6, Republic of Turkey Prime Ministry General Directory of State Archives, 2–9.

piasters only. To put these figures in perspective, his wage increased by two thirds, while consumer prices increased threefold. Mümin made his first formal complaint in July 1946 under such dire conditions:

> [Your] servant has been working at the factory for nine years and nine months (nine years in the yarn department and nine months in the maintenance department as assistant foreman). Although I have been working for such a [long] time, I have received only five piasters increase. My family of four suffers in poverty because the money I am earning is not enough to live on. My counterparts, even the apprentices I teach, earn fifty piasters. Because of the high cost of living, I respectfully ask your high office to stop my suffering by taking into consideration that I have been working for so many years non-stop and paying me the same wage as my friends.

Similar to the earlier examples I cited, Mümin begins his petition by drawing upon meritocratic discourses, but he then presents a different logic of claims-making. While previous petitioners had addressed questions of distribution between worker and employer, in this first petition as well as his later petitions, Mümin addresses questions of distribution between worker and worker.[47] And he was not the only one. Wage differentials among state workers were so large that, a few months after Mümin's petition, the government announced plans to standardise wages based on job and skill categories.[48] We will come back to this point below, but for now let us follow the fate of his first petition.

Although his foreman and the maintenance department chief supported Mümin, the increase would not come until six months later, in February 1947. By September of the same year, Mümin's wage increase was again delayed. His economic situation further deteriorated that year, when state factories stopped wartime overtime work and began operating three shifts of eight hours.[49] In November 1947, he petitioned again and managed to get a rise. Seven months later, in May 1948, another rise followed. But Mümin was not satisfied. He petitioned once again, but this time he failed to secure the support of his supervisors. Mümin was in a relatively good position, the chief of his department wrote, since "his counterparts have not received an increase in the last one and

47 Richard Hymand and Ian Brough, *Social Values and Industrial Relations: Study of Fairness and Inequality* (Oxford: Basil Blackwell, 1975), 11.

48 Abidin Daver, "İşçi Vergilerini Hafifletmek Lazımdır," *Türk İşçisi*, 8 March 1947.

49 "24 Saat Çalışma," *Cumhuriyet*, 5 February 1947; Sedat Toydemir, "Türkiye'de İş İhtilaflarının Tarihçesi ve Bugünkü Durumu," *İçtimai Siyaset Konferansları*, no. 4 (1951), 56.

a half to two years, [thus] he should wait." And thus began the fight between Mümin and the factory management over the notion of fairness among workers. Having worked at the factory for ten years by then, Mümin began to seriously question managerial decision-making. How long did he have to wait? How were wage decisions made exactly? Finally, in the spring of 1951, he took his petitioning to the next level and stormed the factory. But before that, a much larger storm would hit the country.

The general elections in May 1950 ended the CHP's twenty-seven years of uninterrupted rule. By June, the new government had already begun transferring ownership of state factories to private capital to end "the unfair competition" suffered by private business under etatism. Mismanagement, corruption, and low productivity plagued state enterprises, government representatives claimed.[50] In this tense atmosphere surrounding state factories, Mümin wrote a petition to an unprecedented addressee: the prime minister. His petition made its entry into this inflammable situation like a drop of nitroglycerine.

Negotiations in shop-floor industrial relations do not take place in isolation from the wider political context. Subaltern petitioners often resort to exploiting perceived fissures within the ruling classes and appeal to a higher, central authority to advance their case against their immediate superiors.[51] In Mümin's example, addressing the prime minister was a strategy to bypass the factory and Sümerbank bureaucracy and demand justice directly from the top powerholder, a move for which he would pay dearly later on. His file unfortunately did not include this petition, but it did include a one-of-a-kind, almost theatrical document that presents the workplace as "a stage on which the cross-currents of interests, supported by varying degrees of power, are mediated by appeals to value systems and moral perspectives."[52] Entitled "The Transcript of the Investigation of the Petition," this document registered a seemingly unmediated dialogue between worker and manager, revealing the former's perception of managerial authority and the latter's exercise of disciplinary rhetoric.

---

50 "Fabrikaların Hususi Eşhasa Devri," *Cumhuriyet,* 8 June 1950; "Hususi Teşebbüs ve Devlet Fabrikaları," *Cumhuriyet,* 20 June 1950; "Devlet Fabrikaları Devri Meselesi," *Cumhuriyet,* 23 June 1950; "Sanayi İşletmelerinin Devri Meselesi," *Cumhuriyet,* 29 June 1950; "Fabrikaların Hususi Teşebbüse Devri," *Cumhuriyet,* 7 July 1950; "Satışa Çıkarılacak Devlet Fabrikaları," *Cumhuriyet,* 12 August 1950; "Devredilecek Devlet Fabrikaları," *Cumhuriyet,* 17 August 1950; "Yeni Sanayi Kanun Tasarısı," *Cumhuriyet,* 24 August 1950; "Tekel Kibrit ve Şarap Fabrikaları Satılacak," *Cumhuriyet,* 9 September 1950.

51 Lex Heerma van Voss, "Introduction," *International Review of Social History* 46 (Supplement No. 9: Petitions in Social History, 2001), 4, 6.

52 Peter J. Armstrong, John F.B. Goodman, and Jeffrey D. Hyman, *Ideology and Shop-floor Industrial Relations* (London: Croom Helm, 1981), 15.

Below, I cite this transcript in full and then offer a close reading to elucidate workers' and managers' values and notions of fairness, as well as the legitimising principles that underpin the continuous processes of workplace industrial relations.

4 The Investigation

Fuat Ader [director of auxiliary operations, F.A. from here on]: You wrote a petition to the Prime Ministry. Let's talk about it. I will now read it in the presence of Mr Aziz and Mr Şükrü and Mr Hayri. You are not an assistant foreman of fourteen years at the maintenance department as you wrote in your petition.

Mümin [M. from here on]:	No, I am not.
F.A.:	Who is your apprentice getting a higher wage than you?
M.:	No, I meant to say friends. And they are those operators who are my counterparts.
F.A.:	Let me transfer you to the operations department then as well, shall I?
M.:	I do not want it.
F.A.:	You spoke of a mistake in your petition, explain.
M.:	There is no mistake. What I intended to mean was a comparison with my friends in the operations department.
F.A.:	I do not know any apprentice who earns eighty piasters an hour [as you suggested] in the factory. You tell me if there is any.
M.:	I did not say apprentice; it was written wrong.
F.A.:	Is the signature on the stamp yours?
M.:	Yes, it is mine
F.A.:	Are there any apprentices earning seventy-one piasters an hour among the ones you supervise?
M.:	No, there are not any.
F.A.:	Do you think sixty-seven piasters an hour is a low wage?
M.:	I am entitled to ten more piasters.
F.A.:	You are an assistant foreman, aren't you?

M.: Yes.

F.A.: You know all the things that an assistant foreman is supposed to know. Tell me, how do you measure an area?

M.: I don't know how to take measurements.

F.A.: Can you use the measuring stick–the calliper?

M.: No.

F.A.: Describe a joint. Can you find a screw based on a description? (Holding a sample in his hand)

M.: (He did not answer)

F.A.: How is a screw described?

M.: We measure it.
(He was given a calliper.)

M.: I do not know the calliper and I cannot measure.

F.A.: How many types of screws are there?

M.: One is finger type and the other one is millimetric.

F.A.: What is a finger screw?

M.: I don't know.

F.A.: What type is the head of the screw in your hand?

M.: It is bone-shaped.

F.A.: Şükrü, you define the screw in Mümin's hand. [Şükrü Yalçın, assistant foreman at the maintenance department, S.Y. from now on]

S.Y.: It is a 5/16, round-headed screw.

F.A.: Tell me now. Do you really deserve the wage you demand?

M.: I have not gone to school, sir.

F.A.: You said you have been working here for fourteen years, how come you do not know this?

M.: Sir, I have been working for fourteen years, but I do not know this screw.

F.A.: Do you really deserve this money?

M.: I am also illiterate; I leave [the decision] to your conscience.

F.A.: Does your friend deserve a higher wage, Şükrü, what do you think?

S.Y.: You'd know it better.

F.A.: You say Aziz. [Aziz Öz was an assistant foreman at the maintenance department]

A.Ö.: He cannot work on his own, but he can work under a foreman.
Has been read and jointly signed.

The transcript can be divided roughly into three parts. In the first part, addressing Mümin by the informal, second-person singular pronoun "*sen*," the director explains the reason for the meeting and introduces those present. He immediately begins questioning Mümin's claims of unfairness, projecting a powerful definition of the situation as a disciplinary hearing and putting Mümin on the defensive from the outset. The second part focuses on skill evaluation. In the third part, the two parties deploy moral principles on wage determination.

Mümin's main legitimising arguments had not changed since his first petition back in 1946: seniority-based wages and fair distribution among workers. These arguments proved difficult for Mümin to maintain in the actual confrontation with the manager, who, in turn, also appealed strongly to principles of equity and fairness to defend managerial decision-making. He repeatedly asked Mümin to name the apprentices earning more than the assistant foreman, for example, to disprove his accusation of random wage determination. Rule adherence constituted the legitimate bargaining ground for both parties, rendering the outright dismissal of Mümin's complaint impossible.

If operators earned more, would Mümin then want to be transferred to a production department? His answer was a clear no. But why? There are two archival documents that could possibly answer this question. The first, an excerpt from an anonymous handwritten document on the working conditions in different departments of the factory, describes the conditions in the weaving and dyeing departments.[53] The weavery sounded like "cats screeching during a fight," the author writes; the noise was so loud that "the roaring in our ears was still continuing [long after we left]." A weaver attended to twenty-four looms, they noted with disbelief. The dyeing department was extremely damp; a foreman told the author that the factory "took very good care of the workers here" by giving them half a litre of milk every day and new work clothes and boots every year. Their social insurance premiums were also higher than workers in other departments. Signed by a textile worker, who would go on to become a trade unionist, the second document argues for the acceptance of arthritis, tuberculosis, and eye and kidney problems as occupational illnesses, especially for spinnery workers.[54] After more than thirteen years at the factory, Mümin must have been well aware of these harsh working conditions. He did want a higher wage, but he was not willing to work in one of these departments.

The director then moved on to his next point, that is, whether Mümin actually deserved a higher wage. Did Mümin really think that sixty-seven piasters an hour is low? In 1951, the director of the Bakırköy Factory, Şefkati Türkekul, calculated the daily subsistence wage for a worker with two children—like

---

53 "Dokuma tezgâhı dairesine girer girmez," (n.d.), *Kemal Sülker Papers*, Folder no. 402, IISH.

54 Hayri Erdost, "İşçilere zarar temin eden sigorta kanunları," 30 July 1949, *Kemal Sülker Papers*, Folder no. 384, IISH.

Mümin—to be 490 piasters.[55] Mümin earned almost ten per cent higher than this figure, yet he claimed he was "entitled to ten more piasters." The difference in word choice from the previous petitions could hardly be more striking. Here was a worker not begging in order to avoid damnification, but advancing his claim to a higher wage on the basis of his experience and skill. He could not have foreseen, however, that his was the answer the director had hoped for.

FIGURE 23 Head foremen with technicians and engineers in the factory garden, c. 1950
COURTESY OF TURGAY TUNA

In the previous chapter, I showed that, in the absence of skill evaluation and vocational training, management assigned jobs randomly at the factory. The director's on-the-spot skill evaluation reveals that the problem still persisted at the beginning of the 1950s. To discredit Mümin's claims, the director turns to the two other assistant foremen, Mümin's famous "counterparts," who were present at the investigation to witness the restoration of the negotiated order of the workplace. With the air of a schoolboy caught smoking in the lavatory, Mümin's demand rapidly crumbles after that point. The director's final blow comes in the form of a rhetorical question that turns wage bargaining into a moral deliberation: "Do you really deserve the wage you demand?" In response,

55 Şefkati Türkekul, "Mensucat İşletmelerinde Ücret Problemleri," *Mensucat Meslek Dergisi* 4, no. 8 (1951), 8.

Mümin retreats to familiar ground, deploying the deferential language of the desperate, poor worker at the mercy of his superiors.

The case was thus closed. The factory wrote to the Sümerbank General Directorate that Mümin's claims had been investigated and found to be groundless, reassuring the central industrial authority, once again, that factory management followed the formal rules and regulations on promotion and wage increases. Insulted and humiliated, Mümin fell into silence, at least according to his file. He would continue working at the factory for years to come. But there was a second worker, who started petitioning around the same time, who would refuse to bow his head.

5 Questions of Dignity: Mustafa versus Management

Mustafa's first appearance on the shop floor was in 1944, and evidently it was short. His record was erased due to absenteeism within the same year, as we learn from later-dated correspondence. He was rehired in January 1945 with a rather unusual note on his contract: he would be fired if he should engage in undisciplined behaviour. His file remains silent until a work accident in September 1946, which sets off a long and tense conflict between Mustafa and the factory management.

Mustafa lost part of his index finger and the last nodal of his middle finger on his right hand in a sizing machine. If there was one good thing about this terrible accident, it was the timing. After a ten-year delay, work injury insurance had come into force two months before Mustafa lost parts of his fingers. The 1936 Labour Code had stipulated the establishment of an insurance corporation to handle accidents and employment hazards, maternity, old age, unemployment, illness, and death benefits within one year of the code's entry into force.[56] In 1939, the International Labour Organization assisted the Turkish government in drawing up a plan of legislative and technical action for a workers' insurance body.[57] But the establishment of the social insurance system had

56 Donald Everett Webster, *The Turkey of Atatürk: Social Process in the Turkish Reformation* (Philadelphia: The American Academy of Political and Social Science, 1939), 252–258; "Türk Raporu," *Çalışma Dergisi Istanbul Yakın ve Orta Doğu Bölge Çalışma Toplantısı Sayısı*, no. 24 (1947), 71; Ali Güzel, "3008 sayılı İş Yasasının Önemi ve Başlıca Hükümleri," *Sosyal Siyaset Konferansları*, no. 35–36 (1986), 215; Talas, *Sosyal Politika Tarihi*, 119.

57 United States of America, Department of State, "International Conference on Safety of Life at Sea," (London, 23 April 23–10 June 1948), 70; Antony Evelyn Alcock, *History of the International Labour Organization* (London: Palgrave Macmillan, 1971), 148.

to wait until the end of the war.[58] On 27 June 1945, the Law of Work Accidents, Occupational Diseases and Maternity (*İş Kazalariyle Meslek Hastalıkları ve Analık Sigortaları Kanunu*) introduced insurance to cover industrial accidents, occupational diseases, and maternity. This branch of insurance came into force on 1 July 1946. The insuring body, the Workers' Insurance Institution, was established by the law of social insurance (*Sosyal Sigortalar Kurumu Kanunu*) on 16 July 1945. The insurance covered workers employed in establishments subject to the labour code, that is, all establishments regularly employing at least ten people, including non-manual workers. According to an estimate, the number of insured workers reached almost three hundred thousand by 1948.[59] The social security system expanded further during 1949 and 1950 with the adoption of pension funds and the addition of health insurance to the existing maternity insurance programme.

Mustafa's case was one of the 4,091 cases of work accidents and occupational diseases submitted to the insurance institution in the latter half of 1946.[60] The accident report concluded that he had lost fifteen per cent of his general bodily strength and could not work for forty days. His return date was 29 October, but although his wound had still not healed, he started a day earlier because he needed the money. The law stipulated that unskilled and semi-skilled workers would receive half wages, whereas skilled workers and foremen would receive full wages during their accident leave.[61] But, Mustafa's daily accident allowance was almost one third of his daily wage in 1945, and Mustafa had not been able to make ends meet even before the accident. He had worked his yearly seven-day holiday for extra pay, meaning that by the time of the accident, he had been working non-stop for at least one full year.[62]

---

58 "İşçi Sigortaları Kurumu Genel Kurul Toplantısı," *Çalışma Vekâleti Dergisi*, no. 4 (1946), 51–54; Sadi Irmak, "Sosyal Sigortalarımızda Gelişme," *Çalışma Vekâleti Dergisi*, no. 16 (1947), 1–2.

59 International Labour Office, "*Labour Problems in Turkey*," *Report of a Mission of the International Labour Office* (Geneva: ILO, 1950), 73.

60 Between 1937 and 1943, the average number of work accidents was 8,423. See: Ahmet Makal, *Türkiye'de Çok Partili Dönemde Çalışma İlişkileri: 1946–1963* (Ankara: İmge Kitabevi, 2002), 392. In 1949, the number of cases increased to 17,289. The number of occupational disease cases increased from 55 to 434 during the same period. The amount of work accident and occupational sickness insurance premiums paid by employers increased fourfold in the same period. See: *İşçi Sigortaları Kurumu 1953 Yılı Çalışma Raporu ve Bilançosu* (Ankara: İşçi Sigortaları Kurumu Genel Müdürlüğü, 1954), 52.

61 Şefik Ungun, "Hayat Pahalılığı Karşısına Devlet İşletmelerinde İşçi Ücretleri ve Sosyal Yardımlar," *Feshane Mensucat Meslek Dergisi* 2, no. 6 (1949), 94.

62 The right to paid annual leave was part of the Ministry of Labour's five-year work programme in 1946. But the legislation came only in 1960. At a 1947 labour committee meeting held by the Ministry of Labour, workers demanded paid annual leave. See: "İş ve İşçi

In April 1947, eight months after the accident, Mustafa found himself in the same situation as Mümin when state factories switched to three shifts of eight hours. Mustafa reported on this change from the shop floor:

> While I was working eleven hours a day three months ago, I now work on average for eight hours a day and I am in a terrible situation. I was promised an increase, [but] I have waited for a long time and I have been victimised. I kindly request with utmost respect that my hourly wage is increased in light of my situation.

The petition was successful and Mustafa's wage increased from thirty to thirty-five piasters an hour. For the next sixteen months, Mustafa worked on the same wage, and as we understand from his petition dated 20 August 1948, he made several complaints during this time:

> I have been working as a [machine oiler] in different departments of the factory for the last four years. During this period, I have not abstained from doing all the work of different departments with my conscience and efforts. I have not fallen behind in the job. It is because of the care I have given to my duty lately that I got caught in the cogwheel and have lost my future. But I still do the same job in the weavery. I have been deceived by my foreman, my superintendent, and the chief of operations with wage increase promises for the last two or three months. At my last attempt, they told me that I will get a raise when the time comes and showed me the way out in a threatening way. They pointed [the responsibility for the delay] to [the Sümerbank General Directorate in] Ankara, then the chief of operations, and finally said the factory director did not approve [the raise]. I have been waiting for you. I have been waiting amid all these doubts hoping that [the increase] would come at any time. I have become obliged to write this petition upon Your Worship's return from leave. I present [the situation to you] and request that the concerned offices are ordered to give me a raise.

Despite Mustafa's claims to hard work and obedience, things were nowhere near as peaceful as he portrayed. In the summer of 1947, he had been fined

---

Hayatı Bakımından Önemli Toplantılar," *Türk İşçisi,* 3 May 1947. State factories and some large private factories gave workers yearly paid leave of ten to fifteen days. See: "Türk Raporu," 57–59. But, according to their files, many Bakırköy workers chose to work during their annual leave instead.

two hundred piasters—more than seventy per cent of his daily wage—for stopping work twenty minutes early. In January 1948, management confiscated Mustafa's attendance card after five consecutive days of absenteeism. Mustafa was in prison for fifteen days:

> [During the three years I worked at the factory] I have not been absent even for one day. This one time, I became drunk in Istanbul, and was imprisoned for fifteen days. [I have heard that] they confiscated my card because I was absent. Since it is impossible that such a case will happen again, I kindly ask for my card to be returned.

An investigation followed, the result of which did not support Mustafa's claims to being a good worker. Both his foreman and his fellow workers confirmed that Mustafa "has a rebellious character" but worked well. Mustafa was hired once again on the same condition: he would be fired on the first incidence of disobedience. Through his repeated attempts to secure a raise in 1948, it was likely that Mustafa was a well-known worker in the management offices.

In his August 1948 petition, Mustafa combines the narrative of the good worker with his work accident as leverage for his claim to a higher wage. He even attributes the accident to his devotion to the factory. As an aside, he notes that he continued doing the same job even after losing parts of his fingers. In light of these remarks and the style in which he addresses the factory director, he seems to be strategically appealing to the highest authority in the factory, the director. In advancing his claims on the basis of managerial ideology, Mustafa uses one strand of it against another. Mustafa tries to convey his faith in fairness on the shop floor by putting the blame on the lower levels of management. But his strategy failed, and tensions on the shop floor only escalated. The following month, Mustafa confronted the engineers:

> An increase was not given to Mustafa Arap, a worker in the maintenance department, because he has not been working. On 11 September 1948, he came to the machine engineering department and demanded a raise. He was told that he should first work, and he could get an increase after he is appreciated by his foreman and engineers; he had to go back to his work. He refused, uttered threats, and shouted: "Tell me the person refusing to give me the raise." Although he was once again advised in a calm way to go back to work, he was seen waiting in the corridor two hours later. He was warned that he would get a wage cut because although he punched his card, he had not been at work since the morning. He again threatened and said: "Fine me two days' wages if you wish, I am not leaving." We report

> that this worker, who does not work, does not obey orders, and who dares to threaten even the engineers, cannot work at our department.

On the very same day, the personnel department issued Mustafa with another warning, to which Mustafa immediately replied with yet another petition. This time, however, he demanded more than a simple wage increase:

> I have been working at the factory for the last four years. Due to my superiors' approval, I have received a wage raise three times so far. Thank you, but this last time I again applied for an increase. Unfortunately, our chief put me off and threatened me multiple times. Finally, today he treated me inhumanely, put me in a bad position by making accusations against me, and refused to give a raise. I kindly ask you to protect my right.

FIGURE 24 Senior engineers at the factory clubhouse, 1950
COURTESY OF ERGİN AYGÖL

In the two accounts of the incidence, the engineers' office focuses on workplace hierarchy and rules, while Mustafa places the emphasis on justice on the shop floor. By the end of the 1940s, state workers were increasingly demanding respectful treatment in the workplace.[63] If the reader remembers that Mustafa returned to work early after the accident because of his poor finances, his reply to the threat of a wage cut shows that the issue had become a matter of dignity for him. As the formulation of his last sentence suggests, Mustafa resorts one last time to the strategy of appealing to higher levels of management, but he failed again. The following day, he received yet another warning detailing the rules of conduct on the shop floor while repeating the threat that he would be fired.

After this series of petitions in September 1948, things seemed to have calmed down for about nine months. In June 1949, Mustafa was fined to the amount of his day wage for disobeying the foreman. Here, Mustafa acted in another unprecedented way and refused to sign the wage deduction notice. Was this a protest against the foreman with whom Mustafa was already cross? Or did he think he could avoid legal sanctions by not signing? Later events would reveal that this was a conscious move. In the closing scene of Mustafa versus management, an important actor of the shop floor enters the picture: the workers' representative.

The 1936 Labour Code outlawed strikes and lockouts and created a new means of managing class conflict through formalised negotiation procedures. The government adopted compulsory arbitration as the national labour relations policy and, thereby, appeared as a third principal party in all industrial disputes until the legalisation of strikes in 1963.[64] By 1939, the Labour Department had received almost five thousand labour dispute cases.[65] The government then promulgated the Charter of Reconciliation and Arbitration of Labour Disputes in 1939, and built a system to represent employees' interests around workers' representatives.[66] Representatives would be selected by workers at each enterprise, the number varying according to the size of the establishment. As the first step in the compulsory arbitration procedure,

63 Tevfik Erdem, "Kısımlarda Eli Kamçılı Beyler," *Sendika Yolu*, no. 8 (1948); "İç Hizmetler Şefliğinin Nazar-ı Dikkatine," *Gayret: Kayseri Tekstil Sanayii İşçileri Sendikası Organı*, no. 35 (1951); "Gece Postası Gazetesi Yazı İşleri Müdürlüğü Yüksek Makamına," 10 July 1955, *Kemal Sülker Papers*, Folder no. 402, IISH.

64 Cahit Talas, *İçtimai İktisat* (Ankara: S.B.F. Yayınları, 1961), 299; Talas, *Sosyal Politika Tarihi*, 104.

65 Lütfü Erişçi, *Türkiye'de İşçi Sınıfının Tarihi* (Ankara: Kebikeç Yayınları, 1997), 24.

66 Official Gazette of the Republic of Turkey, No. 4,165, 24 March 1939.

workers' representatives are expected to seek to reach an agreement through direct negotiation with the employer in an effort to settle any collective or individual dispute that may arise, and to seek means of avoiding disputes. If the conciliation fails in an individual dispute, that is, a dispute involving fewer than ten or fewer than one fifth of employees, legal proceedings will follow. In the case of a collective dispute, which would involve at least one fifth of all employees at a given enterprise, negotiations continue with the assistance of a conciliation officer. If these negotiations should also fail, the dispute is taken to the arbitration boards.

Because the code did not offer adequate provisions designed to protect representatives from discharge or other discriminatory treatment, representatives were often reluctant to take action. In February 1947, a worker representative at the Bakırköy Factory claimed that workers did not have any complaints, but in his next sentence, he mentioned that a few workers had demanded a wage rise. "They did not know that the management was about to increase the wages," he added; "now everyone is happy."[67] The election mechanism did not offer much protection for workers' representatives either. Candidates needed the approval of their employer and workers had to sign the ballot paper.[68] These representatives continued to represent workers independently of the trade union after the enactment of the Trade Union Act in 1947 because the unions did not have the right to represent their members in negotiations. Under such cramped conditions, the arbitration mechanism remained mostly on paper until the 1950s; between 1939 and 1950, only forty-one industrial dispute cases were submitted to the High Board of Arbitration.[69] By the end of the 1940s, workers were increasingly complaining of the pressures on workers' representatives and demanded their legal protection.[70] In January 1950, four

67 Salahattin Güngör, "97 Yıl Önce Kurulan Bir Fabrika," *Türk İşçisi*, 22 February 1947.

68 Bülent Nuri Esen, *Türk İş Hukuku* (Ankara: Ankara Üniversitesi Hukuk Fakültesi Yayınları, 1944), 148; Rahmi Alp, "İşçi Mümessillerinin Durumu," *Türk İşçisi*, 31 May 1947; M. Koyulhisarlıoğlu, "İşçi Temsilcilerinin Mukaderatı," *Türk İşçisi*, 20 September 1947; "İ.E.T.T. İşçileri Birinci Mümessili Mehmet İmanlı'dan Aldığımız Mektup," *Türk İşçisi*, 18 October 1947; İlhami Coşkundeniz, "Toplulukla İş İhtilafları, Hazırlanması ve Yürütülmesi," *Sosyal Siyaset Konferansları, 7. Kitap* (1955), 67.

69 Toydemir, "Türkiye'de İş İhtilaflarının Tarihçesi," 56; Orhan Tuna, "Türkiye'de Cebri Tahkim Sistemi ve Tatbikatı, 1939–1963," *İstanbul Üniversitesi İktisat Fakültesi Mecmuası* 26, no. 1–4 (1967), 42.

70 Hikmet Kümbetlioğlu, "İş ve İşçi Hayatı Bakımından Önemli Toplantılar," *Türk İşçisi*, 3 May 1947; Sait Kesler, "Eyüp Mensucat İşçileri Sendikası," *Türk İşçisi*, 13 September 1947; Sait Kesler, "İstanbul'da Bir Günde 6 Sendika Kongresi yapıldı," *Türk İşçisi*, 11 October 1947; "İşçi Mümessilleri İçin Yeni Hükümler ve Sigorta İşi!," *İkdam-Gece Postası*, 25 December 1948; "Beyoğlu Mensucat İşçilerinin Üzerinde Durdukları Meseleler," *Kemal Sülker Papers*,

months before the general elections, the CHP government amended the labour code to institute yet another change in the external regulation of labour. This was another instance of government support for the extension of workplace bargaining. The changes provided for protection for workers' representatives by giving them the right to object in cases of firing. More importantly, the new code granted trade unions the right to represent in collective industrial disputes. A dramatic increase in collective labour disputes would follow these stipulations.[71]

6 A Reverse Order: from *İşçi* to *Amele*

Mustafa's own appeal to the workers' representative– also unprecedented in the workers' files I have analysed—came two months after these stipulations, suggesting that he once again was quick to take advantage of the changes in the external regulation of labour that strengthened his bargaining position on the shop floor. In March 1950, after another prison sentence, Mustafa wrote to his workers' representative:

> I was imprisoned for twenty-seven days because of a minor incident I was involved in on 6 March 1950 outside [the factory]. I kindly request you to take the required procedure to avoid the termination of my employment.

A month later, Mustafa was working again at the factory, but in a rather strange position. He submitted another petition via his representative:

> I was working as an oiler in the weavery when I was sent to court for drunkenness and sentenced to a 150-lira fine and one month in prison. I notified the personnel department in a petition via the workers' representative. Although I applied to resume my job after having finished my prison sentence, they keep saying "leave today and come back tomorrow" and are not giving me my job back. I am working as an *amele* for three liras a day in the garden. Since it is extremely difficult to live on this low wage, I kindly request to be assigned to my previous job.

---

19 June 1949, Folder no. 148, IISH; "Mümessil Seçiminde Dikkat Edilecek Noktalar," *İkdam-Gece Postası*, 2 April 1949, *Kemal Sülker Papers*, Folder no. 148, IISH.

71 Melih Göktan, "Türkiye'de İş İhtilafları ve İşgücü ile Münasebetleri," *Kemal Sülker Papers*, Folder no. 347, IISH.

Mustafa's use of the term *amele* deserves our attention. Originally an Arabic word, *amele* derives from "*amel,*" meaning both "job" and "intent." In Ottoman Turkish, the term meant simply "workers," but it gradually acquired a pejorative undertone denoting a labourer doing unskilled heavy work. At the 1923 Izmir Economic Congress, workers demanded the use of the modern Turkish word for "worker," *işçi,* instead of *amele,* but the term remained in use until the 1940s.[72] By the time Mustafa used it as a rebuke, *amele* indicated an unskilled worker in toil.[73] Mustafa wanted an industrial job, not only for the better pay but because, as we have seen repeatedly, he took pride in being a good worker.

Two weeks later, he was back to being an industrial worker again. But not exactly the kind he wanted. Despite his missing fingertips, Mustafa was rehired as a carrier in the roving department, and he revolted. On 11 May 1950, Mustafa "punched his card but did not do the task he was assigned to and walked around in other departments," the chief of operations wrote, asking for him to be given a warning. A note on this petition suggests that management were alert to Mustafa's attempts to endanger formal procedures: "Make sure he receives a written warning each time." According to the chief of operations, the management rehired Mustafa because he could not find a job elsewhere.

By the end of summer 1949, unemployment was soaring in Istanbul due to drought-induced migration from Anatolia. Between August and September, the number of jobseekers in the city increased from twenty thousand to twenty-five thousand.[74] One month before Mustafa's petition, the Istanbul office of the Ministry of Labour had shortened the working day in textile factories and increased the workforce in order to curb unemployment.[75] Pressures under the threat of unemployment resulted in a violent accident at the factory during the time of Mustafa's imprisonment. Abdülkadir, a carpenter foreman, had been fired for beating a young female worker. He first threatened the head foreman, Ahmet, who turned to inserting a piece of metal under his overalls to protect himself from a potential attack.[76] Abdülkadir then showed up with his

---

72 A. Afet İnan, *İzmir İktisat Kongresi: 17 Şubat-4 Mart 1923* (Ankara: Türk Tarih Kurumu Yayınları, 1989), 51; "Amele," *Türkiye Sendikacılık Ansiklopedisi,* vol.1 (Istanbul: Kültür Bakanlığı ve Tarih Vakfı Ortak Yayını, 1996), 38–39; A. Gündüz Ökçün, *Türkiye'de İktisat Kongresi: 1923 İzmir-Haberler, Belgeler, Yorumlar* (Ankara: Sermaye Piyasası Kurulu Yayınları, 1997), 358–361.

73 "Amele," 38; Said Kesler, "İşçi ve Amele; Bizde Bu Tabirler Ne Zaman Kullanılmaya Başlanıldı?" *Türk İşçisi,* 28 December 1946; S. Oflaz, "İşçi Mi Yoksa Amele Miyiz?" *Sendika Yolu,* 1 April 1949.

74 "Istanbul'da İşsizler Çoğalıyor," *Cumhuriyet,* 17 September 1949.

75 "İş İhtilafları ve Alınan Tedbirler," *Cumhuriyet,* 4 February 1950.

76 Ergin Aygöl (Ahmet's son), interview by the author, online, 15 February 2022.

wife at the director's office, begged to be rehired but was rejected. He waited in the garden until the lunch break and stabbed the director with a switchblade multiple times, causing him minor injuries.[77]

But even the increasingly depressing textile labour market trends did not deter Mustafa from adopting a new form of resistance: task bargaining. In his taxonomy of worker responses, Robin Cohen cites task and time bargaining as a hidden worker response directed against managerial control of the labour process, and defines it as workers' efforts to "reduce [their] exploitation by adhering overstrictly to job specifications and rules detailing [their] work."[78] In Mustafa's case, this hidden response escalated into a final and overt conflict on the shop floor.

7 From the Logic of Escape to the Logic of Control

In June 1950, Mustafa received a dismissal notice effective as of 15 June 1950. Three weeks later, he wrote his most strongly worded petition yet:

> I have been notified about the management's decision, dated 1 June 1950 and based on the labour law, about my dismissal effective from 15 June 1950 on the grounds that I have not regularly attended my job during work hours, I disobeyed my superiors' orders to return to my post, and I did not improve my behaviour despite numerous verbal and written warnings. I kindly ask your permission to state that I have never shown such undisciplined behaviour or received a warning from my superiors to return to my post.

From the very beginning, this petition differs from earlier ones in terms of its tone, length, and structure. His much shorter, grammatically problematic, and rather sloppy early petitions tended to give the impression that they were penned rather quickly, and appeal to the superiors' benevolence without paying much attention to logic or reasoning. Mustafa begins here with a clear and concise summary of management's claims and his counterargument. He opts for highly official, impersonal language instead of the colloquial and conversational tone of the earlier petitions. After this formal introduction, Mustafa goes on to refute each of the three claims set out in his dismissal note in turn:

77 "Bakırköy Bez Fabrikası'nda Bir Hadise," *Cumhuriyet*, 7 March 1950.

78 Robin Cohen, *Contested Domains: Debates in International Labour Studies* (London: Atlantic Highlands, 1991), 101.

> 1) I have never disobeyed orders on the shop floor during the eight years I have worked at the factory. Nor have I been warned or scolded by the departmental chiefs. If I had received, as it was claimed, multiple warnings and reprimands, in this considerably long period of employment, based on the charter of internal regulations, there should exist written records of them.

Our speculation was correct: Mustafa did know that a warning becomes official when it is signed by the two parties involved. If they had warned him, where was the proof? If he had disobeyed orders, why did not the management punish him? His self-confident tone appears even more striking when contrasted with the deferential third-person self-references such as "your servant" or "this person in destitution" that were common usage only a few years before. That tone gains even more strength in his second point:

> 2) I have recently had the misfortune of being imprisoned for a month because of a strife outside the enterprise and the working hours. Upon my return to the factory, I was rehired, without any explanation, as a carrier, a task that has no similarity with my original job and I am totally unfamiliar with it. I formally objected with a petition and asked to be given my old job. It is unacceptable to consider the objection of a worker—who served the factory for eight years and had the misfortune to lose his fingers—to being employed as a carrier and his demand to return to his old job as a crime that defies the labour law. It is obvious that [illegible] is merciless and unfair and causes me unjust suffering.

Let us pause here and compare Mustafa's reaction with those of three other workers who found themselves in similar situations. The first example concerns two brothers, Ali, a "weaver candidate" as his foreman called him, and his older brother, who worked as a weaver. In 1941, the two brothers teamed up against the foreman when he ordered Ali to clean his loom and take the woven cloth to the control department. The brothers confronted the foreman, stating that Ali would not do this because these were not his tasks. The furious foreman immediately wrote a petition, demanding that the two brothers be punished for violating the authority of the foreman and the discipline of the factory. This was a must, he added, in order not to set a bad example on the shop floor. The chief of weavery responded quickly and fined Ali a week's wages, an outrageous amount for such an act of disobedience. Ali had worked at the factory for more than a year before the incident without any problems, according to his file. Twenty days after the incident, his record was erased due to absenteeism.

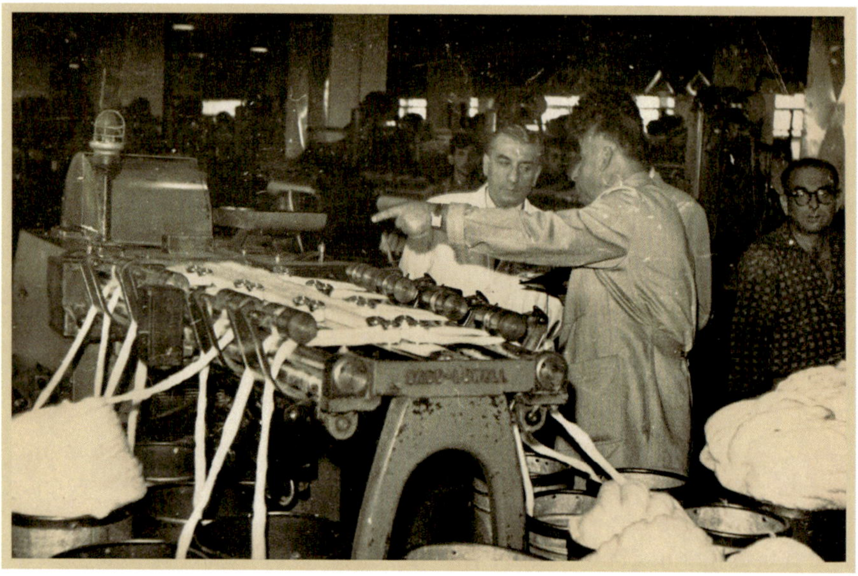

FIGURE 25 An engineer and head foreman in conversation, c. 1950s
KEMAL SÜLKER PAPERS, BG A63/89, IISH

The second example involves a now-familiar worker, Süleyman. Above, we read that he left the factory in 1944, after only three months because he could not make ends meet. Three years later, however, he returned to work for an even lower wage in another position. He worked for another five months and disappeared once again. Cemil, our third example, wrote in 1945 that he had to go back to his hometown after only five months of employment. When he returned in March 1947, he submitted a document indicating that he had been working at a private factory. His subsequent period of employment was short-lived and he resigned after only four months as mentioned above.

In these earlier examples, Ali, Süleyman, and Cemil each left the factory in search of better pay despite the highly fluctuating labour market conditions and the war-induced worsening of economic conditions. Their behaviour exemplifies the logic of escape expressed in the form of absenteeism and worker mobility. Escape is one of the two options available to newly proletarianised workers, argue Jeff Henderson and Robin Cohen.[79] Similar to Albert

79 Jeff W. Henderson and Robin Cohen, "Work, Culture and the Dialectics of Proletarian Habituation," *Papers in Urban & Regional Studies*, no. 3 (1980), 6.

O. Hirschman's earlier conceptualisation of exit as the voluntary separation from the job, escape is an expression of the belief that an improvement in the situation is unlikely.[80] Mustafa, for his part, did not leave even after he was dismissed, as can be seen in the third and final point he makes:

> 3) Unless official documents on the allegations I refuted in the first point above are presented, I cannot be convinced that I have received a fair treatment based on the charter of internal regulations and the labour law. Thus, I kindly ask to be returned to my old job.

In defying the decision to dismiss him, Mustafa followed the logic of control, the second option defined by Henderson and Cohen.[81] He challenged management's disciplinary practices on the basis of a worker's right to have knowledge of rules and penalties, to introduce evidence into disciplinary action, and to appeal a decision.[82] In questioning the system of rules and regulations as well as managerial discretion over job assignment, he was pushing for more bureaucratic procedures. The incident is reflective of the audacity with which some of the workers were confronting their managers. The factory management's reply to Mustafa came in the form of a point-by-point refutation of his arguments, supported by documentation of the fines and warnings he had received. The dismissal was not only just; it was also delayed thanks to the management's benevolence:

> Although the Labour Code gives the employer the right to terminate the labour contract [on the basis of these documentation], our factory acted out of conscience and tried to protect you from falling into hunger on the streets. The final decision about you had to be made in light of your intolerable behaviour.

With this last document in his file, the factory gate closed forever on Mustafa. Despite his assertiveness and decisiveness, and his knowledge of his legislative rights as a worker, he was bound to fail in a repressive industrial environment that discouraged workplace bargaining and crippled collective bargaining. Still, the fact that a state worker was deploying such a self-conscious language

---

80 Albert O. Hirschman, *Exit, Voice and Loyalty: Responses to Decline in Firms, Organisations and State* (Cambridge, MA: Harvard University Press, 1970).

81 Henderson and Cohen, "Work, Culture and the Dialectics," 6.

82 Sanford M. Jacoby, *Employing Bureaucracy: Managers, Unions, and the Transformation of Work in the 20th Century* (London: Routledge, 1985), 200.

of class by the end of the 1940s reveals the extent to which production and social relations had changed in the factories since the 1930s.

8 Conclusion

If one were to choose a single word to describe the atmosphere in postwar Turkey in most general terms, that word would be "tension." The second half of the 1940s was a prolonged period of simmering tensions, both in state politics and in the workplace, and this had direct implications for the long-term structure of industrial relations. Combined with the international postwar rise of the labour welfare discourse, the regime's need to maintain some semblance of popular consensus resulted in new industrial legislation. As the state moved explicitly toward an extension of its role in industrial relations, the resulting process of legal and political change was a key factor in the extension of shop-floor bargaining.

Against the background of the changing socio-political dynamics, a close reading of the historico-social vocabulary that was available to the Bakırköy workers enabled me to set out two arguments in this chapter. The first built on the material I presented earlier in Chapter 4. Wage rises were slower and in smaller increments, and informal bargaining was a chief determinant of wage differentials on the shop floor. Dissonances between management practices and state policy resulted in opportunities for workers to intervene in management authority over labour processes. Second, state workers were not the docile, content labour force that they were often portrayed to be in the contemporary print media or scholarly literature. They closely followed developments in the external regulation of labour and utilised any leverage these changes created to bargain not only for economic gain, but also for respect on the shop floor. In their petitions, workers were showing increasing commitment to the defence of shop-floor earnings and conditions. They also questioned the legitimacy of managerial discourses by raising notions of fairness and legitimising principles that are central to the process of workplace rule-making. By the late 1940s, a Turkish state factory was as much a contested terrain as any other industrial workplace, despite the seemingly bureaucratic organisational structures and the populist ideology behind etatism.

But what layed beyond these particularistic and private bargaining strategies? The careful reader will have noticed something important missing from the petitions analysed in this chapter. The Bakırköy workers made no reference to trade unions in their petitions, even though the streets of Istanbul were already witnessing frantic union activity in June 1946. But could the trade union movement bring an end to the silencing and privatisation of grievances on the shop floor? The curious reader may consult the next chapter to find out.

CHAPTER 6

Textures of Struggle

Worker Politicisation from the Shop Floor to the Trade Union

"Good riddance, we're saved!" exclaimed the deputy chairman of the Bakırköy Textile Workers Trade Union, teary-eyed, at the general assembly on 25 September 1948. The meeting took place days after an anonymous newspaper article had accused the union management of betraying workers' interests in submitting to the control of the ruling party. The author, Enver Tenşi, whose identity was later revealed at the meeting, was a foreman in the weaving department of the Bakırköy Factory. Distressed and anguished, Enver desperately tried to convince the Bakırköy workers that he had not meant "our union"; the "traitors" belonged to other textile unions in Istanbul. But instead of curbing tensions, his defence only escalated it because participants from other textile unions ended up joining the protests. In the end, the only way for the management to resume the meeting was to throw Enver out of the clubhouse.[1]

This new-found peace at the trade union did not last long, however. Seven months later, members gathered for an extraordinary general assembly because the same union management that had expelled Enver had resigned due to discord among its members. As soon as the union chair had finished presenting the activity report, which amounted to nothing more than a list of union-subsidised consumer goods, an angry weaver, Ahmet Cansızoğlu, took to the floor. Pressure on union members was increasing on the shop floor, Ahmet said, and the workers' representatives were indifferent to the grave injustices being suffered by the rank-and-file. What is the purpose of a trade union, he asked; was it just about providing cheaper coffee and coats for its members?[2]

The tense atmosphere and the fierce fights at these two meetings were symptomatic of the crisis of the early trade union movement. We saw in the previous chapter how postwar liberalisation led to state recognition of industrial workers as a social and political group. After two decades of repression, these basic political rights were now the cornerstone of a new citizenship regime. Pluralistic politics replaced one-party rule, intensifying the competitive bidding for worker votes while increasing worker politicisation through

1 "Bakırköy Mensucat İşçileri Sendikası Çok Heyecanlı Bir Toplantı Yaptı", *Hürbilek*, September 25, 1948.

2 "Bakırköy Mensucat İşçilerinin Kongresi," *Hürriyet,* April 18, 1949.

union and political party membership. Enver and Ahmet were only two of the many workers to seize the opportunity provided by the extension of political citizenship to the working class. Under the grip of partisan polarisation and early Cold War macrostructures, Enver and Ahmet challenged the trade union movement from the inside, while following two separate political trajectories. Their stories portray the conditions under which state workers entered the political arena and navigated the turbulent waters of the trade union movement. This chapter follows them on the shop floor at trade union and political party meetings, and draws on their lived experience to tease out the connections between collective organisation and political subjectivity and to unearth alternative trade union voices and visions.

Having analysed how changes in state politics affected shop-floor negotiations over the terms of exploitation, I focus here on the interactions between shop-floor politics and the wider trade union politics. I take issue with the characterisation of the history of labour organisation as a gradual unfolding of a politically conscious working class. Such teleological frameworks fail to adequately address the complexities of the historical context. In the case of Turkey, where a regime change violently interrupted the course of the labour movement, any attempt to seek a processual unfolding of independent working-class political action would be naïve if not condescending. Far from a linear growth in trade union organisation and leadership, the history of the workers' movement in Turkey was marked by a series of ruptures and breaks. Workers had to ride the ebb and flow of state repression to attain and maintain political agency. I discuss the repressive waves that both preceded and succeeded the period when Enver and Ahmet joined the trade union movement, and locate their experiences within the broader framework of postimperial state formation.

The early years of the trade union movement is a rich site for exploring the individual dynamics that challenge and complicate, from below, the monolithic view that has so far dominated the literature. I direct my attention to situationally driven worker responses that are difficult to trace in state-produced documents. My aim is to recover organisational and political alternatives within a labour movement that has largely been depicted as static, monolithic, and passive. Historians have identified, and partly explained, the brief moment when the bubbling up of subterranean labour politics turned into a wave, which was crushed in 1946 quicker than it could rise. The undercurrents flowing below the seemingly calm waters, however, have gone largely unnoticed.

My starting point in this chapter is the workplace experience being central to worker politicisation. Political subjectivity is not a static attribute of an objective class position, but an open-ended and contingent process co-determined by the worker's experience on and beyond the shop floor. Building on this premise, I tackle the following questions: How does a worker decide to unionise? Why does he (and in this case, it is unfortunately and always "he") join or resign from a political party? How does his shop-floor experience affect these decisions? What role do personal relations play? How are contestations on the shop floor over the labour process and the mechanisms of control linked to workers' political and organisational behaviour?

I argue that workers' politics were not confined to the fragile structures of trade unions, but shaped by their experience on the shop floor. As discussed in the previous chapter, contrary to their public image, the shop-floor climate in state factories in the 1940s was one of tension and, at times, hostility. With the heating up of electoral politics in the second half of the decade, the shop floor underwent division along political party affiliations, and became even more contentious. Caught between memories of the liberation war, with its accompanying nationalist rhetoric, and rapidly intensifying global Cold War tensions, the trade unionists struggled to find their voice.

1 A Formative Experience: The First Work Stoppage

In October 1938, Ahmet migrated to western Anatolia from a remote and poor northern village after reading about the opening of a new Sümerbank textile factory in Nazilli. Having lived all his life in the mountains, seventeen-year-old Ahmet found his two years in the hot and humid climate in Nazilli a struggle. The reader will remember this factory, and its proximity to a mosquito-infested swamp, from Chapter 3. Like many of his generation, Istanbul would be the young migrant's next destination. After working for a short time at a private textile factory, he moved to the Bakırköy Factory in 1941, where, before leaving for military service in 1943, he had a formative experience on the shop floor. The incident was not recorded in the factory archives, nor was it reported in any of the newspapers. Only an incomplete account exists of what happened before, during, and after the incident, which makes charting a full story difficult. Such stories by necessity appear only in fragments, and rely on informed speculation to be understood in a meaningful way. I treat the following biographical snapshot exactly in this manner: an incomplete but exemplary case of industrial conflict, where a wage dispute turns into a discussion over the possible meanings and political uses of national belonging and citizenship under wartime conditions.

In the previous chapter, I highlighted the concrete issues facing workers during the war, such as longer hours and food shortages. Beyond the practical difficulties on the shop floor, the war also aggravated the legal enforcement of the employment contract, when the enactment of the National Defence Act on 18 January 1940 overturned the protective provisions of the 1936 Labour Code. Work stoppages and collective dismissals had already been banned in 1933 under an amendment to the penal code.[3] The National Defence Act took this one step further and banned employees from leaving their site of work without an acceptable reason. Ahmet's story illustrates the practical impact of these developments. Before he left for the army in 1943, Ahmet had been working twelve hours a day to compensate for the labour shortages resulting from conscription. The war extended the working day, it also changed the material that Ahmet and the other weavers were working with. To meet military demand, the factory switched from a finer canvas to a coarser cotton cloth, which took twice the time to weave. Weavers lost half of their wages because their piece rate was based on the length of the cloth they were able to weave. Early one morning, Ahmet arrived at the factory to find himself in the middle of a work stoppage:

> One morning, at nine o'clock, the workers turned off the looms and stopped working. The foremen, the chiefs, came but we still refused to work … The director of operations summoned us to the directorate, and on the way, he asked for a representative. I volunteered. The director said: "Your behaviour requires [punishment under] martial law.[4] Those cloths you weave are for our army. [Striking] is a serious crime!"[5] I answered back: "We will also join the army soon; we are getting ready for that day. In one or two years, we will also be soldiers and nobody will send us money, we will have to pay for our own expenses. We are saving for that now. I do not accept your allegations." "We," I said, "want our rights. [We] are working people with families." He shouted: "No! You are making a big mistake; you are committing a crime!" He called the Yenimahalle police station: "Sir, workers are on strike here!" The police chief arrived immediately, saluted the director and ordered: "Take these to the station now!" But he wanted me to stay. I objected, saying, "I am the representative,

3 Muhaddere Gönenli, "Türkiyede Sendika Hareketleri," *Çalışma Vekâleti Dergisi 1*, no. 1 (1953), 66.

4 Between 20 October 1940 and 23 December 1947, martial law was in effect in six cities including Istanbul. In the following section, the reader will read how the government resorted to its use to crush the trade union movement in 1946.

5 According to the 1936 Labour Code, a work stoppage by a minimum of three workers constituted a strike.

> I will follow." Little did I know that they were trying to make a strikebreaker out of me ... By then most workers had disappeared, we were only three people left at the police station. I repeated my argument about the wages and demanded either that they give us back the old cloth or increase our wages. We argued for a good three to four hours. In the end, they doubled our wages.[6]

The narrative of events leading up to the strike incorporates a complex configuration of interests and identities based on class and nation. On one level, the issues represent a clearly defined workplace conflict. Viewed within the larger social milieu of the factory, however, they provide an insight into two interrelated points. First, Ahmet recalls that it was the director who used the word "strike"; the workers just said "we are not working." He had never heard the word before. It is impossible to know whether the others knew what a strike was and avoided using it because strikes were illegal; or if they were also hearing it for the first time from the director. The ensuing exchange is instructive as an instance of contested legitimacy. The director begins by projecting a powerful definition onto the situation as a disciplinary hearing rather than a negotiation, and criminalises the strike as a political offense requiring punishment under martial law.[7] He resorts to the common managerial strategy of putting workers on the defensive from the outset, by making the first move.[8] The second point concerns the director's next claim, which shifts from the broader level of industrial relations to the specificities of state factories. The machines, he protests, were not supposed to stop because "[t]hose fabrics you weave are for our army."

---

6 Interview with Ahmet Cansızoğlu conducted by Yıldırım Koç, International Institute of Social History, Amsterdam call no. BGV1/40–54. Although Cansızoğlu does not specify where the incident took place exactly, the two names he gives are in the inventory of the Bakırköy Cloth Factory, which confirms that the factory where this strike took place was Bakırköy, not Nazilli.

7 Orhan Kemal, a prominent social realist of the period, published a short novel *Grev* (Strike), where the factory director's reaction is exactly the same with that of the director of the Bakırköy Factory. Upon hearing about a strike in his factory, Kemal's protagonist also immediately called the police to report the incident. In contrast to Ahmet, the workers in Kemal's story were aware of the danger of striking; they kept their machines running but did not work behind them, and kept walking around. When the infuriated director shut the machines down and told them to get out, the workers shouted: "You are striking! You are breaking the law!" The incident then turned into a fight over whether workers struck first or the owner declared a lockout. See: Orhan Kemal, *Grev* (Istanbul: Everest, 2007), 1–13.

8 P.J. Armstrong, J.F.B. Goodman, and J.D. Hyman, *Ideology and Shop-floor Industrial Relations* (London: Croom Helm, 1981), 202.

This notion of patriotic service was used by industrial policymakers not only as a means of external labour regulation; it also formed an integral part of labour control on the shop floor. It could be expected that referring to the national interest during wartime would enable the director to achieve political authority, the challenging of which would transcend the realm of factory rules and discipline.[9] However, the director did not simply resort to values that were "rooted in ideologies in the wider society beyond the workplace" to use them as "currency" to maintain the rules and practices of the workplace. As a central component of state ideology, etatism concretised these values in state factories; it rendered them an intrinsic element of labour control on and beyond the shop floor.[10]

With this appeal to hegemonic ideology, however, the incident takes on a twist that the director could not anticipate.[11] When Ahmet appropriates the very categories referred to by his opponent and uses them as a basis for claims-making, a wage dispute evolves into a discursive struggle over categories of national identity, belonging, and citizenship. Ahmet refuses to backpedal in response to the director's strategical likening of industrial labour to national service; he also does not adopt a language of benevolence, as was common in workers' petitions in the early 1940s. Instead, he deploys the very principles derived from the dominant ideology, in forcing the director morally to concede to an increase whilst standing on the legitimacy of the national war effort. The basis of citizenship thus shifted from a rhetoric of "equality in sacrifice" to a notion of equal status with respect to the rights and duties that accompany the status. Ahmet turned the Kemalist regime's master narrative into a discursive field where identities of nation and citizenship are constantly being contested and redefined.[12]

---

9 Carter Lyman Goodrich, *The Frontier of Control: A Study in British Workshop Politics* (New York: Harcourt, Brace, 1921), 32.

10 Armstrong et al., *Ideology and Shop-floor*, 15.

11 In using the term "ideology" here, I do not claim that all its adherents shared the same set of beliefs about its conventions. Two reasons preclude me from making an assumption. First, it is not possible to know which historical subject believed in what and to what capacity. The second, and probably more important reason is that they did not necessarily have to subscribe to it fully. I use ideology to denote a political language, or rather a vocabulary, that constrained its subjects "in order to be recognised as competent speakers." See: Joseph Schull, "What is Ideology? Theoretical Problems and Lessons from Soviet-Type Societies," *Political Studies* 40, no. 4 (1992), 729.

12 Yiğit Akın, "Reconsidering State, Party, and Society in Early Republican Turkey: Politics of Petitioning," *International Journal of Middle East Studies* 39, no. 3 (2007), 437, 446.

By using the same discourses that were intended to mobilise state workers as the justification for his resistance to managerial authority, Ahmet echoes what T.H. Marshall defined as one of the pillars of citizenship: "the right to share to the full in the social heritage and to live the life of a civilised being according to the standards prevailing in the society."[13] For Turkish society, these standards referred to the promises implicit in the Kemalist nationalist rhetoric. But Ahmet did not stop there. At the police station, Ahmet made it clear that he perceived state employment not as a relationship of service but as a relationship of contract. "To be working class," Charles Tilly argued, "is to interact with capitalist in one's capacity as the bearer of labour power."[14] As a member of a working class without organisational power, Ahmet had no choice but to combine his control of that capacity with the rhetoric of national belonging as the basis of his claims-making.

In 1943, Ahmet left the factory for his almost four-year-long military service. Upon his return to Istanbul, a twenty-six-year-old Ahmet who had never heard of the word "*sendika*" (trade union) before found a dramatically different political environment. Workers were no longer the audience but were instead becoming the actors, with the trade union movement flourishing once again after the heavy blow it had sustained the year before.[15] Among those to seize that opportunity were the Bakırköy workers.

2 The Return of the Repressed

During the first quarter of the twentieth century, two waves of political turmoil had struck Turkey, and labour protests peaked during both of them. A mixture of protests and celebratory demonstrations and stoppages by labour groups followed the first granting of the right of association under the Ottoman "Declaration of Freedom" in 1908.[16] Fuelled by nationalist sentiment against foreign capital, strikes spread throughout the country and continued until 1909, when they were prohibited with the Work Stoppage Act of 1909 (*Tatil-i Eşgal*

13 T.H. Marshall, *Class, Citizenship, and Social Development* (New York: Doubleday, 1964), 72.

14 Charles Tilly, "Citizenship, Identity and Social History," *International Review of Social History* 40, no. 3 (1995), 12.

15 Korkut Boratav, *Türkiye İktisat Tarihi* (Ankara: İmge, 2005), 93–94.

16 Sedat Toydemir, "Türkiye'de İş İhtilaflarının Tarihçesi ve Bugünkü Durumu," *İçtimai Siyaset Konferansları* 4 (1951), 45–66.

Kanunu).[17] Labour unrest died down, only to be revived in the power vacuum created by the defeat of the empire and the beginning of the Independence War. Between 1918 and 1925, the second wave of labour disturbances and various attempts at organisation took place, some of which were organised by socialists.[18] The suppression of the second wave broke the link between the developmentalist state and the trade union movement, which would shape the course of state-labour relations in the following decades. The fate of the inchoate and transnationally fragmented communist movement played a central role in this history. Last but not least, the complicated relationship between Kemalists and communists, which still has reverberations today, also has its seed in this suppression.

During the formative years of the republic, three separate communist movements developed in Turkey. As one of the oldest communist parties in the Middle East and the first to be made a member of the Comintern, the Communist Party of Turkey (*Türkiye Komünist Partisi,* hereafter the TKP) was founded in 1920 in Baku by Mustafa Subhi. While living in internal exile because of his critical stance on the ruling Committee of Union and Progress, Subhi had fled to Crimea in 1914, and later organised Turkish émigrés and prisoners of war in the Soviet Union to form his own organisation in contact with Moscow. In exchange for Bolshevik support for the Anatolian struggle for independence, Subhi requested permission from Mustafa Kemal to carry on communist activities in Turkey, but did not wait for a positive response. He stepped up his efforts to organise communists in Anatolia from Baku, and returned to Turkey in January 1921, ostensibly to join the struggle for liberation in Anatolia. But shortly after setting foot in the country, he was cast into the Black Sea off Trabzon with a group of TKP leaders.[19]

17 Gündüz Ökçün, *Tatil-i Eşgal Kanunu, 1909: Belgeler, Yorumlar* (Ankara: S.B.F. Yayınları, 1982), 1–4; Yavuz Selim Karakışla, "The 1908 Strike Wave in the Ottoman Empire," *Turkish Studies Association Bulletin* 16, no. 2 (1992), 153–177.

18 Lütfü Erişçi, *Türkiye'de İşçi Sınıfının Tarihi (özet olarak)* (Ankara: Kebikeç, 1997), 14–19; Kemal Sülker, *Türkiye'de Sendikacılık* (Istanbul: Vakit Matbaasi, 1955), 23–25; Oya Sencer, *Türkiye'de İşçi Sınıfı: Doğuşu ve Yapısı* (Istanbul: Habora, 1969), 209–222, 244–264; Erden Akbulut and Mete Tunçay, *Beynelmilel İşçiler İttihadı: Mütareke Istanbul'unda Rum Ağırlıklı Bir İşçi Örgütü ve TKP ile İlişkileri* (Istanbul: Sosyal Tarih Yayınları Istanbul, 2009); Mete Tunçay, *1923 Amele Birliği* (Istanbul: Sosyal Tarih Yayınları, 2009).

19 Walter Z. Laqueur, *Communism and Nationalism in the Middle East* (New York: Frederick A. Praeger, 1956), 205–211; Ivar Spector, *The Soviet Union and The Muslim World, 1917–1958* (Seattle: University of Washington Press, 1959), 66–79; George S. Harris, *The Origins of Communism in Turkey* (Stanford: Hoover Institution Publications, 1967), 41–2.

To this day, the degree of Ankara's complicity in this murder remains unknown.[20]

A second communist party, the People's Communist Party of Turkey (*Türkiye Halk İştirakiyun Fırkası*), grew out of the Green Army, an anti-imperialist force formed by the Ankara government to attract the support of the Soviet Union. Established on 7 December 1920, the party was admitted into the Comintern as a second body representing Turkish communists, in addition to the organisation set up by Subhi. Around the same time as Subhi's murder, the party's leadership was arrested and convicted on charges of unauthorised links to foreign powers. Although the government permitted the party, thanks to strong Soviet representation in March 1922, by then it had lost its critical momentum. The final blow came in September that same year, when Moscow welcomed the Kemalist victory over the Greeks and asserted that Turkish workers would eventually have to turn against the Anatolian government. The party was closed down once again, and remained so.[21]

The third movement started in Germany in September 1919 but came to be known as the Istanbul movement. Turkish students in Germany, heavily influenced by German Marxism, had organised the Workers' Association of Turkey (*Türkiye İşçi Derneği*) with the young workers who had been sent to Germany for technical training, and formed a companion political body, the Turkish Workers and Peasants Party (*Türkiye İşçi ve Çiftçi Fırkası*). They added the appellation of "Socialist" to the party name when they transferred to Istanbul later that year. Following the demise of Subhi's émigré movement, the Istanbul movement became the dominant strand. Şefik Hüsnü Deymer, a medical doctor who had been influenced by the French socialist party, took over its leadership. With the approval of the Comintern, the party initially supported the Kemalist revolution. By 1925, however, both the Comintern and Deymer had become strongly critical of the regime. In 1927, the Kemalist regime initiated a crackdown on the party. After spending one and a half years in prison, Deymer fled the country in 1929. He returned ten years later, and would remain a leading figure in the Turkish communist movement until his death in 1959.[22]

---

20 In fact, Mustafa Kemal set up an "official" Communist Party in October 1920 to exert control over the movement, as well as to gain Moscow's recognition as the legitimate representative of communists in Turkey. The party was disbanded after only a few months, when Moscow rejected its admission to the Third International. See: George S. Harris, *The Communists and the Cadro Movement: Shaping Ideology in Atatürk's Turkey* (Istanbul: ISIS Press, 2002), 47.

21 Harris, *The Communists*, 48–49.

22 Harris, *Origins*, 39–42, 50–1; Erden Akbulut, *Dr. Şefik Hüsnü Deymer: Yaşam Öyküsü, Vazife Yazıları* (Istanbul: TÜSTAV, 2010), 33–106.

A persistent wave of labour protests was the backdrop to this communist activity. In the four years between 1919 and 1922, there were thirty-four strikes in Izmir, Istanbul, and Zonguldak. A wave of workers' protests took place in 1923: twelve thousand miners went on strike at Zonguldak and Ereğli; beer factory workers in Istanbul went on strike in late summer in protest at dismissals; but the strongest workers' action was the October strike at the Eastern Railway Company (*Şark Şimendiferleri*).[23] Between the Treaty of Lausanne in July 1923 and the declaration of the Turkish republic in October 1923, there was a significant upsurge in the labour movement, with more than fifty thousand workers going on strike in Istanbul, Izmit, Zonguldak, and other cities. In the Ereğli-Zonguldak coal basin, miners successfully demanded the introduction of an eight-hour working day, one day off a week, the signing of a collective agreement, and the formation of an insurance fund.[24] Workers at the Bomonti Brewery in Istanbul also won their strike in August 1923, which was later exploited by the Istanbul Labour Union and the government as a source of propaganda for cooperation between labour and capital. Among other strategies, they also resorted to inciting ethnic animosity among workers to prevent the consolidation of the labour movement. Sadly, it worked. For example, in August 1923, the workers of the Istanbul Streetcar and Tunnel Company demanded the immediate dismissal of all foreigners, including non-Muslim workers. Later the same month, workers at a Belgian-owned textile factory in Izmir went on strike because the director had offended their national feelings. They successfully demanded his dismissal as well as the subordination of the factory management to Turkish laws.[25]

---

23 Kadir Yıldırım, *Osmanlı'da İşçiler (1870–1922), Çalışma Hayatı, Örgütler, Grevler* (Istanbul: İletişim Yayınları, 2013), 293–94; Canan Koç and Yıldırım Koç, *Türkiye İşçi Sınıfı ve Mücadeleleri Tarihi* (Ankara: TIB Tüm İktisatçılar Birliği, 1976), 59–60; R. P. Korniyenko, "Cumhuriyet'in Kuruluşundan İkinci Dünya Savaşına Kadar Türkiye'de İşçi Hareketleri: 1923–1939," *Sosyalist Parti İçin Teori-Pratik Birliği*, no. 4 (1971), 52; Mesut Gülmez, *Türkiye'de Çalışma İlişkileri: 1936 Öncesi* (Ankara: Devlet İstatistik Enstitüsü Matbaası, 1991), 444–5; Mete Tunçay, *Türkiye'de Sol Akımlar: 1908–1925*, vol. 1 (Istanbul: İletişim Yayınları, 1991), 187.

24 Lütfi Erişçi, *Türkiye'de İşçi Sınıfının Tarihi* (Ankara: Kebikeç, 1997), 15–17; Radmir Platonovich Korniyenko, *The Labor Movement in Turkey (1918–1963)* (Washington: U.S. Department of Commerce, 1967), 48.

25 Korniyenko, *The Labor* Movement, 49. Although there was no formal break, the ethnic discord between Greeks and Turks spilled into the communist movement during and after the Greek invasion of Anatolia. The party became a Turkish ethnic organisation for the first time only in the 1930s, years after the general exodus of ethnic Greeks after the Turkish victory in the struggle for independence. See: Harris, *Origins*, 52.

In November 1923, 250 workers' representatives, representing almost 45,000 workers, established the General Union of Workers (*Umum Amele Birliği*). Although the union emphasised that it was an exclusively national and economic organisation, as well as an enemy of communism, the government refused to approve its by-laws and the union dissolved in early 1924.[26] Later the same year, several Istanbul unions formed the Society for the Advancement of Turkish Workers (*Türk Amele Teali Cemiyeti*), a nodal organisation for socialist-leaning trade unions.[27] In January 1925, the Turkish Workers and Peasants Socalist Party began publishing its weekly *Orak-Çekiç* (Hammer and Sickle), which would play an important role in mobilising workers.

As strikes in industrialised regions of the country continued in 1925, the Kurdish tribes of eastern Anatolia revolted. In the spring of 1925, the republic was shaken by a revolt among Kurdish peasants, led by religious and tribal chiefs, that rapidly spread across a vast part of eastern Turkey. The reason given for the revolt was the programme of secularisation. The rebels used symbols of a religious nature and the leader, Shaikh Said, after whom the revolt was named, cited mainly religious arguments in village propaganda. But the Turkish authorities, insisting that the rebels intended to establish an independent Kurdish state, crushed the revolt with much bloodshed. Within weeks, parliament had enacted the 1925 Law for the Maintenance of Order and declared a state of emergency, launching a new phase of authoritarianism.[28]

The Ankara government had already broadened the Treason Act in 1920 to embrace political as well as military subversion, and on 4 October 1920, an amendment to the Associations Act gave the government the authority to prohibit organisations "opposing public law and state policy."[29] The victory of the Kemalists in Anatolia in September 1922 meant that they now wielded political power, which they used to crack down on communists in March and May 1923—on charges of "inciting to revolt."[30] But, mainly for the sake of maintaining good relations with the Soviet Union, they could not go as far as they

26 Erişçi, *Türkiye'de İşçi Sınıfının*, 18.

27 Zafer Toprak, *Türkiye'de İşçi Sınıfı 1908–1946* (Istanbul: Tarih Vakfı, 2016), 373.

28 Martin van Bruinessen, "Popular Islam, Kurdish Nationalism, and Rural Revolt: The Rebellion of Shaikh Said in Turkey (1925)," in *Religion and Rural Revolt*, eds. Janos M. Bak and Gerhard Benecke (Manchester: Manchester University Press, 1984), 281–295.

29 Harris, *Origins*, 80. To control the communist movement and channel its energy to nationalist revolution, Mustafa Kemal also set up his own "official" Communist Party in October 1920. The party applied for membership to the Third International but was rejected. It was dissolved in early 1921. See: Dimitri Şişmanov, *Türkiyede İşçi Sınıfı ve Sosyalist Hareketi* (Sofia: Narodna Proveta, 1965), 56.

30 Korniyenko, *The Labor* Movement, 57.

wanted. Two years later, the Kurdish revolt provided the government with the opportunity to get rid of its political opponents once and for all.

"Istanbul descended into an atmosphere of terror," wrote Sabiha Sertel in her memoir, the prominent leftist journalist who had been forced to flee Turkey in the 1950s.[31] Communist journalists and members of the Society for the Advancement of Turkish Workers were among those sent to the Independence Tribunals, the revolutionary courts established in 1920 invested with the supreme authority to try cases of treason and all such activity against the regime. Sertel describes the shock and confusion experienced by leftist intellectuals and workers before this wholescale attack. "Why are they bringing workers into this? Are they also religious reactionaries?" a typesetter asked her. The government, she responded, was trying to kill not two but three birds with one stone. When the revolt broke out, parliament was in the course of one of its many debates on the labour code, as the reader will remember from Chapter 2. The occasional strikes that targeted not only foreign but also domestic capital upset the government and employers. The revolt was an opportunity for the rulers to suppress not only the Kurds, but also the press and the labour movement. The government closed down the communist journals and prohibited propaganda activities, effectively bringing the legal phase of communism in the country to an end. The veteran leadership were either imprisoned or in self-exile, and the remaining cadres were under close surveillance by the authorities.[32]

Workers who had lived through that time told an American academic in the 1950s that the labour movement had enjoyed more freedom and more popular support prior to 1925 than in the 1930s and 1940s precisely because of their identification with the nationalist struggle.[33] Workers had been invited to the Izmir Economic Congress in 1923, for example, where they demanded the freedom to organise unions, the right to strike, and the designation of May 1 as Labour Day.[34] Sporadic strikes and other demonstrations had been reported in the late 1920s, and the constitution of 1924 recognised the right of association. From 1925 onward, however, the scope of worker organisations

31 Sabiha Sertel, *Roman Gibi: Demokrasi Mücadelesinde Bir Kadın* (Istanbul: Belge, 1987), 96–100.

32 Kemal Karpat, *Turkey's Politics: The Transition to a Multi-Party System* (Princeton: Princeton University Press, 1959), 356–35; Margaret Krahenbuhl, "Turkish Communists: Schism Instead of Conciliation," *Studies in Comparative Communism* 6, no. 4 (1973), 407–410; Aclan Sayılgan, *Solun 94 Yılı, 1871–1965* (Ankara: Mars Matbaası, 1968), 190–1.

33 Sumner Maurice Rosen, "Labor in Turkey's Economic Development" (PhD diss., Massachusetts Institute of Technology, 1959), 417.

34 Rosen, "Labor in Turkey," 419.

was legally limited to mutual assistance through welfare and related activities.[35] With this last nail in the coffin, the Turkish case diverged from both the nineteenth-century European and the twentieth-century postcolonial nation-states. In the former, unions emerged against a background of party politics divided along class lines, and workers' political allegiances followed this line of conflict. Through their links with labour parties of various denominations, the unions played a significant role in national political life, both in national parliaments and as representatives of a major interest group. In the latter, the labour movement came out as critical of the cause of anti-colonial nationalism, and enjoyed, albeit not for long, a certain degree of legitimacy derived from that role after independence.[36] Although a temporary alliance between the labour unions and the nationalist party did exist during the Turkish independence struggle, it dissolved shortly after the establishment of the republic. When the labour movement re-emerged simultaneously with the adoption of the competitive party system, unionists' party loyalties also quickly became divided, and a union-party alignment did not develop.

Two pieces of legislation further criminalised class-based politics in the 1930s. First, as we have seen, the 1936 Labour Code established legal penalties for strikes and lockouts and sanctioned compulsory arbitration for labour disputes.[37] Second, two clauses borrowed from the penal code of fascist Italy were introduced into the Turkish penal code, making it illegal to engage in any activities aiming to "establish the hegemony or domination of a social class over the other social classes, or eliminate a social class, or overthrow any of the fundamental economic or social orders established within the country" and to carry out communist propaganda.[38] But strikes and other forms of labour action, such as the 1931 Defterdar strike, the 1934 mineworkers' hunger march, or the 1938 May Day celebrations, took place even under such repressive circumstances. In fact, more than half of the 145 strikes between 1923 and 1960 occurred before 1938, the year in which the Associations Act prohibited

35 Şeyda Oğuz, ed., *1927 Adana Demiryolu Grevi* (Istanbul: TÜSTAV, 2005).

36 Inga Brandell, "Practices and Strategies - Workers in Third-World Industrialization: An Introduction," in *Workers in Third-World Industrialization*, ed. Inga Brandell (New York: Palgrave and Macmillan, 1991), 3; Gareth Curless, "Introduction: Trade Unions in the Global South from Imperialism to the Present Day," *Labor History* 57, no. 1 (2016), 5.

37 Orhan Tuna, "Trade Unions in Turkey," *International Labour Review* 90, no. 5 (1964), 413–4.

38 William Hale, "Ideology and Economic Development in Turkey 1930–1945," *Bulletin British Society for Middle Eastern Studies* 7, no. 2 (1980), 105.

class-based organisations outright.[39] By centralising all power in government hands two years later, the National Defence Act effectively eliminated whatever freedom of organisation remained.

Workers began to call for the right to organise before the official end of the war. In July 1945, tobacco workers wrote a letter describing how the war had made their already dire working and living conditions unbearable. "We need an organisation of our own," they claimed, "we can only communicate our problems and demands to those in power through such an organisation."[40] For more than a year, nothing changed. And when change did come, it was all rather unsensational. On 10 June 1946, the most important revision of labour policy happened not through a major legislative initiative, but through a simple amendment of the Associations Act. Under pressure amid the upcoming local elections in July and unable to foresee the frantic union activity that would ensue, the government overturned the ban on class-based organisations; not only labour unions, but also political parties, including socialist and communist parties, became legal.[41] Only eight days after the amendment, however, the government introduced articles 141 and 142 to the penal code, forbidding subversive—in particular communist—propaganda.[42] The events that followed proved that the right to organise was stillborn, and the extended Turkish political arena would remain off-limits for the radical leftist parties for the coming decades.

Still, the leftists took advantage of the small window of opportunity created by postwar liberalisation. In the early Cold War period, trade unions globally emerged as key sites of communist organisation and quickly evolved into key sites of robust anti-communism.[43] In the Turkish context, too, the 1946 trade

39 Esat Adil Müstecaplıoğlu, "İşçi Sınıfına Pey Sürenler," *Gerçek*, 5 April 1950; Erdal Yavuz, "Sanayideki İşgücünün Durumu, 1923–1940," in *Osmanlı'dan Cumhuriyet Türkiye'sine İşçiler 1839–1950*, eds. Donald Quataert and Eric Jan Zürcher (Istanbul: İletişim, 1998), 172–173; Yüksel Akkaya, "İşçi Sınıfı ve Sendikacılık-1 (Kısa özet)," *Praksis* 5 (2002), 167.

40 "Tütün İşçilerinin Durumu, Dertleri," *Yeni Sabah*, 21 July 1945.

41 The effect on civil society was tremendous. Between 1946 and 1960, the number of associations multiplied eightfold to reach 17,000, and the number of associations per million people increased from forty in 1946 to over one hundred by 1950, and to 620 by 1960. See: Robert Bianchi, *Interest Groups and Political Development in Tur*key (Princeton: Princeton University Press, 1984), 155.

42 Çetin Özek, *141–142* (Istanbul: Ararat Yayınları, 1968), 126–7; Kurthan Fişek, *Türkiye'de Kapitalizmin Gelişmesi ve İşçi Sınıfı* (Istanbul: Doğan Yayınları, 1969), 82; Jacob M. Landau, *Radical Politics in Turkey* (London and New York: Routledge, 2016), 23.

43 Peter Weiler, "British Labour and the Cold War: The Foreign Policy of the Labour Governments, 1945–1951," *Journal of British Studies* 26, no. 1 (1987); Leong Yee Fong "The Impact of the Cold War on the Development of Trade Unionism in Malaya (1948–1957)," *Journal of Southeast Asian Studies* 23, no. 1 (1992); Anthony Carew, "Conflict Within the

unionism brought the class politics that had been simmering at the subterranean levels to the surface. As soon as the requirement to obtain permission to set up an organisation was rescinded, some twenty political parties, including communists, sprang up. Seven parties promoting the interests of peasants and workers were established in 1946. Although most did not survive, they changed the face of the political scene irreversibly.[44] Two of these parties, the Socialist Party of Turkey (*Türkiye Sosyalist Partisi*, hereafter the TSP) and the Socialist Party of the Workers and Peasants of Turkey (*Türkiye Sosyalist Emekçi ve Köylü Partisi,* hereafter the TSEKP), played an important role in the development of a trade union movement, mainly because the preceding two decades of repression had created a vacuum of leadership and experience among workers, which political activists tried to fill.[45]

The TSP, a pro-Western party with a broad leftist orientation, and the TSEKP, a Marxist party following the Soviet line, strongly disagreed on the organisational model of the trade unions.[46] While the TSP followed the industrial branch-based trade union organisational model, the TSEKP advocated for bottom-up organisation and adopted a workplace-based model of trade unionism. The founder of the social democratic and pro-Western TSP, Esat Adil Müstecaplıoğlu, argued in the party publication *Gün* (Day) that craft or industry-based unions should be organised into national federations.[47] In the

ICFTU: Anti-Communism and Anti-Colonialism in the 1950s," *International Review of Social History* 41, no. 2 (1996); Rotimi Ajayi, "The Politicisation of Trade Unionism: The Case of Labour/NCNC Alliance in Nigeria, 1940–1960," *Ufahamu: A Journal of African Studies* 27, no. 1-2-3 (1999); Nicholas White, "The Limits of Late-Colonial Intervention: Labor Policy and the Development of Trade Unions in 1950s Malaya," *Indonesia and the Malay World* 36, no. 106 (2008), 429–49; Dino Knudsen, "The Nordic Trade Union Movement and Transnational Anti-Communist Networks in the Early Cold War," in *Transnational Anti-Communism and the Cold War: Agents, Activities, and Networks,* eds. Luc van Dongen, Stéphanie Roulin, and Giles Scott-Smith (London: Palgrave Macmillan, 2014), 35–49; Jennifer Luff, "Labor Anticommunism in the United States of America and the United Kingdom, 1920–49," *Journal of Contemporary History* 53, no. 1 (2018); Johan Svanberg, "'The Ruhr Remains our Nightmare': The International Metalworkers' Federation and European Integration in the Early Cold War," *International Review of Social History 66*, no. 1 (2021).

44 Tarık Zafer Tunaya, *Türkiye'de Siyasi Partiler, 1859–1952* (Istanbul: Doğan Kardeş Yayınları, 1952), 693–708; H. Karpat, *Turkey's Politics*, 357–8; C. H. Dodd, *Politics and Government in Turkey* (Manchester: Manchester University Press, 1969), 20–54; Arif T. Payaslıoğlu, "Turkey," in *Political Modernisation in Japan and Turkey*, eds. R. E. Ward and D. A. Rustow (Princeton: Princeton University Press, 1964), 411–433; Landau, *Radical Politics,* 113–5.

45 Rosen, "Labor in Turkey," 422.

46 Kemal Karpat, "The Turkish Left," *Journal of Contemporary History* 1, no. 2 (1996), 176; Igor P. Lipovsky, *The Socialist Movement in Turkey, 1960–1980* (Leiden: Brill, 1992), 10.

47 Esat Adil Müstecaplıoğlu, "Sendika Düşmanları," *Gün,* 6 June 1946.

TSEKP newspaper *Sendika* (Trade Union), Deymer referred to trade union organisations in industrialised countries, where the concentration of workers in the workplace was ever increasing, and referred to the acceptance of this organisational model by the World Federation of Trade Unions (hereafter WFTU).[48] In sectors where production is dispersed into smaller workplaces, workers should organise in occupational unions, Deymer argued.[49] But as soon as a factory has two to three hundred workers, a separate trade union should be established, he wrote in another article. In addition to organising into national federations, he continued, these workplace-based unions should also be organised geographically under the name of *Birlik* (Alliance), an association of local unions in a city or region.[50]

Notwithstanding their divergences, both parties were united against the Association of Turkish Workers (*Türkiye İşçiler Derneği*), an overtly nationalist organisation founded on 9 July 1946 to support, as set out in its charter, the Ministry of Labour in better implementing the labour code and to increase

48 These publications were the forerunners of the labour press that quickly developed in the late 1940s. Building on the significant growth of the print media from the mid-1940s onward, many trade unions made use of this building block of the revived public sphere to demand a legalised increase in their industrial bargaining power. See: Kemal Karpat, "The Mass Media: Turkey," in *Political Modernisation in Japan and Turkey*, eds. R. E. Ward and D. A. Rustow (Princeton: Princeton University Press,1964), 255–282; "Sendika Basını," *Türkiye Sendikacılık Ansiklopedisi vol. 3* (Istanbul: Tarih Vakfı, 1996), 12–16; Gavin D. Brockett, "Betwixt and Between: Turkish Print Culture and the Emergence of a National Identity, 1945–1954" (PhD diss., University of Chicago, 2003).

49 Sendikacı (Şefik Hüsnü Deymer), "Memleketimizde Sendikacılık," *Sendika,* 3 August 1946; Sendikacı (Şefik Hüsnü Deymer), "Memleketimizde Sendika Hareketlerinin Teşkilatı Nasıl Olmalıdır?" *Sendika*, 7 September 1946.

50 Sendikacı (Şefik Hüsnü Deymer), "Sendikalarımız Teşkilat Sistemi," *Sendika*, 21 September 1946. In 1950, Esat Adil Müstecaplıoğlu criticised this model for being "overly chaotic." See: Esat Adil Müstecaplıoğlu, "Sendikalar Tarihinden Bir Yaprak," *Gerçek*, 15 February 1950. With hindsight, TSEKP's organisational model resembles the conception of the struggle at plant level as a struggle within the process of exploitation and therefore the factory as the privileged site of anti-capitalist struggle in 1950s Italy. See: G. Contini,"Politics, Law, and Shop Floor Bargaining in Postwar Italy," in *Shop Floor Bargaining and the State: Historical and Comparative Perspectives,* eds. Steven Tolliday and Jonathan Zeitlin (Cambridge: Cambridge University Press, 1985), 212. I would argue that etatism created two specific conditions that rendered the factory-based organisational model advantageous. First, the state owned the factories with the highest labour concentration and presented them as modal spaces for good industrial relations, a far truth from what actually happened on the shop floor. Second, workplace-based organisation could better protect the rank-and-file from management pressure and help the party maintain its influence over the workers.

productivity.[51] The association envisioned a loose national body organised into local *dernek*s (associations), a word that was strategically chosen over trade union.[52] Both *Sendika* and *Gün* protested the CHP-controlled Association of Turkish Workers for seeking to undermine the trade unions.[53] A 1948 CHP report on labour issues vindicated those claims, in admitting that the party was caught unprepared for the surge in communist activity. The two communist parties, the report noted, had quickly organised workers in different industries and brought them under the Alliance of Trade Unions (*Sendikalar Birliği*). By delivering lectures on "materialism, capital and labour conflict, and the history of communism" at trade union centres and publishing a number of magazines, "professional communists poisoned workers, and even university students."[54] In the eyes of the government officials, trade unions were functioning as "schools of [class] war," as Engels once called them.[55] To put a stop to the communist subversion, party members met with state factory directors and worked with them to "protect state workers from communist infiltration." The *dernek*s, which started first in the state tobacco factories, were a product of this collaboration.[56]

The number of trade unions established in 1946 varies depending on the source. According to the Ministry of Labour, there were around a hundred; in the newspapers this number was multiplied by seven. In his defence of the closure of the unions and the persecution of their leaders in a parliamentary meeting, the internal affairs minister complained that thirty-eight of the numerous "trade unions [that] sprawled out in a short period of time in our various cities" had been founded almost entirely by "registered and fanatical communists."[57] A contemporary communist wrote that the TSEKP had

51 *Türkiye İşçiler Derneği Nizamnamesi* (Istanbul: Sinan Matbaası, 1946); M. Şehmus Güzel, *Türkiye'de İşçi Hareketi, 1908–1984* (Istanbul: Kaynak, 1996), 152.

52 Kemal Sülker, *Türkiyede Sendikacılık* (Istanbul: Vakit Matbaası, 1955), 40–47.

53 "Ankara İşçilerini Ayartmaya Çalışıyorlar," *Sendika*, 21 September 1946; "Kömür Havzasında Bir Verem Sanatoryumu Kurulacak," *Sendika*, 9 November 1946; Esat Adil Müstecaplıoğlu, "Sendika Düşmanları," *Gün*, 6 June 1946; Mustafa Börklüce, "Sendikaların Kuruluşu Münasebetle," *Gün*, 21 September 1946, Esat Adil Müstecaplıoğlu, "Sendikaların Gelişmesi Mahzurlu Mudur?" *Gün*, 30 November 1946.

54 Fazıl Şerafettin Bürge, "Partimizin Meslek Teşekkülleriyle Münasebet ve Temasları Hakkında Umumi Mütalaa," in "CHP Genel İdare Kurulu'nun İşçi Raporunun Divan'da Görüşüleceği," 14 February 1948, 490.453.1867.6, Republic of Turkey Prime Ministry General Directory of State Archives, 1.

55 Friedrich Engels, *The Condition of the Working Class in England* (Cambridge: Cambridge University Press, 2010), 224.

56 Fazıl Şerafettin Bürge, "Partimizin," 1.

57 TBMM Tutanak Dergisi (Records of the Grand National Assembly), 29 January 1947, Session 8, Volume 4, Meeting no. 29, 75.

established twenty-five trade unions under the umbrella of five associations and also founded the Istanbul Workers Club, while the TSP had established six sector-based unions as well as the Federation of Turkish Trade Unions.[58] The unions were mainly established in industrial centres such as Adana, Ankara, Eskişehir, Istanbul, Izmit, Zonguldak, and Samsun, where the socialist parties and the TKP had been active earlier, but they also appeared in Kayseri, Trabzon, Sivas, and Malatya.[59] Later, a contemporary prosecutor claimed that socialists had organised as many as ten thousand workers just in Istanbul. In its own publications, the TSP claimed to have registered 4,500 textile workers in a single month.[60]

Among the trade unions organised by the TSEKP was the Bakırköy Textile Workers Trade Union (*Bakırköy Bez Fabrikası İşçileri Sendikası*). The union charter, published in *Sendika* on 26 October 1946, stated that membership was open to workers of all religious, ethnic, and political identities, but closed to those "who spied for and made propaganda for factory management and engaged in racist or fascist activity."[61] Of the nine names given by the newspapers as the founders of the factory union, three are worth mentioning for different reasons. The reader has already met the first, and we will read more about him below: Enver Tenşi. The second name is Sabri Özcan, a fitter whose name made it into a 1950 police report on communist union activity, suggesting that even after the total crackdown, some communist workers continued to be politically active.[62] And the third is a woman: Reyhan Ozan; the only woman working in the iron works department.

Reyhan made it into the pages of *Sendika* on two other occasions. In September 1946, a female journalist interviewed Reyhan and called her "a tough worker, a welding foreman, a Turkish woman."[63] She had fourteen years of experience by the time of the interview. Before Bakırköy, she had worked

58 Cited in Aziz Çelik, *Vesayetten Siyasete Türkiye'de Sendikacılık (1946–1967)* (Istanbul: İletişim, 2010), 89. The last issue of the TSP's *Gün*, published two days before the party was closed down, reported the founding of the Federation of Turkish Trade Unions. See: "Sendikalar Federasyonu Kuruldu," *Gün*, 14 Dec 1946.

59 "Türkiye Sosyalist Partisi Birçok İşçi Sendikalarının Kurulmasına Müzaharet Etmektedir," *Gerçek*, 7 July 1946; Güzel, *Türkiye'de İşçi*, 153; Dimitri Şişmanov, *Türkiyede İşçi ve Sosyalist Hareketi* (Sofia Narodna Prosveta, 1965), 113; Rosen, "Labor in Turkey," 456.

60 Güzel, *Türkiye'de İşçi*, 151.

61 "Bakırköy Bez Fabrikası Ana Nizamnamesi," *Sendika*, 26 October 1946, 2 November 1946, 9 November 1946.

62 Yıldırım Koç, *Türkiye İşçi Sınıfı ve Sendikacılık Hareketi Tarihi* (Istanbul: Kaynak, 2003), 39–40.

63 Neriman Hikmet, "Kaynakçı Ustası Ağır İşçi Türk Kadını Diyor Ki," *Sendika*, 28 September 1946.

at factories in Eskişehir and Ankara. She had been trained by a German foreman, Jeniqe. Two months later, Reyhan was one of two main protagonists in a news story about unionism on the shop floor. The second protagonist was Enver. The reporter joined a conversation between Reyhan and Enver that he had been eavesdropping on. Their union activity, they told the reporter, had stirred up the factory. The foreman had been pressuring them by saying they would soon be fired. They did not know at the time but they had good reasons to be fearful. Hasan Özgüneş, a full-time union officer in the 1950s, was fired from the Sümerbank Adana Cotton Mill because of his involvement in the 1946 union movement. Although he went on to sue the factory and collect a sizeable indemnity, he was never reinstated.[64] Reyhan and Enver told the reporter that the director of the operations department at Bakırköy had taken matters one step further and threatened them: "This is [a] Sümerbank [factory], in other words, it is state territory. How dare you think you would protect workers' rights better than the state?" The reporter found the male worker "highly intimated," but the woman impressed him: "Her voice is still ringing in my ears!" he wrote, "She said to her male colleague: 'My friend! Neither the chief's recognition nor the foreman's satisfaction will save you. Only the trade union can save you!'"[65] Needless to say, she left a lasting imprint on the male journalist, who called her "the brainbox of the cloth factory."

Reyhan and Enver did not have to worry about the pressure on the shop floor for much longer because barely two weeks after the above conversation, the government instigated a crackdown on the trade unions. Accused of communist propaganda, the trade unions and workers' political organisations faced the full brunt of state repression. The two socialist parties, the trade unions, and six newspapers and magazines were closed down indefinitely on 16 December 1946 under the authority of martial law on the allegation that they were violating the penal code by promoting concepts of class struggle.[66] Their leaders were tried for communism and acquitted, but further arrests followed and continued into the 1950s.[67] The suppression was a hard blow for the

64 Rosen, "Labor in Turkey," 456.

65 Hadi Malkoç, "Bez Fabrikasının Fikir Kutusu," *Sendika,* 31 November 1946.

66 Karpat, *"Turkey's Politics,"* 177.

67 "İzmirde Emekçi Partisi Kuranlar Nezaret Altında," *Cumhuriyet,* 20 March 1947; "İzmitte Üç Partici Tevkif Edildi," *Cumhuriyet,* 25 March 1947. The TSP was revived in 1950, but was closed down again in 1952. Its leaders were charged with disseminating communist propaganda, and after an eight-year trial, they were acquitted. See: Tunaya, *Türkiye'de Siyasi Partiler,* 696–706.

communist movement, and communism quickly gained a bad name among the populace.[68]

Three developments caught the CHP off guard in the summer of 1946. First, the Democrat Party won seventy seats in the local elections and continued to intensify their criticism of the CHP. Although the DP shared the CHP's rejection of class conflict on the grounds that "there does not exist in our nation the situation which requires class conflict," it strongly supported both the right of free organisation and the right to strike.[69] Second, late summer saw increased Soviet pressure to institute joint military control of passage through the Turkish Straits. When the Turkish government refused, tensions escalated into what came to be known as the Turkish Straits crisis, which resulted in Turkey's turning to the United States for protection through NATO membership. Third, against the backdrop of early Cold War tensions, the unexpected success of socialist ideology among the trade unions and some of the intelligentsia was becoming a growing concern for the government. The expectation that the government would be able to direct the development of the movement through the new Ministry of Labour and its own Workers Bureau gave way to a cold awakening to the potential of a communist insurgency, despite two decades of lethargy. As a result, although the labour minister declared his full support for the trade unions and underlined his faith that they would "serve the objectives of the ministry" in September 1946, the government had abandoned its policy of laissez-faire by the end of 1946.[70]

By December 1946, the draft Employer and Employee Unions and Union Alliances Act (*İşçi ve İşveren Sendikaları ve Sendika Birlikleri Kanunu*) was ready. The head piece in the penultimate issue of *Sendika* on 7 December fiercely protested, arguing that the draft law was an anti-democratic move targeting independent trade unions.[71] Another critical piece in the final issue argued that, by stating no one could be barred from membership, the draft opened up the trade unions to the risk of infiltration by "fascists." The draft, Şefik Hüsnü Deymer continued, left out many fundamental trade union rights such as control over production and labour supply through collective agreements, as well as the free election of workers' representatives.[72]

---

68 Igor R. Lipovsky, *The Socialist Movement in Turkey 1960–1980* (Leiden: Brill, 1992), 10.

69 Sülker, *Türkiyede Sendikacılık*, 52–53.

70 "Çalışma Bakanının İşçi Sendikaları Hakkındaki Demeci," 25 September 1946, Kemal Sülker Papers, Folder no. 148, IISH.

71 Sendikacı (Şefik Hüsnü Deymer), "Demokrasi var denen yerde böyle kanun yapılmaz," *Sendika*, 7 December 1946.

72 Sendikacı (Şefik Hüsnü Deymer), "İşçiler kanun tasarısını beğenmiyorlar," *Sendika*, 14 December 1946.

Had it not been for the crisis with the Soviet Union and the Cold War, the short-lived 1946 unionism had the potential to change the course of the labour movement, especially with regard to its demands and its international orientation. These unions not only demanded wage increases and old age insurance; they also called for the right to strike and collective bargaining, the right to representation for trade unions, and the amendment of the labour code.[73] As we shall see below, serious disagreements on these points emerged in the later trade union movement, and workers had to wait until the 1960s for these rights. Both the TSP and the TSEKP closely followed and advocated for joining the international trade union movement. The 1946 brochure of the Alliance of Trade Unions, *Bize Göre Görüşler* (In Our Opinion), openly set out the goal of the Turkish unions joining the WFTU.[74] Both *Sendika* and *Gün* covered news related to this international organisation.[75] Besides the expected internationalism of the leftist movement, the strong emphasis on WFTU membership was also a strategy to provide protection against the state. Rasih Nuri İleri, a TSEKP member who was active in the party's trade union activities, cites a conversation between Şefik Hüsnü Deymer and the leader of those activities, Ferit Kalmuk: "Move quick and establish ten alliances of trade unions and a national federation that has to join the WFTU as soon as possible, so that [the CHP] cannot easily shut down the Turkish trade unions."[76] Little did he know that the escalating Cold War tensions would soon divide the WFTU into two camps and that the Turkish trade unions would have to wait a long time even just to join the anti-communist International Confederation of Free Trade Unions (hereafter ICFTU).

The persecutions erased the differences between the socialists and the communists; from then on, the state would approach any left-leaning politics with the suspicion of communism.[77] In 1966, the leader of the trade union federation

73 Güzel, *Türkiye'de İşçi*, 153.

74 İşçi Sendikaları Birliği, *Bize Göre Görüşler* (Istanbul: ISB Neşriyatı, 1946), 8.

75 Sendikacı (Şefik Hüsnü Deymer), "Memleketimizde Sendikacılık," *Sendika*, 31 August 1946; Safa M. Yurdanur, "Dünya Sendika Federasyonu," *Sendika*, 14 September 1946; "Avrupada Bütün Amele Birleşiyor," *Sendika*, 28 September 1946; Esat Adil Müstecaplıoğlu, "Sendika Düşmanları ve İşçi Teşkilatlanmasındaki Zorluklar ve Yanlışlıklar," *Gün*, 6 November 1946; Mustafa Börklüce, "Sendikaların Kuruluşu Münasebetle," *Gün*, 21 September 1946; "Tekel İşçileri Sendikasının Açılış Töreninde Sendika Mümessilleri Tarafından Söylenen Nutuklar," *Gün*, 30 November 1946; Sendikacı (Şefik Hüsnü Deymer), "İşçiler Kanun Tasarısını Beğenmiyorlar," *Sendika*, 14 December 1946.

76 Rasih Nuri İleri, "Önsöz," in *Kırklı Yıllar-5*, ed. Rasih Nuri İleri (Istanbul: TÜSTAV, 2006), IX–XV, XV.

77 Kemal H. Karpat, *Türk Siyasi Tarihi: Siyasal Sistemin Evrimi* (Istanbul: Timaş, 2015), 58. When the Democrat Party government accused the TSP of communism in 1952, the

Türk-İş (more on this below), Seyfi Demirsoy, boasted about the practices they, the anti-communist trade unionists, had used to red-bait and eliminate the communists in the 1940s. "We took control of the unions by beating up the communists," he told participants at the general committee meeting, urging them to stay alert to communist infiltration.[78] In the midst of yet another wave of worker radicalisation, the leader of the national trade union federation was trying to browbeat the unionists into acquiescence through memories of 1946 unionism.

By the end of 1946, it became clear that the trade union movement could not be allowed to grow unchecked. The CHP government faced a two-sided problem: It needed to build a trade union movement that would conform to the expectations of free world trade unionism, but without jeopardising industrial development or paving the way for class politics. The strategy of either rejecting the notion of class politics or reframing it as a national struggle against foreign capitalists and their local agents would no longer work. When the rhetoric of the nation as an indivisible community and the ability of the state to promote class harmony did not hold anymore, the affirmation of workers as a social presence became inevitable. Moreover, the ruling group had lost "the leisure to plan and pursue the most rational path" of progress, as a new vocabulary of political discourse had emerged and labour questions were increasingly more involved in political controversies.[79] The state's task was to remould the union movement to build closer contact and cooperation with workers and facilitate their integration into the postwar political order. To achieve the former, the government created a new legal framework and associated institutions, and for the latter, it continued to lean on nationalism, but in a form that relied increasingly on communism as a magnified enemy.

party's defence was that it was a European-style socialist party, but it could not escape being closed down a second time. See: Hakan Koçak, "Anti-Komünizmin Markajında Emek Mücadelesi: Tekstil İşçilerinin Gerçekleşemeyen Mitingleri," *Toplumsal Tarih* no. 305 (2019), 22–23.

78 Koç, *Türkiye İşçi Sınıfı*, 40.

79 Rosen, "Labor in Turkey," 247; İlkay Sunar, "Populism and Patronage: Democrat Party and its Legacy in Turkey," in *Politics of Modern Turkey, Vol. 1*, eds. A. Çarkoğlu and W. Hale (London: Routledge, 1990), 161–171; Reşat Kasaba, "Populism and Democracy in Turkey, 1946–1961," in *Rules and Rights in the Middle East*, eds. Ellis Goldberg, Reşat Kasaba, and Joel Migdal (Seattle, WA: University of Washington Press, 1993), 43–68.

3 Weakening the Trade Unions, One Step at a Time

Already dazzled by the events of the past six months, the Turkish parliamentarians in the first weeks of 1947 found themselves in an intense legislative debate. In the words of a government critic, there were two reasons behind the rush to put in place trade union legislation. First, the experience of 1946 had shown the need for an effective legal framework to control the labour movement. Second, the government felt under pressure to fulfil its international commitments.[80] To another former member of parliament who had recently fallen out with the CHP, the Trade Union Act was nothing but a rushed effort by a startled government that had taken a dislike to the helmsman of the trade union ship.[81] The labour minister's account of the events of the previous year supported this impression:

> Shortly after [the amendment in the Associations Act], in many places, among them the large cities, we found ourselves face to face with unionist activity that quickly arose and made headway; their numbers approached a hundred. Some called themselves unions, others, assemblies or associations. Yet all, it was clear, shared the motive of advancing class or collective interests and needs. Although they were founded to meet these needs, some shortly strayed far from their duty, and imposed on us the obligation to promulgate a new system of law and order. For example, we saw that in some instances group interests were abandoned; advancing personal interests and securing the posts of leaders occupied the energies of some who carried on political propaganda based on class or occupational concerns. Others suddenly confronted us as alleged spokesmen for the whole nation through their authority as officials of these groups; without any study or observation, those representing their fellows in a particular area presumed to speak for all Turkish workers. The majority of our workers are patriotic and ready to collaborate with the state. They demanded help and guidance to establish the general course [of the labour movement] from the Ministry of Labour. It is out of the question for our [politically] liberal and etatist state to control the trade union movement and treat workers as if they are civil servants; that only happens in totalitarian regimes. [Thus] the need for a separate law in addition to the Associations Act emerged.[82]

---

80 Yıldırım Koç, "1947 Sendikalar Yasası," *Mülkiyeliler Birliği Dergisi*, no. 121 (1990), 10–14.

81 "Sendikalar Kanunu," *Cumhuriyet*, 24 February 1947.

82 Sülker, *Türkiyede Sendikacılık*, 58–59.

The labour minister resorted once again to the tropes of etatism and industrial work as patriotic service in order to achieve policy legitimation. Together, he claimed, these two key characteristics set Turkey apart from both class-based societies and totalitarian regimes. The parliament enacted the Employer and Employee Unions and Union Alliances Act on 20 February 1947 in the midst of heated debate. The act would remain in effect with minimum amendments for the next sixteen years, and only undergo radical changes after the military takeover of governmental power. In the remainder of this chapter, I focus on the three structural determinants of union bargaining power: the fragmented union structure, limited union finances, and leadership problems; the ban on political activity and international affiliations; and the absence of the right to strike and effective collective bargaining. The combination of these three factors would severely hamper the development of the union movement, leaving workers to their own devices on the shop floor.

4 Union Structure: Fragmentation, Finances, and Leadership

Figures show that trade union enrolment kept its momentum the second time around. In 1948, every sixth worker covered by social legislation was a member of a trade union, ten years later, this applied to every third worker. Between March 1949 and August 1952, the number of unions and unionised workers increased from some seventy unions with 75,000 members to some 211 unions with 173,000 members. In percentage terms, this meant that thirty-three per cent of all workers covered by the labour code—or just over twenty-five per cent of all industrial workers—were unionised in 1952, making Turkey the most unionised country in the Near and Middle East after Israel.[83] The number of trade unions increased significantly thereafter, with the establishment of multiple unions in a given branch or regional unit, and reached 354 in 1954.[84]

83 J.A. Hallsworth, "Freedom of Association and Industrial Relations in the Countries of the Near and Middle East: I," *International Labour Review* 70 (1954), 367; J.A. Hallsworth, "Yakın ve Orta Şark Memleketlerinde Sendika Hürriyeti ve İşçi-İşveren Münasebetleri," *Çalışma Vekâleti* 3, no. 1 (1955), 51–80, 55; Cahit Talas, *Türkiye Cumhuriyetinde Sosyal Politika Meseleleri, 1920—1960, Türk İktisadi Gelişmesi Araştırma Projesi No. 1* (Ankara: S.B.F. Yayınları, 1960), 25.

84 The movement grew fast in the three main urban areas, namely, Istanbul, Ankara, and Izmir, in the first years, and became a widespread geographical institution only in the early 1950s. Of the twenty-four unions founded in 1947 in twelve different cities, ten were in Istanbul. The other cities were Ankara, Izmir, Bursa, Eskişehir, Kayseri, Izmit, Samsun, Adana, Iskenderun, Antalya, and Zonguldak. By 1951, seventy-one of the 154 trade unions were Istanbul-based. By 1955, almost half of union membership was found outside these

More than one third of these unions catered for workers on the state railways and in the state monopoly administrations and other state enterprises.[85]

Behind the high number of unions, however, lay a problem. The resulting "union inflation," as the unionists called it, created small and local organisations with few members and little bargaining power.[86] By permitting an unlimited number of organisations in the same industrial branch and allowing membership of multiple organisations, the law encouraged rival unionism, which fragmented the trade union movement. Voluntary union membership was a strategy to prevent the formation of a union shop. Bianchi called this a "debilitating pluralism" that was hidden behind a "façade of associational freedom." The government promoted a multitude of weak and manipulable organisations that were highly vulnerable to the retaliation of hostile governments. The associational regulations were so complex, limiting, and unclear that organisations inevitably violated them and had to seek refuge in political tutelage.[87]

The Trade Union Act allowed the formation of unions by workers either in the same or related industries or practising the same craft in different industries, and extended the same right to employers. Local unions became the lowest level and the predominant form of organisation. Two types of local unions emerged. There were plant-based unions in the larger factories, and multi-shop unions formed where smaller workplaces were the rule. Where more than one union existed in a plant, there were no provisions for selecting one as the bargaining agent. The connection between workers' representatives and unions was also ambivalent because the working relationship between the Trade Union Act and the Labour Code, which defined the mechanism of worker representation on the shop floor, remained unclear.[88]

These local unions could then organise in their branches of activity by establishing federations on a regional or national basis, and they could also come together with local unions in different branches in the same urban or regional area as alliances (*birlik*s).[89] In March 1948, several Istanbul labour unions representing different industries founded the Alliance of Istanbul Trade Unions

---

three urban areas. See: Rosen, "Labor in Turkey," 561, 430–432; United States of America, Department of Labor, *Summary of the Labor Situation in Turkey* (1956), 4.

85 Hallsworth, "Freedom of Association," 376.

86 "İttihattan, Kuvvet Doğar: Türk İşçileri ve Sendikalar, Birleşin," *Gerçek*, 8 March 1950; Sedat Ağralı, *Günümüze Kadar Belgelerle Türk Sendikacılığı* (Istanbul: Son Telgraf, 1967), 55; Hale, "Labour Unions," 62.

87 Bianchi, *Interest Groups*, 114–5.

88 United States Department of Labor, *Summary*, 5.

89 Tuna, "Trade Unions in Turkey," 424.

(*Istanbul İşçi Sendikaları Birliği*). Associations in other cities followed; by the end of 1954 there were fourteen such groups across ten cities.[90] Regional organisation became the most common and influential form of union collaboration, while federations were less frequent. The relative merits of these two forms remained a seriously debated issue throughout the 1950s.

The Act did not define the scope and function of the alliances in precise terms, and in the absence of a confederation, the Istanbul Alliance acted more like a national rather than a regional organisation.[91] Although the alliances did not have a direct role in the wage bargaining machinery, they were important urban political organisations. They attracted the most talented of the local union leaders, providing them with a forum to take the required steps to form nationwide confederations. In 1952, together with other national federations, alliances in large urban centres formed the Confederation of Turkish Trade Unions (*Türk-İş*), which would remain the country's main labour organisation until the establishment of a second confederation in 1967.[92]

Limited union finances were under strict governmental control. For one, the Ministry of Labour limited annual membership dues, restricting union freedom to increase the rate of dues and own property.[93] Checkoff was permitted in many of the state and large private plants, but not in smaller workplaces, resulting in periodic financial crises for many unions.[94] Employers would deduct the union dues from members' wages and forward them to the Ministry of Labour, which then distributed them to the unions.[95] Union headquarters were nothing more than "one or two small rooms in the cheaper rent section of the city," with the exception of some state factories where the management provided adequate space cheaply. But many such unions still preferred to rent smaller spaces on their own outside the factory to emphasise their independence.[96]

Unionism was voluntary and limited in scope to manual workers because the Trade Union Act exclusively applied to those included within the definition of "worker" under the 1936 Labour Code, namely, "a person who performs work that is either exclusively manual or both manual and intellectual." Purely

---

90 Rosen, "Labor in Turkey," 441.

91 Ağralı, *Günümüze Kadar*, 50.

92 Ibid., 48; Rosen, "Labor in Turkey," 445.

93 Tuna, "Trade Unions in Turkey," 414–5.

94 United States Department of Labor, *Summary*, 6.

95 Cahit Talas, Sait Dilik, and Alpaslan Işıklı, *Türkiye'de Sendikacılık Hareketi ve Toplu Sözleşme* (Ankara: S.B.F. Yayınları, 1965), 42.

96 United States Department of Labor, *Summary*, 6.

intellectual workers could form associations under the Associations Act of 1938, but could not form or join trade unions.[97] Because of the legal restriction excluding white collar workers from union membership, union leaders were members of the working class.[98] According to a 1954 questionnaire, out of 251 union leaders, 139 were aged thirty-five or younger. Less than one fifth were born in cities with a major concentration of industrial activity. Their education level also tended to be quite low, with 150 union leaders having only attended primary school. They worked full time in their trade, which meant their union activities were limited to after-work hours. Only sixteen received a salary from their union, which, in any event, was a practice that did not begin until in 1950, meaning that they conducted union affairs "at considerable sacrifice of time and money."[99] In a 1955 piece, one of these leaders, Bahir Ersoy, defined unionists in the 1940s as a mostly illiterate, inexperienced group of men who were exhausted due to continuous overtime work despite protective legislation.[100] "A rank-and-file leadership in every sense," concluded American political economist Sumner Rosen, which made it quite difficult for these men to fulfil positions of authority in a society where prestige depended on education, occupation, age, and social origin.[101]

5 Parties and Politics in the Trade Union Movement

Perhaps the most difficult dilemma the government faced in legislating for the Trade Union Act concerned the relationship between trade unions and political parties. On the one hand, under the pressure of intensifying political competition, the CHP felt obliged to move in the direction of labour incorporation, with the party reports on industrial workers urging the leaders to win workers over. On the other hand, the government had to make sure that neither the communists nor the DP took advantage of the rise of labour as a political category. The highly disputed fifth article of the Trade Union Act was a result of this dilemma, and created a legislative ambivalence that first the CHP, and later the DP, would take advantage of in confining the trade unions to their "legitimate"

97 Hallsworth, "Freedom of Association," 374–5.
98 Tuna, "Trade Unions," 423.
99 Rosen, "Labor in Turkey," 546–50; United States Department of Labor, *Summary*, 6.
100 Bahir Ersoy, "Sendikacılığın İnkişafına Mani Olan Sebepler," *Sosyal Siyaset Konferansları* 7 (1955), 44–45; Ağralı, *Günümüze Kadar*, 53.
101 Rosen, "Labor in Turkey," 287–8.

areas of concern. The two key terms in the fifth article were "political activity" and "national organisations":

> Employees' and employers' trade unions shall not, as such, engage in political activity or political propaganda, or act as an instrument for the activities of any political organisation. The trade unions shall be national organisations. They shall not carry on any activities which are unpatriotic or contrary to the national interest. With the consent of the Council of Ministers, a union may belong to any international organisation.

Responding largely to the short-lived but effective 1946 union movement, these two provisions located unions under strict government control. Union meetings could take place only under the close supervision of the Ministry of Labour. A union in Turkey could be suspended for between three and twelve months, or dissolved by the court, for any one of the various infringements of the law, such as engaging in political activity or resorting to strikes. "But what was the scope of political activity?" a prominent trade unionist wrote in 1955, arguing that the intentional ambiguity of the definition gave rise to tightened state control over trade unions.[102] Parliamentary discussions over the Trade Union Act supported this interpretation, during which it was understood that struggles over the working day and wages were political in nature.[103] Both the CHP and the DP governments exploited the legislative ambiguity around the concept to steer the trade union movement away from dissident political action, as well as to mobilise it for their own political purposes. Union demands to repeal the ban on political activity fell on deaf ears until the 1960s, and both the CHP and the DP governments refused to permit international union affiliations.[104] In 1967, one of the founders of the Confederation of Progressive Trade Unions of Turkey (*Devrimci İşçi Sendikaları-DISK*) criticised the more moderate Confederation of Turkish Trade Unions for holding onto "an idea that exists neither in underdeveloped areas, nor in Europe—that of keeping above party politics."[105]

In his comprehensive book on the development of Turkey's trade unions, Aziz Çelik argues that apolitical trade unionism resulted from the country's

102 Ersoy, "Sendikacılığın İnkişafına," 44; Ağralı, *Günümüze Kadar*, 58.

103 "Mecliste İşçi Sendikalari İçin Tartışmalar," *Cumhuriyet*, 21 February 1947. The political ban became a dividing line within the trade union movement as well.

104 Toker Dereli, *The Development of Turkish Trade Unionism* (Istanbul: Istanbul University, Faculty of Economics, 1968), 61–79.

105 Landau, *Radical Politics*, 94.

internal dynamics, and was not simply a result of external influence, in particular from the United States.[106] While there may not have been any direct influence, there were certainly two interrelated global developments that helped the CHP to steer the nascent movement in the direction of trade union reformism. First, following the rapid and often violent development of trade unions in colonial contexts in the 1930s, colonial officials and trade unionists collaborated in guiding the emerging trade unions along "responsible lines." Underscored by a motivation to cut any possible links between the trade unions and the independence movements, this strategy was institutionalised by the end of the Second World War.[107] "Responsible trade unionism" had already been established as a term by the time the CHP was insisting on apolitical trade unionism. Second, the formative years of Turkish trade unionism coincided with the splitting of the WFTU. In the wake of the breakup of the WFTU, primarily over the Marshall Plan, and the eventual formation of the ICFTU in 1949, Turkey became an even more strategic arena for both organisations. Fearing "a highly possible Soviet breakthrough in the Near East [that] might open three continents to Soviet penetration," the United States government perceived Turkey as the first line of defence, and allocated large amounts of aid and military funding to the country.[108] The growing American influence in the country also boosted anti-communist sentiment, including the proletarian variant, as we shall see below.

While labour unions were banned from engaging in politics, political propaganda, or publishing political views, they remained vulnerable to party control. The state had created a framework in which, in the face of legal ambiguities and state repression, unions depended on the support of local politicians, and because the government controlled the finances, they depended on the ruling party financially.[109] The CHP monitored trade union developments on the ground, especially in mines and state factories. In some cases, advisors from the party handed out exemplary trade union charters to workers, who then became union founders and managers. In the end, many trade unions

106 Çelik, *Vesayetten Siyasete*, 117.

107 Frederick Cooper, *Decolonisation and African Society: The Labour Question in French and British Africa* (Cambridge: Cambridge University Press, 1996), 250–6, 356; Peter Weiler, "Forming Responsible Trade Unions: The Colonial Office, Colonial Labor, and the Trades Union Congress," *Radical History Review* 28–30 (1984), 367.

108 Daniel Yergin, *Shattered Peace: The Origins of the Cold War and the National Security State* (Boston: Houghton Mifflin, 1977), 281; Barın Kayaoğlu, "Strategic Imperatives, Democratic Rhetoric: The United States and Turkey, 1945–52," *Cold War History* 9, no. 3 (2009), 328.

109 United States Department of Labor, *Summary*, 9.

ended up with suspiciously similar charters.[110] The directors of state factories played an active role in this first phase. At the Paşabahçe Glassware Factory, for example, the director summoned twenty head foreman and declared them the founders of the trade union.[111]

Labour journalist and later trade unionist Kemal Sülker reported hesitance among workers to join trade unions because the events of 1946 had bred strong distrust for the government. The CHP established a Workers Bureau under auspices of the Istanbul branch of the party, and appointed Rebii Barkın, the deputy of Zonguldak, the mining region, together with Sabahattin Selek, a resigned military officer, as official labour deputies. The bureau played an active role in the establishment of trade unions in 1947. In Istanbul alone, it was behind the founding of sixteen trade unions. Bureau officers published the trade union newspaper *Hürbilek* (Free Wrist), joined trade union administrative meetings, spoke at general assemblies, and allocated funds to unions, including the Bakırköy Textile Workers Trade Union in September 1947.[112]

The government also launched its own network of unions, which it later subsumed under the Alliance of Istanbul Labour Unions (*İstanbul İşçi Sendikaları Birliği*) in 1948.[113] Discontent over party control of the movement was simmering. In January 1949, for example, the chair of the Istanbul Textile Workers Union (*Istanbul Mensucat İşçileri Sendikası*), whose predecessor, the Eyüp Textile Workers Union (*Eyüp Mensucat İşçileri Sendikası*), did not join the CHP-founded labour union alliance, summarised the suspicions and hesitations over the Workers Bureau activities. "We had long discussions whether the establishment of trade unions by the bureau could really benefit us, the workers," he said, and arrived at the conviction that "a trade union that was not founded and managed by the workers themselves could not benefit the workers." The lack of finances and experience made it difficult to establish independent unions, he continued, but Istanbul textile workers did manage to found their own union in October 1947. The real difficulty, however, began only after that, because, lacking legal knowledge and organisational experience, the union faltered for a long time.[114]

In February 1950, dissident unionists left the Alliance of Istanbul Labour Unions to establish the DP-supported Alliance of Free Labour Unions (*Hür İşçi*

110 Hakan Koçak, *Camın İşçileri: Paşabahçe İşçilerinin Sınıf Olma Öyküsü* (Istanbul: İletişim, 2014), 181.

111 Ersoy, "Sendikacılığın İnkişafına," 44.

112 Sülker, *Türkiyede Sendikacılık*, 69–71.

113 Erişçi, *Türkiye'de İşçi Sınıfının Tarihi.*

114 "Sayın İşçi Arkadaşlar," (n.d.), Kemal Sülker Papers, Folder no. 121, IISH.

Sendikaları Birliği). Prior to 1950, political differences had led to a split among regional organisations in Istanbul, but in the 1950s, splinter groups divided along political rivalries were formed in three of the other regional organisations.[115] The escalating rivalry between the CHP and the DP resulted in divisions among individual unions as well as union organisations into partisan cliques.[116] Such was the background of the heated Bakırköy Textile Workers Trade Union meeting that ended with Enver's dismissal. But his political affiliation resided outside the rivalry between the ruling party and the main opposition.

Enver Tenşi had been born in 1914 in Sliven, southeast Bulgaria, directly after the Balkan Wars had deprived the Ottoman Empire of almost all its remaining territory in Europe.[117] The Tenşi family migrated to Edirne, Turkey, where Enver's father, Mehmet, opened a confectionery shop (see Figure 26). Until 1934, Enver lived in Edirne, studying at the vocational school and helping out in his father's business. He then left the town for his first factory job at the Alpullu Sugar Factory, some seventy kilometres away from the family home. In 1937, he crossed to the other side of the Marmara Sea to work at the Gemlik Artificial Silk Factory, another state enterprise. He met his wife, an émigré from Romania, around this time. Three years of military service followed the marriage. From 1941 onward, he lived and worked in Bakırköy. He grew so fond of the neighbourhood that after his retirement from the Bakırköy Factory, he founded a neighbourhood protection association. During the twenty-nine years he worked at the factory, Enver received praise from his supervisors for his diligence and discipline. It took him less than a year to get promoted from a weaver-helper to foreman. His two children, born in 1940 and 1952, remember watching him trying to construct or repair looms in the factory workshop after working hours, and complain in a bittersweet way that he did not allow himself or others to sit still even for a moment. An incident from 1952 supports their recollection. Enver became furious when his vice-foreman, Halim, gave permission to a female worker to take a break without consulting him first. Accused of lax discipline, Halim blew his fuse, and swore at and beat Enver until he lost consciousness.[118]

115 United States Department of Labor, *Summary*, 7; Rosen, "Labor in Turkey," 442, 500.

116 Ersoy, "Sendikacılığın İnkişafına," 47; Rosen, "Labor in Turkey," 258–9.

117 Biographical information on Enver Tenşi is based on his letter I cite below and the interview I conducted with his son Ersin Tenşi, daughter Esin Tenşi, and grandson Ediz Tenşi on 22 April 2022. My special thanks to the Tenşi family for sharing these details and their family photo album with me.

118 "Bakırköy Bez Fabrikasında," 30 October 1952, and "Bakırköy Bez Fabrikasındaki Hadisenin Mahiyeti," 1 January 1952, Kemal Sülker Papers, Folder no. 148, IISH.

FIGURE 26 Enver Tenşi with his father, 1936
COURTESY OF THE TENŞİ FAMILY

Enver's energetic and vocal personality was not confined to his work. We have seen above that he was one of the nine founders of the Bakırköy Cloth Factory Workers Trade Union in 1946. By that time, he had already joined a political party, and he even ran as a candidate in the July 1946 local elections.[119]

119 "Aday Listeleri: Halk ve Kalkınma Partileri Kimleri Aday Gösterdiler?" *Cumhuriyet*, 24 May 1946.

Interestingly, his choice was not the main opposition party, but a much smaller one. At a party meeting in May 1948, Enver criticised the main opposition: "What did the DP, which has [a similar] programme to the CHP, do so far? Nothing!"[120] His choice seems even stranger if we consider his employment. Enver was a state worker, but the National Development Party (*Milli Kalkınma Partisi*, hereafter the MKP) he joined was fiercely anti-etatist.[121]

The first opposition party in Turkey after the Second World War, the MKP had been established by Nuri Demirağ, a rich Istanbul industrialist, in July 1945 (see Figure 27). The party was also known as the "Lamb Party" because in every city he visited, Demirağ would pay for the ritual slaughtering of a lamb and throw lavish feasts.[122] Demirağ's business career offers a glimpse into how the turbulent political economy of the era affected private investors. Born in a small central Anatolian town in 1886 and orphaned at the age of three, Demirağ began his career as a civil servant at the Bank of Agriculture when he was seventeen. After climbing the bureaucratic ladder during the last years of the empire, he resigned from his position in the treasury, allegedly due to being insulted by the non-Muslim minorities in his office when Istanbul came under British invasion. He started out manufacturing cigarette paper, and branded his product "Turkish Victory," a bold choice of name given the political landscape of the times. After the state monopolised the tobacco industry, Demirağ moved into international trade, and then invested in the expanding railway network. The surname Demirağ, which translates as "Iron Web," was a reference to his railway business.[123] In the 1930s, he developed a passion for the air industry and established an aircraft factory. By the end of the decade, he fell into a series of conflicts with the leader of the CHP, İsmet İnönü, and had to give up on his investments in the air industry. In his eyes, his private business had fallen prey to etatism, hence the MKP's stern opposition to state involvement in the economy.[124]

The party appealed to workers' votes in 1946 by distributing a leaflet titled "Worker Rights that the MKP will Gift to the Country," and found

120 "Parti Haberleri," *Tez Kalkınma,* 28 May 1948.

121 Nezihi Hakarar, "Devletçilik İktisadi Sisteminin Kötü Örnekleri," *Tez Kalkınma,* 18 June 1948; "Madalyonun Ters Tarafı: İzmit Kâğıt Fabrikası Nasıl İşliyor?" *Tez Kalkınma,* 9 July 1948.

122 Şişmanov, *Türkiyede İşçi Sınıfı*, 118.

123 Adopted in 1934, the Surname Law (Soyadı Kanunu) enforced the adoption and registration of hereditary surnames in Turkish.

124 Necmettin Deliorman, *Nuri Demirağ'ın Hayatı ve Mücadeleleri* (Istanbul: Nu. D. Matbaası, 1957); *Milli Kalkınma Partisi 1949 Yılı Umumi Kongresi* (Istanbul: Vakit Matbaası, 1949), 20–21.

FIGURE 27 Enver Tenşi with Nuri Demirağ, c. 1950
COURTESY OF THE TENŞİ FAMILY

considerable support at the Bakırköy Factory.[125] In 1947, Enver became the head of the Bakırköy branch of the party, which had 431 members by the following year.[126] He also wrote for the party's weekly newspaper, *Tez Kalkınma* (Fast Development). Whenever he did not give his name, he would sign off as "a worker who lives in Bakırköy and works at the Sümerbank Bakırköy Factory and who is a member of the textile trade union." In these pieces, Enver mostly described the tensions on the factory shop floor and the problems of trade unionism.[127]

On 2 July 1948, Enver reported on a series of violent events at the factory, including physical fights and broken windows. The latest incident involved a chief, Niyazi, who had been trained in the Soviet Union. According to Enver, Niyazi could come and go as he pleased, and used the resources at the factory

125 "Milli Kalkınma Partisinin Memlekete Hediye Edeceği İşçi Hakları," 1946, National Library of Turkey, 1946 BD 41; "M.K. Partisinin Dünkü Siyasi Toplantısı," *Yeni Sabah*, 19 September 1949.

126 "MKP Bakırköy Kongresinde Konuşulanlar," *Tez Kalkınma*, 4 June 1948.

127 There were also other Bakırköy workers in the party complaining of government control of their union, specifically of the presence of party officers at trade union meetings. See, for example: "MKP Bakırköy Kongresinde Konuşulanlar," *Tez Kalkınma*, 4 June 1948.

workshop for the maintenance of his private car. Although the situation was reported to the management, the workers on the factory payroll continued to attend to Niyazi's car. When a young head foreman, İhsan, refused to work on his car, Niyazi slapped and swore at the head foreman. İhsan took the matter to the management, who simply disregarded it.[128]

In September 1948, eight days before the tumultuous trade union meeting that opened this chapter, *Tez Kalkınma* published a letter by Enver. In his harsh critique of the Bakırköy Textile Workers Trade Union, Enver first notes the low rate of unionisation in the neighbourhood. Of the more than two thousand workers at Bakırköy, the union managed to organise only about three hundred. Some of these members, he goes on, were enrolled by the bosses and "the chiefs," by which Enver means the CHP officers, and these members did nothing more than inform the party about union discussions. The union needs "honest, decent, selfless, and independent leaders," Enver concluded, and it was probably this closing line that offended the union management most.[129]

It appears to be at the famous trade union meeting that the seething tensions between the MKP and the CHP finally surfaced. Published by two prominent figures in the CHP's Workers Bureau, Rebii Barkın and Sebahattin Selek, the trade union newspaper *Hürbilek* described the assembly as an "exciting" meeting attended by the majority of the members.[130] *Tez Kalkınma*, on the contrary, claimed that there were only seventy members present, thirty of which had just joined the union that day. To solve the union's financial crisis, a member suggested that the union dues should be collected by the factory. The letter in *Tez Kalkınma* was fiercely critical of this suggestion, as well as the discussion over establishing a workers' bureau in the factory, claiming that the management and the CHP were slowly building a "yellow union."

Next on the meeting agenda was Enver's accusations. According to *Hürbilek*, the confrontation at that moment could scarcely have been more divisive. On one side was Enver and his allegations against the union management. Opposing him were the entire union conglomeration and the guest participants from other textile unions. Provoking a "storm" of loud exclamations and discordant noises from the members, Enver's allegations united the otherwise divided assembly. The verbal contest that ensued was sharp and, at times, almost nasty, and it demonstrated how trade union politics could stoke tensions on the shop floor. For example, Enver had verbally accused two members of the union management of working for the factory management. When

128 "Bu Ne Cür'et, Bu Ne Tahakküm!" *Tez Kalkınma*, 2 July 1948.

129 "Bakırköy Mensucat Sendikası Ne Halde?" *Tez Kalkınma*, 7 September 1948.

130 " Çok Heyecanlı Bir Toplantı Yaptı."

confronted, he explained that he suspected them because they had been promoted unusually quickly. The members applauded to show their support for the two accused, and Enver was thrown out of the clubhouse. Defeated and insulted, Enver refused to give up. He penned another piece for *Tez Kalkınma* the following month. "With its *Barkın*s and *Selek*s," he wrote, referring to the two directors of the CHP Workers Bureau, the government "is trying to control the unions" for electoral benefit. But its efforts had backfired, he claimed; the workers knew that their interest in the unions was far from sincere, and they refused to join what he called "the CHP's trade unions."[131]

As we saw in the introduction to this chapter, ganging up on Enver did not succeed in soothing the tensions neither on the shop floor nor in the trade union. We will return to this briefly but we should first follow Enver through the eventful days preceding the 1950 general election, "the happy day on which the national will manifest itself," to borrow Enver's words. He announced his candidacy "as a worker citizen" in a public letter addressed to his "self-sacrificing and patriotic fellow workers," and fiercely criticised the conditions of the industrial working class.[132] He described their slave-like status at their workplaces, their dreadful health and housing conditions, the lack of educational opportunities for working-class children, and the calamity in which working-class families found themselves. Those who appealed to workers' votes by bringing their problems up in the runup to the election, he claimed, would forget about them just as soon as they made it to Ankara; "only workers could represent workers." But how could they do this when the accusation of communism hung above their heads like a sword of Damocles?

With this remark, Enver's fierce critique reached its limits. He resorted to the by now familiar tropes of the dedicated nationalist and sacrificial citizen, drawing on the prevailing notions of the regime's master narrative. He had already made nationalist remarks at the beginning of his letter, when he introduced himself as a proud Turkish worker who was carrying out his "sacred military duty," or when he described Turkish workers as "the most self-sacrificing, patriotic, and benevolent workers in the world." When he referred to communism, however, he took things to the next level, arguing that "there is not a single communist among Turkish workers and there can never be." The motivation behind such unfounded allegations directed at workers was to "condemn them to live in fear and suspicion." A nationalist working-class parliamentary representation was the solution, and the MKP provided exactly

131 "Hakikatın Sesi," *Tez Kalkınma*, 8 October 1948.

132 Enver Tenşi, "Sayın Vatandaşlarım," (n.d.), Kemal Sülker Papers, Folder no. 151, IISH.

that, Enver reassured his readers, before he signed off the letter: "Working and striving from us, blessings from God."

Enver was an outsider amid the fierce competition between the government and the main opposition that pervaded the entire social arena, including union politics. But he very much subscribed to the main tenets of Kemalism, much like the unionists Rosen met in the 1950s. "Turkey's union leaders, all of whom are workers," Rosen wrote, "share the fervent nationalism that Atatürk gave his people, and expend considerable energy demonstrating their rejection of communism and class warfare." They have wholeheartedly accepted the premises of society and their role in it.[133] He met only a few union officers who called themselves "socialists," and even then, they meant socialism "in the gradualist tradition of the British Labour Party." He had clearly never met Ahmet.

6 What Are Trade Unions For?

After four long years, Ahmet walked out of the military barracks in Ankara for the last time into the cold, snowy winter. His initial idea was to go to the state iron and steel plant in Karabük, but from his previous experience, he knew finding a job would be difficult during this season. He then headed to Zonguldak to work in the mechanical workshop of a coal mine, where he earned almost thirty per cent more than a miner. It was during this time that he first heard of occupational disease insurance. He had no idea what it meant, and neither did the foreman he approached. He concluded that miners were "a backward bunch" compared with textile workers, and decided to leave. He became the ninetieth member of the Bakırköy Textile Workers Trade Union when he joined in September 1947 (see Figure 28).

An incident he witnessed in Zonguldak confused Ahmet. He had heard that Celal Bayar, one of the founders of the DP, would meet with workers. On his way to such a meeting, he saw gendarmeries herding workers away from the meeting hall. He somehow managed to reach the venue, only to find that the meeting had been cancelled. Later, he read the party's programme in the newspaper, and two clauses grabbed his attention: the recognition of occupational groups as the building blocks of society and the need to legalise strikes. It was especially the latter that appealed to him, he remembered, because of a recent experience he had had at a meeting where a worker asked the labour minister

133 Rosen, "Labor in Turkey," 293.

FIGURE 28 Ahmet (second from the right in the front row) in front of the Bakırköy Textile Workers Trade Union, c. 1949

for his opinion on the right to strike. Ahmet gave a vivid account of the minister's reply and how it caused such confusion:

> [The minister] walked up and down before us like teachers do before their pupils, and said 'Whoever thinks of striking is a traitor, a communist!' The strange thing is, a traitor is one thing, a communist is another. This is how bizarre things were for us. Of course, everybody kept quiet; I mean, who could say anything after such a statement?

It was remarks like this that pushed workers away from the government, according to Ahmet. Around the same time, Ahmet attended a meeting of the Alliance of Istanbul Trade Unions, where he heard Fuat Köprülü, another DP founder, likening a trade union without the right to strike to an army without weapons, and promising to grant it as soon as the party came to power.[134] In

134 Around the same time, Sabiha Sertel paid a home visit to Fuat Köprülü to discuss a monthly magazine the dissidents wanted to publish with the help of leftist journalists. Köprülü was busy writing the party programme, and Sertel took advantage of her timing to ask whether the new party supported the right to strike. The answer was clear and concise: "Of course! I am working on the party programme, which will include all this. If you ask me personally, I would like the country to move toward socialism, but others do not

its defence of the strike ban, the CHP once again referred to etatism and the unique nature of Turkish industrialisation. The Turkish state had caught up with early industrialisers, policymakers claimed, in terms of welfare provision and social protections without workers' having to strike.[135] The Democrats criticised the ban on strikes, blaming the CHP for not believing in the workers' political maturity, and appealed to union support by promising to legalise strikes.[136] Ahmet was convinced; he joined the main opposition party. It was shortly after this that the trade union meeting discussed at the beginning of this chapter took place, where Ahmet raised the profoundly simple question: What are trade unions for?[137]

We had left İhsan Önaslan, in September 1948, crying with relief after Enver had been thrown out of the union meeting. Seven months later, he has resigned as union chair and we meet him describing what it was like to be a unionist in the 1940s: "There is not a single worker among us who could serve the trade union more than one day in the week, because we all had to work at least six days a week to provide for ourselves and our families." Over approximately seven months, İhsan continued, executive committee members devoted twenty-eight days to union activities, sacrificing the time they needed for rest and for their families. Above, I quoted both local and foreign observers on the leadership structure in the trade unions and the problems it generated. İhsan was only one of those workers who took on union duties on top of full-time work. He had a hard time living on the wage he earned from his full-time work, and he was searching for work in the private sector, where, he claimed, he would earn more. According to three petitions he filed between 1946 and 1962, İhsan "could barely provide for his family of six and lived in hardship" and thought he "would earn much more outside." At no point did İhsan, the union chair, appeal to his union for support in dealing with the factory management. One could hardly find more striking evidence of how legislation—more specifically the continuance of compulsory arbitration—hampered the development of trade unions.

Until 1950, the role of the trade unions in the arbitration process was limited to submitting their views and offering suggestions to solve the dispute.

---

agree with me." Knowing the class background, and the previous political positions of the DP founders, Sertel's response was a silent, sarcastic grin. See: Sertel, *Roman Gibi*, 292.

135 Esat Tekeli, "Çalışma Konferasında Türkiye," *Çalışma* 2, no. 20 (1947).

136 Kemal Sülker, *Türkiye'de Grev Hakkı ve Grevler* (Istanbul: TÜSTAV, 2004), 50.

137 In covering this union meeting, I combine information from two newspaper reports and the interview given by Ahmet. See: "Bakırköy Mensucat İşçilerinin Kongresi"; "Bakırköy Mensucat İşçileri Sendikası Pazar Günü Olağanüstü Kongre Yaptı," *Hürbilek*, 20 April 1949.

Although the Trade Union Act authorised trade unions to negotiate and sign collective bargains on behalf of their members, in practical terms trade unions were bound hand and foot. The act did not stipulate restrictions on an employer refusing to recognise his employees' union as the representative of his employees or refusing to negotiate with the union concerning the conditions of employment. Labour unions thus lacked the special legislative protection they needed, especially in the absence of the right to strike.[138]

Two factors precluded the unions from representing their members in negotiating collective conditions of employment. The first concerned the institution of a workers' representative introduced by the 1936 Labour Code. Between 1936 and 1946, when the government had legalised trade unions, only ten cases of wage disputes reached the central arbitration board through the workers' representatives.[139] After the enactment of the Trade Union Act, the existing system of representation substantially precluded the trade unions from the vital activity of representing their members in negotiating collective conditions of employment. Furthermore, because the office of workers' representatives existed independently of the employee organisations, union participation in dispute settlement was kept at a minimum and the role accorded to organised labour in channelling and managing worker protest was very limited. Unions had no role in selecting workers' representatives to participate in the deliberations, which precluded them from representing their members in negotiating collective conditions of employment. A kind of dual representation emerged at the workplace level, where the unions had to compete with non-union representatives as well as the rival unions created by the employers.[140] The CHP also intervened in the election of workers' representatives.[141] From the very beginning, workers protested at these interventions and demanded that their representatives be union members, but both governments turned a deaf ear to their complaints.[142] Second, neither the Associations Act nor the Trade Union Act contained adequate provisions to protect union members from discharge or other discriminatory treatment.[143] In contrast, the labour code permitted employers to terminate a contract of employment with notice and upon

138 International Labour Office, *Labour Problems in Turkey* (Geneva: ILO, 1950), 185–6; Dereli, *Turkish Trade Unionism*, 84.

139 Rosen, "Labor in Turkey," 270.

140 Bahir Ersoy, "İşçi Gözü ile İsçi ve İşveren Münsabetleri," *Sosyal Siyaset Konferansları* 6 (1954), 49; ILO, *Labour Problems*, 201–202.

141 Bürge, "Partimizin Meslek Teşekkülleriyle," 6.

142 Sait Kesler, "İstanbul'da Bir Günde 6 Sendika Kongresi yapıldı," *Türk İşçisi*, 11 October 1947.

143 Ağralı, *Günümüze Kadar*, 52.

payment of compensation. "A period of discharges follows every union congress," wrote Bahir Ersoy in 1955.[144]

Two developments in 1950 strengthened labour's hand to some extent. First, labour courts were transformed into tripartite tribunals.[145] The Labour Courts Act granted trade unions a clear function in labour-management relations for the first time, in that they could file lawsuits to these courts.[146] Second, an amendment to the labour code conceded limited authority to trade unions to initiate disputes on the condition that they have as members a majority of the workers employed in the enterprise concerned and that one fifth (a minimum of ten) of the total number of employees in the enterprise had submitted a written request. In the 1950s, a large proportion of the arbitrated disputes were submitted through this means. Still, trade unions did not have the power to establish a pattern of direct relations with employers; workers' representatives had enough authority to present grievances but not enough to bargain on them; trade union influence over employment conditions remained limited to providing advisory opinions to the courts and arbitration board.[147]

Another amendment in 1954 provided for direct representation of workers' and employers' organisations on arbitral bodies.[148] By the mid-1950s, collective agreements negotiated by trade unions were still very few in number. In its reply to an International Labour Organization survey in 1956, the government claimed that the awards of the arbitration boards should be "looked upon as a form of collective agreement," adding that at the same time it was preparing a bill concerning collective agreements.[149] Collective agreements were rare until the recognition of the right to strike in 1963, rendering the individual contract the main instrument regulating the employment relationship. İhsan's choice to keep his wage grievance separate from his union leadership was but one manifestation of the individualisation of industrial relations.

Disabled in their capacity to represent workers in their relations with employers, trade union activities were largely reduced to those of mutual

144 Ersoy, "Sendikacılığın İnkişafına," 44; ILO, *Labour Problems*, 166.

145 Safa Ş. Erkün, "İş Mahkemeleri Kurulurken Bazı Düşünceler," *İçtimai Syaset Konferansları* 2 (1949), 34–48; International Labour Office, *Legislative Series 1950* (Geneva: ILO, 1953).

146 United States Department of Labor, *Summary*, 11.

147 Tuna, "Trade Unions in Turkey," 424–427; William F. Delaney, *Labor Law and Practice in Turkey* (United States Department of Labor, 1963), 34; Orhan Tuna, "Türkiye'de Cebri Tahkim Sistemi ve Tatbikatı, 1939–1963," *Istanbul Üniversitesi İktisat Fakültesi Mecmuası* 26, no. 1–4 (1967), 42; Dereli, *Turkish Trade Unionism*, 80–107.

148 United States Department of Labor, *Summary* 13–14; Rosen, "Labor in Turkey," 269–271.

149 United States Department of Labor, *Summary*, 12.

benefit societies.[150] And this was exactly what was at the root of Ahmet's frustration at the meeting in April 1949. Having explained how problems of time and energy constrained union work, İhsan continued with the activity report of the resigned management. Union membership had almost doubled from 350 to 650 in seven months, he claimed. We do not have official records to confirm this, nor can we explain exactly what caused this dramatic increase. But the activities İhsan listed afterward could offer a hint. The trade union had opened a non-profit coffeehouse at the factory to provide cheap tea and coffee; it also sold winter coats on credit and represented textile workers at the Republic Day parade with a weaving loom. "In spite of all this," İhsan continued, some workers continued to claim that, being bought off by the management, "the union administration is not defending workers' rights." Ahmet took the critique one step further:

> Trade unions are supposed to defend workers' rights, but there is no sign of this in the activity report we just heard … We elected colleagues that are more educated than us, but it is clear that they cannot do this. I believe they are under pressure. We face grave injustices at the factory. For example, we lose more than half of our wage when there is machine breakage, but workers' representatives do not care. Our representatives are the foremen, and they work for hourly wages. Thus, they do not care about our problems … We should not forget that the law gives us great benefits.

Why and how did trade unions turn into mutual aid societies? A prominent unionist argued that workers joined unions for material and non-material benefits, and not because they believed in the cause of the labour movement.[151] The labour code permitted the transfer of workers' fines to solidarity funds, which are established by trade unions to be used for social benefit. Given workers' low wages, this strategy was successful in recruiting union members. Employers also supported unions' spending their money on social benefits because, first, this saved them fringe benefit expenses, and second, it meant that unions could not save for "the time when workers finally have

150 ILO, *Labour Problems*, 166.

151 Ersoy, "Sendikacılığın İnkişafına," 45–6. The head of the CHP's Workers Bureau, Sebahattin Selek, complained of workers' perception of trade unions as "soup kitchens," but instead of addressing the structural problems faced by trade unions, he put the blame on the workers who "exploited" union funds when they were not in true need of union assistance. See: Sebahattin Selek, "Sendika Aşevi Değildir!" *Hürbilek,* 12 June 1948.

consciousness." The reduction of trade union activities to those of a mutual aid society, Ersoy argued, acted like a drug on workers.[152]

An incident that happened couple months before Ahmet's protest at the union meeting supports Ersoy's critique. Interestingly, this incident was quite similar to Ahmet's first experience of worker resistance during the war. On 30 December 1948, seventy-three weavers failed to show up for the night shift, and were later fined a day's wage. The union, the director proudly reported, managed to get these workers "forgiven" on the condition that they would work on a holiday to make up for the lost working hours. Only nineteen weavers stuck to their promise when the day came. The archive is silent on the reasons behind this incident. But two things are as clear as day. First, shop-floor industrial relations were quite tense, as reported by both Enver and Ahmet. Second, between the first work stoppage during the war and this incident in 1948, trade union involvement had not changed much, because the union's role was limited to pleading to the management. Third, workers did not follow the union, as seen from the weavers' reaction to the union's "solution."

The meeting concluded with the election of the new union administration, which promoted Ahmet to the position of deputy chair. By this time, Ahmet was also head of the Bakırköy branch of the DP. He went on to become the chief workers' representative in 1951, and shortly after that he came head-to-head with the head foreman of the weaving department, who reported that Ahmet had threatened him in front of two weavers: "Let these friends be witness; from now, if you carry out unfair practices or wrongdoing here, I will take legal action. Similarly, if you report any worker or cause anyone to be fired, I will take legal action." Four days later, the chief of the main production units reported the incident to management, and claimed that Ahmet was using his status as union deputy chair to intervene in the management of the weaving department. He left his loom unattended, the chief claimed, and would engage in public fights with the foremen and head foremen, which was having a negative influence on workers and ruining workplace discipline. Five days later, Ahmet received an official warning from the factory director. His behaviour was contrary to both trade union law and the factory rules and regulations; he would be fired if he continued to disrespect his supervisors. And for the first time in a shop-floor conflict at the factory, the trade union intervened.

In November 1951, the union petitioned the factory. Referring to the Trade Union Act and factory regulations, the union refuted the factory management's claim that Ahmet's behaviour was unlawful and demanded that the

152 Ersoy, "Sendikacılığın İnkişafına," 46; Rosen, "Labor in Turkey," 506.

warning be revoked. Because the management had built its case on the rejection of Ahmet's claim to authority, the union petition began by establishing Ahmet's status as the deputy chairman and workers' representative, while defending his right to intervene in worker-management relations on the shop floor on behalf of workers. The correspondence ended with a short note from the factory management jotted on the union petition: "The management does not deem it necessary to reply." The case was closed. But Ahmet continued to challenge the factory management—even more strongly because his political views were changing after the DP's first year in power.

Once in government, the DP backpedalled from its campaign promise to legalise strikes, and switched to an anti-strike stance in June 1951.[153] During discussions on labour issues at a party congress two years later, Ahmet took to the stage to criticise the party's labour policy and publicly resigned "in front of the ministers," unaware of the high price he would pay for this protest. By then, DP supporters had gained power on the shop floor, or, rather, those who already had power had become government supporters. Ahmet lost the workers' representatives elections. But more importantly, he was kicked out of the factory housing cooperative that he had jointly founded.

After the meeting, Ahmet's political route would take yet another turn. Having heard Ahmet's critique of the DP, a lawyer, Orhan Arsal, approached Ahmet. Arsal, together with three trade unionist workers, had established a political party in October 1950.[154] Arsal had decided to establish a new party after falling out with the DP, and aptly named the party the Democrat Labour Party (*Demokrat İşçi Partisi*, hereafter the DİP).[155] The party shared Ahmet's disappointment in the DP's labour policy. The Democrat Labour Party vice-chairman called 14 May, the day the DP had come to power, "the day of betrayal of the workers," and accused the government of forgetting about workers after

153 Karpat, *Turkey's Politics*, 313–4; Ağralı, *Günümüze Kadar*, 58–9; Feroz Ahmad, *The Making of Modern Turkey* (London: Routledge, 1993), 110; Sülker, *Türkiye'de Grev*, 47.

154 Demokrat İşçi Partisinin Programı (Istanbul: Uğur Basımevi, 1950); Tunaya, *Türkiye'de Siyasi Partiler*, 740–742; Sülker, *Türkiyede Sendikacılık*, 141–142; Kemal Sülker, *Sendikacılar ve Politika* (Istanbul: May Yayınları. 1975), 69.

155 At the first general assembly, some members expressed discontent with the similarity between the names of the two parties, and proposed changing it to the Socialist Labour Party following the vice-chairman's explanation of party ideology as "humanitarian socialism." Arsal opposed the suggestion, claiming that the party name protected them against accusations of "fascism or Bolshevism." The party did not aim to establish a dictatorship of the proletariat but rather to attain class equality in the manner required by a complete democracy. See: *Birinci Sarı Çizgili Kitap* (Demokrat İşçi Partisinin Ikinci Genel Kongresi Münasebetiyle Neşrolunmuştur) (Istanbul: n.p. 1953), 15. The party's name changed to Labour Party in 1953.

"stealing [their] votes."[156] He fiercely criticised party controls on organised labour, and claimed that it had created yellow trade unions in which union aristocracy benefited under political party tutelage, and went so far as to prohibiting party members from joining unions.[157] This critique did not appeal to workers. In 1952 the party had only six hundred members, and it disbanded in August 1955.

Ahmet did not elaborate on his decision to join the Democrat Labour Party. In the end, this was a brief interlude in his political life for he could not find his political match here either. Ahmet left the party because he did not believe that Arsal was sufficiently committed to the cause of labour. This short-lived encounter is revealing of the complex political world surrounding Ahmet during his politicisation, with personal connections playing an important role in this process. It was one such connection that would shape Ahmet's next political affiliation and form a bridge between 1946 unionism with that of the 1950s.

Without explaining how, when, and where they had met, Ahmet mentioned an enamel worker, Şükrü, who had been active in the 1946 union movement. A "class-conscious worker" in Ahmet's words, Şükrü "woke us up," Ahmet said, meaning that he taught Ahmet and others what unions were actually for. He also did something else that would change the course of Ahmet's life forever: he introduced Ahmet to Hikmet Kıvılcımlı, a communist theoretician who had been one of the leading cadres of the illegal Communist Party of Turkey in the 1920s. When Ahmet met him in 1953 or 1954, he was fresh out of prison, where he had spent almost twenty years of the previous three decades.

Ahmet was now a communist. But what did it really mean to be a communist in the mid-1950s? A month after coming to power, the DP government conducted a raid on the Society of the Friends of Peace, the Turkish branch of the international peace front that had organic ties with the political traditions of the TKP. Because the Society objected to Turkey's participation in the Korean War, the government jailed its members on charges of spreading communism. In 1951, the DP government modified the criminal code to increase the penalty for "communist activity." A wave of arrests on charges of membership in the underground communist party followed, and a total of 167

156 *Sarı Çizgili*, 18.

157 This repulsive tone seems to have been shared by a majority of party members, as far as we understand from the choice of the design of the party emblem: "Those trade unions which work for other causes than workers' interests are called yellow trade unions because the colour yellow symbolizes betrayal all around the world. This is the reason why we painted the signboard of the DİP yellow and we wrote the name of the party in black to mourn for those unions. Down with yellow trade unions." *Sarı Çizgili*, 5, 12–4, 19.

workers, intellectuals, and professionals were brought to trial for spreading communism. One of these defendants, the leader of the communist movement since the 1920s, Şefik Hüsnü Deymer, was given a prison sentence of over five years, and died in internal exile.[158] Kıvılcımlı was able to avoid this wave of arrests because he had only just come out of prison in 1950 after spending the last twelve years incarcerated. The persecution of leftist activists continued along with authoritarian legislation with severe penalties, such as the 1954 Press Law (*Neşir Yoluyla Veya Radyo İle İşlenecek Bazı Cürümler Hakkındaki Kanun*) and the 1956 Law of Meetings and Demonstrations (*Toplantılar ve Gösteri Yürüyüşleri Hakkında Kanun*), continued for the rest of the decade. The repression of independent labour organisation remained a constant from the single to the multi-party period.

Despite increasing repression and the ongoing prohibition on strikes, labour protests continued. Strikes took place in Istanbul, Izmir, Ankara, Mersin, and other cities in 1951 and 1952. Port workers also went on strike in Iskenderun and Izmit in 1953 and 1954. In addition to economic demands, workers had political demands such as the abolition of the anti-democratic labour legislation and the expansion of trade union rights. In 1953, a year before the parliamentary elections, the tables had turned when the right to strike made it into the programme of the opposition party, the CHP.[159] The DP, on the other hand, stuck to its no-strike policy and expanded state paternalism by increasing fringe benefits for rank-and-file while criminalising union activity.[160] Although Turkey had ratified the ILO's 1949 Right to Organise and Collective Bargaining Convention in 1951, the government maintained the restrictions on strikes.

Labour anti-communism also remained strong (see Figure 29). In fact, the trade union movement played a role in shaping the distinctive character of postwar domestic anti-communism through the development of their own discourses of communist infiltration and subversion. Trade unions organised anti-communist rallies, and whenever a worker would mention that such rallies were against the ban on unions to engage in political activity, others would attack and insult him, arguing that being an anti-communist had nothing to do with politics; it was a national duty.[161] The public hysteria found its strongest expression in a biological discourse built on blood, germs, and contagious diseases. Trade unions used biological metaphors that claimed "the microbe of communism" could not "live in the noble blood in his veins." Unionists used the

158 Sayılgan, *Solun 94 Yılı*, 266-268.

159 Rosen, "Labor in Turkey," ii; Korniyenko, *The Labor Movement*, 100.

160 Bianchi, *Interest Groups*, 123–124; Rosen, "Labor in Turkey," 276.

161 "İşçi Sendikaları Komünizmi Tel'in Mitingine Katılacak," *Son Telgraf*, 21 August 1950.

FIGURE 29 "We are the enemy of communism," Aydın branch of the Textile, Knitting, and Clothing Industry Workers' Union (Türkiye Tekstil, Örme, Giyim ve Deri Sanayi İşçileri Sendikası, TEKSİF), c. 1955
IISH KEMAL SÜLKER PAPERS, BG A63/90

word "Turkish" almost always in an ethnic sense, suggesting that the ethnicised body of the Turkish worker was full of antibodies to combat communism.[162]

Tensions intensified on the shop floor, too. In the interviews given in the 1980s, some trade unionists explained how party membership provided protection for workers against accusations of communism.[163] However, it could also trigger such accusations, since the war against communism was also embroiled in partisan hostility. A DP-supporting worker from the Defterdar Factory sent a complaint to labour journalist Kemal Sülker, reporting the mistreatment he had suffered at the hands of CHP-affiliated foremen and engineers. He wore his party badge with pride on the shop floor, he wrote, but the foremen and engineers kept accusing him of communism.[164] To be accused of

162 "Son Telgraf ve Gece Postası Yazı İşleri Sayın Müdürlüğüne," 24 August 1950, Kemal Sülker Papers, Folder no. 187, IISH; "Türk İşçileri Dün Komünizmi Tel"in Etti," *Vatan*, 27 August 1950; "Komünizme Karşı Istanbul İşçilerinin Dünkü Muazzam Toplantısı," *Milliyet*, 27 August 1950.

163 Yıldırım Koç, *Türk-İş Tarihinden Portreler: Eski Sendikacılardan Anılar Gözlemler* (Ankara: Türk-İş Yayınları, 1999), 26, 33, 47, 103.

164 "Diktatörcesine Haksızlığa Uğrayan bir Türk Vatandaşın Şikayeti," (n.d.), Kemal Sülker Papers, Folder no. 402, IISH.

being a communist in those days, remembered Bahir Ersoy, was akin to being accused of being a national traitor, or even a Soviet spy, and made it extremely difficult for the unionists to communicate with the public.[165]

But perhaps most shockingly, the pent-up shop-floor tensions at the Bakırköy Factory culminated in “a mysterious murder” in March 1952.[166] The series of events that led to three gunshots portray a vivid picture of the political pressures on the shop floor. A twenty-eight-year-old engineer, İhsan, had just returned from the United States, where he had been on a six-month training course on a grant from the Marshall Plan (see Figure 30). He shot another young engineer, Fethi, three times while the two men were having an early lunch in the factory canteen. Nobody witnessed the incident, and by the time the waiters had arrived at the crime scene, Fethi was already dead. İhsan had run out to the back of the factory to jump into the Marmara Sea, but a doorman caught him. He then succumbed to silence, refusing to answer questions from either the police or his family.

People had different theories about the murder motive. Some thought the two men had a common love interest. Some others said that it was because Ferit earned more than İhsan even though İhsan was more qualified as an engineer. Months later, İhsan spoke for the first time in court. Before he had left for the United States, life at the factory had become almost unbearable for him, he said, complaining of two groups at the factory: the communists and the slanderers. Despite his clean past and good intentions, the slanderers had been provoking him. He had been blamed for several cases of arson and sabotage. Then they tried to turn workers against him. Finally, “they painted hammer and sickle and wrote ‘Long live communism!’ on the walls near my office, and blamed it on me,” he claimed. The period he referred to was the time of the communist arrests. On the witness stand, the factory director, Şefkati Türkekul, confirmed that the factory management had indeed been trying to weed out the communists in the factory to no avail. A group of employees, including

165 Interview with Bahir Ersoy by Yıldırım Koç, 1988, video recording *V1/44*, Trade Union Movement in Turkey Oral History Collection, IISH.

166 “Bakırköyde İşlenen Esrarengiz Cinayet,” *Milliyet*, 1 March 1952; “Bir Yüksek Mühendis Diğer Bir Yüksek Mühendisi Öldürdü,” *Cumhuriyet*, 1 March 1952; “Bakırköy Cinayetinin Esrarı Çözülemiyor,” *Milliyet*, 2 March 1952, “Bez Fabrikasındaki Cinayetin Sebebi,” *Cumhuriyet*, 2 March 1952; “Bakırköy Cinayeti,” *Milliyet*, 3 March 1952; “Bakırköy Cinayeti Tahkikatı Dün Yeni Bir Safhaya Girdi,” *Cumhuriyet*, 3 March 1952; “Katil Dün De Konuşmadı,” *Milliyet*, 4 March 1952; “Katil Mühendis Adli Tıbba Sevkedildi,” *Cumhuriyet*, 4 March 1952; “Bakırköy Bez Fabrikası Cinayeti, *Cumhuriyet*, 27 March 1952; “Kaatil Mühendis,” *Milliyet*, 6 May 1952; “Kaatil Mühendis Nihayet Konuştu,” *Milliyet*, 30 September 1952; “Arkadaşını Öldüren Mühendisin Duruşması,” *Cumhuriyet*, 30 September 1952.

FIGURE 30 İhsan Aydın leaving for the United States with a big send-off from his family and factory personnel, c. 1951
COURTESY OF ERGİN AYGÖL

Fethi, had wanted to smear his name because they were jealous, İhsan concluded, and he could not stand it anymore.

Such was the world on and outside the shop floor when Ahmet decided to join Kıvılcımlı in establishing a new communist party. On 22 October 1954, Ahmet was one of the founders, and the first chair, of the Homeland Party (*Vatan Partisi*). After twenty days, he left his seat to Kıvılcımlı at the first party general assembly. Textile workers made up the majority of the party membership, Ahmet noted. The party was not very well organised, but it was active in Taşlıtarla and Zeytinburnu in Istanbul, as well as Izmit and Izmit. In the 1957 general elections, Ahmet announced his candidacy. By then, he was no longer working at the Bakırköy Factory; a new phase of his life had started, one characterised by police surveillance and state violence.

7 The Arrest

On 4 January 1955, while he was on leave to take care of his family after the death of a family member, Ahmet was arrested "on the basis of false allegations," in his words. He had just returned to Istanbul after a visit to his hometown, and was looking for a fountain pen a fellow villager had ordered when an undercover police officer approached and asked Ahmet to follow him to the police station. The police officer questioned him about a speech he had given at a trade union meeting. He referred to Ahmet's mentioning the worker struggles in Europe and the United States for the eight-hour working day, and that the socialist labour parties backed these struggles. Communist parties were in European parliaments, Ahmet had continued, arguing that it was time for the same to happen in Turkey. And there he was at the police station being interrogated for communist propaganda.

The factory management annulled Ahmet's contract immediately after his arrest. In June 1955, after his acquittal, he petitioned the factory, demanding to return to his job. The response was negative: the factory did not need weavers. With this, Ahmet's personnel file enters into twelve years of silence, during which time he is unable to secure stable employment. The last document in his file dates back to 1967, when Ahmet made one last attempt to be recruited. He mentions numerous unsuccessful applications he had made to the factory since 1955, and that he had been unemployed for a long time. The response was again negative.

Two years later, after a speech given by Kıvılcımlı in Eyüp in the wake of the 1957 snap elections, the DP arrested thirty-eight party members, including Ahmet (see Figure 31). The police tortured them; one of them heard Ahmet

FIGURE 31 Ahmet Cansızoğlu in prison with Hikmet Kıvılcımlı and other Homeland Party members, c. 1957
TÜRKİYE SOSYAL TARİH ARAŞTIRMA VAKFI ARŞİVİ

FIGURE 32 Enver Tenşi in front of the prison, c. 1960
COURTESY OF TENŞİ FAMILY

begging for water when the police brutally inflicted bastinado on him.[167] After two years of imprisonment, all members were acquitted and released. The party would exist only on paper afterward. In the 1960s, Ahmet joined the Labour Party of Turkey (*Türkiye İşçi Partisi*). Established in 1961 by progressive labour union leaders, the Labour Party of Turkey has been the largest and most durable of legal socialist parties in Turkey. Ahmet never got his job back at the Bakırköy Factory, and he died a communist.

While Ahmet was experiencing these turbulent times, things were looking stable for Enver. The MKP remained small and ineffective, and finally dissolved in 1958.[168] By then, Enver had already joined the DP. But the DP was also fast

167 *Zehra Kosova: Ben İşçiyim,* ed. Zihni T. Anadol (Istanbul: İletişim, 1996), 120–2; Suat Şükrü Kundakçı: *Bir Ömür Bir Sohbet,* ed. Ersin Tosun (Istanbul: TÜSTAV, 2005), 59.

168 Karpat, *Turkey's Politics*, 148–9; Tunaya, *Türkiye'de Siyasi Partiler*, 638.

approaching its end. Turkey's first military coup d'état happened on 27 May 1960, when the Turkish armed forces overthrew the Democrat Party government and arrested all of its leaders. At the end of the trials, four received death penalties, and three were ultimately hanged. One of the many accusations they faced was inciting the people against the CHP leader, İsmet İnönü, in May 1959. On 18 August 1960, Enver was arrested on the factory grounds and charged with taking part in the attack. He spent a month in prison, was acquitted, and returned to his job at the Bakırköy Factory (see Figure 32).

8 Conclusion

The end of the Second World War ushered in political pluralisation in Turkey. Already shaken during the war years, the CHP's hegemonic grip soon weakened in the postwar period. With the end of the single-party era, labour became a political category, and political leaders began to pursue the option of mobilising workers as a political base far more extensively than before. Beside the simmering tensions in the workplace, workers found themselves in the midst of rapidly escalating political rivalry and an unexpectedly fast-growing and potentially militant union activity. The repeal of the ban on class-based association brought the undercurrents of leftist politics to the surface, making it clear that trade unions could not be allowed to grow unchecked. The challenge, then, was to develop an alternative that would allow the trade union movement to develop within the confines of acceptable bounds that would pose a threat to neither Kemalist political rule nor industrial productivity. By the time the founding party made a move to incorporate the working class into the national political arena, the effort was too little, too late.

Albeit lacking in actual numbers and fervent strength, the potential threat of the communist labour movement shaped the course of labour policy. Trade unionists operated on slippery ground that was constantly being reshaped by two sets of forces. On the one side was the political expansion of citizenship as an enabling force. On the other side were the quickly developing Cold War tensions in the furthest geographical outpost of the non-communist world. As communism became a popular smear word, the trade union movement had to put a foot on the brakes to protect itself from state repression and strong proletarian anti-communism. Furthermore, the absence of strikes and strong collective bargaining, the fragmented nature of unions, and the prohibition on union involvement in politics and its abuses all seriously hindered the growth of effective unionism. These three elements working together made wage and employment negotiations specific and confidential. Workers were left with little recourse for their complaints because the individual contract continued to be the only method used to determine wages.

In this chapter, I followed two Bakırköy Factory workers whose life experiences reflected the tumult of the 1940s and 1950s. Their life stories gave human form to these macrostructural developments, and depict a political atmosphere that was at once chaotic and dangerous, and exciting and hopeful. Their stories also demonstrate the dynamic and processual nature of working-class political identity as an outcome of everyday material and discursive social practices. Both Enver and Ahmet were dissidents who challenged the government and its control over the trade unions, but their political paths diverged completely. While Enver stayed within the hegemonic boundaries of Kemalist nationalism and its authorised discourses, Ahmet gradually became radicalised and became a communist. Both workers ended up in prison at some point in their lives, a commonality that is evidence of the precarious character of working-class politics. But, while Enver's one-month imprisonment in 1960 did not alter the course of his life, Ahmet would pay the price for his politics with a life-long struggle just to get by.

No matter how precarious, subordinated, and controlled they were in most cases, trade unions were not the mouthpiece of the state. Conflicting class interests and organisational alternatives did exist but they were frozen until the mid-1960s within the labour movement. By the end of the 1940s, the existence of workers as a social *and* political force was confirmed. Their existence deeply influenced the politics and, indeed, the whole of society in the following decades. A factory consciousness developed during these years, which played an important role in the privileging of the industrial workplace as a site of class struggle. The foresight of Ersoy in the mid-1950s is striking. Worker education, he said, is the principal job of the trade union until conditions make it possible for unions to actually advance workers' rights. The union's role, he said, will be performed "tomorrow, not today."[169] In 1954, thirty-eight out of forty-nine union leaders supported Ersoy's observation by responding in the negative to the question as to whether one party was clearly more favourable to the unions.[170] But the highly anticipated change was not realised when the old dissidents became the new rulers.

Yet "tomorrow" arrived faster than expected. The trade unions began to play an increasingly important political role after the military takeover in May 1960, and especially after the adoption of the liberal 1961 constitution.

169 Rosen, "Labor in Turkey," 470–1.

170 Rosen, "Labor in Turkey," 98.

The Constituent Assembly of 1961 included six trade union leaders. In 1961, the Confederation of Turkish Trade Unions was permitted as an affiliate member of the ICFTU. The new labour laws of 1963 also granted the trade unions a considerably increased scope of action, including the rights to strike and engage in collective bargaining. As a new period of accelerated industrialisation and planned economic development was beginning, the ruling elite tried to build a more centralised and peaceful system of industrial relations. They failed; the 1960s and 1970s witnessed the politicisation of trade unionism, and the rise of the factory as a privileged site of struggle.[171]

---

171 Aziz Çelik and Zafer Aydın, *Paşabahçe 1966: Gelenek Yaratan Grev* (Istanbul: TÜSTAV, 2006); Özkal Yici, *Kırkbir Uzun Gün: Berec Grevi* (Istanbul: Sosyal Tarih Yayınları, 2010); Zafer Aydın, *"Kanunsuz" Bir Grevin Öyküsü: Kavel 1963* (Istanbul: Sosyal Tarih Yayınları, 2010); Zafer Aydın, *Geleceğe Yazılmış Mektup: 1968 Derby İşgali* (Istanbul: Sosyal Tarih Yayınları, 2012).

Conclusion

Shattering Silence, Deafening Nostalgia: The Legacy of State-Led Industrialisation

"A life where dreams come true." With these words, Doğa Grup, a holding company with investments in education, heavy industry, and mining as well as real estate, announced the construction of Pruva 34, ten luxury seafront residential high-rise buildings in Bakırköy, "one of Istanbul's most desirable locations."[1] The company had bought the lucrative land on the shores of the Marmara Sea in the heart of the city for forty-four million US dollars in 2004. Construction had begun ten years later, after the company secured the zoning permit, which, according to the chair of the Istanbul branch of the Chamber of Architects, increased the value of the land to a billion US dollars.[2] Construction was often interrupted by the surfacing of Byzantium ruins dating back to between the sixth and the thirteenth century, such as the Palace of Justice (*Hebdomon Tribünalis*) and the Summer Palace (*Hebdomon Iucundianea*). At some point, the company, which prides itself on undertaking "successful restoration projects and taking part in social responsibility projects," placed modular panels around the construction site to close it off to public eyes.[3] No trace of these archaeological findings is visible on the site today, except for the marble foundations of a Byzantine church, which was able to avoid destruction because it was located outside the construction site. I tried to visit the site in January 2023 with local historian Turgay Tuna, but security guards refused to let us in. I could only glimpse the church ruins through the high walls and iron bars "protecting" this gated community, where, by 2022, an increasing number of rich migrants from Iraq, Syria, and Afghanistan resided. "The refugee invasion" of the luxury building complex, as the mainstream media called it, disturbed the Turkish property owners, who put their houses on the market because they "did not want to live next to such neighbours."[4]

1 "Pruva34," accessed 20 July 2022, https://doga.com.tr/en/project/pruva-34-2/.

2 "Pruva 34 Bakırköy Sümerbank Arazisinde Yükseliyor!" accessed 20 July 2022, https://emlakkulisi.com/pruva-34-bakirkoy-sumerbank-arazisinde-yukseliyor/252510.

3 Special thanks to local historian Turgay Tuna for sharing this information with me.

4 "İlyas Ayvacı'nın Sahibi Olduğu Pruva 34'e Göçmen İstilasi," accessed 20 July 2022, https://www.ntvmagazin.com/haber/ilyas-ayvaci-nin-sahibi-oldugu-pruva-34-e-gocmen-istilasi-60534.html.

As built manifestations of twenty-first-century real-estate capitalism, Pruva 34 rises on the site of a factory that was at the centre of two rounds of state-led developmentalist policies, one imperial and one republican, in the nineteenth and twentieth centuries: The Bakırköy Cloth Factory. The Ottomans failed in their attempt to build a factory system; their "Turkish Manchester" remained a stillborn project. The Kemalists failed to break the fetters of underdevelopment through state-led, planned industrialisation.

In 2003, a year before the sale of the factory site, Bakırköy workers were on perpetuated paid leave because, the government claimed, there was no work. Fearing unemployment, angry workers refused to leave the factory site, pledging to resist its closure. Trade union leaders argued that workers were being kept idle purely to manipulate public opinion, framing state factories as inefficient investments and state workers as lazy people chasing after easy money.[5] The propaganda worked. Once regarded as the backbone of Kemalist economic modernisation, the state economic enterprises were now viewed as a hunchback on economic efficiency and development. Privatisation as a major instrument of public enterprise reform had already entered the policy agenda almost two decades earlier in 1986. In January 1980, a mere eight months before the military takeover, the Turkish government joined the Washington Consensus announcing a stabilisation and structural adjustment programme, changing economic policy from import-substitution to export-led growth.[6] The ensuing developments would follow the well-known destructive path of neoliberalisation.

In the extremely polarised political atmosphere of present-day Turkey, where past historical experience is a crucial bedrock of contemporary ideological and political debates, the early republican period has become a highly controversial topic with the power to provoke intense interest and passionate opinions. A fierce attack on "the single-party mentality," as President Recep Tayyip Erdoğan puts it, has gained a special place in the political repertoire of his ruling Justice and Development Party (*Adalet ve Kalkınma Partisi*, hereafter the AKP). Even if the Kemalist opposition cannot defend the period in its entirety, it does dearly uphold two pillars of early republican state policy: secularism and etatism. The Erdoğanist attack on the former, especially during the last decade, defies elaboration. As for the question as to who bears political responsibility for the end of state industry, this is more complicated than

5 "Sümerbank İşçisi Nöbette," *Evrensel*, 21 April 2003.

6 Metin R. Ercan and Ziya Öniş, "Turkish Privatisation: Institutions and Dilemmas," *Turkish Studies* 2, no. 1 (2001); Ziya Öniş, "Power, Interests and Coalitions: The Political Economy of Mass Privatisation in Turkey," *Third World Quarterly* 32, no. 4 (2011).

the Kemalist opposition makes out. While they often cite the closure of state factories as evidence of the party's strong neoliberal stance, the adoption of privatisation actually precedes AKP rule, which began in 2002.

Today, the desolated, rundown state factories ignite a feeling of waste, a lost opportunity for Turkey to become a self-sufficient modern industrial nation. Sümerbank products, especially textiles, are remembered with a sense of pride for their quality, and with sorrow over the disappearance of democratic consumption opportunities. "Sümerbank, once upon a time" has become a Kemalist yearning for a past where positive nationalism reigned, where a sense of national duty overcame personal interest, and where the state elite could still be trust. And finally, in terms of working conditions, the term "state factory" conjures up a vision of workers working at a leisurely pace enjoying state protections, secure employment, and fringe benefits. The actual working conditions and work relations at state factories find almost no place in this narrative of shining, happy producers toiling for the reconstruction of their homeland.

In the Shadow of War and Empire debunks the current nostalgic investment in work under etatism. I started with a simple observation: We knew almost nothing about what went on inside Turkish factories during this formative period of Turkish industrial relations. I took up the challenge and pushed the study of Turkish industrialisation in a new direction, namely, toward an analysis of the nature of the work process and the informal organisation of the shop floor in relation to state policy. I argued that an analysis of the organisation of work in state factories is central to our understanding not only of this specific case of peripheral industrialisation, but also of the many meanings of work and working-class politics in the development of modern Turkey. Workers are at the centre of this book; I portray how they experienced industrial work and attempted to make sense of their lives and the wider forces operating in society throughout this formative period of modern Turkey.

Turkish state-led industrialisation is a case worthy of attention, among other reasons for its timing. Globally, it was a product of the interwar crisis of capitalism, which eventually culminated in a global war. Turkey took economic nationalism, an economic doctrine that gained currency in the post-Depression context, to its extreme with the first industrial planning attempt outside the Soviet Union, and ushered in the widespread import substitution industrialisation policies that followed the Second World War. Over the first half of the twentieth century, Turkish industrialisation was subject to the ravages of a decade of uninterrupted wars and external constraints, followed by the exigencies of the Great Depression, the destructive effects of the Second

World War, and, finally, the mounting tensions of the Cold War as the furthest geographical outpost of the non-communist world.

If the timing of etatism within the global conjuncture determined the outer boundaries of its achievements and failures, its local timing determined the internal limitations on its pace and scope. Etatism began barely a decade after the country emerged as the last nation-state from the ashes of the Ottoman Empire. The revolution-from-above in the 1920s, with the aggressive cultural modernisation programme as its engine, had created a political crisis involving threats to territorial integrity. Having witnessed the territorial disintegration of the empire throughout their military and political careers, the Kemalist elite invested their hopes in etatism as a way of transforming what was left of the empire into a nationally integrated economic space. However, the ethnic conflicts associated with Turkish nation-building had resulted in a drastic reduction of skills and entrepreneurial capacity, both of which were disproportionately possessed by the non-Muslim minorities. Shortage of industrial skill and know-how bottlenecked state-led industrialisation. Among other things, etatism depended on a process of discursively reshaping a workforce of which the majority were born as Ottoman imperial subjects and would later in life be recategorised as Turkish national citizens.

Combining a long-term political economy approach with a shop-floor-level analysis of industrial relations, this book analyses the emerging industrial order and the labour regime under etatism. As a result of a complex combination of global developments and locally specified systems of class interactions and power structures, etatism developed as a nationally specific regime of accumulation based on the articulation of a new ideology of work that would shape state, employer, and trade union policies in subsequent decades. Building on a set of labour market and shop-floor discourses, this new ideology constituted the basis for a specific industrial labour control regime combining a new set of external labour regulations with older forms of shop-floor labour control.

Through etatism, Kemalist industrial policymakers created and maintained two main sources of accumulation: the high pricing of consumer goods due to protectionism and the transfer of surplus from agriculture to industry through shifting terms of trade in favour of industrial products.[7] Peasants and industrial workers shouldered the weight of state-led industrialisation, while private capital benefited from the state-sponsored development of the socioeconomic and institutional infrastructure required for an expansion of the

7 Korkut Boratav, "Kemalist Economic Policies and Étatism," in *Atatürk: Founder of a Modern State*, eds. Ali Kazancıgil and Ergun Özbudun (London: C. Hurst & Company, 1981), 183.

sources of capital accumulation and mechanisms of surplus extraction. The state also provided private capitalists with lucrative credit options, an expanding national market, and the transfer of industrial technology and managerial skills from state to private industries. But the contribution of etatism to the general logic of capital accumulation did not stop there. Etatism served as the "nursemaid" of industrial capitalism in Turkey by creating a labour regime based on a state-sponsored ideology of industrial work, a drive system on the shop floor, low wages, and repressive industrial relations.

The production of state and cultural discourses played a central role in the constitution of this labour control regime because they constructed the acceptable social and political vocabularies and imaginations. In Turkish etatism, these strategies mainly took the form of comparisons with a corrupt colonial economy where the Turkish national identity had fallen prey to foreign exploitation. The discursive tropes deployed in this instance ranged from cultural modernity and developmentalism, to economic autarky as part of a prolonged national liberation struggle. The result was a popular understanding of labour's place in the nation-building effort and the moulding of industrial class politics into nation-building in the 1930s, and into a virulent Cold War anti-communism in the 1940s. Official historiography and public memory remained central to state and employer demands for a labour force with patriotic motivations, effectively silencing workers' demands for their share of the spoils of national development. The state factory became a metonymy of the homeland within state discourse on industrial labour relations under etatism, implying the fiction of an integrated society where faithfulness to the nation trumps class distinctions.

As a nationalist historiography of development and a patriotic motive for work underlined the external regulation of labour, a drive system based on the iron fist of the foreman ruled on the shop floor of state factories. A closer look at the everyday practices on the shop floor dims the bright colours in which state factories have been painted, by both contemporaries and the present-day nostalgics. Though they were presented and celebrated as model institutions of national modernity, serious and chronic problems of inefficiency and low productivity characterised the operations of state factories. Industrial managers sought productivity mainly through intensifying work and maintaining worker effort through close supervision and pressure. The strictly authoritarian world of labour on the shop floor diverged from bureaucratised protections and procedures, such as standardisation of job requirements, adoption of promotion ladders and merit-rating systems, and rules concerning discipline and dismissal.

Nationalism and an appeal to patriotic labour in the structuring of class relations has been a significant driver of the cheap labour-based accumulation regime in Turkey. State-led industrialisation initially focused on light manufacturing, but policymakers had already prepared a second five-year plan to achieve industrial deepening. But when the war broke out, wartime conditions did not allow the realisation of this plan; Turkish industrialisation remained restricted to light and labour-intensive industries for which low wages are always a blessing. Industrialists could afford to suppress workers' wages thanks to two sets of state policies: the unfavourable terms of trade for the agricultural sector and the strictly authoritarian industrial relations system. Workers' wages declined by twenty-five per cent between 1934 and 1938, and by a further seventy-five per cent between 1939 and 1946.[8]

Finally, repressive industrial relations gave the etatist labour regime its most defining colours. Turkey implemented the first five-year plan without a labour code because fears over the radicalisation of working-class politics had blocked legislative attempts for fifteen years. When the internal affairs minister proudly announced the 1936 Labour Code, which was modelled after the 1927 fascist Italian legislation, he described it as a "law of regime" that would "wipe out the erroneous roads leading to class consciousness."[9] Although the labour code brought a certain degree of individual protection to workers, the ban on strikes and collective bargaining crippled working-class political agency. Furthermore, workers complained of the poor enforcement of the already limited protection it afforded even in state factories. The state had effectively subordinated labour laws to rapid industrialisation goals, and resorted to comparisons with "colonial" industrial relations under the Ottoman Empire to present the protective legislation as a bestowal to the workers. State factories were central to these labour discourses because they presented an alternative to the conflict-laden Western industrial workplaces. Celebrated as industrial workplaces where *Turkish* workers used *Turkish state* capital to produce for the *Turkish* homeland, state factories offered up a solution to one of the central tensions of Kemalist modernism: the desire to catch up with Western industrial capitalism without having to deal with its accompanying social turmoil or even class divisions.

---

8 Çağlar Keyder, *State and Class in Turkey: A Study in Capitalist Development* (London: Verso, 1987), 104–5; Faruk Birtek, "The Rise and Fall of Etatism in Turkey, 1932–1950: The Uncertain Road in the Restructuring of a Semiperipheral Economy," *Review Fernand Braudel Center* 8, no. 1 (1985), 419.

9 Cited in Kurthan Fişek, *Türkiye'de Kapitalizmin Gelişimi ve İşçi Sınıfı* (Istanbul: Doğan Yayınevi, 1969), 72.

Laden with tensions from the beginning, etatism slowly waned in the late 1940s. By 1947, the CHP had amended the constitutional principle of etatism, limiting its scope. The DP's rise to power in 1950, which was based on an alliance of large landholders, smallholding peasants, and the bourgeoisie, reversed etatist economic policies. Thanks to the DP's laissez-faire approach to industrial development, private investment flourished in the 1950s, increasing the share of private to total manufacturing production from fifty-eight per cent in 1950 to sixty-five per cent in 1954. But the state continued to construct new factories and expand old ones, increasingly investing in ventures jointly with private capital.[10] By the end of the decade, public investment as a percentage of total investment rose to a high of sixty-two per cent.[11]

Starting in the 1950s and intensifying in the following decade, the demographic landscape of Turkey changed as rural-urban migration and urbanisation gained momentum. By 1950, the industrial workforce, including the construction sector, made up 7.4 per cent of the total workforce. This figure increased to 12.2 per cent by 1970.[12] But, although the country underwent profound social, economic, and political transformation, the labour regime remained intact until the 1960s. Neither the political crisis with the ensuing power change by the end of the 1940s nor the economic liberalisation of the 1950s altered the labour regime. But the following decade completely transformed industrial relations.

Planning and import substitution industrialisation returned with a vengeance after the 1960 coup d'état. The National Unity Committee, a military committee formed after the 1960 coup d'état and which subsequently ruled the country until November 1961, set up a State Planning Organisation in September 1960, even before the adoption of the new constitution. Its first five-year development plan came into effect in March 1963. Between 1948 and 1967, industrial production had grown at an average annual rate of about ten per cent, with private enterprise taking the lead. Still, by the early 1970s, approximately forty per cent of manufacturing remained state-owned, with Sümerbank responsible for almost half of all cotton manufacturing.[13] Planning

10 Alec Alexander, "Turkey," in *Economic Development: Analysis and Case Studies*, eds. A. Pepelasis, L. Mears, and I. Adelman (New York, Harper, 1961), 493.

11 Gülten Kazgan, "Structural Changes in Turkish National Income: 1950–1960," in *Middle Eastern Studies in Income and Wealth*, ed. Taufiq M. Khan (New Haven: International Association for Research in Income and Wealth, 1965), 154.

12 William Hale, "Labour Unions in Turkey: Progress and Problems," in *Aspects of Modern Turkey*, ed. William Hale (Essex: Bowker, 1976), 62.

13 Jane Perry Clark Carey and Andrew Galbraith Carey, "Turkish Industry and the Five-Year Plans," *Middle East Journal* 25, no. 3 (1971), 341–6.

in the 1960s, however, substantially differed from etatism in that it recognised the class inequalities as well as the political agency of the industrial working class; the myth of "a classless, fused mass" no longer held up. A discourse of rapid growth and industrialisation re-emerged, but this time with a focus on issues of redistribution in policy discussions.

Under the import substitution industrialisation of the 1960s, working-class politics expanded on the back of increasing trade union strength in industrial relations. Industrial workers became central to electoral politics, and even established their own political party, the Labour Party of Turkey in 1961. On the last day of 1961, more than one hundred thousand workers gathered in Saraçhane Square in Istanbul to demand the long-overdue legislation on the right to strike and collective agreements.[14] The protest took even the socialists aback; the prominent socialist leader Mehmet Ali Aybar described it in awe: "It was as if workers had suddenly woken up from a century-long sleep."[15]

My analysis of the relationships and bargaining at the point of employment, however, portrays a far from deep, uninterrupted sleep. The narrative of a passive, helpless working class has been compelling beyond the sphere of professional historiography. It has become the hegemonic pattern of historical remembrance with regard to etatism, reducing the complexity of the historical moment of early republican Turkey. But from the level of the shop floor, etatism was clearly not a supra-class nationalistic development plan. Behind the façade of the celebratory narratives on etatism, factories, including state-owned ones, simmered with tensions as workers were increasingly contesting industrial relations on the shop floor to bargain not only for economic gains, but also for respect.

Despite rising factory consciousness, however, worker resistance remained individualistic, isolated, and largely ineffective, even after the development of the trade union movement. The fragmented structure of unions, the ambivalent and highly exploited ban on union involvement in politics, and the prohibition of strikes and thus effective collective bargaining severely crippled the development of trade unionism. The combination of these three factors rendered wage and employment bargaining particularistic and private. The individual contract remained the sole mechanism determining wages, leaving workers completely alone in their grievances. By the end of the 1940s, a Turkish state factory was as much a contested terrain as any other industrial workplace

14 *Türkiye Sendikacılık Ansiklopedisi*, vol. 2 (Istanbul: Tarih Vakfı, 1998), 566–568.

15 Cited in Hakan Koçak, "İşçi Hareketinin Örgütsel Kapasitesi ve Ölçeksel Strateji Bağlamında İstanbul İşçi Sendikaları Birliği Örneği (1948–1962)," *Çalışma ve Toplum* 4 (2014), 83.

despite the seemingly bureaucratic organisational structures and the populist ideology behind etatism. And it was on the historically sedimented industrial conflicts of the 1940s and 1950s that the rising working-class militancy at the workplace level in the 1960s and 1970s was built.

With this book, I situate the unique Turkish politico-economic experience of the interwar and immediate postwar period in a global framework and write this history, as it happened, over the course of empire and global capitalism. I chose to look at the history of postimperial late-late industrialisation through the lens of an industrial workplace as a geographically specific, locally integrated place that is situated at the intersection of local, national, and global connections. As the site where class happens and capital, as a social relationship, is produced and reproduced, the industrial workplace offers great potential for the integrated interdisciplinarity of an all-encompassing history of capitalism. At a time when a number of major lines of research are developing in almost complete isolation from one another, this book offers a modest attempt at explanatory integration to understand the interactions between social structures and the material production process on the one hand, and between the processes of nation-building and industrialisation, on the other. I hope that it goes some way toward breaking the shattering silence of the working classes during one of the most formative periods in the history of Turkey.

Bibliography

Archival Sources

International Institute of Social History, Amsterdam

"Bakırköy Bez Fabrikasında," 30 October 1952, Kemal Sülker Papers, Folder no. 148.

"Bakırköy Bez Fabrikasındaki Hadisenin Mahiyeti," 1 November 1952, Kemal Sülker Papers, Folder no. 148.

"Beyoğlu Mensucat İşçilerinin Üzerinde Durdukları Meseleler," 19 June 1949, Kemal Sülker Papers, Folder no. 148.

"Çalışma Bakanının İşçi Sendikaları Hakkındaki Demeci," 25 September 1946, Kemal Sülker Papers, Folder no. 801.

"Diktatörcesine Haksızlığa Uğrayan Bir Türk Vatandaşın Şikayeti," (n.d), Kemal Sülker Papers, Folder no. 402.

"Dokuma Tezgahı Dairesine Girer Girmez," (n.d.), Kemal Sülker Papers, Folder no. 402.

Enver Tenşi, "Sayın Vatandaşlarım," (n.d.), Kemal Sülker Papers, Folder no. 151.

"Gece Postası Gazetesi Yazı İşleri Müdürlüğü Yüksek Makamına," 10 July 1955, Kemal Sülker Papers, Folder no. 402.

Hayri Erdost, "İşçilere Zarar Temin Eden Sigorta Kanunları," 30 July 1949, Kemal Sülker Papers, Folder no. 384.

Interview with Ahmet Cansızoğlu by Yıldırım Koç, 1988, video recording *V1/51*, Trade Union Movement in Turkey Oral History Collection.

Interview with Bahir Ersoy by Yıldırım Koç, 1988, video recording *V1/44*, Trade Union Movement in Turkey Oral History Collection.

Melih Göktan, "Türkiye'de İş İhtilafları ve İşgücü ile Münasebetleri," (n.d.), Kemal Sülker Papers, Folder no. 347.

"Sayın İşçi Arkadaşlar," (n.d.), Kemal Sülker Papers, Folder no. 121.

"Son Telgraf ve Gece Postası Yazı İşleri Sayın Müdürlüğüne," 24 August 1950, Kemal Sülker Papers, Folder no. 187.

Presidency of the Republic of Turkey Directorate of State Archives

Fazıl Şerafettin Bürge. "Partimizin Meslek Teşekkülleriyle Münasebet ve Temasları Hakkında Umumi Mütalaa," in "CHP Genel İdare Kurulu'nun İşçi Raporunun Divan'da Görüşüleceği," 14.02.1948, 490.453.1867.6.

Personnel files of workers at the Bakırköy and Defterdar Factories, unclassified archives of Sümer Holding.

"Sümerbank 1945 Yılı Fabrika Raporları Yönetim Kurulu Kararı Ekleri," 1946, file 730 05 01 EK 1–11 16–111.

Presidency of the Republic of Turkey Supreme Auditory Board Archives

3460 Sayılı Kanuna Bağlı İktisadi Teşekküllerin 1940 Yılı Bilançoları ile Kâr ve Zarar Hesaplarını Tetkik Eden Umumi Murakebe Heyet Zaptı, vol. 3. Ankara: TBMM Matbaası, 1942.

3460 Sayılı Kanuna Bağlı Devlet Ekonomi Kurumlarının 1943 Yılı İşlemleriyle Bilanço ve Kâr ve Zarar Hesaplarını İnceleyen Genel Kurul Tutanağı. Ankara: Başbakanlık Devlet Matbaası, 1945.

Aray, Suat. "Sanayi İşletmelerinde İşçi Hareketleri ve Bunların Zirai Sebeplerle İlgileri," 1950, Register K.A./255.07.02.01.06.1153, Prime Ministry Supreme Auditory Board Archives.

Aydemir, Ş. Süreyya, Bülent Büktaş, Fazlı Turga & Turgut Akkaş. Devlet Endüstrisinde Çalışan Personelin İşletmeler Civarına Yerleştirme Şekilleri Hakkında, 1945. Amb./Db.No: K.A./255.07.02.01.06.1163.

Başvekalet Umumi Murakebe Heyeti. Sümerbank 1943 Yılı Umumi Murakabe Heyeti Raporu. Ankara: 1944.

Bauer, Ivor. "Bakırköy Fabrikası İğleri Hakkında," 1934, Register K.A./255.07.02.01.06.1142.

Bereznitsky. Kayseri Bez Fabrikası Hakkında, 1936. Amb./Db.No: K.A./255.07.02.01.06.1224.

Hösli. Ereğli Bez Fabrikası Hakkında Rapor, 1940. Amb./Db.No: K.A./255.07.02.01.06.1099.

Hösli. Nazilli Bez Fabrikası Hakkında Rapor, 1943. Amb./Db.No: K.A./255.07.02.01.06.1226.

Hösli. Bakırköy Bez Fabrikası Hakkında Rapor, 1943. Archival Collection of the Republic of Turkey Prime Ministry Supreme Audit Board. Amb./Db.No: K.A./255.07.02.01.06.1241.

Hösli. Merinos Fabrikası Hakkında Rapor, 1943. Amb./Db.No: K.A./255.07.02.01.06.1117.

Klopfer. Sümerbank Memur ve Amelelerine Prim ve Ikramiye esasları hak., 1941. Amb./Db.No: K.A./255.07.02.01.06.1263.

Landau, Hans. Kayseri, Ereğli, Nazilli, Merinos Fabrikaları Hakkında (n.p., 1938).

Porten, Max von der. "Bakırköy Bez Fabrikası Hakkında," 1936, Register K.A./255.07.02.01.06.1285.

Porten, Max Von der. "Feshane ve Hereke Fabrikaları Tetkiklerine Dair," 1936, Register K.A./255.07.02.01.06.1285.

Porten, Max von der. "Beykoz Deri ve Kundura Fabrikasında Memur ve Ameleden Ne Gibi Tasarruflar Yapılabileceği Hakkında", 1939, Register K.A./ 255.07.02.01.06.1075.

Porten, Max Von der. "Devlet ve Hususi Sınai İşletmelerin Kontrolü ve Islahı", 1939, Register K.A./ 255.07.02.01.06.1056.

Porten, Max Von der. "Kayseri Fabrikası İplik ve Dokuma Daireleri Hakkında", 1939, Register K.A./255.07.02.01.06.1114.

Sachsenberg, Ewald. "Bakırköy Bez Fabrikası Organizasyonu Hakkında", 1937, Register K.A./255.07.02.01.06.1139.

Sümerbank Birleşik Pamuk İpliği ve Dokuma Fabrikaları Müessesesi 1939 Yılı Umumi Murakebe Heyeti Raporu, in Sümerbank 1939 Yılı Umumi Murakebe Heyeti Raporu (Ankara: Titaş Basımevi, 1940), Amb./Db.No: K.A./ 255.07.02.01.06.3227.

Sümerbank 1939 Yılı Umumi Murakebe Heyeti Raporu (Ankara: Titaş Basımevi, 1940), Archival Collection of the Republic of Turkey Prime Ministry Supreme Audit Board. Amb./Db.No: K.A./ 255.07.02.01.06.3227.

"Sümerbank Birleşik Pamuk İpliği ve Dokuma Fabrikaları Müessesesi 1940 Yılı Raporu," in Sümerbank 1940 Senesi Faaliyet ve Hesap Devresine Ait İdare Meclisi Raporu, Bilanço, Kâr ve Zarar Hesabı.

Sümerbank 1941 Yılı Umumi Murakebe Heyeti Raporu, Archival Collection of the Republic of Turkey Prime Ministry Supreme Audit Board. Amb./Db.No: K.A./ 255.07.02.01.06.3236.

"Sümerbank Fabrikaları İçtimai Teşkilat 1940 Yılı Raporu," in Sümerbank 1940 Senesi Faaliyet ve Hesap Devresine Ait İdare Meclisi Raporu, Bilanço, Kâr ve Zarar Hesabı. Ankara: TBMM Matbaası, 1941.

Sümerbank Fabrikalarının İşçi Meseleleri ve İçtimai Teşkilatı Hakkında Rapor (1941). Archival Collection of the Republic of Turkey Prime Ministry Supreme Audit Board. Amb./Db.No: K.A./255.07.02.01.06.3236.

"Sümerbank İplik ve Dokuma Fabrikaları Müessesesi 1941 Yılı Raporu," In 1941 Yılı Umumi Murakebe Heyeti Sümerbank Raporu. Ankara: Alaaddin Kıral Basımevi, 1942.

"Sümerbank'ın 1940 yılı Muamelatile Bilanço, Kâr ve Zarar Hesaplarının Tetkikine Dair Olan Umumi Murakebe Heyeti Raporu Hakkında İktisat Vekâleti Mütaelası," In 1941 Yılı Umumi Murakebe Heyeti Sümerbank Raporu. Ankara: Alaaddin Kıral Basımevi, 1942.

"Sümerbank 1942 Yılı Umumi Murakebe Heyeti Raporu", in Sümerbank 1942 Senesi Faaliyet ve Hesap Devresine Ait İdare Meclisi Raporu, Bilanço, Kâr ve Zarar Hesabı (Ankara, 1943). Amb./Db.No: K.A./230.1/338.4, Prime Ministry Supreme Auditory Board Archives.

Sümerbank 1943 Umumi Murakebe Heyeti Raporu. Archival Collection of the Republic of Turkey Prime Ministry Supreme Audit Board. Amb./Db. No: K.A./ 255.07.02.01.06.3246.

Sümerbank 1944 Yılı Umumi Murakebe Heyeti Raporu. Ankara: Başbakanlık Devlet Matbaası, 1945.

"Sümerbank 1944 Senesi Faaliyet ve Hesap Devresine Ait İdare Meclisi Raporu, Bilanço, Kâr ve Zarar Hesabı," in Sümerbank 1944 Yılı Umumi Murakebe Heyeti Raporu (Istanbul: Ankara Başbakanlık Devlet Matbaası, 1945), 8, Amb./Db.no: K.A./ 255.07.02.01.06.3251, Sümer Bank Murakebe Raporu 1944.

"Sümerbank İşletmelerinde İşletmede İnsan ve İşçi Meseleleri 1945 Yılı Umumi Murakebe Heyeti Raporu," Archival Collection of the Republic of Turkey Prime Ministry Supreme Audit Board. Amb./Db.No: K.A./255.07.02.01.7462.

"Sümerbank İplik ve Dokuma Fabrikaları Müessesesi 1945 Yılı Raporu," in Sümerbank 1945 Senesi Faaliyet ve Hesap Devresine Ait İdare Meclisi Raporu, Bilanço, Kâr ve Zarar Hesabı (Ankara: Başbakanlık Devlet Matbaası, 1946).

"Sümerbank İplik ve Dokuma Fabrikaları Müessesesi 1948 Yılı Raporu," In Sümerbank 1948 Senesi Faaliyet ve Hesap Devresine Ait İdare Meclisi Raporu, Bilanço, Kâr ve Zarar Hesabı. Izmit: Selüloz Basımevi, 1949.

Sümerbank 1948 Senesi Faaliyet ve Hesap Devresine Ait İdare Meclisi Raporu, Bilanço, Kâr ve Zarar Hesabı (Izmit: Selüloz Basımevi, 1949).

"Sümerbank Bakırköy Sanayii Müessesesinin 1949 Yılı Raporu," in Başbakanlık Umumi Murakebe Heyeti 1949 Yılı Raporları (Ankara: Başbakanlık Devlet Matbaası, 1950).

Tesal, Necip T., Milli Korunma Mevzuatı ve Kiralar Hakkında (1952). Archival Collection of the Republic of Turkey Prime Ministry Supreme Audit Board. Amb./Db.No:K.A./ 255.07.02.01.06.1287.

"Umumi Murakebe Heyeti Sümerbank Fabrikalarının İşçi Meseleleri ve İçtimai Teşkilatı 1941 Yılı Raporu Hakkında Mütalaalar," In 1941 Yılı Umumi Murakebe Heyeti Sümerbank Raporu. Ankara: Alaaddin Kıral Basımevi, 1942.

Wegenstein, W.O. and Käser, G.W. "Management and Organisation of the Turkish State Monopolies," Başvekalet Umumi Murakebe Heyeti Kitaplığı, No. 222. 1958.

Records of the Grand National Assembly of Republic of Turkey

TBMM Tutanak Dergisi (Records of the Grand National Assembly), 8 June 1936, Session 5, Volume 12, Meeting no. 75.

TBMM Tutanak Dergisi (Records of the Grand National Assembly), "1937 yılı muvazenei umumiye kanunu layihası ve Bütçe encümeni mazbatası" (1/702), 28 May 1937, Session 5, Volume 18, Meeting no. 67.

TBMM Tutanak Dergisi (Records of the Grand National Assembly), "İş Kazaları ile Mesleki Hastalıklar ve Analık Sigortaları Hakkında Kanun Tasarısı ve Geçici Komisyon Raporu" (1/316), 13 June 1945, Session: VII, Volume 18, Meeting no. 2.

TBMM Tutanak Dergisi (Records of the Grand National Assembly), "İş kazaları ile Mesleki Hastalıklar ve Analık Sigortaları Hakkında Kanun Tasarısı ve Geçici Komisyon raporu" (1/316), 15 June 1945, Session 7, Volume 18, Meeting no. 2.

TBMM Tutanak Dergisi (Records of the Grand National Assembly), "Çalışma Bakanlığı Kuruluş ve Görevleri Hakkında Kanun Tasarısı ve Ekonomi ve Bütçe Komisyonları Raporları" (1/508), 26 November 1945, Session 7, Volume 21, Meeting no. 3.

TBMM Tutanak Dergisi (Records of the Grand National Assembly), 29 January 1947, Session 8, Volume 4, Meeting no. 29.

The US National Archives and Record Administration

Giesen, Alexander. "National, Economic and Cultural Work in the New Turkey" (5 December 1917), Records of the Department of State Relating to Internal Affairs of Turkey, Economic Matters, 2 June 1910 – 17 December 1929, Decimal File 867.50, NARA, accessed 1 May 2020, https://go.gale.com/ps/retrieve.do?tabID=Manuscripts&resultListType=RESULT_LIST&searchResultsType=SingleTab&searchType=AdvancedSearchForm&currentPosition=1&docId=GALE%7CSC5111519615&docType=Manuscript&sort=Relevance&contentSegment=GDSC221&prodId=GDSC&contentSet=GALE%7CSC5111519615&searchId=R11&userGroupName=cumhurb&inPS=true&ps=1&cp=1.

Letter from Robert P. Skinner to US Department of State (28 June 1932, Ankara), Records of the Department of State Relating to Internal Affairs of Turkey 1930–1944, Economic Matters., 30 June 1932 – 14 April 1938, Decimal File 867.50, National Archives and Record Administration (NARA), accessed 29 April 2020, https://link.gale.com/apps/doc/SC5111457718/GDSC?u=cumhurb&sid=GDSC&xid=093827ec.

Letter from Robert P. Skinner to US Department of State (7 August 1934, Istanbul), Records of the Department of State Relating to Internal Affairs of Turkey 1933–1935, Economic Matters, Turkey, Economic Adviser, 19 January 1933 – 8 April 1935, Decimal File 867.50A,Decimal File 867.50A, NARA, accessed 29 April 2020, https://link.gale.com/apps/doc/SC5111457416/GDSC?u=cumhurb&sid=GDSC&xid=093827ec.

Letter from Wallace Murray to Dr Sumner Schlichter (25 February 1933), Records of the Department of State Relating to Internal Affairs of Turkey 1930–1944, Economic Matters., Turkey, Economic Adviser, 19 January 1933 – 8 April 1935, Decimal File 867.50A, NARA, accessed 28 April 2020, https://go.gale.com/ps/retrieve.do?tabID=Manuscripts&resultListType=RESULT_LIST&searchResultsType=SingleTab&searchType=AdvancedSearchForm&currentPosition=2&docId=GALE%7CSC5111457416&docType=Manuscript&sort=Relevance&contentSegment=GDSC221&prodId=GDSC&contentSet=GALE%7CSC5111457416&searchId=R5&userGroupName=cumhurb&inPS=true&ps=1&cp=2.

Ravndal, G. Bie. (compiled by). *Turkey: an Economic Handbook* (unpublished, 1924), 347, Records of the Department of State Relating to Internal Affairs of Turkey, Economic Matters, 2 June 1910 – 17 December 1929, Decimal File 867.50, NARA, accessed 1 May 2020, https://go.gale.com/ps/retrieve.do?tabID=Manuscripts&resultListType=RESULT_LIST&searchResultsType=SingleTab&searchType=AdvancedSearchForm&currentPosition=1&docId=GALE%7CSC5111519615&docType=Manuscript&sort=Relevance&contentSegment=GDSC221&prodId=GDSC&contentSet=GALE%7CSC5111519615&searchId=R11&userGroupName=cumhurb&inPS=true&ps=1&cp=1.

Interviews

Atalay, Muazzez, interview by the author, 4 June 2019.
Aygöl, Ergin, interview by the author, online, 15 February 2022.
Kocabaş, Asım, interview by the author, 3 August 2009.
Öden, İlhan, interview by the author, 6 December 2022.
Sevme, İbrahim, telephone interview by the author, 27 July 2009.
Tenşi, Ediz; Tenşi, Ersin and Tenşi Esin, interview by the author, 22 April 2022.
Yılmaz, Hüseyin, interview by the author, 4 August 2009.
Yürekli, Sebahat, interview by the author, 4 June 2019.

Newspapers

Cumhuriyet
Evrensel
Gayret
Gece Postası
Gerçek
Gün
Haber-Akşam Postası
Hürbilek
Hürriyet
İkdam-Gece Postası
İşçi Hakkı
Kadın Gazetesi
Milliyet
Nazilli
Sendika
Sendika Yolu
Son Posta
Son Telgraf
Tez Kalkınma
Türk İşçisi
Ulus
Vakit (*Yeni Gazete*)
Vatan
Yeni Sabah

Contemporary Literature and Memoirs

1955 Population Census of Turkey (Ankara: Republic of Turkey, Prime Ministry, General Statistical Office, 1957).

Abasıyanık, Sait Faik. *Tüneldeki Çocuk* (Istanbul: Türkiye İş Bankası Kültür Yayınları, 2019).

Adıvar, Halide Edib. *Turkey Faces West: a Turkish View of Recent Changes and Their Origin* (New Haven: Yale University Press, 1930).

Ağaoğlu, Samet and Hüdaioğlu, Selahattin. *Türkiye'de İş Hukuku: İş Hukuku Tarihi,* vol. 1 (Istanbul: Merkez Basımevi, 1938).

Atatürk'ün Söylev ve Demeçleri, vol. I–III (Ankara: Türk Tarih Kurumu Basımevi, 1989).

Aydemir, Şevket Süreyya, *İkinci Adam,* vol. 1 (Istanbul: Remzi Kitabevi, 1984).

Barker, James M. *The Economy of Turkey: an Analysis and Recommendations for A Development Program* (Baltimore: The Johns Hopkins Press, 1951).

Birinci Sarı Çizgili Kitap (*Demokrat İşçi Partisinin Ikinci Genel Kongresi Münasebetiyle Neşrolunmuştur*) (Istanbul: n.p., 1953).

Cillov, Haluk. *Denizli El Dokumacılığı Sanayi* (Istanbul: Istanbul Üniversitesi İktisat Fakültesi, 1949).

Coşkundeniz, İlhami. "Toplulukla İş İhtilafları, Hazırlanması ve Yürütülmesi." *Sosyal Siyaset Konferansları, 7. Kitap* (1955).

"Çalışma Hayatımızda Çocuklu Kadınlar ve Kreş İhtiyacı." In *Çalışma Bakanlığı: İlk Yılı ve İlk Hedefleri* (Ankara: T.C. Çalışma Bakanlığı Yayınları, 1946).

"Çalışma Meclisi Raporu." *Çalışma Vekâleti Dergisi,* no. 17 (1947).

Delaney, William F. *Labor Law and Practice in Turkey* (United States Department of Labor, 1963).

Demokrat İşçi Partisinin Programı (Istanbul: Uğur Basımevi, 1950).

Derin, Haldun. *Türkiye'de Devletçilik* (Istanbul: Çituri Biraderler, 1940).

Derviş, Suat. *Bu Roman Olan Şeylerin Romanıdır* (Istanbul: İthaki, 1936).

"Dünya Basınında Akisler." *Çalışma Vekâleti Dergisi,* no. 22 (1947).

Düstur, Üçüncü Tertip vol. 17 (Başvekalet Neşriyat Müdürlüğü, Teşrinisani 1935-Teşrinievvel 1936).

Düstur Üçüncü Tertip vol. 31, Nov. 1949-Oct. 1950 (Ankara: Başbakanlık Devlet Matbaası, 1950).

Erişçi, Lütfü. *Türkiye'de İşçi Sınıfının Tarihi* (*özet olarak*) (Ankara: Kebikeç, [1951] 1997).

Erkün, Safa Ş. "İş Mahkemeleri Kurulurken Bazı Düşünceler." *İçtimai Siyaset Konferansları* 2 (1949).

Ersoy, Bahir. "İşçi Gözü ile İşçi ve İşveren Münasebetleri." *Sosyal Siyaset Konferansları* 6 (1954).

Ersoy, Bahir. "Sendikacılığın İnkişafına Mani Olan Sebepler." *Sosyal Siyaset Konferansları* 7 (1955).

Esen, Bülent Nuri. *Türk İş Hukuku* (Ankara: Ankara Üniversitesi Hukuk Fakültesi Yayınları, 1944).

Fındıkoğlu, Ziyaeddin Fahri. "Türk İçtimai Siyasetinin İlk Zaferi." *İş,* no. 60 (1946).

Fındıkoğlu, Ziyaeddin Fahri. "Türkiye'de İçtimai Siyaset." *Çalışma Vekâleti Dergisi*, no. 24 (1947).

Fındıkoğlu, Ziyaeddin Fahri. "Türkiye'de Sınai Sosyoloji Araştırmaları 1-Defterdar Fabrikası." *Feshane Mensucat Meslek Dergisi* 2, no. 12 (1954).

Fındıkoğlu, Ziyaeddin Fahri. *Defterdar Fabrikası Hakkında Bir Tatbiki Sınai Sosyoloji Denemesi* (Istanbul: Türkiye Harsi ve Araştırmalar Derneği Yayını, 1955).

Fındıkoğlu, Ziyaeddin Fahri. "Karabük'ün Teşekkülü ve Bazı Demografik ve İktisadi Meseleler." *Istanbul Üniversitesi Sosyoloji Konferansları Dergisi*, no. 1 (1960).

"Foremen and Superintendents." *Scientific American* 22, no. 6 (1870).

Godfrey, Hollis. "The Foreman." *The Annals of the American Academy of Political and Social Science* 85 (1919).

Hanson, A. H. *The Structure and Control of State Enterprises in Turkey* (Ankara: Public Administration Institute for Turkey and The Middle East, 1954).

Hanson, A. H. *Public Enterprise and Economic Development* (London: Routledge, 1959).

Hallsworth, J.A. "Freedom of Association and Industrial Relations in the Countries of the Near and Middle East: I." *International Labour Review* 70 (1954).

Hallsworth, J.A. "Yakın ve Orta Şark Memleketlerinde Sendika Hürriyeti ve İşçi-İşveren Münasebetleri." *1955 Çalışma Vekâleti* 3, no. 1 (1955).

Hines, Walker. *Türkiye'nin İktisadi Bakımdan Umumi Bir Tetkiki, 1933–1934* (Ankara: Mehmed İhsan Matbaası, 1936).

Hines, Walker. "Conclusions and Recommendations." *A General Economic Survey of Turkey, 1933–1934*, vol. 1 (Ankara: Ekonomi Bakanlığı, 1934).

International Labour Office, *Labour Problems in Turkey Report of a Mission of the International Labour Office* (March-May 1949) (Geneva, 1950).

International Labour Office, *Legislative Series 1950* (Geneva, 1953).

Irmak, Sadi. "Beveridge Planına Göre Sosyal Dayanışma." *Çalışma Vekâleti Dergisi*, no. 1 (1945).

Irmak, Sadi. "İşçi Sigortaları Kurumu Genel Kurul Toplantısı." *Çalışma Vekâleti Dergisi*, no. 4 (1946).

Irmak, Sadi. "Istanbul Çalışma Konferansı." *Çalışma Vekâleti Dergisi*, no. 24 (1947).

Irmak, Sadi. "Sosyal Sigortalarımızda Gelişme." *Çalışma Vekâleti Dergisi*, no. 16 (1947).

İstatistik Yıllığı 1931–1932 (Istanbul: Başbakanlık İstatistik Genel Müdürlüğü, 1932).

İşçi Sendikaları Birliği, *Bize Göre Görüşler* (Istanbul: ISB Neşriyatı, 1946).

"İşçi Sigortaları Kurumu Genel Kurul Toplantısı." *Çalışma Vekâleti Dergisi*, no. 4 (1946).

İşçi Sigortaları Kurumu 1953 Yılı Çalışma Raporu ve Bilançosu (Ankara: İşçi Sigortaları Kurumu Genel Müdürlüğü, 1954).

Kemal, Orhan. *Grev* (Istanbul: Everest, [1954] 2007).

Kerwin, Robert V. "Private Enterprise in Turkish Industrial Development." *Middle East Journal* 5, no. 1 (1951).

Kessler, Gerhard. "İşçi Hareketlerinin Hedefleri ve Yolları." *Çalışma Vekâleti Dergisi*, no. 16 (1947).

Kessler, Gerhard. "Zonguldak ve Karabükteki Çalışma Şartları." *İstanbul Üniversitesi İktisat ve İçtimaiyat Enstitüsü ayrı bası*, no. 11 (İstanbul: Kenan Matbası, 1949).

Kolker, Kenneth K. "The Changing Status of the Foreman." *Bulletin of the Business Historical Society* 22, no. 3 (1948).

Kosova, Zehra. *Ben İşçiyim* (ed). Zihni Anadol (Istanbul: İletişim Yayınları, 1996).

Kundakçı, Suat Şükrü. *Bir Ömür Bir Sohbet,* ed. Ersin Tosun (Istanbul: TÜSTAV, 2005).

Kurtay, Muammer. "İçtimai Emniyetin Temelleri." *Çalışma Vekâleti Dergisi*, no. 16 (1947).

"Labour Problems in Turkey." *Report of a Mission of the International Labour Office* (March-May 1949).

Lingeman, E. R. *Turkey: Economic and Commercial Conditions in Turkey* (London: His Majesty's Stationary Office, 1948).

Linke, Lilo. *Allah Dethroned: A Journey Through Modern Turkey* (London: Constable and Co., 1937).

Linke, Lilo. "Social Changes in Turkey." International *Affairs* 16, no. 4 (1937).

MacFarlane, Charles. *Turkey and Its Destiny: The Result of Journeys Made in 1847 and 1848 to Examine into the State of That Country,* vol. 1 and vol. 2 (London: John Murray, 1850).

Mallary, Benjamin E. "The Foreman-His Training and Education." *The Annals of the American Academy of Political and Social Science* 91 (1920).

Mayo, Elton. *The Human Problems of an Industrial Civilisation* (New York: MacMillan, 1933).

Mayo, Elton. *The Social problems of an Industrial Civilisation* (London: Routledge&Kegan Paul, 1949).

"Milletlerarası Çalışma Konferansında Türkiye (Bir Radyo Konusması)." *Çalışma Vekâleti Dergisi*, no. 22 (1947).

Milli Kalkınma Partisinin Memlekete Hediye Edeceği İşçi Hakları, 1946, National Library of Turkey, 1946 BD 41.

Milli Kalkınma Partisi 1949 Yılı Umumi Kongresi (Istanbul: Vakit Matbaası, 1949).

Motassian, Mary. "Ideologies of Delayed In dustrialisation: Some Tensions and Ambiguities" *Economic Development and Cultural Change* 6, no. 3 (1958).

Muntz, T.G.A. *Turkey: Economic and Commercial Conditions in Turkey.* (New York: Philosophical Library, 1951).

Myers, Charles A. *Labor Problems in the Industrialisation of India*. (Cambridge, MA: Harvard University Press, 1958).

Official Gazette of the Republic of Turkey, no. 4165, 24 March 1939.

Ökte, Faik. *Varlık Vergisi Faciası* (Istanbul: Nebioğlu Yayınevi, 1951).

Özeken, Ahmet. "Türkiye'de Sanayi İşçileri." *Sosyal Siyaset Konferansları Dergisi,* no. 1 (1948).

Özeken, Ahmet. "Türkiye Sanayiinde İşçiyi Barındırma Problemi," *Sosyal Siyaset Konferansları Dergisi*, no. 3 (1950).

Pardoe, Julia. *The City of the Sultan: Domestic Manners of the Turks in 1836* (London: Henry Colburn, 1837).

Parker, John and Smith, Charles. *Modern Turkey* (London: Routledge, 1940).

Pole, William. *The Life of Sir William Fairbairn* (London: Gale and The British Library, 1877).

Reuter, Ernst. "Türkiye'de Şehirlileşmenin Temayülleri." *Siyasi İlimler Mecmuası* no. 126 (1941).

Rogers, Allen. "The Technically Trained Foreman." *Scientific American* 105, no. 12 (1911).

Ruthenburg, Louis. "Training the foremen of a manufacturing organisation." *SAE Transactions* 20 (1925).

Sarc, Ömer Celal. *Tanzimat ve Sanayimiz* (Istanbul: Maarif Matbaası, 1940).

Sarc, Ömer Celal. "The Economic Policy of the New Turkey." *Middle East Journal* 2, no. 4 (1948).

Sarc, Ömer Celal. *Türkiyede Şehirleşme Temayülleri* (Istanbul: İsmail Akgün Matbaası, 1949).

Scigliano, Robert G. "Trade-Unionism and the Industrial Foreman." *The Journal of Business* 27, no. 4 (1954).

Sertel, Sabiha. *Roman Gibi: Demokrasi Mücadelesinde Bir Kadın* (Istanbul: Belge, 1987).

Sufrin, Sidney C. "Foremen and Their Social Adjustment." *Industrial and Labor Relations Review* 4, no. 3 (1951).

Talas, Cahit. "Mesken Davamız." *Ankara Üniversitesi SBF Dergisi* 10, no. 1 (1955).

Talas, Cahit. *Türkiye Cumhuriyetinde Sosyal Politika Meseleleri, 1920—1960, Türk İktisadi Gelişmesi Araştırma Projesi, no. 1* (Ankara: S.B.F. Yayınları, 1960).

Talas, Cahit. *İçtimai İktisat* (Ankara: S.B.F. Yayınları, 1961).

Talas, Cahit, Sait Dilik and Alpaslan Işıklı. *Türkiye'de Sendikacılık Hareketi ve Toplu Sözleşme* (Ankara: S.B.F. Yayınları, 1965).

T.C. Ekonomi Bakanlığı, *Türkiye Milli Geliri* (Ankara: Başvekalet Matbaası, 1937).

Tekeli, Esat. "Çalışma Konferansında Türkiye." *Çalışma Vekâleti Dergisi*, no. 20 (1947).

Thornburg, Max Weston, Spry, Graham and Soule, George. *Turkey: an Economic Appraisal.* (New York: The Twentieth Century Fund, 1949).

Tör, Vedat Nedim. "Müstemleke İktisadiyatından Millet İktisadiyatına." *Kadro* 1, no. 1 (1932).

Türkiye İşçiler Derneği Nizamnamesi (Istanbul: Sinan Matbaası, 1946).

Tuna, Orhan. "Trade Unions in Turkey." *International Labour Review* 90, no. 5 (1964).

Tuna, Orhan. "Türkiye'de Cebri Tahkim Sistemi ve Tatbikatı, 1939–1963" *Istanbul Üniversitesi İktisat Fakültesi Mecmuası* 26, no. 1–4 (1967).

Tuna, Orhan. "Türkiye'de Sendikacılık ve Sendikalarımız." *Sosyal Siyaset Konferansları Dergisi*, no. 20 (1969).

"Türk Raporu." *Çalışma Dergisi Istanbul Yakın ve Orta Doğu Bölge Çalışma Toplantısı Sayısı*, no. 24 (1947).

Türkekul, Şefkati. "Mensucat İşletmelerinde Ücret Problemleri." *Mensucat Meslek Dergisi* 4, no. 8 (1951).

Tüzün, Gürel, ed. *Vehbi Koç Anlatıyor: Bir Derleme* (Istanbul: Yapı Kredi, 2018).

Ungun, Şefik. "Hayat Pahalılığı Karşısına Devlet İşletmelerinde İşçi Ücretleri ve Sosyal Yardımlar." *Feshane Mensucat Meslek Dergisi* 2, no. 6 (1949).

United Nations, *Review of Economic Conditions in the Middle East 1951–1952* (New York, 1953).

United Nations Department of Economic and Social Affairs, *The Development of Manufacturing Industry in Egypt, Israel and Turkey* (New York, 1958).

United States of America, Bureau of Labor Statistics, *Summary of the Labor Situation in Turkey* (Washington: International Cooperation Administration Office of Labor Affairs, 1956).

United States of America, Department of State, "International Conference on Safety of Life at Sea" (London, 23 April – 10 June 1948).

Webster, Donald Everett. *The Turkey of Atatürk: Social Process in the Turkish Reformation* (Philadelphia: The American Academy of Political and Social Science, 1939).

White, Charles. *Three Years in Constantinople: Or, Domestic Manners of the Turks in 1844*, Vol II (London: Henry Colburx, 1845).

Whyte, William F. and Burleigh B. Gardner. "Facing the Foreman's Problems." *Applied Anthropology* 4, no. 2 (1945).

Wray, Donald E. "Marginal Men of Industry: The Foremen." *American Journal of Sociology* 54, no. 4 (1949).

Wyatt, S.C. "Turkey: The Economic Situation and the Five-Years Plan." *International Affairs* 13, no. 6 (1934).

Zaim, Sabahaddin. *Istanbul Mensucat Sanayiinin Bünyesi ve Ücretler* (Istanbul: Istanbul Üniversitesi İktisat Fakültesi Yayını, 1956).

Contempororary Bulletins, Journals, and Magazines

Arkitekt

Çalışma Dergisi

Çalışma Vekâleti Dergisi

Erciyes Halkevi Dergisi

Feshane Mensucat Meslek Dergisi

Istanbul Sanayi Odası Dergisi

Istanbul Üniversitesi İktisat Fakültesi Mecmuası

İktisadi Yürüyüş

Kadro

Nuh'un Gemisi

Sümerbank
Ülkü
Vakıflar Dergisi
Yeni Yazı

Academic theses

Arıtan, Özlem. "Kapitalist/Sosyalist Modernleşme Modellerinin Erken Cumhuriyet Dönemi Mimarlığının Biçimlenişine Etkileri: Sümerbank KİT Yerleşkeleri Üzerinden Yeni Bir Anlamlandırma Denemesi" (doctoral dissertation, Dokuz Eylül Üniversitesi, 2004).

Asiliskender, Burak. "Modernleşme ve Konut; Cumhuriyet'in Sanayi Yatırımları ile Kayseri'de Mekansal ve Toplumsal Değişim" (doctoral dissertation, Istanbul Teknik Üniversitesi, 2008).

Brockett, Gavin D. "Betwixt and Between: Turkish Print Culture and the Emergence of a National Identity, 1945–1954" (doctoral dissertation, University of Chicago, 2003).

Buluş, Abdülkadir. "Osmanlı Tekstil Sanayi Hereke Fabrikası" (doctoral dissertation, Istanbul University, 2000).

Barsoumian, Hagop Levon. "Armenian Amira Class of Istanbul" (doctoral dissertation, Colombia University, 1980).

Clark, Edward C. "The Emergence of Textile Manufacturing Entrepreneurs in Turkey, 1804–1968" (doctoral dissertation, Princeton University, 1969).

Kırlı, Engin. "Osmanlı Tekstil Sektöründe Meydana Gelen Gelişmeler Çerçevesinde Basma Fabrikası'nın Kuruluşu ve Faaliyetleri, 1846–1876" (doctoral dissertation, Marmara University, 2015).

Köksal, Gül. "Istanbul'daki Endüstri Mirası için Koruma ve Yeniden Kullanım Önerileri" (doctoral dissertation, Istanbul Technical University, 2005).

Müller-Wiener, Wolfgang. "15–19. Yüzyılları Arasında İstanbul'da İmalathane ve Fabrikalar," Istanbul: Istanbul Üniversitesi Edebiyat Fakültesi Yayınları, 1992. Quoted in Didem Boyacıoğlu, "Osmanlı Fabrika Yapılarının Kentsel Mimari Analizi" (doctoral dissertation, Istanbul Technical University, 2013).

Nacar, Can. "Working Class in Turkey during the World War II Period: Between Social Policies and Everyday Experiences" (master's thesis, Boğaziçi University, 2004).

Rosen, Sumner Maurice. "Labor in Turkey's Economic Development" (doctoral dissertation, Massachusetts Institute of Technology, 1959).

Tezel, Yahya Sezai. "Turkish Economic Development 1923–1950; Policy and Achievements" (doctoral dissertation, University of Cambridge, 1975).

Handbooks and Encyclopedias

Baydar, Oya, ed. *Türkiye Sendikacılık Ansiklopedisi* (Istanbul: Kültür Bakanlığı ve Tarih Vakfı Ortak Yayını, 1996).

"Dünden Bugüne." *Istanbul Ansiklopedisi,* vol. 7 (Istanbul: Tarih Vakfı Yurt Yayınları, 1995).

Göktürk, Hakkı. "Bahariye Adaları." *Istanbul Ansiklopedisi,* vol. 4 (Istanbul: Koçu Yayınları, 1960).

Istanbul Ansiklopedisi, vol. 4 (Istanbul: Koçu Yayınları, 1960).

İnsel, Ahmet. "Devletçiliğin Anatomisi." *Cumhuriyet Dönemi Türkiye Ansiklopedisi,* vol. 2 (Istanbul: İletişim Yayınları, 1984).

İnsel, Ahmet and Cengiz Aktar. "'*Devletin Bekası*' İçin Yürütülen Çağdaşlaşma Sürecinin Toplumsal Sorunları." *Toplum ve Bilim* 31, no. 39 (1987).

Koçu, Reşad Ekrem. *Istanbul Ansiklopedisi,* vol. 4 (Istanbul: Koçu Yayınları, 1960).

Oxford English Dictionary, 2nd ed. (Oxford: Oxford University Press, 2004).

Pamukçiyan, Kevork. "Dadyan Ohannes Bey." *Istanbul Ansiklopedisi,* vol. 8 (Istanbul: Koçu Yayınları, 1966).

Pamukçiyan, Kevork. "Dadyan veya Dad (Arakel Amira)." *Istanbul Ansiklopedisi,* vol. 8 (Istanbul: Koçu Yayınları, 1966).

Toprak, Zafer. "Tanzimatta Osmanlı Sanayi." *Tanzimattan Cumhuriyete Türkiye Ansiklopedisi* vol. 5. (Istanbul: İletişim Yayınları, 1985).

Websites

"İlyas Ayvacı'nın sahibi olduğu pruva 34'e göçmen istilasi." Accessed 20 July 2022. https://www.ntvmagazin.com/haber/ilyas-ayvaci-nin-sahibi-oldugu-pruva-34-e-gocmen-istilasi-60534.html

Interview with Carlo Ginzburg by Nicolas Weill. Accessed 28 February 2023. https://www.versobooks.com/blogs/5536-carlo-ginzburg-in-history-as-in-cinema-every-close-up-implies-an-off-screen-scene

Pruva34." Accessed 20 July 2022. https://doga.com.tr/en/project/pruva-34-2/

"Pruva 34 Bakırköy Sümerbank arazisinde yükseliyor!" Accessed 20 July 2022. https://emlakkulisi.com/pruva-34-bakirkoy-sumerbank-arazisinde-yukseliyor/252510

Research Literature

50 Yılda Türk Sanayii (Ankara: Sanayi ve Teknoloji Bakanlığı, 1973).

Agarwal, Prerna "The War at The Workplace: Calcutta's Dockworkers and Changing Labour Regime, 1939–1945." *International Review of Social History,* FirstView (Published online by Cambridge University Press, 2002).

Ağralı, Sedat. *Günümüze Kadar Belgelerle Türk Sendikacılığı* (Istanbul: Son Telgraf, 1967).

Ahmad, Feroz. *The Turkish Experiment in Democracy* (London: C. Hurst, 1977).

Ahmad, Feroz. "Vanguard of a Nascent Bourgeoisie: The Social and Economic Policy of Young Turks 1908–1918." In *Türkiye'nin Sosyal ve Ekonomik Tarihi,* edited by Osman Okyar and Halil İnalcık (Ankara: Meteksan, 1980).

Ahmad, Feroz. "The Progressive Republican Party, 1924–1925." In *Political Parties and Democracy in Turkey*, edited by Metin Heper and Jacob Landau (London: I. B. Tauris, 1991).

Ahmad, Feroz. *The Making of Modern Turkey* (London: Routledge, 1993).

Ahmad, Feroz. "The Development of Class Consciousness in Republican Turkey, 1923–45." In *The Workers and the Working Class in the Ottoman Empire and Turkish Republic 1839–1950*, edited by Donald Quataert and Erik Jan Zürcher (London and New York: I.B. Tauris in association with the International Institute of Social History, Amsterdam, 1995).

Ahuja, Ravi. "A Beveridge Plan for India? Social Insurance and the Making of the 'Formal Sector'." *International Review of Social History* 64, no.2 (2019).

Ahuja, Ravi. "Produce or Perish: The Crisis of the Late 1940s and the Place of Labour in Post-Colonial India." *Modern Asian Studies* 54, no.4 (2020).

Ajayi, Rotimi. "The Politicisation of Trade Unionism: The Case of Labour/NCNC Alliance in Nigeria, 1940–1960." *Ufahamu: a Journal of African Studies* 27, no. 1–2–3 (1999).

Akbulut, Erden and Tunçay, Mete. *Beynelmilel İşçiler İttihadı: Mütareke Istanbul'unda Rum Ağırlıklı Bir İşçi Örgütü ve TKP ile İlişkileri* (Istanbul: Sosyal Tarih Yayınları Istanbul, 2009).

Akbulut, Erden. *Dr. Şefik Hüsnü Deymer: Yaşam Öyküsü, Vazife Yazıları* (Istanbul: TÜSTAV, 2010).

Akçay, Faik. *Zeytinburnu: Gerçek Yönleriyle Bir Gecekondu Kenti* (Istanbul: Çelikcilt Matbaası, 1974).

Akgöz, Görkem, Richard Croucher and Nicola Pizzolato. "Back to the Factory: The Continuing Salience of Industrial Workplace History." *Labor History* 61, no. 1 (2020).

Akgöz, Görkem. "Experts, Exiles, and Textiles: German 'Rationalisierung' on the 1930s Turkish Shop Floor." *International Review of Social History* 66, no. 2 (2021).

Akgöz, Görkem. "Between State Feminism and Work Intensification: Gendered Labour Control Regimes in Turkish Textile and Tobacco Industries." In *Power at Work: A Global Perspective on Control and Resistance*, eds. Marcel van der Linden and Nicole Mayer-Ahuja (Oldenbourg: De Gruyter, 2023).

Akgöz, Görkem. "Metaphorical Machines or Mindless Consumers: Young Working-Class Femininity in Early Post-War Turkey." *International Labor and Working-Class History* 104 (2023).

Akın, Yiğit. "Erken Cumhuriyet Dönemi Emek Tarihçiliğine Katkı: Yeni Yaklaşımlar, Yeni Kaynaklar." *Tarih ve Toplum*, no. 2 (2005).

Akın, Yiğit. "Reconsidering State, Party, and Society in Early Republican Turkey: Politics of Petitioning." *International Journal of Middle East Studies* 39, no. 3 (2007).

Akın, Yiğit "The Dynamics of Working-Class Politics in Early Republican Turkey: Language, Identity, and Experience." *International Review of Social History IRSH* 54 (2009).

Akkaya, Yüksel. "İşçi Sınıfı ve Sendikacılık-1 (Kısa özet)." *Praksis* 5 (2002).

Aktar, Ayhan. *Kapitalizm, Az Gelişmişlik ve Türkiye'de Küçük Sanayi* (Istanbul: Afa Yayınları, 1990).

Aktar, Ayhan. *Varlık Vergisi ve Türkleştirme Politikaları* (Istanbul: İletişim Yayınları, 2001).

Alcock, Antony Evelyn. *History of the International Labour Organization* (London: Palgrave Macmillan, 1971).

Alexander, Alec. "Turkey." In *Economic Development: Analysis and Case Studies,* eds. Adamantios Pepelasis, Leon Mears, and Irma Adelman (New York: Harper & Brothers Publishers, 1961).

Alexander, Catherine. "The Factory: Fabricating the State." *Journal of Material Culture* 5, no.2 (2000).

Altenried, Moritz. *The Digital Factory: The Human Labor of Automation* (Chicago: Chicago University Press, 2022).

Anderson, Benedict. *Imagined Communities: Reflections on the Origin and Spread of Nationalism* (New York: Verso, 2016).

Andrijasevic, Rutvica and Devi Sacchetto, "China may be far away but Foxconn is on our doorstep." Accessed 5 June 2013 https://www.opendemocracy.net/rutvica-andrijasevic-devi-sacchetto/china-may-be-far-away-but-foxconn-is-on-our-doorstep.

Andrijasevic, Rutvica and Devi Sacchetto, "Made in the EU: Foxconn in the Czech Republic." *WorkingUSA: The Journal of Labor and Society* 17 (2014).

Anscombe, Frederick F., "Islam and the Age of Ottoman Reform." *Past and Present* 208, 1 (2010).

Archer, Rory and Goran Musić, "Approaching the socialist factory and its workforce: Considerations from fieldwork in (former) Yugoslavia." *Labor History* 58, no. 1 (2017).

Archer, Rory and Musić, Goran. "Not All Canteens Are Created Equal: Food Provision for Yugoslav Blue-Collar Workers in Late Socialism." In *Brotherhood and Unity at the Kitchen Table? Cooking, Cuisine and Food Culture in Socialist Yugoslavia*, edited by Ruža Fotiadis, Vladimir Ivanović, and Radina Vučetić (Zagreb: Srednja Europa, 2020).

Armstrong, P.J, Goodman, J.F.B and Hyman, J.D. *Ideology and Shop-floor Industrial Relations* (London: Croom Helm, 1981).

Arnold, Caroline E. "In the Service of Industrialisation: Etatism, Social Services and the Construction of Industrial Labour Forces in Turkey (1930–50)." *Middle Eastern Studies* 48, no. 3 (2012).

Atabaki, Tauraj and Zürcher, Erik J. *Men of Order: Authoritarian Modernisation Under Atatürk and Reza Shah* (London: I.B. Tauris, 2003).

Aydın, Zafer. *"Kanunsuz" Bir Grevin Öyküsü: Kavel 1963* (Istanbul: Sosyal Tarih Yayınları, 2010).

Aydın, Zafer. *Geleceğe Yazılmış Mektup: 1968 Derby İşgali* (Istanbul: Sosyal Tarih Yayınları, 2012).

Azak, Umut. *Islam and Secularism in Turkey: Kemalism, Religion and the Nation State* (London: I.B. Tauris, 2010).

Bain, Peter and Phil Taylor, "Entrapped by the 'Electronic Panopticon'? Worker Resistance in the Call Centre." *New Technology, Work and Employment* 15, no. 1 (2000).

Banani, Amin. *The Modernisation of Iran 1921–1941* (Stanford: Stanford University Press, 1961).

Barkey, Henry J. *The State and the Industrialisation Crisis in Turkey* (New York: Routledge, 1990).

Barlas, Dilek. *Etatism and Diplomacy in Turkey: Economic and Foreign Policy Strategies in an Uncertain World, 1929–1939* (Leiden: Brill, 1998).

Basualdo, Victoria "Shop-Floor Labor Organisation in Argentina From Early Peronism to the 'Proceso' Military Dictatorship." *WorkingUSA: The Journal of Labor and Society* 14, no. 3 (2011).

Batstone, Eric, Ian Boraston and Stephen Frenkel. *Shop Stewards in Action: The Organization of Workplace Conflict and Accommodation* (Oxford: Blackwell, 1979).

Behar, Cem. *Osmanlı İmparatorluğu'nun ve Türkiye'nin Nüfusu 1500–1927* (Ankara: T.C. Başbakanlık Devlet İstatistik Enstitüsü, 1996).

Beinin, Joel. "Formation of the Egyptian Working Class." *Middle East Research and Information Project*, no. 94 (1981).

Beland, Daniel, Marchildon, Gregory P., Mioni, Michele and Petersen, Klaus. "Translating Social Policy Ideas: The Beveridge Report, Transnational Deffusion, and Post-War Welfare State Development in Canada, Denmark and France." *Social Policy and Administration* 56, no. 2 (2022).

Berberoğlu, Berch. *Turkey in Crisis: from State Capitalism to Neo-colonialism* (London: Zed Books, 1982).

Bergquist, Charles. "Labor History and Its Challenges: Confessions of a Latin Americanist." *The American Historical Review* 98, no. 3 (1993).

Bhattacharya, Sabyasachi. Introduction to *India's Labouring Poor: Historical Studies c.1600–2000,* edited by Rana Behal and Marcel van der Linden (New Delhi: Cambridge University Press India, 2007).

Bianchi, Robert. *Interest Groups and Political Development in Turkey* (Princeton: Princeton University Press, 1984).

Biggs, Lindy. *The Rational Factory: Architecture, Technology and Work in America's Age of Mass Production* (Baltimore: The Johns Hopkins University Press, 2002).

Bilgin, İhsan. "Anadolu'da Modernleşme Sürecinde Konut ve Yerleşme." In *Tarihten Günümüze Anadolu'da Konut ve Yerleşme*, edited by Yıldız Sey (Istanbul: Tarih Vakfı Yayınları, 1996).

Bilgin, İhsan. "Modernleşmenin Toplumsal Hareketliliğin Yörüngesinde Cumhuriyetin İmarı", *75 Yılda Değişen Kent ve Mimarlık*, edited by Yıldız Sey (Istanbul: Tarih Vakfı Yayınları, 1998).

Birtek, Faruk. "The Rise and Fall of Etatism in Turkey, 1932–1950: The Uncertain Road in the Restructuring of a Semiperipheral Economy." *Review Fernand Braudel Center* 8, no. 1 (1985).

Bonne, Alfred. *Studies in Economic Development* (London: Routledge, 1998).

Boratav, Korkut. *100 Soruda Gelir Dağılımı* (Istanbul: Gerçek Yayınları, 1969).

Boratav, Korkut. "Büyük Dünya Bunalımı İçinde Türkiye'nin Sanayileşme ve Gelişme Sorunları: 1929–1939" In *Tarihsel Gelişimi İçinde Türkiye*, edited by Orhan Kurmuş et al. (Ankara: Makina Mühendisleri Odası, 1977).

Boratav, Korkut. "Kemalist Economic Policies and Étatism." In *Atatürk: Founder of a Modern State*, edited by Ali Kazancıgil and Ergun Özbudun (London: C. Hurst & Company, 1981).

Boratav, Korkut. *Türkiye İktisat Tarihi 1908–2009*. (Istanbul: İmge, 2005).

Boratav, Korkut. "İktisat Tarihi (1908–1980)." In *Türkiye Tarihi 4: Çağdaş Türkiye 1908–1980*, edited by Sina Akşin (Istanbul: Cem Yayınevi, 2008).

Boratav, Korkut. *Türkiye'de Devletçilik* (Ankara: İmge Kitabevi, 2017).

Bosworth, Richard. *Mussolini's Italy: Life Under the Dictatorship* (London: Penguin Books, 2005).

Bouquet, Olivier Bouquet, "Is it Time to Stop Speaking about Ottoman Modernisation?" In *Order and Compromise: Government Practices in Turkey from the Late Ottoman Empire to the Early 21st Century*, edited by M. Aymes, B. Gourisse and É. Massicard (Leiden: Brill, 2015).

Bozdoğan, Sibel. *Modernism and Nation Building: Turkish Architectural Culture in the Early Republic* (Seattle: University of Washington Press, 2002).

Bozdoğan, Sibel. "Industrial Architecture and Nation-building in Turkey: a Historical Overview." In *Workplaces: The Transformation of Places of Production-Industrialisation and the Built Environment in the Islamic World*, edited by Mohammad al-Asad (Istanbul: Istanbul University Press by the cooperation with the Aga Khan Award for Architecture, 2010).

Brandell, Inga. "Workers in Third-World Industrialization: An Introduction." In *Workers in Third-World Industrialization*, edited by Inga Brandell (New York: Palgrave and Macmillan, 1991).

Brecher, Jeremy. "Uncovering the Hidden History of the American Workplace." *Review of Radical Political Economics* 10, no. 4 (1978).

Breman, Jan. "The Formal Sector: An Introductory Review." In *The Worlds of Indian Industrial Labour*, edited by Jonathan P. Parry, Jan Breman and Karin Kapadia (New Delhi: Sage Publications, 1999).

Brody, David. "Labor History in the 1970s." In *The Past before Us: Contemprorary Historical Writings in the United,* edited by Michael Kammen (Ithaca: Cornell University Press, 1980).

Bruinessen, Martin van. "Popular Islam, Kurdish Nationalism, and Rural Revolt: The Rebellion of Shaikh Said in Turkey (1925)." In *Religion and Rural Revolt,* edited by Janos M. Bak and Gerhard Benecke (Manchester: Manchester University Press, 1984).

Burawoy, Michael. *Manufacturing Consent: Changes in the Labour Process Under Monopoly Capitalism* (Chicago: University of Chicago Press, 1979).

Burawoy, Michael. "Between the Labor Process and the State: The Changing Face of Factory Regimes under Advanced Capitalism." *American Sociological Review* 48, no. 5 (1983).

Burawoy, Michael. *The Politics of Production: Factory Regimes under Capitalism and Socialism* (London: Verso, 1985).

Carew, Anthony. "Conflict Within the ICFTU: Anti-Communism and Anti-Colonialism in the 1950s." *International Review of Social History* 41, no. 2 (1996).

Carey, Jane Perry Clark and Carey, Andrew Galbraith. "Turkish Industry and the Five Year Plans." *Middle East Journal* 25, no. 3 (1971).

Chandavarkar, Rajnarayan. "'*The Making* of the Working Class': E. P. Thompson and Indian History." *History Workshop Journal* 43, no. 1 (1997).

Chibber, Vivek. "From Class Compromise to Class Accommodation: Labor's Incorporation into the Indian Political Economy." In *Social Movements and Poverty in India: Poverty, Power and Politics,* edited by Mary Falased Katzenstein and Raka Ray (New York: Rowman and Littlefield Publishers, 2005).

Clark, Edward C. "The Ottoman Industrial Revolution." *International Journal of Middle East Studies* 5, no. 1 (1974).

Clarke, Jackie. "Closing Moulinex: Thoughts on the Visibility and Invisibility of Industrial Labour in Contemporary France." *Modern and Contemporary France* 19, no. 4 (2011).

Cohen, Robin. *Contested Domains: Debates in International Labour Studies* (London: Atlantic Highlands, 1991).

Contini, G. "Politics, Law, and Shop Floor Bargaining in Postwar Italy." In *Shop Floor Bargaining and the State: Historical and Comparative Perspectives,* edited by Steven Tolliday and Jonathan Zeitlin (Cambridge: Cambridge University Press, 1985).

Cooper, Frederick. *Decolonisation and African Society: The Labour Question in French and British Africa* (Cambridge: Cambridge University Press, 1996).

Coopey, Richard and McKinlay, Alan. "Power Without Knowledge? Foucault and Fordism, c. 1900–50." *Labor History* 51, no. 1 (2010).

Cox, Jeffrey. "Labor History and the Labor Movement." *Journal of British Studies* 25 (1986).

Cunnison, Sheila. "The Manchester Factory Studies, the Social Context, Bureaucratic Organization, Sexual Divisions and Their Influence on Patterns of Accommodation between Workers and Management." In *Custom and Conflict in British Society*, ed. R. Frankenberg (Manchester: Manchester University Press, 1982).

Cucu, Alina-Sandra. *Planning Labour: Time and the Foundations of Industrial Socialism in Romania* (New York: Berghahn, 2019).

Curless, Gareth. "Introduction: Trade Unions in the Global South from Imperialism to the Present Day." *Labor History* 57, no. 1 (2016).

Çağaptay, Soner. "Reconfiguring the Turkish Nation in the 1930s." *Nationalism and Ethnic Politics* 8, no. 2 (2002).

Çakır, Serpil. *Osmanlı Kadın Hareketi* (Istanbul: Metis Yayınevi, 1994).

Çelik, Aziz. *Vesayetten Siyasete Türkiye'de Sendikacılık (1946–1967)* (Istanbul: İletişim, 2010).

Çelik, Aziz and Zafer Aydın. *Paşabahçe 1966: Gelenek Yaratan Grev* (Istanbul: TÜSTAV, 2006).

Çelik, Zeynep. *19. Yüzyılda Osmanlı Başkenti: Değişen İstanbul* (Istanbul: Tarih Vakfı Yurt Yayınları, 1998).

Çizakça, Murat. "Incorporation of the Middle East into the European World-Economy." *Review (Fernand Braudel Center)* 8, no.3 (1985).

Danielson, Michael N. and Keleş, Ruşen. *The Politics of Rapid Urbanisation* (New York: Holmes & Meier, 1985).

Darley, Gillian. *Factory* (London: Reaktion Books, 2004).

Dayıoğlu, Kadir. *Kayseri'de Ticaret ve Sanayi* (Kayseri: Kayseri Büyükşehir Belediyesi Kültür Yayınları, 2019).

De Grazia, Victoria. "Beyond Time and Money." *International Labour and Working-Class History* 43 (1993).

Deliorman, Necmettin. *Nuri Demirağ'ın Hayatı ve Mücadeleleri* (stanbul: Nu. D. Matbaası, 1957).

Dereli, Toker. *The Development of Turkish Trade Unionism* (Istanbul: Istanbul University, Faculty of Economics, 1968).

Dereli, Toker. *Aydınlar, Sendika Hareketi ve Endüstriyel İlişkiler Sistemi.* (Istanbul: Istanbul Üniversitesi İktisat Fakültesi Yayını, 1974).

Deringil, Selim. "The Ottoman Origins of Kemalist Nationalism: Namık Kemal to Mustafa Kemal." *European History Quarterly* 23 (1993).

Deshpande, Satish. "Imagined Economies: Styles of Nation-Building in Twentieth Century India." *Journal of Arts and Ideas* 25, no. 26 (1993).

Dilik, Sait. "Atatürk Döneminde Sosyal Politika." *Ankara Üniversitesi SBF Dergisi* 40, no.1 (1985).

Dina, Makram-Ebeid. "Between God and State: Class, Precarity, and Cosmology on the Margins of an Egyptian Steel Town." In *Industrial Labor on the Margins of Capitalism*, edited by Chris Hann and Jonathan Parry (New York: Berghahn, 2018).

Dodd, C.H. *Politics and Government in Turkey* (Manchester: Manchester University Press, 1969).

Doğan, Çağatay Emre. "Nazilli Basma Fabrikası Yerleşimi: Tarihçe ve Yaşantı." In *Fabrika'da Barınmak: Erken Cumhuriyet Dönemi'nde Türkiye'de İşçi Konutları: Yaşam, Mekan ve Kent*, edited by Ali Cengizkan (Ankara: Arkadaş, 2009).

Dölen, Emre. *Tekstil Tarihi* (Istanbul: Marmara Üniversitesi Teknik Eğitim Yayınları, 1992).

Drinot, Paulo. *The Allure of Labor: Workers, Race, and the Making of the Peruvian State* (Durham: Duke University Press, 2011).

Edwards, P.K. "Understanding Conflict in the Labour Process: The Logic and Autonomy of Struggle." In *Labour Process Theory*, edited by D. Knight and H. Willmott (London: Palgrave Macmillan, 1990).

Ekin, Nusret. "Memleketimizde İşçi Devri Mevzuunda Yapılan Araştırmalar ve Ortaya Koydukları Neticeler." In *Sosyal Siyaset Konferansları Dokuzuncu, Onuncu, Onbirinci Kitap* (Istanbul, 1960).

Ekin, Nusret. "Türkiye'de Endüstri İlişkilerinin Gelişimi ve 1936 İş Kanunu." *Sosyal Siyaset Konferansları Dergisi*, no. 35–36 (1986).

Eldem, Vedat. *Osmanlı İmparatorluğu'nun İktisadi Şartları Hakkında Bir Tetkik* (Istanbul: Türkiye İş Bankası Kültür Yayınları, 1970).

Eley, Geoff and Keith Nield, "Farewell to the Working Class?" *International Labor and Working-Class History* 57, no. 1 (2000).

Emmett, Isabel and D.H.J. Morgan, "Max Gluckman and the Manchester Shop-Floor Ethnographies," In *Custom and Conflict in British Society*, edited by R. Frankenberg (Manchester: Manchester University Press, 1982).

Emrence, Cem. "Turkey in Economic Crisis (1927–1930): A Panaromic Vision." *Middle Eastern Studies* 39, no. 4 (2003).

Emrence, Cem. *99 Günlük Muhalefet: Serbest Cumhuriyet Fırkası* (Istanbul: İletişim Yayınları, 2006).

Engels, Friedrich. *The Condition of the Working Class in England* (Cambridge: Cambridge University Press, 2010).

Epstein, James. "Rethinking the Categories of Working-Class History." *Labour/Le Travail* 18 (1986).

Eralp, Atilla. "The Politics of Turkish Development Strategies." In *Turkish State and Turkish Society*, edited by Andrew Finkel and Nükhet Sirman (London: Routledge, 1990).

Ercan, Metin R. and Öniş, Ziya. "Turkish Privatisation: Institutions and Dilemmas." *Turkish Studies* 2, no. 1 (2001).

Eroğul, Cem. *Demokrat Parti: Tarihi ve İdeolojisi* (Ankara: İmge Kitabevi, 1990).

Fink, Leon. "The Great Escape: How a Field Survived Hard Times" *Labor: Studies in Working-Class History of the Americas* 8, no. 1 (2011).

Fişek, Kurthan. *Devlete Karşı Grevlerin Kritik Tahlili* (Ankara: Ankara Üniversitesi Siyasal Bilgiler Fakültesi Yayınları, 1969).

Fişek, Kurthan. *Türkiye'de Kapitalizmin Gelişimi ve İşçi Sınıfı* (Istanbul: Doğan Yayınevi, 1969).

Fong, Leong Yee. "The Impact of the Cold War on the Development of Trade Unionism in Malaya (1948–1957)." *Journal of Southeast Asian Studies* 23, no. 1 (1992).

Foster, John. *Class Struggle and the Industrial Revolution* (London: Routledge, 1974).

Frader, Laura L. "Dissent over Discourse: Labor History, Gender and the Linguistic Turn." *History and Theory* 34, no. 3 (1995).

Frank, Andre Gunder. *Capitalism and Underdevelopment in Latin America: Historical Studies of Chile and Brazil* (New York: Monthly Review Press, 1967).

Frank, Andre Gunder. "The Development of Underdevelopment." In *Latin America: Underdevelopment or Revolution*, edited by Andre Gunder Frank (New York: Monthly Review Press, 1969).

Freeman, Joshua B. *Behemoth: A History of the Factory and the Making of the Modern World* (New York: W. W. Norton & Company, 2018).

Genç, Mehmet. "Ottoman Industry in the Eighteenth Century: General Framework, Characteristics, and Main Trends." In *Manufacturing in the Ottoman Empire and Turkey, 1500–1950*, edited by Donald Quataert (Albany: State University of New York Press, 1994).

Goodrich, Carter Lyman. *The Frontier of Control: A Study in British Workshop Politics* (New York: Harcourt, Brace, 1921).

Gorz, André. *Farewell to the Working Class: An Essay on Post-Industrial Socialism* (London: Pluto Press, 1982).

Göymen, Korel. "Stages of Etatist Development in Turkey: The Interaction of Single-Party Politics and Economic Policy in the 'Etatist Decade,' 1930–1939, " *Gelişme Dergisi* 10 (1976).

Guha, Ranajit. *Dominance Without Hegemony: History and Power in Colonial India* (Cambridge: Harvard University Press, 1997).

Gülalp, Haldun. "Patterns of Capital Accumulation and State-Society Relations in Turkey." *Journal of Contemporary Asia* 15, no. 3 (1985).

Gülalp, Haldun. "Capitalism and the Modern Nation-State: Rethinking the Creation of the Turkish Republic." *Journal of Historical Sociology* 7, no. 2 (1994).

Gülalp, Haldun. "The Eurocentrism of Dependency Theory and the Question of 'Authenticity': A View from Turkey." *Third World Quarterly* 19, no. 5 (1998).

Gülmez, Mesut. 1936 *İş Yasası'nın Hazırlık Çalışmaları* (Istanbul: Istanbul Üniversitesi İktisat Fakültesi, 1986).

Gülmez, Mesut. *Türkiye'de Çalışma İlişkileri: 1936 Öncesi* (Ankara: Devlet İstatistik Enstitüsü Matbaası, 1991).

Güran, Tevfik. "Tanzimat Döneminde Devlet Fabrikaları." In *150. Yılında Tanzimat,* edited by Hakkı Dursun Yıldız (Ankara: Türk Tarih Kurumu Yayınları, 1992).

Gürboğa, Nurşen. "Compulsory Mine Work: The Single-Party Regime and the Zonguldak Coalfield as a Site of Contention, 1940–1947." *International Review for Social History* 54 (2009).

Güzel, Ali. "3008 Sayılı İş Yasasının Önemi ve Başlıca Hükümleri." *Sosyal Siyaset Konferansları,* no. 35–36 (1986).

Güzel, Mehmet Şehmus. "Çalışma Bakanlığının Kuruluşu-Çalışma Hayatında İngiliz Etkisi." *Tarih ve Toplum* 9, no. 50 (1988).

Güzel, Mehmet Şehmus. "1940'larda İşgücünün (İşçilerin) Özellikleri." *Mülkiyeliler Birliği Dergisi,* no. 119 (1990).

Güzel, Mehmet Şehmus. *Türkiye'de İşçi Hareketleri 1908–1984* (Istanbul: Kaynak Yayınları, 1996).

Güzel, Mehmet Şehmus. "İkinci Dünya Savaşı Boyunca Sermaye ve Emek." In *Osmanlı'dan Cumhuriyet Türkiye'sine İşçiler,* edited by Donald Quataert and Erik Jan Zürcher, translated by Cahide Ekiz (Istanbul: İletişim Yayınları, 1998).

Hale, William. "Labour Unions in Turkey: Progress and Problems." In *Aspects of Modern Turkey,* edited by William Hale (Essex: Bowker, 1976).

Hale, William. "Ideology and Economic Development in Turkey 1930–1945." *Bulletin British Society for Middle Eastern Studies* 7, no.2 (1980).

Hale, William. *The Political and Economic Development of Modern Turkey* (London: Croom Helm, 1981).

Hale, William. *The Traditional and the Modern in the Economy of Kemalist Turkey: The Experience of the 1920s* (London: Routledge, 1984).

Hammad, Hanan. *Industrial Sexuality: Gender, Urbanisation, and Social Transformation in Egypt* (Austin: University of Texas Press, 2016).

Hanioğlu, M. Şükrü. *A Brief History of the Late Ottoman Empire* (Princeton: Princeton University Press, 2008).

Harris, George S. *The Origins of Communism in Turkey* (Stanford: Hoover Institution Publications, 1967).

Harris, George S. *The Communists and the Cadro Movement: Shaping Ideology in Atatürk's Turkey* (Istanbul: ISIS Press, 2002).

Hart, Charles W. M. *Zeytinburnu Gecekondu Bölgesi,* translated by Nephan Saran (Istanbul: Istanbul Ticaret Odası Yayınları, 1969).

Heilperin, Michael A. *Studies in Economic Nationalism* (Geneva: Publications de L'Institut Universitaire de Hautes Etudes Internationales, 1960).

Henderson, Jeff W. and Cohen, Robin. "Work, Culture and the Dialectics of Proletarian Habituation." *Papers in Urban and Regional Studies,* no. 3 (1980).

Heper, Metin. *The State Tradition in Turkey* (Walkington: Eothen Press, 1985).

Herod, Andrew. "Workers, Space, and Labor Geography." *International Labor and Working-Class History*, no. 64 (2003).

Hershlag, Zivi Yehuda. *Introduction to the Modern Economy of the Middle East* (Leiden: Brill, 1964).

Hershlag, Zivi Yehuda. *Turkey: The Challenge of Growth* (Leiden: E.J. Brill, 1968).

Hershlag, Zivi Yehuda. *The Contemporary Turkish Economy* (London: Routledge, 1988).

Hetherington, Kevin. *The Badlands of Modernity: Heterotopia and Social Ordering* (London: Routledge, 1997).

Hirschman, Albert O. *Exit, Voice and Loyalty: Responses to Decline in Firms, Organizations and State* (Cambridge, MA: Harvard University Press, 1970).

Hobsbawm, Eric. *Industry and* Empire (Suffolk: Penguin, 1969).

Hobsbawm, Eric. "The Forward March of Labour Halted?" *Marxism Today* 22, no. 9 (1978).

Holzberg, Carol S. and Maureen J. Giovannini, "Anthropology and Industry: Reappraisal and New Directions," *Annual Review of Anthropology* 10, no. 1 (1981).

Hudis, Peter. *The Complete Works of Rosa Luxemburg*, vol. 1 (London: Verso, 2013).

Hymand, Richard and Ian Brough. *Social Values and Industrial Relations: Study of Fairness and Inequality* (Oxford: Basil Blackwell, 1975).

İleri, Rasih Nuri. "Önsöz." In *Kırklı Yıllar-5*, edited by Rasih Nuri İleri (Istanbul: TÜSTAV, 2006).

İlkin, Selim. "Devletçilik Döneminin İlk Yıllarında İşçi Sorununa Yaklaşım ve 1932 İş Kanunu Tasarısı." In *Türkiye İktisat Tarihi Üzerine Araştırmalar-Gelişme Dergisi 1978 Özel Sayısı* (1978).

İlkin, Selim. "Birinci Sanayi Planının Hazırlanışında Sovyet Uzmanlarının Rolü." *ODTÜ Gelişim Dergisi* 1979–1980 Özel Sayısı (1981).

İlkin, Selim. "Birinci Sanayi Planı Döneminde ABD'li Uzmanlara Hazırlatılan 'Türkiye'nin İktisadi Bakımdan Umumi Bir Tetkiki' Adlı Rapor." In *Atatürk Döneminde Türkiye Ekonomisi Semineri* (Istanbul: Yapı Kredi, 1982).

İlkin, Selim. "Birinci Sanayi Planının Hazırlanışında Sovyet Uzmanlarının Rolü." In *Cumhuriyetin Harcı 2-Köktenci Modernitenin Gelişimi,* edited by Selim İlkin and İlhan Tekeli (Istanbul: Bilgi, 2004).

İnal, Vedit. "The Eighteenth and Nineteenth Century Ottoman Attempts to Catch Up with Europe." *Middle Eastern Studies* 47, no. 5 (2011).

İnalcık, Halil. "Osmanlı Pamuklu Pazarı, Hindistan ve Ingiltere: Pazar Rekabetinde Emek Maliyetinin Rolü," *ODTU Gelişme Dergisi*, special issue (1979–80).

İnalcık, Halil "Turkey Between Europe and the Middle East." *Foreign Policy* 7 (1980).

İnalcık, Halil. *Osmanlı İmparatorluğu: Toplum ve Ekonomi* (Istanbul: Eren Yayıncılık, 1996).

İnalcık, Halil. *Türkiye Tekstil Tarihi Üzerine Araştırmalar* (Istanbul: İş Bankası Yayınları, 2008).

İnan, A. Afet. *İzmir İktisat Kongresi: 17 Şubat-4 Mart 1923* (Ankara: Türk Tarih Kurumu Yayınları, 1989).

İnsel, Ahmet. "Devletçiliğin Anatomisi." *Cumhuriyet Dönemi Türkiye Ansiklopedisi*, vol. 2 (Istanbul: İletişim Yayınları, 1984).

İnsel, Ahmet. *Düzen ve Kalkınma Kıskacında Türkiye, Kalkınma Sürecinde Devletin Rolü* (Istanbul: Ayrıntı Yayınları, 1996).

Issawi, Charles. "De-industrialisation and Re-industrialisation in the Middle East Since 1800." *International Journal of Middle Eastern Studies* 12, no.4 (1980).

Issawi, Charles. *The Economic History of Turkey, 1800–1914* (The University of Chicago Press: Chicago, 1980).

Issawi, Charles. *An Economic History of the Middle East and North Africa* (New York: Colombia University Press, 1982).

Jacoby, Sanford M. *Employing Bureaucracy: Managers, Unions, and the Transformation of Work in the 20th Century* (London: Routledge, 1985).

Joshi, Chitra. "Kanpur Textile Labour: Some Structural Features of Formative Years." *Economic and Political Weekly* 16, no. 44/46 (1981).

Joshi, Chitra. "Histories of Indian Labour: Predicaments and Possibilities." *History Compass* 6, no. 2 (2008).

Kalfa, Ceren. "Planlamada Sümerbank Modeline Geçiş." In *Türkiye Cumhuriyeti İdare Tarihi Araştırması* (TIDATA), edited by Birgül A. Güler et al. (Ankara: Ankara Üniversitesi, 2007).

Karakışla, Yavuz Selim. "The 1908 Strike Wave in the Ottoman Empire." *Turkish Studies Association Bulletin* 16, no. 2 (1992).

Karal, Enver Ziya. *Osmanlı Tarihi: Islahat Fermanı Devri, 1856–1861*, vol. 6 and vol, 7 (Ankara: Türk Tarih Kurumu, 2007).

Karpat, Kemal. "The Mass Media: Turkey." In *Political Modernisation in Japan and Turkey*, edited by R. E. Ward and D. A. Rustow (Princeton: Princeton University Press,1964).

Karpat, Kemal H. *The Gecekondu: Rural Migration and Urbanisation* (Cambridge: Cambridge University Press, 1976).

Karpat, Kemal. "The Turkish Left." *Journal of Contemporary History* 1, no. 2 (1996).

Karpat, Kemal. *Türk Siyasi Tarihi: Siyasal Sistemin Evrimi* (Istanbul: Timaş, 2015).

Karpat, Kemal H. *Turkey's Politics: The Transition to a Multi-Party System* (New Jercey: Princeton University Press, 2016).

Kasaba, Reşat. "Populism and Democracy in Turkey, 1946–1961", In *Rules and Rights in the Middle East*, edited by Ellis Goldberg, Reşat Kasaba, and Joel Migdal (Seattle, WA: University of Washington Press, 1993).

Katznelson, Ira. "Working-Class Formation: Constructing Cases and Comparisons." In *Working-Class Formation: Nineteenth-Century Patterns in Western Europe and the United States*, edited by Ira Katznelson and Aristide R. Zolberg (Princeton: Princeton University Press, 1986).

Kayaoğlu, Barın. "Strategic Imperatives, Democratic Rhetoric: The United States and Turkey, 1945–52." *Cold War History* 9, no. 3 (2009).

Kazgan, Gülten. "Structural Changes in Turkish National Income: 1950–1960." In *Middle Eastern Studies in Income and Wealth*, edited by Taufiq M. Khan (New Haven, International Association for Research in Income and Wealth, 1965).

Kazgan, Gülten. *Tarım ve Gelişme* (Istanbul: Fakülteler Matbaası, 1977).

Kazgan, Gülten. "Türk Ekonomisinde 1927–35 Depresyonu, Kapital Birikimi ve Örgütleşmeler." In *Atatürk Döneminin Ekonomik ve Toplumsal Tarihiyle İlgili Sorunlar Sempozyumu* (Istanbul: IITIA, 1977).

Kazgan, Gülten. *Türkiye Ekonomisinde Krizler (1929–2001): "Ekonomi Politik" Açısından bir İrdeleme* (Istanbul: Bilgi Üniversitesi Yayınları, 2005).

Keleş, Ruşen. *Urbanisation in Turkey* (New York: Ford Foundation, 1971).

Kepenek, Yakup and Nurhan Yentürk. *Türkiye Ekonomisi* (Istanbul: Remzi Kitabevi, 1994).

Kerr, Clark, John T. Dunlop, Frederick H. Harbison, and Charles A. Myers, *Industrialism and Industrial Man: The Problem of Labor and Management in Economic Growth.* (Cambridge: Harvard University Press, 1960).

Keskinok, H. Çağatay. "Urban Planning Experience of Turkey in the 1930s." *METU JFA* 27, no.2 (2010).

Keyder, Çağlar. "The Political Economy of Turkish Democracy." *New Left Review* 1, no. 115 (1979).

Keyder, Çağlar. *The Definition of a Peripheral Economy: Turkey 1923–1929* (Cambridge: Cambridge University Press, 1981).

Keyder, Çağlar. *State and Class in Turkey: A Study in Capitalist Development* (London: Verso, 1987).

Kezer, Zeynep. *Building Modern Turkey: State, Space and Ideology in the Early Republic* (Pittsburgh: University of Pittsburgh Press, 2015).

Kılınçoğlu, Deniz T. *Economics and Capitalism in the Ottoman Empire* (New York: Routledge, 2015).

Kirin, Renata and Marina Blagaić, "The Ambivalence of Socialist Working Women's Heritage: A Case Study of the Jugoplastika Factory." *Narodna Umjetnost* 1, no. 150 (2013).

Klubock, Thomas Miller. *Contested Communities: Class, Gender, and Politics in Chile's El Teniente Copper Mine, 1904–1951* (Durham, NC: Duke University Press, 1998).

Knudsen, Dino. "The Nordic Trade Union Movement and Transnational Anti-Communist Networks in the Early Cold War." In *Transnational Anti-Communism and the Cold War: Agents, Activities, and Networks* edited by Luc van Dongen, Stéphanie Roulin, Giles Scott-Smith (London: Palgrave Macmillan, 2014).

Koç, Canan and Koç, Yıldırım. *Türkiye İşçi Sınıfı ve Mücadeleleri Tarihi* (Ankara: TIB Tüm İktisatçılar Birliği, 1976).

Koç, Yıldırım. "1947 Sendikalar Yasası" *Mülkiyeliler Birliği Dergisi* no. 121 (1990).

Koç, Yıldırım. "1923–1950 Döneminde CHP'nin İşçi Sınıfı Korkusu." *Mülkiyeliler Birliği Dergisi*, no. 170 (1994).

Koç, Yıldırım. "Türkiye'de 1923–1946 Döneminde Mülksüzleşme ve İşçi Sınıfının Oluşumu." *Mülkiyeliler Birliği Dergisi*, no. 174 (1994).

Koç, Yıldırım. *Türkiye'de İşçi Sınıfı ve Sendikacılık Tarihi: Olaylar-Değerlendirmeler* (Ankara: Türkiye Yol-İş Sendikası Yayınları, 1996).

Koç, Yıldırım. *Türk-İş Tarihinden Portreler: Eski Sendikacılardan Anılar Gözlemler* (Ankara: Türk-İş Yayınları, 1999).

Koç, Yıldırım. *Türkiye İşçi Sınıfı ve Sendikacılık Hareketi Tarihi* (Istanbul: Kaynak, 2003).

Koçak, Cemil. *Belgelerle İktidar ve Serbest Cumhuriyet Fırkası* (Istanbul: İletişim Yayınları, 2006).

Koçak, Hakan. *Camın İşçileri: Paşabahçe İşçilerinin Sınıf Olma Öyküsü* (Istanbul: İletişim, 2014).

Koçak, Hakan. "İşçi Hareketinin Örgütsel Kapasitesi ve Ölçeksel Strateji Bağlamında İstanbul İşçi Sendikaları Birliği Örneği (1948–1962)." *Çalışma ve Toplum* 4 (2014).

Koçak, Hakan. "Anti-Komünizmin Markajında Emek Mücadelesi: Tekstil İşçilerinin Gerçekleşemeyen Mitingleri." *Toplumsal Tarih*, no. 305 (2019).

Kofman, Jan. "How to Define Economic Nationalism: A Critical Review of Some Old and New Standpoints." In *Economic Nationalism in East-Central Europe and South America 1918–1939*, edited by Henryk Szlajfer (Geneva: Droz, 1990).

Kofti, Dimitra. "*Moral Economy of Flexible Production: Fabricating Precarity Between the Conveyor Belt and the Household.*" *Anthropological Theory* 16, no. 4 (2016).

Koraltürk, Murat. *Erken Cumhuriyet Döneminde Ekonominin Türkleştirilmesi* (Istanbul: İletişim Yayınları, 2011).

Korniyenko, Radmir Platonovich. *The Labor Movement in Turkey (1918–1963)* (Washington: US Department of Commerce, 1967).

Korniyenko, Radmir Platonovich. "Cumhuriyet'in Kuruluşundan İkinci Dünya Savaşına Kadar Türkiye'de İşçi Hareketleri: 1923–1939." *Sosyalist Parti İçin Teori-Pratik Birliği*, no. 4 (1971).

Kotkin, Stephen. *Magnetic Mountain: Stalinism as a Civilisation* (Oakland: University of California Press, 1997).

Kotkin, Stephen. "Modern Times: The Soviet Union and the Interwar Conjunction," *Kritika: Explorations in Russian and Eurasian History* 2, no. 1 (2001).

Krahenbuhl, Margaret. "Turkish Communists: Schism Instead of Conciliation." *Studies in Comparative Communism* 6, no. 4 (1973).

Kuban, Doğan. *Istanbul an Urban History: Byzantion, Constantinopolis, Istanbul* (Istanbul: The Economic and Social History Foundation, 2004).

Kuromiya, "The Commander and the Rank and File: Managing the Soviet Coal-Mining Industry, 1928–33." In *Social Dimensions of Soviet Industrialisation*, edited by William G Rosenberg and Lewis H Siegelbaum (Bloomington: Indiana University Press, 1993).

Kurt, Mustafa, Kuzucu, Kemalettin, Çakır, Baki and Demir, Kemal. "19. Yüzyılda Osmanlı Sanayi Sürecinde Kurulan Devlet Fabrikaları: Bir Envanter Çalışması." *OTAM* 40 (2016).

Kuruç, Bilsay. *Mustafa Kemal Döneminde Ekonomi.* (Istanbul: Bilgi Yayınevi, 1987).

Kuruç, Bilsay. *Belgelerle Türkiye İktisat Politikası 1929–1932*, vol. 1 (Ankara: Ankara Üniversitesi Siyasal Bilgiler Fakültesi Yayınları, 1988).

Kuruç, Bilsay. *Belgelerle Türkiye İktisat Politikası, 1933–1935*, vol. 2 (Ankara: Ankara Üniversitesi Yayınları, 1993).

Küçükerman, Önder. *Hereke Fabrikası* (Istanbul: Sümerbank, 1987).

Küçükerman, Önder. *Geleneksel Türk Dericilik Sanayi ve Beykoz Fabrikası: Boğaziçi'nde Başlatılan Sanayi* (Istanbul: Sümerbank, 1988).

Landau, Jacob M. *Radical Politics in Turkey* (London and New York: Routledge, 2016).

Laqueur, Walter Z. *Communism and Nationalism in the Middle East* (New York: Frederick A. Praeger, 1956).

Leys, Colin. "Underdevelopment and Dependency: Critical Notes." *Journal of Contemporary Asia* 7, no.1 (1977): 92–107.

Lewis, Bernard. *The Emergence of Modern Turkey* (London: Oxford University Press, 1968).

Lipietz, Alain. *Mirages and Miracles: The Crisis in Global Fordism* (New York: Verso, 1987).

Lipovsky, Igor P. *The Socialist Movement in Turkey, 1960–1980* (Leiden: Brill, 1992).

Lipp, Carola and Krempel, Lothar. "Petitions and the Social Context of Political Mobilisation in the Revolution of 1848/49: A Microhistorical Actor-Centred Network Analysis." *International Review of Social History* 46, no. S9 (2001).

Lovejoy, Paul E. *Transformations in Slavery: A History of Slavery in Africa* (New York: Cambridge University Press, 2012).

Luff, Jennifer. "Labor Anticommunism in the United States of America and the United Kingdom, 1920–49." *Journal of Contemporary History* 53, no. 1 (2018).

Ma, Tehyun. "A Chinese Beveridge Plan: The Discourse of Social Security and the Post-War Reconstruction of China." *European Journal of East Asian Studies* 11, no. 2 (2012).

Makal, Ahmet. *Türkiye'de Tek Partili Dönemde Çalışma İlişkileri: 1920–1946* (Ankara: İmge Kitabevi, 1999).

Makal, Ahmet. "Türkiye'nin Sanayileşme Sürecinde İşgücü Sorunu, Sosyal Politika ve İktisadi Devlet Teşekkülleri: 1930'lu ve 1940'lı Yıllar." *Toplum ve Bilim*, no. 92 (2002).

Makal, Ahmet. *Ameleden İşçiye: Erken Cumhuriyet Dönemi Emek Tarihi Çalışmaları* (Istanbul: İletişim Yayınları, 2007).

Makal, Ahmet. "Türkiye'de Kadın Emeğinin Tarihsel Kökenleri: 1920–1960." In *Geçmişten Günümüze Türkiye'de Kadın Emeği*, edited by Ahmet Makal and Gülay Toksoz (Ankara: Ankara Üniversitesi Yayınevi, 2012).

Mardin, Şerif. "Center–Periphery Relations: A Key to Turkish Politics?" *Daedalus*, no. 102 (1972).

Martykanova, Darina. *Reconstructing Ottoman Engineers: Archaeology of a Profession (1789–1914)* (Lungarno Pacinotti: Pisa University Press, 2012).

Marshall, T.H. *Class, Citizenship, and Social Development* (New York: Doubleday, 1964).

Meyer, John W. and Rowan, Brian. "Institutionalized Organisations: Formal Structure as Myth and Ceremony." *American Journal of Sociology* 83, no. 2 (1977).

Mihm, Stephen. "Interchange: The History of Capitalism." *Journal of American History* 101 (2014).

Minassian, Anahide Ter. *A Family of Armenian Amiras: The Dadians* (MA: Armanian Review, 1992).

Mitchell, Timothy. "Fixing the Economy." *Cultural Studies* no. 12 (1998).

Mitchell, Timothy. "Rethinking Economy." *Geoforum* 39, no. 3 (2008).

Mollona, Massimiliano. "Factory, Family and Neighbourhood: The Political Economy of Informal Labour in Sheffield." *The Journal of the Royal Anthropological Institute* 11, no. 3 (2005).

Montgomery, David. *The Fall of the House of Labor: The Workplace, the State, and American Labor Activism, 1865–1925* (New York: Cambridge University Press, 1987).

Musić, Goran. *Making and Breaking the Yugoslav Working Class: The Story of Two Self-Managed Factories* (Budapest: Central European University Press, 2021).

Myrdal, Gunnar. *Asian Drama: An Inquiry into the Poverty of Nations* (New York: Pantheon Books, 1972).

Nacar, Can. "Our Lives Were Not as Valuable as an Animal: Workers in State-Run Industries in WorldWar-II Turkey." *International Review of Social History* 54, no. 17 (2009).

Nacar, Can. "Labour Activism and the State in the Ottoman Tobacco Industry." *International Journal of Middle East Studies* 46, no. 3 (2014).

Neve, Geert De. "Towards an *Ethnography* of the *Workplace*: Hierarchy, Authority and Sociability on the South Indian Textile Shop Floor." *South Asia Research* 21, no. 2 (2001).

Nichols, Theo and Erol Kahveci. "The Condition of Mine Labour in Turkey: Injuries to Miners in Zonguldak, 1942–90." *Middle Eastern Studies* 31, no. 2 (1995).

Nolan, Mary. "Das Deutsche Institut für Technische Arbeitsschulung und die Schaffung des: Neuen Arbeiters." In *Rationale Beziehungen? Geschlechterverhältnisse im*

Rationalisierungsprozess, edited by Dagmar Reese, Eve Rosenhaft, Carola Sachse, and Tilla Siegel (Frankfurt am Main: Suhrkamp, 1993).

Nolan, Mary. *Visions of Modernity: American Business and the Modernisation of Germany* (Oxford: Oxford University Press, 1994).

Oğuz, Şeyda, ed. *1927 Adana Demiryolu Grevi* (Istanbul: TÜSTAV, 2005).

Oktar, Tiğinçe. *Osmanlı Toplumunda Kadının Çalışma Yaşamı: Osmanlı Kadınları Calıştırma Cemiyet-i İslamiyesi* (Istanbul: Bilim Teknik, 1998).

Okyar, Osman. "The Concept of Etatism." *Economic Journal* 75, no. 297 (1965).

Ökçün, Gündüz. *Tatil-i Eşgal Kanunu, 1909: Belgeler, Yorumlar* (Ankara: S.B.F. Yayınları, 1982).

Ökçün, Gündüz. *Osmanlı Sanayi İstatistikleri: 1913–1915* (Istanbul: Hil Yayınları, 1984).

Ökçün, Gündüz. *Türkiye'de İktisat Kongresi: 1923 İzmir-Haberler, Belgeler, Yorumlar* (Ankara: Sermaye Piyasası Kurulu Yayınları, 1997).

Ölçen, Ali Nejat. "1923–1938 Döneminde Birinci ve İkinci Sanayi Planları." In *Atatürk Dönemi Ekonomi Politikası ve Türkiye'nin Ekonomik Gelişmesi Semineri* (Ankara: SBF Yayınları, 1982).

Öncü, Emre and Sırrı Çölmekçi, "Yeni Araştırmalar: Bakırköy Eski Sümerbank Arazisinde Yürütülen Arkeolojik Kazılar." *Mimar.ist* 18, no. 61 (2018).

Öniş, Ziya. "Power, Interests and Coalitions: The Political Economy of Mass Privatisation in Turkey." *Third World Quarterly* 32, no. 4 (2011).

Önsoy, Rıfat. *Tanzimat Dönemi Osmanlı Sanayii ve Sanayileşme Politikası* (Ankara: Türkiye İş Bankası Kültür Yayınları, 1988).

Özek, Çetin. *141–142* (Istanbul: Ararat Yayınları, 1968).

Özden, Barış Alp. "Health, Morality and Housing: The Politics of Working-Class Housing in Turkey." *New Perspectives on Turkey*, no. 49 (2013).

Özgür, M. Erdem, and Eyüp Özveren, "Turkey's Attempt to Break the Fetters Before the Ladder Was Kicked Away, 1929–1947." In *Political Economy of Development in Turkey 1838–Present*, edited by Emre Özçelik and Yonca Özdemir (London: Palgrave Macmillan, 2022).

Öztürk, Nazif. "XIX. Yüzyılda Osmanlı İmparatorluğu'nda Sanayileşme ve 1827'de Kurulan Vakıf İplik Fabrikası." *Vakıflar Dergisi*, no. 21 (1990).

Öztürk, Saygı. *İsmet Paşa'nın Kürt Raporu* (Istanbul: Doğan, 2007), 24, 59–60.

Özvar, Erol. "Osmanlılar Zamanında Zeytinburnu." In *Surların Öte Yanı, Zeytinburnu*, edited by Burçak Evren and Alper Çeker (Istanbul: Zeytinburnu Belediye Başkanlığı, 2003).

Palairet, Michael. *Balkan Ekonomileri, 1800–1914: Kalkınmasız Evrim*, translated by Ayse Edirne (Istanbul: Sabancı Üniversitesi Yayınevi, 2000).

Pamuk, Şevket. "Political Economy of Industrialization in Turkey." *Middle East Research and Information*, no. 93 (1981).

Pamuk, Şevket. *The Ottoman Empire and European Capitalism, 1820–1913* (Cambridge: Cambridge University Press, 1987).

Pamuk, Şevket. *Turkey's Response to the Great Depression in Comparative Perspective, 1929–1939* (San Domenico di Fiesole: European University Institute, 2000).

Pamuk, Şevket. *Osmanlı-Türkiye İktisadî Tarihi 1500–1914* (Istanbul: İletişim Yayınları, 2005).

Pamuk, Şevket and Jeffrey G. Williamson. "Ottoman De-Industrialisation, 1800–1913: Assessing the Magnitude, Impact, and Response." *The Economic History Review* 64, no. 1 (2011).

Pamuk, Şevket. *Uneven Centuries: Economic Development of Turkey since 1820* (Princeton: Princeton University Press 2018).

Parla, Taha and Andrew Davison. *Corporatist Ideology in Kemalist Turkey: Progress or Order?* (Syracuse: Syracuse University Press, 2004).

Parry, Jonathan. "The Sacrifices of Modernity in a Soviet-built Steel Town in Central India." In *On the Margins of* Religion, edited by Frances Pine and João Pina-Cabral (New York: Berghahn, 2008).

Parry, Jonathan and Christian Strümpell. "On the Desecration of Nehru's 'Temples': Bhilai and Rourkela Compared." *Economic and Political Weekly* 43, no. 19 (2008).

Parry, Jonathan. "*Sex, Bricks and Mortar*: *Constructing Class in a Central Indian Steel Town*." *Modern Asian Studies* 48, no. 5 (2014).

Pasetti, Matteo. "The Fascist Labour Charter and Its Transnational Spread." In *Corporatism and Fascism: The Corporatist Wave in Europe*, edited by Antonio Costa Pinto (London: Routledge, 2017).

Payaslıoğlu, Arif T. "Turkey." In *Political Modernisation in Japan and Turkey*, edited by R. E. Ward and D. A. Rustow (Princeton: Princeton University Press, 1964).

Price, Richard. "'What's in a Name?' Workplace History and 'Rank and Filism'." *International Review of Social History* 34, no. 1 (1989).

Quataert, Donald. "The Social History of Labour in the Ottoman Empire." In *The Social History of Labour in the Middle East*, edited by Ellis Jay Goldberg (Boulder: Westview Press, 1966).

Quataert, Donald. *Manufacturing and Technology Transfer in the Ottoman Empire: 1800–1914* (Istanbul and Strasbourg: The Isis Press, 1992).

Quataert, Donald. *Ottoman Manufacturing in the Age of Industrial Revolution* (Cambridge: Cambridge University Press, 1993).

Quataert, Donald. "Women Households and Textile Manufacturing 1800–1914." In *The Modern Middle East*, edited by Albert Hourani et al. (London: I.B. Tauris, 1993).

Quataert, Donald. "Introduction." In *Manufacturing in the Ottoman Empire and Turkey, 1500–1950*, edited by Donald Quataert (Albany: State University of New York Press, 1994).

Quataert, Donald. "Ottoman Manufacturing in the Nineteenth Century." In *Manufacturing in the Ottoman Empire and Turkey, 1500–1950,* edited by Donald Quataert (Albany: State University of New York Press, 1994).

Quataert, Donald. "The Workers of Salonica." In *The Workers and the Working Class in the Ottoman Empire and Turkish Republic 1839–1950*, edited by Donald Quataert and Erik Jan Zürcher (London and New York: Tauris Academic Studies in Association with the International Institute of Social history, Amsterdam, 1995).

Quataert, Donald. "Clothing Laws, State, and Society in the Ottoman Empire, 1720–1829." *International Journal of Middle East Studies* 29, no. 3 (1997).

Quataert, Donald. "19. Yüzyıla Genel Bakış: Islahatlar Devri, 1812–1914." In *Osmanlı İmparatorluğu'nun Ekonomik ve Sosyal Tarihi, 1600–1914*, ed: Halil İnalcık and Donald Quataert, translated by Ayşe Berktay, Süphan Andıç, and Serdar Alper (Istanbul, Eren Yayıncılık, 2004).

Rosen, Sumner Maurice. "Turkey." In *Labor in Developing Economies*, edited by Walter Galenson (Berkeley and Los Angeles: University of California Press, 1963).

Richards, Alan, John Waterbury, Melani Cammett, and Ishac Diwan. *A Political Economy of the Middle East* (Boulder: Westview Press, 2013).

Rifkin, Jeremy. *The End of Work: The Decline of the Global Labor Force and the Dawn of the Post-Market Era* (New York: Tarcher, 1995).

Robinson, Richard D. "Turkey's Agrarian Revolution and the Problem of Urbanisation." *Public Opinion Quarterly* 22 (1958).

Robinson, Richard D. *The First Turkish Republic* (Cambridge: Harward University, 1963).

Rose, M. and B. Jones. "Managerial Strategy and Trade Union Responses to Work Reorganisation Schemes at Establishment Level." In *Job Redesign: Critical Perspectives on the Labour Process,* edited by David Knights, Hugh Willmott, and David Collinson (Brookfield: Gower, 1985).

Roy, Srirupa. *Beyond Belief: India and the Politics of Postcolonial Nationalism* (Durham: Duke University Press, 2007).

Sailer, Anna. *Workplace Relations in Colonial Bengal: The Jute Industry and Indian Labour 1870s-1930s* (London: Bloomsbury, 2022).

Sarıbay, Ali Yaşar. "The Democratic Party, 1946–1960." In *Political Parties and Democracy in Turkey*, edited by Martin Heper and Jacob M. Landau (New York: I.B. Tauris, 1990).

Sayılgan, Aclan. *Solun 94 Yılı, 1871–1965* (Ankara: Mars Matbaası, 1968).

Schull, Joseph. "What is Ideology? Theoretical Problems and Lessons from Soviet-Type Societies." *Political Studies*, no. XL (1992).

Seccombe, Wally. *Weathering the Storm: Working-Class Families from the Industrial Revolution to the Fertility Decline* (London: Verso, 1995).

Sencer, Oya. *Türkiye'de İşçi Sınıfı, Doğuşu ve Yapısı* (Istanbul: Habora Kitabevi Yayınları, 1969).

Serin, Necdet. "Industrialisation Policy of Turkey Since 1923." *Ankara Üniversitesi SBF Dergisi* 20, no. 2 (1965).

Seton-Watson, Hugh. *Nations and States: An Enquiry into the Origins of Nations and the Politics of Nationalism* (London: Methuen & Co. Ltd., 1977).

Scott, James. *Seeing Like a State: How Certain Schemes to Improve the Human Condition Have Failed* (London: Yale University Press, 1998).

Shaw, Stanford J. and Ezel Kural Shaw. *History of the Ottoman Empire and Modern Turkey-Reform, Revolution, and Republic: The Rise of Modern Turkey 1808–1975*, vol. 2 (Cambridge: Cambridge University Press, 1977).

Shehata, Samer S. *Shop Floor Culture and Politics in Egypt* (Albany: SUNY Press, 2009).

Shorter, Frederic C. "Turkish Population in the Great Depression." *New Perspectives on Turkey* 23 (2000).

Siegelbaum, Lewis H. "Masters of the Shop Floor: Foremen and Soviet Industrialisation." In *Stalinism: Its Nature and Aftermath. Studies in Soviet History and Society*, edited by Nick Lampert and Gábor T. Rittersporn (London: Palgrave Macmillan, 1992).

Siegelbaum, Lewis H. and Michael Morgan, "'State' versus 'Society' in Tsarist and Soviet History." *Radical History Review* 28, no. 30 (1984).

Silier, Oya. *Türkiye'de Tarımsal Yapının Gelişimi: 1923–1938* (Istanbul: Boğaziçi Üniversitesi, 1981).

Silver, Beverly. *Forces of Labor: Workers' Movements and Globalisation Since 1870* (Cambridge: Cambridge University Press, 2003).

Singer, Morris. *The Economic Advance of Turkey: 1938–1960* (Ankara: Turkish Economic Society Publications, 1977).

Sipahi, Ali. "Convict Labor in Turkey, 1936–1953: A Capitalist Corporation in the State?" *International Labor and Working-Class History* 90 (2016).

Spector, Ivar. *The Soviet Union and the Muslim World, 1917–1958* (Seattle: University of Washington Press, 1959).

Statistical Indicators: 1923–1990 (Ankara: Başbakanlık Devlet İstatistik Enstitüsü Yayınları, 1991).

Stedman-Jones, Gareth. *Languages of Class: Studies in English Working Class History, 1832–1982* (Cambridge, Cambridge University Press, 1983).

Stephanov, Darin. "Sultan Mahmud II (1808–1839) and the First Shift in Modern Ruler Visibility in the Ottoman Empire." *Journal of the Ottoman and Turkish Studies Association* 1, no. 1–2 (2014).

Strümpell, Christian. "Law Against Displacement: The Juridification of Tribal Protest in Rourkela, Orissa." In *Law Against the State: Etnographic Forays into Law's Transformations*, edited by Julia Eckert, Brian Donahoe, Christian Strümpell, and Zerrin Özlem Biner (Cambridge: Cambridge University Press, 2012).

Strümpell, Christian. "The Anthropology of *Work* and *Labour*." *Ethnoscripts* 19, no. 2 (2017).

Sunar, İlkay. *State and Society in the Politics of Turkey's Development* (Ankara: Ankara University Faculty of Political Science, 1974).

Sunar, İlkay. "Populism and Patronage: Democrat Party and its Legacy in Turkey." In *Politics of Modern Turkey 1*, edited by A. Çarkoğlu and W. Hale (London: Routledge, 1990).

Sugar, Peter. "Economic and Political Modernisation: Turkey." In *Political Modernisation in Japan and Turkey,* edited by Robert E. Ward and Dankward. A. Rustow (Princeton: Princeton University Press, 1964).

Sussitzki, A.J. "Ethnic Division of Labour." In *The Economic History of the Middle East (1800–1914)*, edited by Charles Issawi (Chicago: The University of Chicago Press, 1966).

Sülker, Kemal. *Türkiye'de Sendikacılık* (Istanbul: Vakit Matbaasi, 1955).

Sülker, Kemal. *Sendikacılar ve Politika* (Istanbul: May Yayınları. 1975).

Sülker, Kemal. *100 Soruda Türkiye'de İşçi Hareketleri* (Istanbul: Gerçek Yayınları, 1978).

Sülker, Kemal. *Türkiye'de Grev Hakkı ve Grevler* (Istanbul, TÜSTAV, 2004).

Svanberg, Johan. "'The Ruhr Remains our Nightmare': The International Metalworkers' Federation and European Integration in the Early Cold War." *International Review of Social History* 66, no. 1 (2021).

Szlajfer, Henryk, ed. *Economic Nationalism in East-Central Europe and South America 1918–1939* (Geneva: Droz, 1990).

Şişmanov, Dimitri. *Türkiyede İşçi Sınıfi ve Sosyalist Hareketi* (Sofia: Narodna Proveta, 1965).

Şiviloğlu, Murat R. *The Emergence of Public Opinion: State and Society in the late Ottoman Empire* (New York: Cambridge University Press, 2018).

Talas, Cahit. *Türkiye'nin Açıklamalı Sosyal Politika Tarihi* (Ankara: Bilgi Yayınevi, 1992).

Tekeli, İlhan. *Gecekondulu, Dolmuşlu, İşportalı Şehir* (Istanbul: Cem Yayınevi, 1976).

Tekeli, İlhan. *Türkiye'de Yaşamda ve Yazında Konut Sorununun Gelişimi* (Ankara: T.C. Başbakanlık Toplu Konut İdaresi Başkanlığı, 1996).

Tekeli, İlhan. "Atatürk Türkiye'sinde Kentsel Gelişme ve Kent Planlaması." *Arredamento Mimarlık* 10 (1998).

Tekeli, İlhan. "Türkiye'de Cumhuriyet Döneminde Kentsel Gelişme ve Kent Planlaması." In *75 Yılda Değişen Kent ve Mimarlık,* edited by Yıldız Sey (Istanbul: Tarih Vakfı Yayınları, 1998).

Tekeli, İlhan and Selim İlkin. *Savaş Sonrası Ortamında 1947 Türkiye İktisadi Kalkınma Planı* (Ankara: ODTÜ Yayınları, 1974).

Tekeli, İlhan and Selim İlkin. *1929 Dünya Buhranında Türkiye'nin İktisadi Politika Arayışları* (Ankara: Orta Doğu Teknik Üniversitesi, 1977).

Tekeli, İlhan and Selim İlkin. *Uygulamaya Geçerken Türkiye'de Devletçiliğin Oluşumu* (Ankara: ODTÜ İdari İlimler Fakültesi, 1982).

Tekeli, İlhan and Selim İlkin. "War Economy of a Non-Belligerent Country: Cotton Textiles: from Production to Consumption." *Turcica* 22 (1988).

Tekeli, İlhan and Selim İlkin. *Dr. Max von der Porten'in Türkiye'deki Çalışmaları ve İktisadi Devlet Teşekkülleri Sisteminin Oluşumu* (Istanbul: Friedrich Ebert Vakfı, 1992).

Tekeli, İlhan and Selim İlkin. "Osmanlı İmparatorluğu'nda 19. Yüzyıl'ın İkinci Yarısında Nafia Programları ve Teknoloji Gelişimi Üzerine," *Dünü ve Bugünüyle Toplum ve Ekonomi*, no. 3 (1993).

Tezel, Yahya Sezai. *Cumhuriyet Döneminin İktisadi Tarihi (1923–1950)* (Istanbul: İş Bankası, 2015).

Tharu, Susie. "Citizenship and Its Discontents." In *A Question of Silence? the Sexual Economics of Modern India,* edited by Mary E. John and Janaki Nair (New Delhi: Zed Books, 1998).

"The Ottoman Tobacco Industry." *Journal of the Society of Arts* 42, no. 2,173 (1894).

Therborn, Göran. *What does the Ruling Class do When It Rules? State Apparatuses and State Power under Feudalism, Capitalism and Socialism?* (London: New Left Books, 1978).

Thompson, Edward Palmer. "The Crime of Anonymity." In *Albion's Fatal Tree: Crime and Society in Eighteenth-Century England* by Douglas Hay, Peter Linebaugh, John G. Rule, E. P. Thompson and Cal Winslow (London: Verso, 2011).

Thompson, Paul and Chris Smith, "Labour Power and Labour Process: Contesting the Marginality of the Sociology of Work." *Sociology* 43, no. 5 (2009).

Tilly, Charles. "Citizenship, Identity and Social History." *International Review of Social History* 40, no. 3 (1995).

Timur, Taner. *Türkiye'de Çok Partili Hayata Geçiş* (Istanbul: İletişim Yayınları, 1991).

Topal, Alp Eren. "Tanzimat Politics Revisited: New Sources and Novel Approaches." *Journal of the Ottoman and Turkish Studies Association* 8, no. 1 (2021).

Toprak, Binnaz. "The State, Politics, and Religion in Turkey." In *State, Democracy and the Military: Turkey in the 1980's*, edited by Metin Heper and Ahmet Evin (Berlin: Walter de Gruyter, 1988).

Toprak, Zafer. *Türkiye'de Milli İktisat: 1908–1918* (Ankara: Yurt Yayınları, 1982).

Toprak, Zafer. "Tanzimattan Cumhuriyet'e Osmanlı Ekonomisinde Gelişmeler: Tarım, Ticaret, Sanayi." In *1885–1985 Türkiye Ekonomisinin 100 Yılı ve Izmir ve Izmir Ticaret Odası Sempozyumu* (Izmir: Izmir Ticaret ve Sanayi Odası, 1986).

Toprak, Zafer. "Tanzimat'ta Osmanlı Sanayii." In *Tanzimat'tan Cumhuriyet'e Türkiye Ansiklopedisi* V (Istanbul: İletişim, 1986).

Toprak, Zafer. *Sümerbank* (Istanbul: Creative Yayıncılık, 1989).

Toprak, Zafer. "National Economy and Ethnic Relations in Modern Turkey." In *State Formation and Ethnic Relations in the Middle East,* edited by Usuki Akira (Osaka: The Japan Center for area Studies, 2001).

Toprak, Zafer. *Türkiye'de İşçi Sınıfı 1908–1946* (Istanbul: Tarih Vakfı, 2016).

Toydemir, Sedat. "Türkiye'de İş İhtilaflarının Tarihçesi ve Bugünkü Durumu," *İçtimai Siyaset Konferansları*, vol. 4 (1951).

Toynbee, A. J. "The Ottoman Empire's Place in World History." In *The Ottoman State and Its Place in World History*, edited by Kemal Karpat (Leiden: Brill, 1974).

Trentmann, Frank. "Beyond Consumerism: New Historical Perspectives on Consumption." *Journal of Contemporary History* 39, no. 3 (2004).

Tronti, Mario. "Factory and Society," trans. Guio Jacintoh, *Operaismo in English*, accessed 17 January 2022, https://operaismoinenglish.wordpress.com/2013/06/13/factory-and-society/.

Tuğlacı, Pars. *Dadyan Ailesi'nin Osmanlı Toplum, Ekonomi ve Siyaset Hayatındaki Rolü* (Istanbul: Pars Yayın, 1993).

Tunaya, Tarık Zafer. *Türkiye'de Siyasi Partiler, 1859–1952* (Istanbul: Doğan Kardeş Yayınları, 1952).

Tunçay, Mete. *Türkiye'de Sol Akımlar: 1908–1925*, vol. 1 (Istanbul: İletişim Yayınları, 2009).

Tunçay, Mete. *1923 Amele Birliği* (Istanbul: Sosyal Tarih Yayınları, 2009).

Tümertekin, Erol. *Istanbul Sanayiinde Kuruluş Yeri* (Istanbul: Istanbul Üniversitesi Coğrafya Enstitüsü Yayınları, 1972).

Türesay, Özgür. "The Political Language of Takvīm-i vekayi: The Discourse and Temporality of Ottoman 'Reform' (1831–1834)." *European Journal of Turkish Studies* 31 (2020).

Türkeş, Mustafa. "A Patriotic Leftist Development-Strategy Proposal in Turkey in the 1930s: The Case of the Kadro (Cadre) Movement." *International Journal of Middle East Studies* 33, no. 1 (2001).

Türkiye'de Toplumsal ve Ekonomik Gelişmenin 50 Yılı (Ankara: DIE Yayınları, 1973).

Uhl, Karsten. *Humane Rationalisierung? Die Raumordnung der Fabrik im Fordistischen Jahrhundert* (Bielefeld: Transkript Verlag, 2014).

Upadhyay, Shashi Bhushan. "Cotton Mill Workers in Bombay, 1875 to 1918: Conditions of Work and Life." *Economic and Political Weekly* 25, no. 30 (1990).

Ussishkin, Daniel. "The 'Will to Work': Industrial Management and the Question of Conduct in Inter-war Britain," In *Brave New World: Imperial and Democratic Nation-building in Britain between the Wars*, eds. Laura Beers and Geraint Thomas (London: University of London Press, 2011).

Uyar, Hakkı. "CHP Izmir İşçi ve Esnaf Cemiyetleri Birliği (1935)/Devletin İşçi Sınıfı ve Örgütlenme Girişimi." *Tarih ve Toplum*, no. 160 (1997).

Uyar, Hakkı. "Devletin İşçi Sınıfı ve Örgütlenme Girişimi: CHP İzmir İşçi ve Esnaf Cemiyetleri Birliği (1935)." *Tarih ve Toplum* 27, no. 157 (1997).

Ülker, Erol. "Turkish National Movement, Mass Mobilization, and Demographic Change in Istanbul, 1922–1923." In *Contemporary Turkey at a Glance II: Turkey Transformed Power, History, Culture*, edited by Meltem Ersoy and Esra Özyürek (Wiesbaden: Springer VS, 2017).

van der Linden, Marcel, ed. *The End of Labour History?* (Cambridge: Cambridge University Press, 1994).

van der Linden, Marcel. "Labour History: The Old and the New and the Global." *African Studies* 66, no. 2–3 (2007).

van der Linden, Marcel. *Workers of the World: Essays toward a Global Labour History* (Leiden: Brill, 2008).

van der Linden, Marcel. "Labour History Beyond Borders." In *Histories of Labour: National and International Perspectives*, edited by Joan Allen, Alan Campbel and John Mcllroy (Decatur: Merlin Press, 2010).

van der Linden, Marcel. "The 'Globalization' of Labor and Working-Class History and Its Consequences." In *The Global History of Work: Critical Readings: vol. 1: Work and Workers in Context*, edited by Marcel van der Linden (London: Bloomsbury Publishing, 2019).

van Voss, Lex Heerma. "Introduction." *International Review of Social History* 46 (Supplement No. 9: Petitions in Social History) (2001).

van Voss, Lex Heerma. "Whither Labour History? Histories of Labour: National and International Perspectives." *International Review of Social History* 58, no.1 (2013).

Varlık, M. Bülent. "Izmir Sanayi İşçileri Birliği-1932." *Mülkiyeliler Birliği Dergisi*, no.155 (1995).

Varlık, M. Bülent. "Izmir İşçi-Esnaf Kurumlar Birliği Yardım Talimatnameleri (1935–1936)." *Kebikeç-İnsan Bilimleri İçin Kaynak Dergisi*, no. 4 (1996).

Varlık, M. Bülent. "Izmir İşçi ve Esnaf Birlikleri Genel Bürosu Nizamnamesi (1935)." *Kebikeç-İnsan Bilimleri İçin Kaynak Dergisi*, no. 5 (1997).

Vergara, Angela. *Copper Workers, International Business, and Domestic Politics in Cold War Chile* (University Park, PA: Pennsylvania State University Press, 2008).

Vernon, James. *Hunger: A Modern History* (Cambridge: Harvard University Press, 2007).

Vito, Christian G. De and Anne Gerritsen. "Introduction." In *Micro-Spatial Histories of Global Labour*, edited by Christian G. De Vito and Anne Gerritsen (London: Palgrave Macmillan, 2018).

Waldner, David. *State Building and Late Development* (Ithaca: Cornell University Pres, 1999).

Ward, Chris. "Languages of Trade or a Language of Class? Work Culture in Russian Cotton Mills in the 1920s." In *Making Workers Soviet: Power, Class, and Identity*, edited by Lewis H. Siegelbaum and Ronald Gregory Suny (New York: İthaca, 1994).

Weigert, Oscar. "The New Turkish Labour Code." *International Labour Review* 35, no. 6 (1937).

Weiker, Walter F. *Political Tutelage and Democracy in Turkey: The Free Party and Its Aftermath* (Leiden: Brill, 1973).

Weiler, Peter. "Forming Responsible Trade Unions: The Colonial Office, Colonial Labor, and the Trades Union Congress." *Radical History Review* 28–30 (1984).

Weiler, Peter. "British Labour and the Cold War: The Foreign Policy of the Labour Governments, 1945–1951." *Journal of British Studies* 26, no. 1 (January 1987).

White, Nicholas. "The Limits of Late-Colonial Intervention: Labor Policy and the Development of Trade Unions in 1950s Malaya." *Indonesia and the Malay World* 36, no. 106 (2008).

Winant, Gabriel, Andrew Gordon, Sven Beckert and Rudi Batzell. "Introduction: The Global E.P. Thompson." *IRSH* 61 (2016).

Winn, Peter. *Weavers of the Revolution: The Yarur Workers and Chile's Road to Socialism* (Oxford: Oxford University Press, 1986).

Wolf, Diane Lauren. *Factory Daughters:* Gender, *Household Dynamics, and Rural Industrialization* in *Java* (Berkeley: University of California Press, 1992).

Wolfe, Joel. "Populism and Developmentalism." In *A Companion to Latin American History,* edited by Thomas H. Holloway (Oxford: Wiley-Blackwell, 2011).

Wolfgang, Müller-Wiener. "15–19. Yüzyılları Arasında Istanbul'da İmalathane ve Fabrikalar." In *Osmanlılar ve Batı Teknolojisi: Yeni Araştırmalar, Yeni Görüşler*, edited by Ekmeleddin İhsanoğlu. (Istanbul: Edebiyat Fakültesi Basımevi, 1992).

Yalçın, İrfan. *Ölümün Ağzı* (Istanbul: Adam Yayınları, 1979).

Yalman, Galip. "The Turkish State and Bourgeoisie in Historical Perspective: A Relativist Paradigm or a Panapoly of Hegemonic Strategies?" In *The Politics of Permanent Crisis; Class, Ideology and State in Turkey,* edited by Neşecan Balkan and Sungur Savran (New York: Nova Science Publishers Inc., 2002).

Yavuz, Erdal. "The State of the Industrial Workforce, 1923–40." In *Workers and the Working Class in the Ottoman Empire and the Turkish Republic,* edited by Donald Quataert and Erik Jan Zürcher (London: Tauris Academic Studies, 1995).

Yavuz, Erdal. "Sanayideki İşgücünün Durumu, 1923–1940." In *Osmanlı'dan Cumhuriyet Türkiye'sine İşçiler 1839–1950,* edited by Donald Quataert and Eric Jan Zürcher (Istanbul: İletişim, 1998).

Yaycıoğlu, Ali. *Partners of the Empire: The Crisis of the Ottoman Order in the Age of Revolutions* (Stanford: Stanford University Press, 2016).

Yaycıoğlu, Ali. "Guarding Traditions and Laws-Disciplining Bodies and Souls: Tradition, Science, and Religion in the Age of Ottoman Reform." *Modern Asian Studies* 52, no. 5 (2018).

Yelvington, Kevin. *Producing Power: Ethnicity,* Gender, *and Class in a Caribbean Workplace* (Philadelphia: Temple University Press, 1996).

Yerasimos, Stefanos. *Az Gelişmişlik Sürecinde Türkiye* (Istanbul: Belge Yayınları, 1986).

Yerasimos, Stefanos. "The Monoparty Period." In *Turkey in Transition: New Perspectives,* edited by Irvin C. Schick and Ertuğrul Ahmet Tonak (New York: Oxford University Press, 1987).

Yergin, Daniel. *Shattered Peace: The Origins of the Cold War and the National Security State* (Boston: Houghton Mifflin, 1977).

Yici, Özkal. *Kırkbir Uzun Gün: Berec Grevi* (Istanbul: Sosyal Tarih Yayınları, 2010).

Yıldırım, Kadir. *Osmanlı'da İşçiler (1870–1922): Çalışma Hayatı, Örgütler, Grevler* (Istanbul: İletişim Yayınları, 2013).

Yıldız, Gültekin. *Neferin Adı Yok: Zorunlu Askerliğe Geçiş Sürecinde Osmanlı Devleti'nde Siyaset, Ordu ve Toplum (1826–1839)* (Istanbul: Kitapevi, 2009).

Zaim, Sabahaddin. *Istanbul Mensucat Sanayiinin Bünyesi ve Ücretler* (Istanbul: Istanbul Üniversitesi İktisat Fakültesi, 1956).

Zaim, Sabahaddin. "Türkiye Mensucat Sanayiinde Ücretler." *Sosyal Siyaset Konferansları*, Sekizinci Kitap (1956).

Zaim, Sabahaddin. *Bölge ve Şehir Planlaması Yönünden Istanbul Sanayi Bölgeleri* (Istanbul: Istanbul Üniversitesi Yayınları, 1971).

Zürcher, Erik J. *Turkey: A Modern History* (London: I. B. Tauris, 2015).

Index

Printed in the United States
by Baker & Taylor Publisher Services